The African American Struggle for Secondary Schooling, 1940–1980

Closing the Graduation Gap

The African American Struggle for Secondary Schooling, 1940–1980

Closing the Graduation Gap

JOHN L. RURY
SHIRLEY A. HILL

Teachers College, Columbia University
New York and London

To African American students: past, present, and future.

Published by Teachers College Press, 1234 Amsterdam Avenue, New York, NY 10027

Copyright © 2012 by Teachers College, Columbia University

All rights reserved. No part of this publication may be reproduced or transmitted in any form or by any means, electronic or mechanical, including photocopy, or any information storage and retrieval system, without permission from the publisher.

Library of Congress Cataloging-in-Publication Data

Rury, John L., 1951–
 The African American struggle for secondary schooling, 1940–1980: closing the graduation gap / John L. Rury.
   p. cm.
 Includes bibliographical references and index.
 ISBN 978-0-8077-5277-7 (pbk.) — ISBN 978-0-8077-5278-4 (hardcover)
 1. African Americans—Education. 2. African Americans—Education (Secondary) 3. Academic achievement—United States. 4. Segregation in education—United States. 5. School integration—United States. I. Title.
 LC2717.R87 2011
 371.829'96073—dc23

2011027417

ISBN 978-0-8077-5277-7 (paper)
ISBN 978-0-8077-5278-4 (hardcover)

Printed on acid-free paper
Manufactured in the United States of America

19 18 17 16 15 14 13 12   8 7 6 5 4 3 2 1

Contents

Acknowledgments vii

Introduction 1
   Racial Convergence in Secondary School Attainment 3
   Setting Attainment in Context 6
   Improving Black Secondary Education 10
   Moving to Opportunity, and to Crisis 14
   Building Toward the Future 16
   Plan of the Book 18

PART I: EXPANDING ACCESS

1. The South in the 1940s 25
   Stark Inequity: The Rural Countryside 26
   A Shaky Foundation: Elementary Education 31
   Making the Best of Hard Times 34
   City Schools 38
   Accreditation Struggles 45
   Conclusion: Struggling Against a Legacy of Inequity 50

2. Sea Change: "Equalization" and Secondary Schooling 52
   Race, Education, and Regional Development 52
   Mounting Restiveness 55
   Shifting Social and Political Conditions 57
   A New Day for High Schools 60
   Rising Levels of Attainment 63
   A Grassroots Movement 67
   The Good Black High School 71
   White Resistance and Black Skepticism: The Limits of Reform 76
   Conclusion: Building a Foundation for the Future 81

3. Inequity, Discrimination, and Growth Outside the South, 1940–1960 83
   Blacks and Secondary School Attainment in 1940 85
   Going to High School in the North and West, 1940 88
   Racial Conflict in High Schools 91

In Search of Tolerance	95
Segregated Secondary Schooling, North and West	98
Parsing the Academic Layer Cake	104
Black Secondary School Attainment in 1960	108
Conclusion: Growing Attainment and Persistent Inequality	111

PART II: FIGHTING FOR EQUALITY

4. Black Youth and the Urban Crisis — 115
A Changing Urban Scene	117
Discovery of the "Dropout"	119
Continuing Progress in Attainment	122
Learning Under Difficult Circumstances	127
Serving the "Disadvantaged"	132
An Era of Conflict and Protest	136
Conclusion: Coming of Age in the 1960s and 1970s	143

5. Battling Segregation — 145
Integration in the 1940s and 1950s	146
Changing High Schools in Kansas City	151
Desegregation and Protest Across the North	157
Pyrrhic Victory in the South	162
Integration and Student Conflict	168
Inequity Within the Schools	171
Conclusion: Trial by Fire	174

Conclusion: The African American High School Experience in Perspective — 176
The High School in the History of Black Education	177
High Schools and Social Status	180
Dilemmas of Integration	183
A Legacy of Protest	188
The Elusive Goal of Equality	191
The Imperative of Educational Change	197

Appendix A: Oral History Interviews and Other Sources of Information — 200

Appendix B: Logistic Regression Analysis of Secondary School Attainment — 204

Notes — 208
Index — 251
About the Authors — 262

Acknowledgments

SCHOLARLY RESEARCH AND WRITING is an inherently collective enterprise and we certainly have benefitted from a great deal of assistance in this undertaking. Our collaboration began with Lizette Peter's recommendation that we work together during a visiting semester in the Sociology Department at the University of Kansas. We discussed our respective but related fields of urban education and social inequality, giving rise to a successful proposal to the Spencer Foundation and eventually to a long journey through the history of Black high school experiences. Ultimately it led us to write this book together, a task that has proven both enlightening and gratifying.

Our research took us to a number of locations South and North, and we were greeted with hospitality and helpful assistance everywhere. In Atlanta, Wayne Urban and Regina Werum proved gracious hosts to the city. We encountered supportive staff members at the Georgia State Archives in Morrow, the Auburn Avenue Research Library in Atlanta, and the Woodruff Library at Emory University. We owe a special debt to Lalita Washington and Principal Carter Coleman of Booker T. Washington High School in Atlanta, for helping us locate alumni and use school facilities in conducting interviews. In North Carolina we were guests of former KU colleague Shirley Harkess, and Jim LeLoudis of the University of North Carolina at Chapel Hill provided guidance to the campus and its library collections, along with stimulating lunch and dinner conversation. Librarians at the Southern Historical Collection in the Wilson Library were especially helpful, as were staff members of the North Carolina State Archives in Raleigh and librarians at North Carolina State University. Gabriel Lee was a sympathetic research compatriot in Raleigh and a sociable lunch companion. In Mississippi we were assisted by staff members at the State Archives in Jackson and the Center for Oral History and Cultural Heritage in the McCain Library at the University of Southern Mississippi in Hattiesburg. John Brown, assistant to the mayor of Hattiesburg, helped arrange interviews at a local community center. Emily Noble introduced us to Gene Young, an especially genial host in Jackson, who offered insights into the history of Lanier High School and shared a memorable lunch in a renowned neighborhood eatery.

We received congenial assistance in the North as well. In Chicago we met very obliging staff members at the archives of the Public School System, the Harold Washington Library Center, the Carter G. Woodson Regional Library, and the Chicago Historical Society. We also would like to thank DuSable High School and Charles Mingo for allowing us use of facilities for interviews with alumni of the Chicago Public Schools. In New York we were assisted by librarians at the Schomburg Center for Black Culture, and in Washington by staff members at the Library of Congress. When visiting Washington we enjoyed the hospitality of Cindy Rury and daughters Emily and Jenny. Librarians at the University of Missouri in Columbia and the University of Kansas also were very helpful, especially Deborah Dandridge at KU's Spencer Research Library, as were those in the Kansas City Public Library's Missouri Valley Special Collections Division.

It is also important to acknowledge our gratitude to the dozens of individuals who took time to share memories of high school with us in the form of oral history interviews. As indicated above, many of these conversations occurred in the schools being discussed, but others took place in homes, restaurants, and other public places. We provide a description of interview procedures in the book's appendix, but the fact that our subjects have been granted anonymity in this account does not mean that their contributions have been minor. Interviews were one dimension of our research, and perhaps not the most decisive one, but they have added significantly to our comprehension of the high school experience and the meaning it held for different generations of students. Without the support of the people who shared their memories with us, this aspect of the study would not have been possible.

Similarly, we would like to express our gratitude to the Integrated Public Use Microdata Series (IPUMS) program of the Minnesota Population Center at the University of Minnesota. Publicly available and easily utilized IPUMS samples of United States Census data are an invaluable resource for historians and other social scientists, and especially for studying the history of American education. IPUMS has been critical to this study; these data should be used more widely in the field.

As indicated above, the Spencer Foundation provided financial support to the project, as did the School of Education and the General Research Fund at the University of Kansas. We are very grateful for this crucial assistance; without it the research for this book would not have been possible. Sheryl Lang and her colleagues in the Institute for Educational Research and Public Service were most obliging in helping obtain and manage our research funds.

Acknowledgments

We also benefitted from a number of students, friends, and colleagues who assisted with the research or read all or portions of our work and provided helpful feedback. Colleagues and staff in the Departments of Educational Leadership and Policy Studies and Sociology at KU have been very supportive. Graduate students Kevin Lee, Aaron Rife, and Kip Smilie assisted with research. Shade Little, Jeff Mirel, Hilary Moss, Jennifer Ng, Bill Reese, Argun Saatcioglu, Barbara Shircliffe, Bill Tuttle, Vanessa Siddle Walker, and Kim Warren provided a range of useful reactions and suggestions for the study, as did anonymous reviewers working with the press. Derrick Darby and Donna Ginther hosted a stimulating discussion of our work at KU's Hall Center for the Humanities. Portions of the research were presented at meetings of the American Educational Research Association, the History of Education Society, and the Midwest Sociological Society, and we received helpful commentary in each instance. All this assistance and feedback was enormously helpful, but the customary caveats about responsibility for interpretations, errors, infelicities, and other problems in the book resting solely with the authors apply in this instance as well.

We also would like to thank Brian Ellerbeck, Lori Tate, and their colleagues at Teachers College Press for their interest in this project and support throughout the publication process. They have helped us to produce a considerably better book, one that has largely fulfilled our goals for the project.

Finally, we would like to thank our colleagues, friends, and family members who have supported this project, cheerfully or not, for the past fours years. In particular, we are grateful to our spouses, who have endured many absences for research, the project's slow gestation over several years, and our more recent preoccupation with finally completing the manuscript. We hope this acknowledgment of our appreciation and affection will be a small recompense for the sustenance and love they have provided through thick and thin.

Introduction

IN THE SPRING OF 1951, all 450 Black students walked out of Farmville, Virginia's segregated Moton High School to protest the local school board's failure to provide them a new facility. In the wake of rapidly rising enrollments, the original brick building became overcrowded and three "temporary frame structures" had been erected, "covered with tar paper," with the promise of a new building. The students charged that these structures were impossible to heat and leaky in the rain. They also pointed to a high school that had recently been built for Whites and demanded a facility at least equivalent. Doubting the White superintendent's claim that plans were underway, they ignored their principal's pleas to return, resolving to hold out "a long time" to achieve their goals.[1]

This event came at a pivotal time in the history of Southern schooling and has been widely celebrated by historians. When the National Association for the Advancement of Colored People (NAACP) told the student strikers that it no longer litigated to improve segregated schools, they voted by a narrow margin to demand admittance to the White school. The resulting lawsuit, *Davis v. County School Board of Prince Edward County*, was rejected by state courts on the grounds that Virginia's recently announced campaign to equalize schools made integration unnecessary. The case was eventually bundled with four others by NAACP lawyers and taken to the U.S. Supreme Court, where it became a part of the *Brown v. Board of Education* decision of 1954, declaring segregating schooling to be unconstitutional.[2] Although a decade of struggle would pass before Black students in Prince Edward County would achieve the goal of attending the White high school, they were among the first in the South to attend fully integrated schools.

In the history of Black secondary education, this case is telling in a number of respects. First, it began as a struggle over improving a high school. With students taking the lead, a Black community demanded better education for the growing numbers of youth interested in study beyond the elementary level. Second, initial demands focused on making equal facilities available and improving schools within the framework of segregation. This was a widespread concern among Blacks throughout the region, especially with respect to high schools, and Southern state authorities took up "campaigns" for equalization as a way of forestalling integration. Finally, the case ultimately was about integration, which eventually was seen in Black communities as the sure way to achieve equality in education. Prescient students and community members in Prince Edward County recognized this earlier than others, but eventually the logic of integration proved irresistible as a means of gaining access to a range of educational opportunities. These students and their supporters were among the pioneers, but they were hardly alone.

Davis thus encapsulated various phases of the history of Black secondary schooling in the postwar era, particularly in the South but elsewhere as well. It also highlighted the significance of conflict as a theme in the process of change. Like those at Moton High School, African Americans across the South encountered resistance as they sought improvements to woefully underfunded schools, even in the midst of the so-called equalization campaigns by the states. Activists in other parts of the country met opposition as well. The growth of secondary education for the nation's African American youth did not occur spontaneously or because of White compassion, but rather from prolonged struggle for the cause of educational equity. At a time when high school was becoming a near universal facet of life for White Americans, Black communities wanted the same for their children. In this book, we examine the factors that eventually led to expanded access to high schools, more integrated education, and, ultimately, to realizing the limits of racial equity in secondary schooling.

This introductory chapter highlights our principal focal point—the narrowing Black-White gap in high school graduation between 1940 and 1980—and describes the circumstances that led to greater racial parity in high school attendance and success. This extension of the "high school movement" to include African Americans has been overshadowed by accounts of racial integration and continuing racial disparities, thus its role in expanding the earning power, aspirations, and size of the Black middle class, and in abetting the civil rights movement, has been neglected. Our research examines the struggle to increase high school graduation among Black youth, in its regional variants, and the many obstacles and challenges encountered along the way. It was a long road, but a journey marked by undeniable progress. We also consider some of the outcomes of this struggle, both positive and problematic, for African Americans and the nation as a whole. The remainder of this chapter provides an overview of the book.

RACIAL CONVERGENCE IN SECONDARY SCHOOL ATTAINMENT

The high school is an institution that many Americans take for granted today, a familiar stage of life for most teenagers. Although some students do not graduate, virtually everyone now attends secondary schools and more than 80% eventually receive a diploma or equivalent certificate. But as recently as the mid-20th century, the high school served much smaller numbers of youth and fewer than half graduated. Lacking a diploma was less of an impediment then, as many jobs did not require one, but it also meant that future opportunities would be limited, and it was impossible to even consider college. Thus, having a chance at secondary school and graduation was a big advantage for many, even if it was still not a widespread norm. It was an aspect of inequality in American life, moreover, linked clearly to the question of race.[3]

Formal education for African Americans had long been subject to appalling inequality, especially in the South, where about 8 of 10 Blacks lived prior to World War II. In a classic study, historian Louis Harlan documented the brute suppression of Black education there during the opening years of the 20th century. As James Anderson and others have established, Black elementary schooling experienced a revival with assistance from Northern philanthropists, but secondary education did not follow suit. By the time of World War I, fewer than 40 public high schools served a Black population of nearly 9 million across the region, and most states of the Deep South, where the vast majority lived, had none. During the 1920s, the number of secondary institutions serving African Americans increased, principally in the larger cities, and growth continued into the following decade. Even so, the scope of Black secondary schooling remained far behind White institutions throughout the South. Conditions elsewhere were only a little better. Few high schools welcomed African American students, and those permitting their attendance generally did not treat them kindly.[4]

In 1940, on the eve of World War II, African American teenagers graduated from high school at a rate just a third that of their White counterparts, 14% compared with 46%.[5] It was a striking disparity that reflected a number of circumstances. Nationally, secondary enrollments had increased dramatically in the 1920s and 1930s, particularly in the wake of the Great Depression, which drove thousands of youth out of the job market.[6] With few alternatives, White teens turned to the schools, many hoping that additional education would prove helpful in finding employment. High school enrollments swelled as a consequence. The biggest jumps occurred in the cities, however, especially the industrial centers where young men and women had historically taken factory jobs. In other settings, such as the rural South, high schools were few and far between, and enrollments did not advance nearly as rapidly. Because African Americans still lived predominantly in the Southern countryside at the time, where hardly any Black high schools existed, they remained isolated from these developments. Black youth thus had little opportunity to join the ranks of America's rising tide of secondary graduates. While the rest of the country was increasingly going to high school, the nation's Black population was left behind.[7]

Over the next 4 decades, this changed. The graduation disparity between Black and White Americans decreased dramatically, as secondary enrollment rates for both groups climbed rapidly. By 1980, the White rate was only about 20% higher than the African American rate, 78% percent compared with 64%, based on calculations using census data. Although Blacks had not completely caught up, this decrease in the gap represented a major advance in African American education, paving the way for striking increases in college attendance and improved earning power after 1960.[8] It marked an instance in recent history when an immense racial disparity in educational attainment was largely closed, an accomplishment clearly linked to the subsequent social and economic success of African Americans.[9]

This process is evident in the enrollment patterns depicted in Figure I.1. Although graduation rates increased for youth from both races, attainment levels improved more dramatically for Blacks than Whites, especially in the years following 1960. These were national trends, of course, and there were important regional differences within these patterns. But the overall picture of convergence in attainment is unmistakable. It represented a vast process of change, as graduation for African Americans went from being limited to a small minority to reaching a clear majority. It was the time when Black youth as a group started going to high school. After this period, however, this process of convergence ceased and a significant racial gap continued to exist in graduation rates, largely due to new social, economic, and political challenges affecting African American communities, especially in the nation's largest cities.[10]

Despite great interest in contemporary Black-White education "gaps," not much attention has been given the process by which the historic secondary graduation gap was narrowed. This may partly be due to the scale of change this represented, and the seemingly gradual quality of its development, extending across nearly half a century and involving millions of people. On the other hand, the question of school integration drew enormous interest as it became a national preoccupation, just as the secondary attainment gap was finally diminishing. As a number of scholars

FIGURE I.1. Graduation Rates, by Decade, for 19-Year-Old Youth

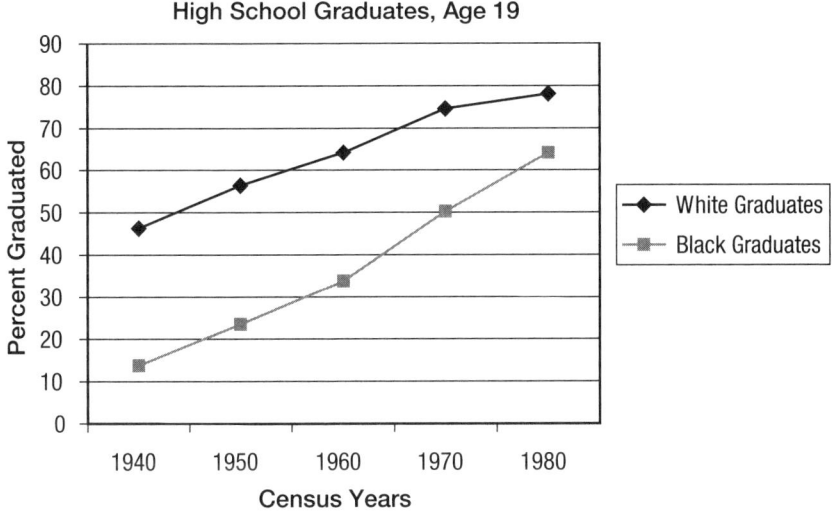

Note: Calculated with IPUMS data.

have noted, the story of school integration has become a dominant narrative in historical research on Black education.[11] Indeed, it probably is accurate to say that so much attention was given to controversies about desegregation and integration that the rise in African American graduation was largely overlooked, both by contemporaries and subsequent generations.[12]

The attainment of secondary schooling for most Black Americans may not have garnered much notice, but it was hardly a trouble-free process. As suggested by Moton High School, it entailed great conflict, and almost constant confrontation on the part of activists and supporters concerned with improving Black education. This was true in all parts of the country, but especially in the South. In many respects, there were distinctive regional stories regarding Black high schools. Shifting patterns of attainment also were linked to the mass migration that marked African American experience during World War II and its aftermath, extending through the 1960s. In this respect, high school graduation rates were clearly affected by the urbanization of the Black population and corresponding changes to the Southern countryside. And as suggested earlier, secondary schooling also was inevitably linked to integration, often a volatile issue where teenagers were concerned and hence rarely without conflict.

In short, the growth of Black secondary attainment was a multifaceted process, linked to many other changes in the lives of African

Americans. It occurred at a time of expanding horizons, but also a time of violence and cruelty motivated by White racism and "massive resistance" to change.[13] Popular education was a longstanding feature of American life, but the expectation that it should be fundamentally equal for all was still gaining currency. The NAACP's decision to make education a focal point of its campaign for civil rights is well known, but improvements in schooling had long been sought by Black communities to enhance their children's future. In this respect, African American education, particularly in high schools, was an integral element of social change. Rising educational attainment was part and parcel of advancing Black status in American society, tangible evidence of a better day coming.[14]

For these reasons, we believe it apposite to view changes to Black secondary education during this time as an aspect of what Jacquelyn Dowd Hall has described as the "Long Civil Rights Movement." Unequal education for African Americans, after all, was not simply a matter of neglect; it was an intrinsic element of the regime of systematic racial discrimination and exploitation in the South, and blatantly unequal provision of educational resources elsewhere. The achievement of educational equity—at least with respect to attainment—was the consequence of a long, sustained campaign for justice with respect to educational opportunity. It was an issue that mobilized untold numbers of students, parents, and community members across the period. Their many achievements speak to the determination and resourcefulness employed in bringing a new educational order into view. It also helped to cast the question of equity in educational attainment for a wide range of additional groups in a new light, including other ethnic minorities and the poor.[15] As such, it can be justifiably described as one of the more remarkable accomplishments in the history of American education. And it has come to represent a foundation upon which the education of subsequent generations of African Americans has been built.

SETTING ATTAINMENT IN CONTEXT

Born in 1934 in Atlanta, Herschel Summers graduated from the city's first Black high school, Booker T. Washington, in 1951. After attending nearby Morehouse College for a semester, he dropped out and joined the armed forces. Upon returning 4 years later, Summers was able to finish college with aid from the GI Bill, and found employment with the federal government. Summers enjoyed a long and productive career in law enforcement and security services, working for years after his retirement from the government. Looking back, he credited his high school experiences for much of his success. Without attending an institution as large and comprehensive as Washington, his path would have been considerably steeper. Among the first wave of Blacks to graduate in the postwar era, at a time when less than a quarter did so, Summers led the way for others to follow. School and military service provided a way to escape the limited opportunities of the segregated South. Like many other African Americans, he was able to find employment in the public sector. Summers's subsequent career pointed to the improving prospects of those who possessed the requisite educational credentials.[16]

A parallel story can be told about Mabel Fountain. Born in 1941, also in Atlanta, she attended Henry McNeil Turner High, a school built during Georgia's campaign to raise the level of Black education. Fountain graduated in 1959, and after attending Clark University without graduating, she got married and had children, making extra money by sewing clothes at home. When her children reached school age, she decided to become a telephone operator. In taking this step, she was among the first African Americans to benefit from a new openness to racial diversity in large American corporations.[17] Fountain spent the next 30 years at the phone company, moving into management and eventually becoming a team leader for diversity training. As with Herschel Summers, her secondary diploma opened doors for her occupationally, and skills and knowledge she gained in school helped in her career. Without the opportunity to graduate from high school, her pathway to work-related and personal success would have been considerably harder.[18]

The high school is often labeled a peculiarly American educational institution. Occupying a strategic position between the elementary or grade school and the college or university, it historically has functioned as a critical arbiter of who succeeds in the education system. Unlike early secondary institutions in 19th-century Europe, American high schools traditionally were open to all students who met requisite academic standards. In the parlance of the time, they were "people's colleges," providing instruction in the "higher branches" to anyone who studied hard, without regard to social or economic background. Fueled by this democratic ethos, the high school spread rapidly, and at the start of the 20th century, the United States had more students enrolled in secondary institutions than any other country in the world.[19]

Economists Claudia Goldin and Lawrence Katz have described the high school as an engine of economic development in American history, providing millions with essential skills that boosted economic development in the first half of the 20th century. This was the result of a process of sustained growth in secondary education that Goldin and Katz have labeled "the high school movement," establishing schools across the country and creating conditions for educational development in subsequent decades. Expansion was particularly noteworthy during the 1930s, when the Great Depression severely constrained job opportunities for teenagers. By 1940, over half of the nation's White youth were attending high school. Most of this change occurred in the Northeast and Midwest; the least developed school system was in the South. It was there, of course, that the vast majority—more than 80%—of African American youth lived at the time.[20]

As indicated earlier, because so many Blacks lived in the South and Whites controlled resources there, Black youth were largely excluded from these critical stages of high school expansion. As Southern school systems grew, White secondary institutions outnumbered those for Blacks ten to one. As suggested above, the number of Black high schools remained quite limited during the opening years of the 20th century. Historians have clearly established that by the end of the 1930s, secondary education remained the principal element of the public school system that excluded the vast majority of Black students. Consequently, African Americans were largely denied the manifold economic and social benefits offered by the high school movement. This eventually became a potentially debilitating handicap for Black youth from this period, as they later confronted a changing national job market in the postwar era. But the experiences of those who did succeed in gaining a secondary education illuminated a path for others. The expansion of Black high school enrollments did not happen overnight, but once it started in earnest, the tempo of growth in attainment accelerated quickly.[21]

Economists have devoted considerable attention to improvements in Black education during the postwar era and gains in the earning power of African American workers. By and large, this body of research indicates that enhancements to Black schools, such as longer school terms and lower student–teacher ratios, had a substantial impact on reducing income gaps between the races following 1960. Improvement in the quality of African American schools was accompanied by the rapid rise in enrollments noted above, and this permitted Black wage earners in the years to follow to keep pace with rising incomes for the rest of the country. And as we will document below, developments in African American secondary education went well beyond the factors typically utilized in econometric analyses of these questions. Given this, even the best of these estimates may well understate the positive economic effects of educational change for Blacks during this era.[22]

The experiences of Herschel Summers and Mabel Fountain highlight the critical role that the high school came to play. The fact that their high schools were urban institutions with regional (rather than state) accreditation meant that more doors were open to them than most other Black graduates. Even if Washington and Turner high schools were overcrowded and poorly equipped compared to most White schools, they had sizable libraries, serviceable science laboratories, large auditoriums, and a number of other amenities that contributed directly to the quality of student experiences. Both Summers and Fountain described their teachers as well prepared and highly dedicated, holding high expectations for students and devoting considerable effort to their success. Although he was a "B student" and not among the academic leaders of his class, Summers gained the skills necessary to succeed in the Air Force, to finish college, and to enjoy a long career in law enforcement. The high school also broadened his vision of the world, and subsequent experiences took him away from the South, exposing him to people and places he might otherwise never have encountered. Had he not finished secondary school, the likelihood of Summers being able to take advantage of these opportunities would have been severely constrained. In Fountain's case, her high school record, along with some college experience, enabled her to gain employment at Southern Bell at a time when few African Americans had done so. The skills she had acquired served her well, helping her advance through the ranks of a large modern corporation. For her, the high school also was a critical gateway to success.[23]

As these cases suggest, a significant role of the high school was preparing students for college, even if they never completed a degree program. Even having an exposure to collegiate life was an advantage, as relatively few students went on to postsecondary study. In 1940, the propensity of Black high school graduates to attend college was almost exactly the same as that of White graduates, about 15% for both groups.[24] Of course, this meant that many more Whites went to college than Blacks, simply because White high school graduates were so numerous. The fact that Black secondary graduates were just as likely to go to college, however, points to the critical role that the high schools played as arbiters of educational advancement. For most Blacks living at the time in the rural South, high schools simply were not available, especially accredited institutions that could prepare them for collegiate study. The development of secondary schools for the nation's Black youth, particularly in the South, made it possible for the first large increase in Black college enrollment to occur in the 1960s. This, too, augmented Black earning power, contributing to the development of a middle-class lifestyle that emerged in the latter 1960s and 1970s. But it also contributed to the civil rights movement, as thousands of Black college students played a pivotal role in confronting Jim Crow policies and practices across the South, and helped to organize protests in other parts of the country. It was these students, for instance, who launched waves of dramatic sit-ins, beginning in Greensboro, North Carolina, in 1960 and sweeping the South thereafter. They also played critical roles in the years to follow, often providing a range of new perspectives on issues of the day. Without a dramatic increase in Black secondary attainment, however, this simply would not have been possible. The high schools helped to produce a generation of activists that contributed significantly to the development of the movement.[25]

Accordingly, there appears to have been considerably more to the impact of education than simply enhanced earning power, as important as income was, particularly in the impoverished South. As suggested earlier, this was a period of widespread upheaval over the social and political rights of African Americans. Who is to say what the role of greater and higher-quality education was in the unfolding of this momentous development? Here, we refer to the majority of high school students who never attended college. As a general proposition, people with higher levels of education were more likely than others to be politically active, as suggested in the behavior of college students. In the case of African Americans, there is evidence that higher attainment raised the propensity of individuals to participate in civil rights activities. Sociologist Doug McAdam, for example, has suggested that rising Black education levels led to greater political "insurgency" in the South in particular, even in the period prior to 1960, a tendency noted by other observers as well.[26] Education represented more than just another occasion for Black Americans to protest inequity; it also became a potentially invaluable resource in the struggle to gain greater equality and respect in all spheres of life.

IMPROVING BLACK SECONDARY EDUCATION

As suggested above, the campaign for racial equity in education became inescapably linked to integrated schooling in the postwar era. As McAdam's research suggests, it was an issue that quickly came to command public attention, especially following the Supreme Court's 1954 *Brown* decision. But at the same time there was another, initially more pervasive campaign for educational equity focused on expanding opportunities for Black Americans regardless of segregation. For many—perhaps most—African Americans, this was the more telling question: Just what kind of an education were Black students going to receive? Getting better schools and the opportunity for an education more or less equivalent to that of other children was the first order of business for many. If integration was seen as essential to that goal, it became an issue to consider, but a widespread, informal movement to raise the quality and availability of education—and high schools in particular—for Black communities also marked this era. It did not generally receive the attention that was given to desegregation, which held important implications for Whites as well as Blacks. But in the end, it was this less publicly celebrated campaign for educational equity that may have had the most pervasive

Introduction

FIGURE I.2. Regional Trends in Black High School Enrollment, 14- to 18-Year-Old Students, 1940–1980

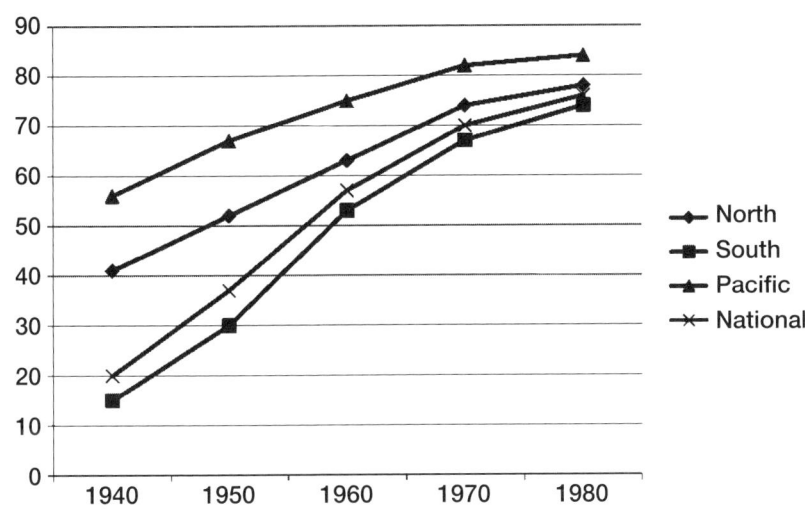

Source: Calculated with IPUMS data.

impact on African American education at the time.[27]

It is impossible, of course, to discuss the history of African American schooling without considering regional differences in educational experience. Figure I.2 depicts three distinctive regional profiles of Black secondary enrollment between 1940 and 1980. It is important to remember that the vast majority of African Americans lived in the South at the outset of this period, and despite large-scale migration, most still lived there 40 years later.

Several patterns are immediately evident in these enrollment profiles. First, it is clear that the most dramatic improvements occurred in the South, where fewer than one in six Black adolescents attended high school in 1940. Rates were considerably higher in other parts of the country, particularly in the Pacific states, which had a relatively small and highly urbanized African American population. Enrollments also were fairly strong in the North (East North Central, Middle Atlantic, and New England census regions), where the Black population was mainly urban as well. At the outset of the period, in that case, there was considerable regional inequity in overall levels of African American secondary enrollment.

Another trend is regional differences in the timing of growth and the convergence of rates across the period. In the South, where most Black youth lived, the decade following 1950 was a period of especially rapid expansion. This, of course, was a time of considerable ferment, highlighted by the historic *Brown* decision, but also before any meaningful desegregation occurred. Enrollment increased more rapidly in the South than elsewhere in subsequent decades, contributing to the convergence evident in Figure I.2. Growth was steady but less dramatic elsewhere, and by 1970, regional differences had diminished a great deal. The national trend closely mirrored that of the South, reflecting the fact that a preponderance of the country's Black population lived there. There can be little doubt, in that case, that changes in the South were the principal driver of rapid improvement evident in these data. To capture much of the story of change, it is necessary to look to that section of the country.

In recent years, an emerging body of research and writing has focused on the development of particular African American secondary institutions during this period, principally in the South. Drawing upon school records and the recollections of educators and former students of the schools, these studies have emphasized the positive role that these institutions played in their communities and in the lives of the youth attending them. The so-called "good Black high school" literature has directed attention to the commitment of educators who worked in these settings, and the dedication to accomplishment that students encountered there.[28] Our research complements this line of work, building on the insights gained from these studies and offering additional perspective on the range of institutions that existed during the pre-integration era and the students who attended them. In this respect, we contribute to the story told in a number of case studies of such schools, providing a context for interpreting the development of Black education in the South. At the same time, we also address the question of whether integrated schools were seen as necessary to advancing African American educational achievement. Although the many positive contributions of all-Black schools must be recognized, it also is important to acknowledge their limitations, such as inadequate resources and inferior facilities. For many African American communities, integration was a step taken only after it became clear that truly equal education could not be realized without it.

Change occurred elsewhere, too, and there is a growing literature on the civil rights movement outside of the South. A number of studies have considered the high school experiences of African Americans in other parts of the country, and to grasp changes in Black secondary attainment it is important to consider these settings as well. Segregation was not legally mandated in most non-Southern school systems, and most Black youth attended secondary schools alongside White students. In many other respects, however, the issues facing Black communities in the North and West were similar to those in the South. Although segregated and unequal education was not formally required, longstanding patterns of residential segregation were abetted by school-district policies to placate White prejudice, which usually prevented meaningful integration. Districts in many instances also discriminated against institutions that served African Americans by limiting their resources and curricular options. And if Black students were conscious of discrepancies in excellence within their own districts, they also became painfully aware of contrasts between the institutions they attended and those serving affluent suburban communities.[29]

Despite such inequities, predominantly Black high schools in Northern cities also developed loyal followings over the years, becoming known as institutions that served their constituencies ably, sending thousands off to work, college, and careers as community leaders. Perhaps somewhat less celebrated than well-known Southern institutions, these schools became important signposts on the urban landscape in Chicago, Philadelphia, Detroit, Milwaukee, Cleveland, Indianapolis, and elsewhere. Like their Southern counterparts, these institutions must also be appraised both in terms of their successes and their shortcomings. After all, they, too, were part of an educational system with great disparities in both human and financial resources. Despite their proud traditions, moreover, these schools also suffered many of the manifold problems that beset their communities.[30]

These pervasive patterns of social and educational inequality prompted protest in the North and West, just as segregation and inequity did in the South. The character of these confrontations was somewhat different across regions, however, especially regarding the involvement of students. In the South, protest occurred on a somewhat larger scale, at least in the early years, and to some extent was less confrontational. Walkouts like the one at Moton High in 1951 were unusual in the beginning, as students irregularly took initiative in registering complaints. It was only later, in the latter half of the 1960s, that Northern Black protest began to emerge on a large scale. These differing patterns of student activism represent yet another facet of Black high school experience that calls for explanation. As much as anything else, these expressions of student concern about their schools and communities reflected just how important the high school had become as an aspect of Black aspirations. If students were angry and frustrated with the condition of these institutions, it was because of the critical role they believed formal education would play in their futures.[31]

Making improvements to Black secondary schooling, in that case, entailed a wide range of activities, extending from quiet community organizing for better schools to raucous student demands for immediate change. In most cases, however, the impulse for improvement came from local Black communities, whether expressed by adults or youth. To a considerable degree, it is accurate to say that the high school movement among African Americans was built from the bottom up. In this respect, it can be considered both an element of the larger civil rights movement that appeared at this time and a reflection of an enduring American tradition of localism in educational policy and practice. Without grassroots initiative, much of the change in Black attainment at this time simply would not have occurred.

MOVING TO OPPORTUNITY, AND TO CRISIS

In 1946, Princeton Elroy's family moved from Skene, Mississippi, to Kansas City, Missouri when he was 13 years old. They had worked as sharecroppers, plowing the land with mules and planting and picking cotton by hand. Elroy recalled attending school just 3 months out of the year, and working the rest of the time. After his stepfather found a job up north, his mother decided to follow him with the children, "to have a better opportunity for education." Elroy was put back two grades by the Kansas City schools, but finally made it to high school at age 17. Although he never graduated, joining the Army in 1950, he learned enough to later earn a General Equivalency Diploma (GED) and eventually complete a degree at a public university in Missouri. He then started a lengthy career in education, working first in the public schools and spending many years as a faculty member teaching social science at a community college.[32]

For Princeton Elroy and his family, the move away from the cotton fields of Mississippi, where they endured conditions "a cut above slavery," was indeed a step toward a better future. Although initially behind his Northern classmates, he had the opportunity to attend high school and college, and to enjoy a long, rewarding career as an educator.[33] Like many others, leaving the impoverished conditions of the rural South provided him access to educational opportunities that were scarcely imaginable to prior generations of African Americans. This experience was also the story of improved Black secondary attainment during this period.

As suggested earlier, this was an era of large-scale relocation for African Americans, with as many as 5 million leaving the South and millions more moving from the countryside to Southern cities. As in other parts of the country, the youth labor market was shifting in the wake of the Great Depression and World War II. Movement to industrial centers and changes in agricultural technology, particularly mechanical cotton harvesting, altered demand for unskilled labor. As the numbers of African American youth looking for jobs diminished, demand for education increased, putting pressure on the schools. In the North and West, Black migrants settled in the cities, crowding into old African American neighborhoods and creating new ones defined by shifting local real estate markets. By 1970,

Introduction

three out of four Black teenagers lived in metropolitan areas, a big change from just 30 years earlier, when nearly two-thirds (63%) did not. At the same time, Black schooling went from being defined by rural and small town settings to being increasingly associated with urban education.[34]

Many of the Black migrants in this era were young, and most appear to have been relatively well educated, at least compared with those left behind. Their arrival put great pressure on city school systems, as the number of Black students rose with expanding African American neighborhoods. Moving from rural to urban communities, per the experience of Princeton Elroy, meant better educational opportunities, especially with respect to secondary schooling. School-building campaigns occurred in districts across the country to address these shifts, even if they often failed to keep pace with population growth. At the same time, enrollments everywhere increased due to the baby-boom generation starting shortly after the war, the first wave arriving in high schools in 1960. Districts scrambled to keep pace, especially in the cities where students came and went each year. All of this was made even more complicated by shifting neighborhood boundaries that altered the racial profile of existing schools. At the same time, growing demands for school integration from Black communities, along with resistance from Whites, raised the pressure on school leaders. It was a time of rapid change, for African American and other students alike, and their education was invariably affected, for better or worse.[35]

These were the conditions that defined the "crisis" in urban education first identified in the early 1960s. Predominantly Black high schools often were labeled as failing institutions, plagued by higher dropout rates and lower test scores than schools dominated by Whites. The contrast was especially striking in schools that transitioned from White to Black in a relatively short time, the experience of many urban secondary institutions during these years. As African American students moved into a neighborhood, some of them having attended impoverished rural institutions, it appeared as though the schools changed for the worse. For many observers, such changes signaled "deteriorating" local institutions, falling behind both in academic standards and student conduct.[36] But in fact, the urban schools that Black students attended were often a considerable improvement over the smaller, inadequately funded Southern institutions that previous generations had known.

This certainly had been the case for Princeton Elroy, and it was true for many who followed in his footsteps. What was a "crisis" in one set of observers' eyes, consequently, often represented a fresh start for others. Even though dropout rates were higher for African American students than Whites, their graduation rates were improving. Blacks were often placed in so-called "general track" courses of study or in vocational classes, with lower academic standards, but many managed to learn a good deal nonetheless. Large numbers of White students, after all, were enrolled in such classes too, and even if Blacks were more likely to be assigned to them, such racial differences appear to have gradually changed.[37] By the end of the 1970s, Black graduation rates were closer to those of Whites than at any time in American history, even in the cities. And because most Blacks lived in urban settings by then, much of this advancement was accomplished in the very urban schools that had been so widely derided in previous years.[38]

Migration to the cities represented a new source of educational opportunity for many African American families, an improvement over what they experienced in the past, along with a host of other changes. It was often motivated by the search for an improved life through better schools. The high school was an integral part of this, and large numbers of Black youth like Elroy benefitted from exposure to the larger, better-equipped institutions available to them in the cities. Just how much of the movement of Black families from the countryside to the cities, or from one part of the country to another, can be linked to the quest for better schooling is hard to say. But there can be little doubt that it was a vital aspect of the transformation in Black attainment that occurred during this time.

BUILDING TOWARD THE FUTURE

African Americans' embrace of secondary education, in all of its various manifestations, represented a big change. In taking this step, Black families and their children not only contributed to their own well-being, but also helped establish a new level of attainment upon which the education of subsequent generations could advance. It is a well-established historical pattern, after all, that the offspring of parents with a given level of education have a propensity to attain at least the same level of schooling, if not a higher one. In this case, the children of Black parents who had graduated from high school in this period attended secondary schools in greater numbers and began to close the longstanding racial gap in academic achievement that became a focal point of national attention in the latter 20th century. That ultimately may be the most significant outcome of the period, an underappreciated contribution that the educational accomplishments of this generation of African Americans ultimately came to represent.

In his interview for this study, Herschel Summers proudly noted that three of his four children were high school graduates and that two held graduate degrees. Mabel Fountain also had four children, all of whom finished high school, and two of whom graduated from college. These

Introduction

FIGURE I.3. Black-White Trends in NAEP Reading Scores, 1971–1988

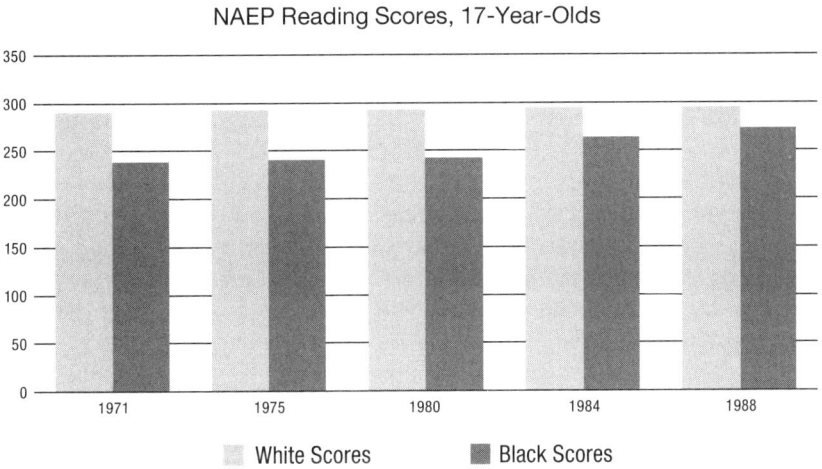

parents and countless others like them raised their children with the expectation that they would complete at least as much education as their parents had.[39] The result, as indicated in Figure I.1, was a steady rise in Black educational attainment that extended to the 1980s and ultimately played a major role in the expansion of the Black middle class. At the same time, there was also evidence of improved Black performance on standardized tests of academic achievement, most notably the National Assessment of Educational Progress (NAEP). It was during the decade of the 1980s that African American teenage students achieved their highest scores on the NAEP exams in both reading and mathematics, registering the smallest "gap" between Black and White students in the history of these tests.[40]

NAEP has been collecting comparable test results broken down by race since 1970. Although is it not possible to isolate scores for particular states from the early years, national trends mark a pattern of improvement that can be linked to rising Black attainment. As suggested above, there is a well-known rise in the mathematics and reading scores of African American 17-year-olds during the 1980s, the decade immediately following the final year in this study. As many scholars have pointed out, the Black-White gap shrank by about 50% in less than 10 years. This reduction is displayed in Figure I.3, showing national trends in NAEP reading scores. The Black-White gap among 17-year-olds reached its lowest point in 1986, before widening slightly. The students who reached this milestone were the offspring of the first generation of African Americans who were mostly secondary graduates. Their parents also came of age during the turbulent 1960s, when the battle for civil rights—including equal educational opportunity—was in full bloom. A number of analyses have concluded that these developments were clearly connected. It was the children of the 1960s Black high school students who closed the racial achievement gap to its narrowest point in history.[41] They were also a highly conflicted generation, as we will see below, and subsequent generations of Black students have not sustained the gains made in these years.[42]

Of course, these are national data and trends that might have been a bit different in urban and rural areas and across regions, given the attainment patterns seen in various parts of the country. Still, David Armor has shown that Black students in large cities were just as likely to exhibit achievement gains as those outside the cities. There also is the question of timing. By and large, the period of dramatic improvement in Black NAEP scores lagged behind attainment increases by at least a decade, if not more. But this suggests that the trends were related across generations. Sociologists Mark Berends, Samuel Lucas, and Roberto Peñaloza estimate that about 40% of the reduction in the Black-White gap in NAEP scores was due to changes in parental and family status of Black students' families, much of it associated with higher levels of educational attainment.[43] In short, rapid improvements in attainment were followed by achievement gains in the children of high school graduates. Other social scientists examining the cohort of Black students who came of age in the 1980s have argued that the educational level of their parents was a major factor in their academic success.[44]

This suggests that the attainment gains of the 1960s and 1970s had a significant impact on the educational accomplishments of subsequent generations. Even if Black achievement trailed that of Whites during these critical decades, improved attainment provided a base upon which further advances in academic achievement could be made. If the stories of improving African American attainment and achievement are linked in this way, attainment levels accomplished by students in the era of "urban educational crisis" marked the beginning of a critically important process, one that may deserve greater attention than it has received to date.

PLAN OF THE BOOK

In the chapters that follow, we examine many steps in closing the racial attainment gap across 40 years. As suggested above, this process touched upon all parts of the country but was most profoundly associated with the South. It is little wonder that our story begins in that region, examining the conditions that Black adolescents faced as they contemplated secondary schooling at the height of the Jim Crow era.

Introduction

The book is divided into two parts, the first dealing with the years between 1940 and 1960 and the second concerning the 1960s and 1970s. We have titled the first part "Expanding Access" because the principal concern of the time was sending larger numbers of African American youth to high school and enabling them to graduate. Equity was a major issue, of course, but we believe greater access was the prevailing theme. The second part is titled "Fighting for Equality," as it deals with the 1960s and 1970s, during the height and immediate aftermath of the civil rights movement. Equality became the principal focal point in struggles over schools, particularly regarding the issue of desegregation. Access continued to be a concern, but the quality of education became the predominant concern of the day.

Part I includes three chapters, the first two focusing on developments in the South and the third dealing with the rest of the country. The years prior to 1960 marked a critical time of growth in African American secondary education, and these chapters describe how this process unfolded in different social and economic contexts. It opens with a chapter describing conditions at the start of the period, focusing on the South and the struggles that African Americans faced in gaining access to high schools. We examine the characteristics of Black students and the many constraints of their institutions. Although secondary education was advancing, its pace was deliberate and measured compared with what would soon follow. These circumstances were compounded by the arrival of the war, which diverted resources and attention away from education and other domestic concerns, at least for a while.

Chapter 2 covers the years between the latter 1940s and 1960, when Black secondary enrollment expanded at a sustained and rapid rate in the South. This was the time of "equalization" campaigns, when states poured resources into making Black schools more equivalent to those for Whites, hoping to forestall pending litigation over integration. Hundreds of new high schools were built across the region, fueling a surge in African American attainment levels. It also marked a substantial improvement in the quality of schooling, with better facilities, smaller class sizes, and enhanced curricular options.

Despite these positive developments, however, these were also years of debate within Black communities regarding the virtues of "equalization" as opposed to integration. Growing numbers of African Americans wondered whether Southern Whites would ever support Black schools at a level comparable to their own institutions. As the equalization campaigns unfolded in the 1950s and 1960s, it became increasingly clear that the answer was no. Eventually, sentiment favoring separate but equal schools gave way to a broad push for integration as the resolution to nearly a century of systematic racial inequality in education.

In Chapter 3, we turn our attention to African American high school experiences outside of the South between 1940 and 1960. Although de jure segregation did not affect most institutions, many suffered the effects of segregated residential settlement, resulting in a high degree of racial inequality for Black students. This was especially true in the larger cities, where the majority of African Americans lived in Northern and Western states. About a third of non-Southern Blacks lived outside of the major cities, and their lives were somewhat different, with less informal segregation in secondary schools but fewer job opportunities for those who graduated. The advent of large-scale migration of Blacks out of the South during and after the war intensified the urbanization of Northern Blacks, but African American suburbanization in the West raised attainment to new heights by the latter 1950s. The result was a pattern of growing inequity in schooling, especially evident at the secondary level, as some institutions that served Black students became overcrowded and were beset with a host of problems, while others provided a new level of educational quality for African American youth.

Part II of the book examines thematic questions in African American education during the years following 1960, focusing on struggles over equity in secondary schooling. This was the time when a widely publicized "crisis" began to emerge in American urban education, a phenomenon principally associated with the North and places such as New York, Detroit, and Chicago, although certainly not limited to that region or the largest cities. In Chapter 4, we consider the urban crisis of the 1960s and 1970s. High schools frequently were cited as examples of urban problems, beset with poor attendance, low academic achievement, petty crime, and truancy, capped by high dropout rates. Although much criticism certainly was warranted, there is also evidence of considerable success in these schools, particularly in the years between 1960 and 1970. This was a time of substantial investment in urban schools on the part of private foundations, state and federal agencies, and a variety of other organizations, much of it focused on the secondary level. This took the form of "dropout prevention" programs, alternative schools, new curricula, and other measures to boost graduation rates, and they seem to have experienced some success.

In the latter years of the 1960s, high school students became an especially volatile factor in the development of African American secondary education. Demanding a wide range of changes to the schools, including curricular reforms and the hiring of Black teachers and administrators, they managed to bring about a significant shift in the character of these institutions in a relatively short time. Although confined largely to cities in the North and West, these activities had a national impact. In certain

Introduction 21

respects, this generation of students helped to reshape the high school to reflect themes of Black pride and cultural awareness, at least for a time.

In Chapter 5, we examine the question of school integration and its impact on high schools across the country. Desegregation proceeded through various phases, from integration of small groups of Blacks in largely White schools to larger numbers later on. Apart from cases such as Little Rock, Arkansas, and Clinton, Tennessee, where violence erupted, most White resistance did not get national attention. Of course, this did not mean that it was ineffective. Even when they were finally forced to accept integration in principle, most Whites eventually abandoned the schools, making true desegregation an elusive quest through much of the period. We devote particular attention to Kansas City, Missouri, which was typical of many "border" and Northern cities, witnessing rapid transition from integrated to highly segregated high schools in a matter of years. We also consider the massive desegregation in the South following 1968, when states across the region finally began wholesale integration of public education, including high schools. Studies from this period found that after a time of adjustment, high school students adapted to the new reality of Southern education with varying degrees of success. Although there was considerable conflict at first, White and Black students eventually learned to live with integration, which seems to have enhanced learning outcomes in many instances.

In the book's Conclusion, we touch upon the principal themes discussed in earlier chapters and examine the closing years of the 1970s, when the desegregation movement began to reach an apogee in terms of its influence. The term "White flight" became a popular way to describe the process of change in urban school districts, and a growing number of big-city high schools were becoming predominantly African American, particularly in the North. At the same time, however, widespread integration, especially in the South, meant that more Black youth attended largely White secondary schools than at any prior time in American history. African American graduation rates continued to improve into the decade, and there is evidence that achievement—as measured in test scores—increased as well. This development, along with rising Black college graduation rates and the emergence of a substantial African American middle class, were the clearest manifestations of the educational advances accomplished during this era. The Black struggle for secondary education may have been difficult and protracted, but there can be little doubt that it contributed materially to the accomplishments of African Americans evident in the closing decades of the 20th century.

The book closes with a brief look beyond 1980 to the period when the Black-White attainment gap ceased closing, followed by a widening of the achievement gap as well. We suggest that a number of factors can be linked to these developments, but one of them may be the arrival of a new era in the history of African American life, where the high school is no longer an object of struggle and large numbers of youth are living in high-poverty inner-city settings. The shifting context in which these children grew up, particularly the loss of jobs and a changing family structure, appears to have contributed to this halt in progress. There is obviously more to this, but for future generations of African American educators and students, one of the biggest tasks may be returning a sense of accomplishment to these communities and to their schools. Despite the many problems of inner-city schools, they continue to represent a critical gateway to success for many thousands of African American youth in a society that is largely defined by educational credentials. Revisiting the struggles of the past may be a useful starting point, to restore a degree of hope and faith in secondary schooling as a transformative and liberating experience once again.

Finally, Appendix A gives details of the research methods employed in collecting data for this book. The sources we drew upon—quantitative data sets, oral history interviews, newspaper articles, high school yearbooks, and other archival data—are described, along with our reflections on these sources and process of analysis we undertook in utilizing them. Appendix B provides tables with additional information about some of the statistical analyses performed throughout the book.

Part I

EXPANDING ACCESS

CHAPTER 1

The South in the 1940s

WHITE AMERICANS WENT to high school in large numbers during the first half of the 20th century, but the same was not true for the nation's Black population. Although Black elementary school enrollments expanded, the vast majority of African American youth did not attend secondary institutions before the 1950s. Historian James D. Anderson has described this as "one of the fundamental reasons that the educational progress of Black Americans lagged far behind that of other Americans."[1] By any measure, progress was slow. At the end of the 1920s, secondary students numbered less than 5% of Black enrollments. By the start of World War II, that figure had roughly doubled, but according to one estimate, fewer than 4% of those starting school in 1932 graduated 12 years later. This was less than one-sixth the rate for Whites. Even in major cities, where secondary schools for African Americans could be found, enrollments and graduation rates lagged behind district norms.[2] If the high school's growth was a "second transformation" of American education, contributing materially to middle-class prosperity for millions, it largely excluded Blacks.[3]

To grasp changes in African American secondary schooling in the postwar era, it is necessary to begin with the South. This was where more than three-quarters of the nation's Black youth lived, and it was their experiences that represented most of Black education. The early 1940s were a time of hardship as the country emerged from the Great Depression, especially in the impoverished South, but there was also hope as economic conditions began to improve. For many African Americans, life continued to be a struggle, but they, too, held aspirations for a brighter future. Resources were scarce but communities banded together to make improvements to their local institutions and plan for a better quality of life. Perhaps the most visible manifestation of such changes was the schools, and few enhancements were as significant as establishing a high school. Secondary education, after all, held the promise of a future beyond the often bleak conditions of the agricultural South, and an opportunity for subsequent generations to realize their highest potential.

This chapter describes the Black-White racial disparity in high school attendance and completion in the South prior to the civil rights era, along with differences in the quality and level of education. As we will see, the opportunity to attend high school varied considerably across states and among youth from different backgrounds. For Black and White youth, for example, living in non-farming and property-owning households increased the probability of school attendance. A gender gap in high school attendance favoring daughters also existed for both groups, if more so among Blacks. But race was the major factor shaping the opportunity to attend school and the quality of schools available. Access to schooling was more precarious for Blacks, and their schools lacked critical resources. Whereas White schools were consolidated and modernized, and had buses to transport students, most Black schools remained small and isolated. During the 1940s, these differences were increasingly contested by Black parents, communities, and organizations such as the NAACP. These were portents of changes yet to come.

STARK INEQUITY: THE RURAL COUNTRYSIDE

At the start of this period, the condition of Black secondary education varied across the South, but similar problems existed everywhere. In general, high schools were far less readily available for Blacks than for Whites, and their quality was inferior on most observable counts. A 1938 report noted the rapid increase in overall enrollments, but especially among Black students, whose numbers had increased fivefold since the latter 1920s. Even so, Black attainment levels lagged considerably behind those of Whites. In 1939, Doxey Wilkerson observed that Black secondary enrollment in the 18 Southern states was just one-third that of Whites, with Mississippi, South Carolina, and Georgia registering the lowest levels. Many believed the lack of transportation for rural Blacks was a problem, but Wilkerson pointed to an even more fundamental question: the absence of high schools in rural districts, where two-thirds of the Black population lived at the time. He counted 425 Southern counties with large Black populations and no secondary schools for African Americans.[4] Counties with smaller Black populations also had few opportunities.[5] Despite promising signs, education for Black youth clearly had a long way to go.

The challenges facing Black secondary schooling in the rural South were manifold and extended well beyond availability. There also were questions regarding the level and quality of schooling. Students with access to high schools were likely to attend one that offered instruction for just 1 or 2 years and no diploma. A study in 1935 found that a slight ma-

TABLE 1.1. High School Enrollment in the South, Ages 14–18, 1940 (in percentages)

Household Status	Portion of Region Teen Population		Teen Secondary Enrollment Rate		17-year-old Junior Enrollment Rate	
	Black	White	Black	White	Black	White
Non Farm; Home Owner	15	24	32.3	55.7	20.8	45.5
Non Farm; Non Owner	35	33	16.9	37.8	9.6	28.4
Farm; Landowner	11	23	16.7	40.1	8.1	29.9
Farm; Non Landowner	39	20	5.4	22.3	1.7	14.1
Total Region	100	100	14.6	39.3	7.9	30

Source: IPUMS data (Blacks 25% of youth population).

jority of Black rural secondary schools offered 2 years or less of instruction. Most appear to have been extensions of elementary schools, offering a few subjects beyond the 8th grade.[6] The profile of White schools, on the other hand, was quite different. Most were 3- or 4-year institutions, even though many offered shorter programs. Although there was variation in the number and type of schools, the weak condition of rural secondary education was a theme in state reports and other commentaries. It affected both races. In 1943, the Virginia Chamber of Commerce described the offerings of all such schools as "very meager," and failing "to meet the varied needs of the pupils attending them."[7] If this was true of White high schools, it was doubly so for Black institutions with substantially fewer resources.

This is evident in enrollment figures. Table 1.1 displays secondary enrollment rates for teenagers in 1940, divided according to household status and race, derived from 1% Integrated Public Use Microdata Samples (IPUMS) of U.S. Census data. Home ownership and farm status represent global indicators of social and economic conditions, along with rural versus urban residence.[8] The largest number of Black youth, nearly 40%, lived in households where farming was a major source of income, and property, including the domicile, was rented. This group represented the poorest echelon of Southern society, and it had the lowest secondary enrollment. Most were tenant farmers, living on land rented annually, largely at subsistence by growing crops—typically cotton—for the market. In the words of Black sociologist E. Franklin Frazier, they survived "under a modified form of the plantation economy" with little change from the past.[9] At less than 6%, these youth attended at less than half the rate of the next category, farm households that owned property. The meager representation of Black farm teenagers in high schools, whether their families owned property or not, is prima facie evidence of the shortage of institutions to serve them.

High school enrollment for White youth, closer to natural norms, provides a telling contrast to the Black rates. Overall, White enrollment was more than two and a half times greater than Black rates, and among tenant farm households it was more than four times higher. This, too, points to the lack of education opportunities for Black youth, especially in rural districts, a problem for decades.[10] It also was symptomatic of deprivation experienced by Black tenant families, who were twice as likely to suffer poverty as their White counterparts.[11] White enrollment rates were slightly higher for females, but not to the same extent as African Americans. In other respects, Black and White enrollment was closer, but only non-farm home-owning Blacks attended at rates more than half those of Whites. This, too, may have reflected the availability of secondary schooling, but it doubtless was a function of wealth and educational background as well. By and large, households in this category represented an urban middle class, such as it was, which could best afford to send children to school well into their teens. It is hardly a surprise that youth in such households from both races attended high school at the highest rate. Among African Americans, these were students whose educational experiences probably most closely mirrored those of Whites.

These patterns also are evident among youth approaching the age of high school completion. The figures in the right-hand column of Table 1.1 represent the proportion of 17-year-olds enrolled in the junior year (grade 11) or higher, a measure of readiness for graduation.[12] For Blacks in tenant farm households, fewer than 2% were in this category, reflecting the many rural institutions that lacked a curriculum beyond 2 years. For youth in other categories, the numbers reaching this level of attainment were far higher, closer to overall secondary enrollment, typically more than half. Even among White teens in tenant farm households, the proportion reaching this level was nearly two-thirds the overall secondary enrollment rate. Their institutions offered a more complete curriculum than those serving Blacks in analogous circumstances.

Youth living in more affluent households in non-farm settings appear to have had more school success among both Blacks and Whites. More than one out of five Black 17-year-olds from property-owning, non-farm households were on track to graduate, but this group of persistent and successful students comprised less than 3% of Southern African American youth. Although they were somewhat privileged for Blacks, students in this category registered attainment well below the regional average for

TABLE 1.2. Percentage of Southern High School Students Who Were Female, by Race, Farm Status, and Property Ownership, 1940 (in percentages)

Category	BLACK			WHITE		
	Owner	Renter	Total	Owner	Renter	Total
Farm	62.9	72.5	67.9	55.6	58.2	56.5
Non-Farm	61.4	58.3	59.7	54.6	56.5	54.5
Total	61.8	62.1	62	53.8	56.9	55.2

Source: IPUMS data.

Whites. They may have represented an advance guard of African American education, but even these youth had a long way to go in reaching prevailing standards. This, too, was evidence of the underdeveloped state of Black secondary schooling.

As noted earlier, another feature of African American secondary schooling was a rather pronounced gender imbalance in favor of young women. As indicated in Table 1.2, more than 60% of Black high school students were female, and more than two-thirds among farm families. It was among tenant farm households, however, that the degree of student feminization was greatest, with nearly three-quarters being female. This meant that just 3% of male teenagers in these households attended high school, compared to nearly 8% of young women. It was symptomatic of the expectations and requirements of farm labor, which required physical strength and impeded schooling. And because of the difficulties facing families in these circumstances, the labor of children was often critical. On tenant farms, consequently, the majority of male teenagers worked, most as laborers, with a third classified in the census as "unpaid family workers." This foreclosed the option of high school for most. This also was true for property-owning Black farm households, but not to the same degree. Among White tenant families, more than a third of teenage males worked, with paid laborers representing 30%. For property-owning Whites, the numbers were a bit lower, but more than a quarter of their teenage boys worked as laborers, too. Agricultural work was a fact of life in the rural South, but African American farmers relied more on their sons than Whites, and it was reflected in the schools.[13]

The female enrollment margin also may have reflected an interest in teaching as a vocational option. In the Southern countryside, most teachers were women, and a secondary education was often required for such positions. A quarter of Black teachers outside of metropolitan areas had no collegiate training in 1940, and the number was even higher in rural districts.[14] A high school diploma, or even a year or 2 of secondary courses, could lead to work as a teacher. Teaching was widely considered female work and relatively few alternatives existed for young women. This contributed to the feminization of secondary institutions, especially in communities with a preponderance of tenant farmers.

In other settings, the gender imbalance appears to have been less severe. Among non-farm secondary students, girls represented just 60% of enrollments, not as one-sided a majority. As suggested above, employment was a major alternative to school, and for young men job prospects apparently were more appealing than for women. Judging from figures in Table 1.2, this appears to have been the case among Whites as well, although not to the same degree. As had been true elsewhere in earlier times, Southern high schools were predominantly female institutions in 1940, but particularly for African Americans.[15]

As important as they were, however, such gender and status distinctions affected a relatively small number of individuals. For the vast majority of Southern Black youth, secondary schooling simply was not in the cards. Regardless of their gender or social standing, living in the country in poor communities meant that going to high school was a luxury few could realize.

This was especially true in counties spanning the lower tier of the South geographically, the so-called Cotton Belt, where farm tenancy was a prevailing way of life. It was perhaps most clearly evident in Mississippi, Alabama, and Georgia, where less than one in five Black youth lived on family-owned property, the lowest numbers in the region.[16] As indicated in Table 1.3, these states, along with Louisiana and South Carolina, had the weakest African American secondary enrollment rates. Across 15 Southern states, the bivariate correlation between property ownership and secondary enrollments was statistically significant at .65, accounting for more than 40% of the interstate variance and pointing to a broad relationship between these facets of social status.[17] This finding is consistent with Wilkerson's observations at the time, and highlights the critical shortage of Black high schools in rural areas, especially where farm tenancy predominated.

Educational opportunities were better in towns and cities, but economic uncertainty plagued African Americans in these settings, too. As a consequence, most Black youth entered the labor market as soon as possible, regardless of where they lived. With nearly a third holding jobs, their likelihood of employment was more than 50% greater than Whites, whose teen employment rate was under 20%. The numbers were highest on farms, where more than 37% worked, but more than a fifth of non-farm Black teenagers had jobs, too.[18] This would change in years to come, but significant improvements in the availability and quality of schooling would not come easily. The readiness of many African Americans to em-

TABLE 1.3. Black Property Ownership and Secondary School Enrollment, Ages 14–18, by Southern State, 1940

State	Share of Families Owning Property	High School Attendance Rate	Black 14–8 Population Size
Virginia	.4526	.1556	77,862
Alabama	.1992	.1115	106,850
Arkansas	.2397	.1038	52,623
Florida	.3327	.1631	50,261
Georgia	.1592	.0957	115,465
Louisiana	.2611	.0863	86,095
Mississippi	.1943	.0683	106,382
North Carolina	.2771	.1660	119,589
South Carolina	.2289	.1003	102,689
Texas	.3208	.2127	92,149
Kentucky	.3729	.2230	19,258
Maryland	.2839	.2268	27,863
Oklahoma	.3691	.1910	17,718
Tennessee	.2727	.1837	50,529
West Virginia	.2558	.1996	10,804
Total	.2623	.1338	1,036,137

Source: IPUMS data.

brace the high school was hardly evident, as more immediate concerns took precedence in their lives.

A SHAKY FOUNDATION: ELEMENTARY EDUCATION

One reason that many African American youth did not succeed in high school, even if opportunities existed, was weak preparation at the elementary level. As historians have established, a combination of local Black initiative, state support, and philanthropic contributors, particularly the Rosenwald Fund, greatly expanded elementary education across the South. Between 1915 and the end of the 1920s, nearly 4,000 rural schools were erected, replacing dilapidated and dangerous older structures and providing buildings on new sites. At the same time, a bigger share of state school funds was devoted to Black education, narrowing the gap with White expenditures somewhat. School terms were lengthened and teacher pay improved, in some instances even reaching parity with White standards. Certain states benefitted more than others; North Carolina and Mississippi saw more than a quarter of the new schools while Georgia got less than 1%.[19] The greatest concentration of students lived in an area extending from North Carolina to Mississippi, five states with more than 40% of the region's Black student population and about half the new school buildings. This was also where cotton production, farm tenancy, and the demand for agricultural labor were greatest, and where improved schooling was most needed.

Although conditions had improved significantly since the latter part of the 19th century, by 1940 problems abounded. Across the region, elementary facilities were in poor condition following the Great Depression, and children were frequently kept out of school for work or other reasons, which did not auger well for attainment. "It was not an unusual scene," wrote a South Carolina official in 1945, "to see children who should be in school gathering cotton as late as March in fields that had never been picked." Such demands made it difficult if not impossible to "progress normally in their school lives," even if reasonably good schools were available.[20] Sounding a similar note, Georgia's state superintendent lamented the "irregular attendance" that prevented most elementary students from advancing to higher grades.[21] It was hardly surprising that Black enrollment in secondary schools lagged behind that of Whites in every Southern state, although there was considerable variation in course offerings and the quality of institutions. High schools were slow to develop partly because elementary education was itself insufficiently supported, especially in poor rural districts.

The problem of substandard school facilities for Black children had been voiced for decades, but came to light in dramatic fashion during 1946 in Lumberton, North Carolina. Black children and parents staged a boycott against the decaying and hazardous condition of the local school, a 40-year-old frame building formerly known as the Redstone Academy. The incident began at the urging of an NAACP organizer and word quickly spread to the state's larger newspapers, which sent reporters and photographers to investigate. When stories appeared with pictures highlighting the crumbling and unsanitary state of the building, Dr. Carl V. Reynolds, the state's health commissioner, decided to inspect the school. Within days, the Charlotte and Raleigh newspapers featured Reynolds declaring the Lumberton facility "a disgrace," speculating that as many as 500 other Black schools suffered similar conditions. Perhaps more important, Reynolds also pointed out that health risks posed by such structures were a danger to the state's entire population, not just Blacks. This may have made the question of Black schools a bit more urgent for many Whites.[22] At the very least, it called attention to the deplorable state of African American schools across the region.

The Lumberton incident was resolved when the local school board abruptly found funds for a new building, but progress in other rural areas throughout the South was much slower. Protests occurred elsewhere over a range of issues, a sign of growing frustration in the face of inequities that had existed for decades, particularly in the Deep South.[23] In 1942, a Mississippi Methodist Conference report estimated that just 37 cents of every dollar allocated to Black education was actually spent on African American schools, with the rest going to White institutions. Five years later, things had not changed much, as another report noted the slapdash condition of the state's 3,345 Black schools, "nearly half [of which] are housed in churches, tenement houses or any other type of building possible." Yet another bulletin alluded to the haphazard circumstances of the schools, warning that they should not be located too close to highways, lest vagabonds spend the night, burning fuel and destroying books.[24] In neighboring Alabama, a similar report counted half the state's Black schools as one-room buildings, many of them "shacks" with "no provisions made for water, toilets and health facilities."[25] A review of conditions in Georgia found that more than 90% of Black facilities were "either incapable of remodeling or would require extensive repairs to meet a reasonable standard of efficiency," circumstances affecting less than 20% of White schools. Echoing this, a 1949 survey reported that only 12% of the state's Black schools had "water under pressure on school grounds," and that many of these did not have "satisfactory drinking fountains" or toilets.[26] Even in North Carolina, 2 years after Lumberton, Nathan C. (N.C.) Newbold, the White director of the state's Division of Negro Education, publicly lamented the overall "dreariness and forbidding general atmosphere" of its many rural Black schools, echoing observations across the region.[27]

Poor one- or two-room schools also existed for Whites, but numbered far fewer because of consolidation campaigns in earlier decades, and they were rapidly disappearing. In 1947, Mississippi officials counted little more than 100 White one-teacher schools in the state, as opposed to 2,000 Black ones. Figures from other states were not as extreme, but the differences were great.[28] By and large, consolidation of smaller schools into larger, newer facilities was a practice reserved for White institutions prior to the latter 1940s. "Consolidation was a white man's pattern of operating schools," declared one Mississippi Black principal.[29] It often was facilitated with aid from the state, which helped to finance larger, modern buildings, including high schools. These facilities were typically organized into districts controlled at the county level. Consolidation also required considerable investment in school buses, and many more White than Black students were bussed in the South prior to the 1950s. Georgia, for instance, reported spending some 14 times more on transporting White students in 1949 than it did on Blacks, and similar inequities were noted throughout the region.[30] In North Carolina, Newbold observed that most White students attended consolidated schools, and the statewide value of their facilities, on a per-pupil basis, was several times that of Black schools. The relatively poor state of Black education in the rural districts, he concluded, was the result of prolonged neglect and underfunding for facilities, transportation, and a range of other factors.[31] A 1947 report from Alabama noted that the number of one- and two-teacher White schools had fallen by some 80% since the 1920s, while the decline in similar Black schools had been only 18%.[32] A Georgia legislative report the same year counted 50% more Black schools across the state than White ones. Since White enrollments were higher, their schools were correspondingly larger.[33] Consolidation often led to the expansion of high school facilities or building new ones, so Whites attended larger, modern institutions funded in part with state assistance. The development of Black education, on the other hand, was generally dependent on the districts and their immediate communities.

In rural areas across the region, the result was an excruciatingly gradual pace of improvement, as African Americans struggled in these circumstances to enhance their children's educational prospects. Conditions may have been worst in the more heavily Black states of the Deep South, but African American school expenditures lagged across the region, with differences greatest in the rural districts. Since the majority of Black children lived in the countryside, the quality of their preparation for study at the secondary level was not very high indeed.

MAKING THE BEST OF HARD TIMES

Despite these problems, the 1930s and 1940s were years of rising secondary schooling among African Americans.[34] High schools were growing across the country and there was increased interest in them throughout the South. This was abetted, certainly, by the changing cotton economy, and the idea of moving to other parts of the country where secondary education could be advantageous.[35]

The arrival of war in 1941 put a temporary pause on enrollment growth as thousands of American teenagers left school to take jobs in a labor market that was suddenly enlivened by defense spending. Altogether, secondary enrollments appear to have declined by nearly 15% during the first several years of war, but the drop in African American attendance was considerably lower. Howard University's Walter Daniel estimated that Black secondary enrollment in the South declined by less than 3%.

No doubt, fewer job opportunities beckoned to African American youth because of discrimination, and the numbers of Black secondary students was low to start with. Black youth had considerably less education than Whites, particularly in the South, and this surely hurt them as well. Those fortunate enough to attend a high school were less inclined than Whites to seek employment. This may have reflected the prejudice they faced, but for some it also could have signaled a strong commitment to making the most of their schooling.[36]

Enrollment growth returned following the war, but it was still hard to find Black secondary institutions, especially in rural areas. This gradually changed as high schools for African Americans began to multiply. Although they were surely encouraged by certain state officials and school leaders, most such endeavors were launched by local educators and community members who were interested in expanding educational possibilities for their youth. Long-time Black Mississippi principal N. R. Burger maintained that such efforts were most likely to succeed with "a group of progressive Black farmers who had land and resources and supported the school." He declared the prospects greater for "educational opportunities for blacks in a community where independence exists than in a community where dependence is a way of life." This observation corresponded with the regional patterns in property ownership and enrollments evident in Table 1.3. Other commentators agreed that land-owning Blacks across the South generally took the greatest initiative in promoting secondary education.[37] Growing enrollments and a rising number of institutions were testimony to their success.

Secondary education was expensive, however, and regardless of how much land and other resources a community controlled, establishing a high school was rarely easy. Most Black communities, of course, were not affluent, so a variety of strategies were employed. The most common approach to providing students with secondary classes was simply to add them to an elementary school. This was a practice observed in both White and Black schools, but far more frequently in the latter. Indeed, it had been a strategy for leveraging school resources practiced for decades, if not longer.[38] It also was the source of most of the region's 1- or 2-year secondary institutions, chiefly due to local initiative. Even if the level of instruction in these extensions of primary schools was modest, it represented a beginning upon which subsequent improvements could be made.

County training schools were another type of institution that frequently adapted to offer secondary instruction. With support from Northern foundations, these schools were established throughout the South to provide basic preparation for Black teachers at the elementary level. Since they often represented the highest stage of instruction in a large area, many were considered natural sites for expanding secondary education. Some of these institutions evolved into freestanding high schools; others offered only limited instruction beyond the elementary grades.[39]

More often, however, whether in an elementary school or a training institute, the Black high school was grafted onto an existing institution, offering just 1 or 2 years of additional instruction. Funds typically were raised by a special committee or board of "trustees" from the local Black community, and used for building materials, books, and the salaries of additional teachers if necessary. As such, these measures represented a form of additional or "double" taxation for educational purposes, a longstanding tradition in these communities.[40] The result often was secondary education at a rudimentary level, but in the countryside it was an opportunity that had not existed for earlier generations of Black youth.

In 1947, Jasper Jones graduated from the Colored High School in Angleton, Texas, which he described as a "jumpstart school" of four rooms attached to an elementary building. When he was in grade school, the town lacked a Black secondary school, so older youth went to Houston to high school. That changed in the early 1940s, when "Professor Wright," an "outstanding orator," arrived declaring, "If Henry Ford can build cars and they can go around the world, why couldn't they teach Black kids in America?" Jones described the addition as an immediate success, with 75 or 80 students "coming from everywhere." The school started with a bus, and Jasper and his brother rode 13 miles there daily. The curriculum was basic, with few vocational courses, but Jones recalled teachers caring deeply about students and felt he received a good education. Although he missed 40 days of instruction one year to farm work, he kept up with assignments that his brother brought home. After graduation, Jones attended Texas Southern University in Houston, and eventually graduated from Prairie View A&M.

The "jumpstart school" that Jones attended was typical of much Black secondary education at the time. The realities of limited resources often made such local accommodations necessary, but state education officials also urged this approach, even in larger districts. In one instance, Robert Cousins, the White director of Georgia's Division of Negro Education, urged Macon's superintendent to adapt a newly built elementary facility to meet rising demand for secondary instruction, adding a vocational annex of eight rooms. Although clearly not an equitable solution, since a sizable White high school already existed, it was a politically expedient response given the relatively modest resources involved. As Cousins noted, he would be "greatly surprised" if the district were to spend "much of its own money on new school buildings in the next few years," especially for Black students.[41] Starting a high school in this fashion was clearly better than not starting one at all. It enabled African American elementary graduates to continue their studies, even if only for a couple of years, and established a starting point for developing a more fully realized secondary institution. Of course, it perpetuated White advantages in education as well.

Because of circumstances such as these, facilities often were modified to serve more than one purpose, typically combining elementary and secondary classes under a single roof. Sometimes called "union schools," these hybrid institutions extended limited secondary instruction to students who wanted to remain in school or offered a start to those interested in continuing their studies elsewhere.[42] Such arrangements represented the bulk of 1- and 2-year Black "high schools" throughout the region. Consequently, Louisiana listed just 10 freestanding Black high schools out of 102 institutions offering secondary courses in 1946. Likewise, Mississippi reported in 1949 that 261 of the state's 3,159 Black schools (8%) were "doing some high school work," 108 of them unaccredited at the secondary level.[43] It was the latter group that represented most of the state's newest high schools, as well as its smaller and academically weaker ones. But all of them reflected some measure of local determination to provide secondary instruction to students interested in advancing their education. Even if scholastic offerings were meager, theses courses represented a foundation upon which future African American attainment ultimately would be realized.

Facilities were hardly the only resources stretched by high school growth. Throughout the South, concerns were widely expressed over finding capable administrators to lead these institutions, along with qualified secondary teachers.[44] In the face of shortages, a number of improvised solutions were found. Georgia's Robert Cousins complained about the practice of cash-strapped districts hiring agricultural education teachers as principals, simply because their salaries were paid by federal Smith-Hughes funds that required 12-month contracts. He believed such arrangements made for neither effective administration nor good vocational instruction, as "teachers of agriculture were spending too much time getting up public programs, coaching basketball teams, and the like."[45] Whether local communities had the same concerns, of course, was a different matter. Many were happy to have the resources to hire any kind of leader on a year-round basis, even one who was not fully prepared, while others were looking for administrators with training and experience. There is little evidence, moreover, that agricultural education was a big concern for African American students and their parents. It was considered no great loss, in that case, to use these funds for an administrator, even one who doubled as a vocational teacher.

Experienced and skilled leaders, on the other hand, were usually in short supply. One group of Blacks wrote to Cousins seeking several teachers and a principal with a bachelor's or master's degree. "We need one," they declared, "to raise the standard of this school." For his part, Cousins was able to recommend a couple of names and send along a list of state accreditation requirements.[46] But beyond getting such basic information, it was up to local communities to find the personnel to staff their budding institutions. It was not easy, as the number of Black secondary schools was increasing and veteran administrators and teachers were rare in the countryside. As N. R. Burger observed, many Black educators felt that using state vocational funds to hire a leader was a creative solution to such problems. Finding an energetic and ambitious beginner with a subsidized year-round salary generally was considered a blessing in most rural districts.[47]

With many schools opening under these circumstances, the number of Black secondary institutions increased more rapidly in the 1930s and 1940s than White schools, which began to decline in number due to consolidation campaigns. A report from North Carolina, for instance, showed that in 15 years following 1937, some 41 union schools for Whites closed and 20 started for Blacks. At the same time, 12 freestanding White high schools were shuttered, while four Black high schools opened. Altogether, this represented a loss of more than 50 White secondary schools and a gain of two dozen Black ones, as enrollments for both groups continued to expand. Similar developments occurred elsewhere, marking a substantial increase in opportunities for Blacks at the secondary level. In 1939, there were 19 counties in South Carolina with no Black high schools; 10 years later, there were none, and secondary enrollment had increased by nearly 70%. At the same time, the number of Black youth in high school more than doubled in Georgia, Alabama, and Mississippi.[48] Even if the circumstances of most secondary institutions were quite modest, this represented a dramatic widening of the higher branches of instruction. Rising enrollment also signaled widespread belief in the value of education and hope for the future.

CITY SCHOOLS

The condition of Black schools was considerably better in the Southern cities, although problems existed there, too. The most prominent and successful Black secondary institutions were located in principal urban centers. By the 1920s, many large Southern cities had at least one sizable high school for African Americans, providing educational experiences comparable in many respects to those offered by White institutions. In the 1930s, it was these schools that provided the bulk of secondary instruction to African Americans in the South. Edward Redcay estimated in 1935 that urban institutions enrolled two-thirds of the region's Black high school students, but served just a third of its Black teenage population.[49] These flagship schools grew to be quite large, enrolling as many as 2,000 or more students by the 1940s. The curriculum they offered was correspondingly expansive, especially compared to the meager offerings of rural institutions.[50] They employed scores of teachers, administrators, librarians, counselors, and other professionals, representing a key segment of the urban Black middle class.

Wilbur Johnson graduated from Atlanta's Ashford Street School in 1945 and entered Booker T. Washington High in the fall to begin 7th grade. Raised by his mother and grandmother, Johnson was not an especially good student, and felt himself drawn by the "street life." With the adults in his household working almost constantly, he and his brother were often left to their own devices. He credited his peers for eventually exerting a positive influence, pointing out the advantage of staying in school, along with several teachers who served as role models. He graduated from high school in 1950 and went to college for a couple of years before being trained as an accountant and eventually forging a career in the clothing business. In retrospect, he readily acknowledged the importance of the education he received at Washington, even if he occasionally lost sight of it at the time. Even though his family did not particularly stress the importance of education, the school's proximity and the variety of social activities it offered, along with the relationships he developed there, helped keep him enrolled and eventually helped him to graduate.

For countless other students like Johnson, large urban secondary schools like Booker T. Washington represented a major benefit. These institutions were centers of activity that drew youth from all directions, regardless of their social and economic circumstances. For social elites in the community, like Martin Luther King Jr., who attended Washington with Wilbur Johnson, these schools were a gateway to higher education and the professions. The son of a highly visible leader, King was considered excessively studious, even bookish, by many classmates. But Atlanta's only Black high school offered him an opportunity to hone his academic skills, just as it afforded Johnson and many others the chance for a more conventional secondary education.

In this regard, there can be little doubt that such schools functioned as important community anchors, both in terms of their middle-class staff and the academic opportunities they offered, along with extracurricular activities, particularly in sports and musical performance. School activities were routinely covered in local Black newspapers, especially sports but also receptions, dances, and award ceremonies.[51] Institutions such as Atlanta's Washington, Lanier in Jackson, Parker High in Birmingham, and dozens of others were well regarded by Blacks throughout their states and across the region.⁵² Former students recalled classmates who came to the city, living with relatives or family friends, just to attend one of these schools. Such substantial institutions provided strong models of what Black high schools might become, and a potent source of training and guidance for thousands of ambitious youth.⁵³

The big cities also attracted the best Black teachers, or at least those with the most education. Although the average age of city teachers was just a year older than those outside of metropolitan areas, more than half (56%) were college graduates, as opposed to only a third (33%) in smaller communities. Only 9% of city teachers had graduate training, but they represented more than two-thirds of all Southern Black teachers with such advanced preparation. While it is probably safe to assume that the urban Black high schools were able to employ the teachers with the best credentials, only a select few had any significant graduate training. In this respect, their staffs appear to have been generally comparable to those of White institutions, as less than one in five urban White teachers had done graduate work.⁵⁴ If most African American teachers were behind their White counterparts with respect to formal credentials, they did not lag very far in the region's principal cities.

Notwithstanding their size and stature, however, the city high schools exhibited many of the difficulties facing Black education in the South. Dropout rates were high, often 50% or more over a 4-year period.⁵⁵ Johnson may have managed to keep attending, but many of his peers did not. Although often housed in impressive buildings, these schools struggled with overcrowding and the challenges of maintaining and expanding their facilities with limited resources. The books they assigned to students, along with many in the libraries, were typically handed down from the White schools, and were often in poor repair and marked by previous users. The same was true of furniture and lab equipment, which almost always was older and more worn and dilapidated than in White schools. And conditions in the immediate neighborhood were not always positive.⁵⁶ Students were well aware of these differences, and felt the sting of exclusion from competition in sports and other extracurricular activities with the White schools. Athletics teams and bands were required to journey long distances, sometimes to neighboring states, in order to compete against and perform with other Black schools. Many of the most successful and active students found this especially galling, as they felt perfectly capable of competing with the very best that White schools had to offer, certainly in terms of athletics and musical performance.⁵⁷

Some of the strengths and limitations of the big-city Black high schools are evident in enrollment figures reported in Table 1.4, based on IPUMS data from Southern metropolitan areas in 1940. These figures exclude youth living in towns and smaller cities whose circumstances also could

TABLE 1.4. Southern Metropolitan Teenage High School Enrollment, 1940 (percent in high school or graduated, ages 14–18) *

Household Status	Portion of Metro Teen Population		Teen Secondary Enrollment Rate		17-Year-Old Junior + Enrollment Rate	
	Black	White	Black	White	Black	White
Urban Home Owner	17.5	29	50.4	62.8	23.8	45.3
Urban Renter	52	43	23.7	42.7	10.7	23.9
Suburban Home Owner	13	19	20.6	53.5	14	36.9
Suburban Renter	17.5	9	16.3	36.8	11.6	21.5
Total Metro	100	100	26.7	50	13.6	32.3

* Sample excludes individuals classified as "central city status unknown" or "metro status not identified."
Source: IPUMS data (Blacks 28% of youth population).

be considered urban but not in or near a large city. Altogether, fewer than a quarter of Southern Black youth lived in metropolitan areas, which was less than half of the non-farm population, so their circumstances cannot be considered typical. But there can be little question that living in these settings afforded greater access to secondary education.

Perhaps the most striking feature reported in Table 1.4 is the high proportion of youth from home-owning households enrolled in high school. At 50%, this figure was the same as overall White metropolitan enrollment, and 80% of the White city rate of nearly 63%. It suggests that going to secondary school had become a modal experience for this segment of the Black population, just 4% of the region's total. As home owners in the South's largest cities, the parents of these youth represented the Black urban middle class, and it appears that they clearly valued education. They undoubtedly were a critical constituency of the flagship Black high schools in these communities. The largest group of urban Black youth, on the other hand, was made up of the sons and daughters of renters, who outnumbered the home owners by nearly a three to one margin. Their secondary enrollment rate was less than half that of their wealthier counterparts, but because of their numbers they comprised a slight majority (58%) of the students in these institutions. Although it is hard to say how differences in wealth and status may have affected student experiences, there does seem to have been a range of backgrounds represented.

Attending high school was one thing, of course, but graduating was another. As indicated in the right-hand column of Table 1.4, less than a quarter of Black 17-year-olds with homes owned by their parents were on track to graduate in city schools. The figure for renters was barely one in 10. Altogether, just 14% of Black 17-year-olds in the largest Southern cities had reached the junior year or higher, as opposed to nearly a quarter of their White counterparts. This discrepancy points to the dropout rate in these schools, and the proportion of students lagging behind an age-appropriate grade level. Overall, the likelihood of big-city Black students reaching this level of attainment was less than half that of their White counterparts. This was even true among those living in owner-occupied residences, despite relatively high levels of overall enrollment. There is evidence that some eventually graduated, as the census figures indicate that one of five Black 19-year-olds in central cities had completed school in 1940. But that figure may overstate the urban graduation rate, especially if some graduates did not attend city schools but instead had moved there after school. Although the flagship urban institutions afforded many Black youth the opportunity to attend high school, they hardly guaranteed success.

The other geographic category in Table 1.4 is "suburban" residence, which included all youth living within metropolitan areas but not in central cities. While the term *suburban* may have a particular meaning and resonance today, it was hardly the same in the South at the start of the 1940s. As a number of historians have demonstrated, these extra-urban communities varied widely in their character and status, ranging from relatively poor and isolated hamlets to thriving towns connected directly to the city.[58] It is telling, in that case, that secondary enrollments for both Blacks and Whites were lower in the suburbs than the cities, although the White rates were similar in both settings. Although Black students who did attend high school in these communities seem to have succeeded at a higher rate than those in the city, their numbers were small by comparison. Perhaps those circumstances contributed to the success of some students, but little is known about the institutions these students attended. In the end, with a 19-year-old graduation rate of 14%, it appears that a relatively modest number of African Americans in these circumstances were able to graduate from high school.

Because a significant portion of the Black metropolitan teen population attended high school, it is possible to perform a somewhat more telling statistical analysis of the factors contributing to their success. Figure 1.1 presents the results of a binary logistic regression analysis of factors related to success in school for African American and White 17-year-olds in 1940. The results indicate a logarithmic expression of the odds—or probability—of an individual with each of the listed characteristics attending school. A value of 0 indicates even chances, a likelihood neither higher nor lower than those individuals without the characteristic in question. A

FIGURE 1.1. Logistic Regression, Factors Contributing to High School Enrollment, Youth, 14–18, Metropolitan South, 1940

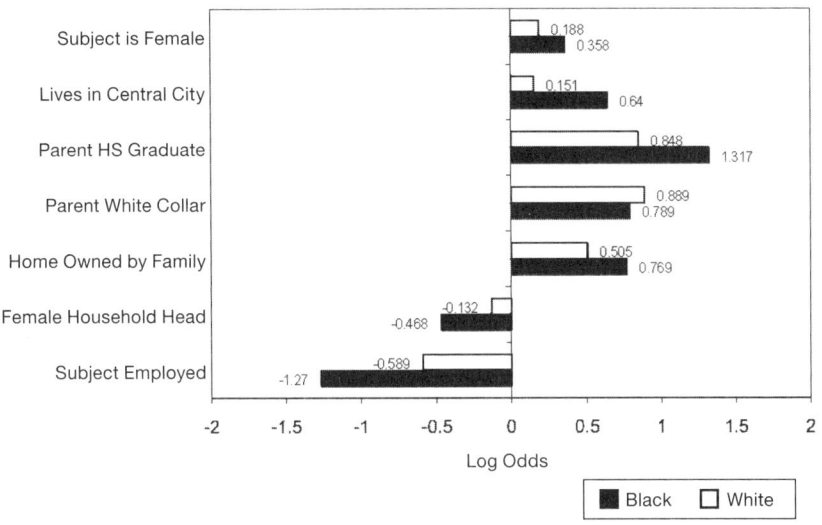

Dependent variable: Enrollment (or not) in high school. All variables are significant at .001 level except Female Household Head for Whites, which is significant at .05 level.

positive value indicates a greater likelihood of attending with that characteristic; a negative value indicates lower odds than individuals without the characteristic. Further information on this analysis and similar ones for other years is provided in Appendix B. This technique makes it possible to consider the *independent* effect of each variable, holding the others constant. The dependent variables are the likelihood of teenage (14 to 18) Black and White youth being enrolled in high school, or having already graduated, in a Southern metropolitan area.

Although just a relatively narrow range of factors are considered in Figure 1.1, the results are revealing on a number of counts. Four of the included variables were associated with an increased likelihood of secondary enrollment (those with positive coefficients) and two with reduced odds for both groups (with negative coefficients). Being female and living in a household with enough wealth to own the family dwelling were clearly advantages. The same was true of households where one or both parents were high school graduates, which was relatively rare at the time, or having at least one parent in a white-collar job, including clerical work. Not surprisingly, parental education had the strongest association with secondary enrollment, a finding consistent with other studies of attainment in the 20th century.[59] It also was advantageous to live in a central city, where the largest and most renowned Black high schools were located.

Living in a household headed by a female, on the other hand, was a disadvantage, a result that also is consistent with a large body of research. The biggest drawback to succeeding in school for both White and Black youth, but particularly for the latter, was having a job. Indeed, the strong negative association between employment and attainment points to the difficult choices facing large numbers of Black youth and their families. Hard times made secondary schooling an option that many African American households could ill afford. Even if youth did not contribute directly to the family budget, the fact that they could more or less support themselves was often a blessing. Turning down the opportunity for employment to stay in school clearly was a tough proposition for many Black teens, more than for their White counterparts.

Other factors in Figure 1.1 underscore these points. The wealth represented by home ownership undoubtedly helped youth of both races to stay out of the job market. For girls of both groups, employment options were relatively narrow, but especially so for African Americans who worked predominantly as domestics. Consequently, schooling for them entailed somewhat lower opportunity costs, or foregone earnings. For youth in households lacking a male head, more pressing needs almost certainly took precedence over schooling, even if employment was not an immediate option. In the case of Wilbur Johnson, the fact that his mother did not urge him to drop out of school to find work made his experience unusual. For most others in his cohort, living in a single-parent household meant that high school was out of the question.

Comparing the coefficients for each variable, it is clear that the factors utilized for this analysis loomed larger in the lives of Black youth than they did for Whites, with the exception of parental occupational status, which varied less for Blacks. This was partly due to greater availability of secondary schooling for Whites, especially outside of the central cities, but also because of their superior social and economic circumstances. Attending high school and graduating were simply more difficult for African Americans because these factors had a greater impact on their ability to succeed in school. Because of their general level of destitution, Black youth needed greater relative advantages than Whites to succeed in school.

Regardless of the opportunities that these institutions offered, in that case, and the accomplishments of their students, these high schools also were constant reminders of the inferior status of Black education. Even the best African American high schools faced daunting challenges as they struggled to serve the youth of their growing urban communities. For students in these settings, going to high school was a mark of social status in itself, but most fell behind in their studies or dropped out altogether. Consequently, graduating was an even a finer point of distinction, limited to those with the good fortune and determination to persist and succeed. Although their education gave them few advantages in the labor market, they represented an elite segment of the region's Black population. They, too, faced daunting challenges in the Jim Crow social structure, despite the many changes that lay ahead in the not-too-distant future.

ACCREDITATION STRUGGLES

As noted earlier, the majority of Black secondary institutions in the 1930s and 1940s offered just 2- or 3-year programs, and began with very few assets. A 1942 Georgia report declared these smaller high schools "a valuable link in the educational chain," especially "where there are not enough high school pupils to justify a plant and a staff for a four year school."[60] Since it was difficult for many districts to "justify" a freestanding Black high school, however, this principle was applied far more frequently to Black students than to Whites. This made it relatively easy to open a new secondary school, but most of them were quite small. In North Carolina, one in five Black high schools in 1944 had just one or two teachers, as opposed to just 8% of White institutions. Only a quarter of Black secondary schools had more than six teachers, while some 38% of White ones did.[61] Inequities on these counts were even greater in other states.[62] In Georgia in 1948, White high schools averaged about seven teachers while Black ones averaged four. Nearly two-thirds of White schools were 4-year institutions, and about the same proportion of Black schools (63%) offered 3 years or less of secondary work.[63] The latter institutions mainly served rural Black communities, of course, and most had small staffs and very limited resources.[64]

Such arrangements naturally raised questions about the character and quality of instruction. A 1947 Louisiana school bulletin ruled that if "a high school department operated in the same building with an elementary school, separate classrooms must be provided for the exclusive use of the secondary grades." It also specified that it must enroll no fewer than 50 "bona fide" students.[65] This, of course, often called for building an addition to an existing school, even if it comprised only one or two classrooms. Additionally, such small numbers of students, fewer than 200 in most cases, posed significant educational challenges. Perhaps foremost was a severely restricted curriculum, usually limited to a narrow range of academic subjects. Thus, despite a longstanding emphasis on the most immediately practical subjects, or as one Mississippi official put it, a focus on "above everything else *health* and *vocations*" (emphasis in original), most Black high schools featured courses that were largely academic in orientation.[66] This undoubtedly accounted for the sparse curriculum required by most Southern states, typically just a few units of English and history. Teachers with other specialties, such as sciences and foreign language, could be hard to find and expensive. It was a problem that was widely recognized, but usually unavoidable due to school size and tight budgets.[67] This was secondary education at a rudimentary level, but it did afford elementary graduates an opportunity to keep studying.

Apart from students and classrooms, there were other expectations for high schools, many of them honored in the breach by African American institutions. Standards existed in practically all states regarding the ratio of students to teachers, teacher qualification, the size of libraries, and lab equipment for teaching science. In Louisiana, 4-year schools were required to have at least four teachers, all certified in their subjects, with each one teaching classes adding up to no more than 750 students per week, or an average of 150 each day. They also were supposed to have at least a part-time librarian, and a collection with at least five books per each pupil enrolled. Schools also were directed to ensure "adequate provision for laboratory instruction in each of the sciences" offered, if possible in rooms designated for such purposes. Officials reported that very few Black high schools had any lab facilities.[68] Beyond that, there was the question of vocational and fine arts subjects, which also required provisions. Even the principal's office was required to meet certain specifications, particularly with respect to maintaining school records.[69] Expectations such as these spanned the region, and although they were considerably less stringent than standards elsewhere, they represented a formidable challenge to impoverished rural districts.

Since these requirements were associated with accreditation, educators devoted a good deal of attention to addressing them. In general, there were two types or levels of official recognition for Southern high schools to seek. The first was the state requirements, which generally corresponded to those described above in Louisiana. Although they had been applied to White schools across the region since the turn of the century, they were first applied to Black schools following World War I. Requirements for this type of recognition represented major hurdles for many Black schools, as they required additional resources. A second level of accreditation was offered by the Southern Association of Colleges and Secondary Schools (SACS), a regional body that published even more exacting requirements, including a variety of curricular expectations. Although the SACS had refused to consider Black schools when the association began such reviews early in the century, by the early 1930s it allowed them to apply for evaluation. While the SACS did not formally accredit

Black schools, it did extend approval to those meeting its criteria for accreditation by a parallel organization for Black institutions, the Association of Colleges and Secondary Schools.[70] As a rule, these requirements for teacher qualifications and teaching loads, average class size, library and lab facilities, and curricular depth and breadth were more stringent than those of the states. This meant that the number of schools qualifying for this level of recognition was always smaller than the number of those with state accreditation.

For most White high schools, gaining state accreditation was not difficult, so regional endorsement represented a more telling distinction. Community pride in the excellence of local schools was at issue, of course, but there also was the question of coursework and diplomas being accepted by collegiate institutions. Although local colleges were likely to accept credentials from state accredited high schools, those from outside the state often demanded regional certification when evaluating students for admission. This was particularly true of more prestigious private institutions and leading state universities.[71] Accreditation, in that case, was more than a matter of local honor. It held important implications for the students of a particular high school, chiefly regarding the weight that their diploma would carry upon graduation.

For Black high schools, consequently, the question of accreditation was hardly insignificant. It was a point of recurring discussion among educators and a source of ongoing concern for state officials overseeing the schools. The reason for this, however, went well beyond the matter of pride and eligibility for college. As long as a single standard was used to evaluate Black and White schools, the numbers of institutions succeeding at different levels of recognition served as an inescapable point of comparison between the races. School reports across the region routinely published lists of schools with asterisks or other indicators to identify those with state or SACS approval. Every year, the numbers at each level were far apart, with the vast majority of White institutions accredited by the states and a growing number at the regional level. Although a number of Black high schools were able to secure state accreditation by the 1940s, and their ranks were growing, regional recognition remained an elusive goal. This highlighted differences in resources available to each set of schools and reinforced popular attitudes about the inferiority of Black institutions and their students' academic accomplishments.[72]

Early on, educational leaders recognized the difficulty that common accreditation standards posed for African American schools. Addressing the problems of meeting SACS expectations, a superintendent in Mississippi wrote to Georgia's Robert Cousins in 1939, declaring that "pressed as all of your schools are going to be for funds, it will be quite remarkable if any of your Negro high schools can continue to meet any kind of standard."[73] For his part, Cousins was interested in exploring the possibility of relaxing certain SACS standards for Black institutions, in light of their meager resources. There were explicit guidelines about salary levels, which were considerably higher than many schools could afford, along with requirements for full-time librarians. Considering this, it seemed reasonable to suggest that a different set of criteria be applied to Black schools.

In the end, however, neither SACS officials nor the principals of regionally accredited Black high schools expressed much interest in pursuing the idea of a different set of standards. Even educators in non–regionally accredited institutions were cautious about the idea. In an era when Black schools struggled with widespread perceptions of inferiority and received little public support, the thought of a double standard in evaluation held little appeal.[74] Of course, state authorities also realized that explicitly acknowledging lower standards for Black schools would inevitably be subject to challenge under the "separate but equal" doctrine that governed segregationist policies. Besides, as Cousins noted in a letter to SACS commissioner W. A. Robinson, the standards were useful in garnering support for school improvements from local and state authorities. And what, many educators wondered, would be the prospects for ever attaining equality in funding if Black schools were held to lower requirements?[75] For better or worse, the challenge of accreditation would remain a critical stumbling block and a telling point of assessment for high schools in years to come.

In the main, only larger Black high schools in cities and towns were able to achieve SACS approval, at least in the early years. And even these institutions encountered difficulties with respect to overcrowding and numbers of students assigned to teachers.[76] Libraries also were a recurring dilemma, as the regional requirements typically were higher than those of the states. The SACS criteria called for principals with graduate degrees, or at least to be working on them, and this, too, was a problem for many Black schools. In 1947, Alabama reported that just 15 of its 138 Black high schools were accredited by SACS.[77] In Mississippi, it was just eight out of 233. Most White high schools in the region also failed to meet the more exacting requirements of regional accreditation. In Mississippi, for instance, 88 White high schools received regional accreditation, out of a total of 551, or about 15%. In Georgia, the numbers were 153 accredited by SACS out of nearly 500, less than a third. It was a widely discussed problem, pointing to the comparatively weak state of secondary education for students of both races.

For most Black institutions, however, recognition from SACS was hardly the most pressing issue; large numbers struggled to meet state requirements that were considerably less demanding. As indicated in Table

TABLE 1.5. High Schools Approved by the Southern Association of Colleges and Secondary Schools, 1939–40

State	Accredited White Schools	Approved Black Schools	% Approved Schools Black	% Teens Black in State
North Carolina	55	18	24.6	29.3
Alabama	68	10	12.2	35.5
Georgia	119	14	10.5	35.1
South Carolina	48	5	9.4	48.1
Virginia	82	8	8.9	27.2
Kentucky	145	11	7.0	6.6
Tennessee	93	5	5.1	16.7
Texas	245	12	4.6	15.2
Mississippi	81	3	3.6	46.5
Louisiana	141	4	2.7	36.1
Florida	120	3	2.4	28.4

Source: W. A. Robinson, "Some Problems in the Administration, Support, and Accreditation of Negro Secondary Schools," *The Journal of Negro Education*, Vol. 9, No. 3 (July 1940), pp. 474–481. Black teen population figures calculated from IPUMS data.

1.5, in many states the number of SACS-approved Black high schools was a tiny fraction of the accredited White ones, especially in the Deep South. The situation was almost as dire with respect to state accreditation. Across the region, a substantial majority of Black high schools failed to meet these basic accreditation standards through the latter 1940s, and the conditions were worst in states with the largest Black populations. In 1947, South Carolina reported "approximately 170 Negro schools doing high school work, of which 66 are accredited." The fact that the exact number of these institutions was not known, and that nearly two-thirds of them were unaccredited, pointed to the precarious condition of secondary instruction in much of the state.[78] In Alabama, only 39 institutions (28%) that offered secondary instruction to Blacks were accredited by the state. The state's Department of Education reported that the chief reasons were overcrowding and excessive teaching loads, poorly equipped libraries and laboratories, inadequate supervision by principals, and lack of properly trained teachers, especially librarians.[79] Similar conditions existed in Georgia, Mississippi, and Louisiana. Even in North Carolina, which had the largest number of accredited Black high schools, Newbold reported nearly two dozen on the verge of losing accreditation in 1944 due to these issues, particularly a shortage of classroom space. Three years later, he announced that 16 schools "hung in the balance . . . near losing their state accredited rating." Once again, the main problems were related to buildings and furnishings, "not enough room nor equipment, and what they had was desperately poor."[80] At the same time, of course, additional secondary schools and departments were being opened throughout the region. The failure of most Black institutions to gain this level of official recognition was a glaring reminder of their second-class status.[81] And most of the deficiencies that held them back were a consequence of inadequate resources.

By contrast, the vast majority of White secondary programs, typically 80% or more, were accredited by the states. Howard University's Walter Daniel reported that Black accredited high schools represented just 8% of all approved public secondary schools across the region in 1944.[82] This was largely due to conspicuous discrepancies in basic school assets. The number of books in Georgia's White secondary libraries in 1948, for instance, outnumbered those in Black institutions by more than six to one. The value of lab equipment in White schools exceeded that in Black ones by nearly a nine to one ratio. Even funds used for vocational education, traditionally held as a focal point for Black institutions, were nearly nine times greater in White schools. Although White secondary enrollments were three times higher than corresponding Black figures, these disparities indicated unequal resources across the state.[83] The numbers from other states on these matters were similar.[84] The general pattern across the region was plain: Secondary education for African Americans may have been expanding rapidly, but it was still far removed from even the most basic standards of state and regional accrediting agencies. If Southern Black high schools were to eliminate longstanding racial attainment and achievement gaps, they clearly had a long way to go.

CONCLUSION: STRUGGLING AGAINST A LEGACY OF INEQUITY

Black communities across the South were clearly interested in improving the educational opportunities available to their youth. For many, this meant establishing secondary institutions with extremely meager resources, often grafting them onto existing schools by means of makeshift additions or annexes, providing the bare essentials of instruction and materials to support the curriculum. When confronted by resistance from White school boards, they raised funds themselves, sometimes to see those resources misspent or simply stolen by Whites.[85] Still, they persisted, and the steadily rising numbers of Black secondary institutions in the 1940s is testimony to their vision and determination, and to the youth who attended these institutions in ever-increasing numbers.

Black high school students and the educators who served them struggled under a host of difficult conditions. Even when they had comparatively good facilities, as in many larger cities, their schools were often overcrowded and provisioned with secondhand textbooks and laboratory equipment. Because of their greater community poverty and lower adult education levels, Black students fell behind in grade and dropped out of school at a higher rate than their White counterparts. Because few employment options existed for educated African Americans, many found it difficult to see the point of remaining in school to graduate. This would change in the years ahead, but it would take a revolution in Southern education to alter the experiences of Black secondary students. Although few could see such a development in the early 1940s, important changes were on the horizon and a new world of opportunity was about to be revealed.

CHAPTER 2

Sea Change: "Equalization" and Secondary Schooling

B{LACK SECONDARY SCHOOL ENROLLMENTS} in the South grew throughout the early 20th century but in the latter 1940s the pace of change began to pick up considerably. This was due to a number of developments, including extensive movement out of the agricultural economy and increased attention to inequality in education and other aspects of social life, by both local Black communities and state authorities. It was during this period that some of the most dramatic changes occurred in African American secondary schooling. If a certain time and place was critical to the growth of Black attainment, it was the postwar South.

This important development occurred under specific historical circumstances. They included regional population loss, a declining farm economy and the rise of industry, migration from the countryside to cities, and a challenge to ideologies of racial supremacy following World War II. In this context, calls to improve Black education grew, including demands for secondary schooling, helping to launch a period of unprecedented increases in Black high school enrollments. White education officials were frequently critical allies in the process, along with assorted other groups. In the end, it was the vitality of widespread Black interest in schooling, the effectiveness of legal challenges to unequal education, and a new level of responsiveness on the part of White authorities that led to these changes.

RACE, EDUCATION, AND REGIONAL DEVELOPMENT

The South faced many challenges in years immediately following World War II. Like the rest of the country, it had benefited from the economic stimulus of the war effort, although not nearly to the extent of other regions. As demand for labor increased elsewhere, the South suffered population loss during the war. In the latter 1940s, worldwide production of cotton was increasing, exerting downward pressure on the region's principal crop, one that was integral to the livelihood of many African Americans. One response was the mechanization of cotton production, which would lead many Black families to leave the land, looking for other forms of work. Between the economic impact of the war and changing demands for labor in its aftermath, the number of African Americans engaged in farm work dropped precipitously by 1960, as millions migrated to nearby cities or left the South altogether. Noting that the number of Black farm workers had declined 25% between 1940 and 1950, the *Daily Minutes* of a Tuskegee principals workshop 1957 declared that the "old order of the South is gradually disappearing." The *Minutes* also asserted that segregated schools were ill suited to the changing economy, and that to strengthen the South "some generation must suffer . . . the discomfort and pain that this transition requires."[1]

Economic development was the region's greatest need, and forward-looking business leaders and politicians recognized that the old cotton economy would eventually give way to an urban industrial future. Race relations remained a critical question, however, particularly as African Americans pressed for greater equity and more economic opportunities. Although there had long been a liberal faction of White leadership in the South, there were signs of its ascendency in the immediate postwar years. As historians have noted, traditionally White supremacist ideology was becoming anachronistic in the wake of World War II and the battle against Nazism. The appointment of President Truman's Commission on Civil Rights in 1946 and the subsequent publication of its report, *To Secure These Rights*, which was sharply critical of Jim Crow brutality and the exploitation of Blacks, signaled a new tone in race relations.[2] Beyond that, there was the ever-present question of economic growth. A growing number of Whites recognized that the region was unlikely to move ahead unless African Americans could enhance their skills and contribute more directly to the economy.[3] A big part of this, of course, hinged decisively on the schools. Unless access to education was improved, and the quality of Black schools was enhanced, the South would have problems competing with other parts of the country for industrial investment and other forms of development.

During the years immediately following the war, there were signs of a subtle shift in the thinking of state officials concerning Black education. "A modern democratic state," declared Mississippi's White director of Negro Education, "cannot hope to reach its true destiny with one half of its people educated and trained and the other half neglected and left in ignorance and superstition." In particular, he cited the need for improved facilities and teacher preparation, and establishing "at least one good high school in each county" with a substantial Black population. It would take years for this goal to be realized, of course, as Mississippi had the region's most poorly developed Black school system.[4] But remarks such as these would become more commonplace in the years to come. A 1947 commentary on improving Black education in Alabama argued that it "can play an important part in the development of the entire state," and that a lack of attention to it "can retard the development of the entire state." In the end, it concluded, money spent in this way "is neither charity, nor was it philanthropy. It is an investment."[5] Such remarks had been made before, but they appeared to obtain greater resonance in the immediate postwar years. N. C. Newbold regularly made similar points in North Carolina, focusing on the need for greater attention to the depressed state of Black schools.[6] A special commission in the border state of Maryland declared in 1949 that the state was "faced with a legal as well as a moral obligation to provide for the Negro student facilities equivalent to those available to the White student." It concluded somewhat ominously that "the only alternative would be the complete or partial abandonment of its segregation policy."[7] While the report was principally concerned with higher education, these questions applied to all schooling in the region.

It was not just educational leaders who were interested in such matters. The *Atlanta Constitution* editorialized in 1948 that the state had an obligation to fund improvements in Black schools, as a matter of basic principle. "Southern States have been served notice repeatedly that the courts will not tolerate unequal education opportunity because of race," the editors wrote. "Prompt and positive action must be forthcoming if the traditional segregation of races is to be maintained." Even letters written by skeptical Whites were cautiously supportive, clearly favoring improvements to Black schools over integration, widely associated with "race-mixing." "I believe most people of good will and education desire to see the Negro given better industrial education, more training in vocations and skilled trades, more economic security as citizens, and a greater opportunity to develop all possible talents in music, drama and self-respect," wrote one woman in 1946. "But to advocate social equality, which presupposes intermarriage, should be regarded by any intelligent American, white or black, as nothing short of enemy propaganda (of both races)."[8]

This, of course, was a source of great misgiving to many recalcitrant Whites, along with the belief that improved education could encourage African Americans to question their servile status. It was also telling that the letter advocated vocational education for Blacks, a vision with deep historical roots.[9] But as fears of judicial interventions grew in the wake of legal challenges to unequal funding, the weight of opinion among Southern officials began to change. Although they had effectively resisted efforts to increase state support for Black education in the past, limiting it to vocational training and the bare minimum necessary to appear even-handed, it was becoming increasingly difficult to do so. A new day was dawning and a fresh perspective on the question of race and education was coming into view.

This is not to say that there was consensus on these questions among Whites across the region; considerable debate occurred between those who favored more or less traditional views of race relations. But before the historic *Brown* decision put White liberals on the defensive, and added fuel to conservative fears of assertive African Americans, it appeared that significant enhancements to Black schooling were possible. In the end, however, it took a concerted push by Blacks to make significant changes a reality.

MOUNTING RESTIVENESS

Accompanying this was a surge of interest among African Americans in upgrading their schools. In 1950, the Georgia Division of Negro Education noted "a growing dissatisfaction on the part of Negro citizens with the educational opportunities afforded their children, as evidenced by the filing of petitions and suits for equal facilities, services and opportunities."[10] These concerns were also evident in the Black press, where a growing number of stories were devoted to the question of schools and educational opportunities. As the Black *Atlanta Daily World* proclaimed in a 1946 editorial, "Negro children must have busses. They must have longer school terms and better facilities."[11] In short, a comprehensive program of improvement was called for at all levels of education.

The term widely employed throughout the period was *equalization*, although its meaning differed from one context to another. It had first appeared in Southern education as early as the 1930s regarding teacher salaries. As a number of historians have noted, litigation over unequal pay was joined in several states and these challenges eventually led to dramatically improved compensation for many African American teachers.[12] Equalization also referred to establishing uniform lengths in Black and White school terms, which was largely achieved by the early 1940s.[13] But in a few years, the term had acquired a broader meaning, referring to efforts to make Black and White schools equivalent in most practical respects. Among the biggest issues, of course, was the quality of facilities, and amenities such as libraries and laboratories, critical matters in accreditation reports. As Newbold noted in one of his many speeches on the question, the improvement of Black schools had become perhaps the most decisive race question of the time.[14]

Most Southern Whites probably disagreed with Newbold and other officials who endorsed equalization, however, and ultimately it was the threat of legal action—and the commencement of lawsuits—that proved decisive in paving the way to wholesale change. This was the case in salary equalization in all states except North Carolina, and following the war, Black communities began to weigh the option of lawsuits to gain additional improvements to their schools. The tactics of striking and protest, as seen in Lumberton, Farmville, and other communities, were augmented by legal briefs outlining the unequal treatment of Black institutions, or the lack of equal opportunities for Black students. These developments, of course, were influenced by the ongoing legal battles being waged by the NAACP on the national stage. This was a part of a broad strategy to challenge inequity associated with Jim Crow policies rather than attacking segregation itself, which would come later. NAACP leaders hoped that by pursuing equalization, the cost of maintaining segregation would become prohibitive.[15] Through a series of highly publicized cases, starting with the U.S. Supreme Court's 1938 *Gaines v. Canada* decision against segregated professional education, the focus shifted to disparities that Black communities had endured for generations.[16] It is little wonder that litigation became a more widely utilized tactic in the struggle to gain better schools.

Using the precedent established in *Gaines*, the NAACP launched a campaign against inequity in the public schools, focusing first on teacher salaries and later addressing the dilapidated facilities and lack of secondary education that plagued the rural South. The salary equalization struggle started in Maryland and met early success, but ran into determined resistance in the Deep South. It took the better part of a decade, and court battles across the region, to establish the principle that teachers should be paid a single scale regardless of race, although discrepancies were still widely observed.[17] Toward the end of the 1940s, the NAACP broadened its attack by challenging unequal facilities. Virginia became a focal point, as more than 100 equalization lawsuits were filed across the state.[18] The most widely publicized and consequential cases, however, occurred elsewhere and focused on higher education. *Sweatt v. Painter* and *McLaurin v. Oklahoma* resulted in 1950 Supreme Court decisions requiring Texas and Oklahoma to admit Blacks to their graduate and professional schools. This signaled that it was no longer permissible to simply offer African Americans just any segregated institution. For states that had deprived Black schools for generations, the handwriting was clearly on the wall.

In August 1948, Federal District Judge Sterling Hutcheson issued a restraining order against school boards in Virginia's King George and Gloucester counties to prevent them from operating inferior secondary facilities for Blacks. Noting resistance from local Whites, NAACP attorney Martin A. Martin declared, "Unless these Virginia School Boards and Superintendents change their attitudes, colored and white children will be attending the same high schools in September." Even though there were almost as many Black students in each county as White, secondary enrollments were much lower for African Americans because neither district provided a freestanding Black high school. Eventually, White officials in these largely rural counties were cited for contempt, even as they admitted that inequality existed and appealed to state authorities for funds to build new facilities. Plans were drawn up but funding appeared uncertain, especially as other districts across the state faced similar legal challenges. Eventually, new facilities were built, marking improvements to Black schools and ending the dispute, although true equalization was never accomplished. In many respects, these events at opposite ends of the Chesapeake Bay foreshadowed developments in districts throughout the South. The confrontational tone that started the conflict signaled a new political dynamic in Southern education, and Whites were on notice that the familiar unequal manner of running the schools no longer was acceptable.[19]

The King George and Gloucester cases were among the opening salvos in a broad-based campaign against inequality in public schools that gained momentum with considerable fanfare. "Five legal actions were instituted in four states last week," declared the *Chicago Defender* in 1949, "in the rapidly growing fight for equalization of school facilities and teachers salaries." The article announced new lawsuits in Texas, Mississippi, Virginia, and North Carolina, several of which specifically mentioned the need for new or improved high schools.[20] These and similar cases throughout the South were reported widely in the Black press.[21] It represented a veritable bombardment of litigation aimed squarely at redressing the longstanding racial disparity in public schooling. One of the key issues, of course, was secondary education; in light of the shortage of African American high schools, equalization represented a powerful impetus to change.[22]

SHIFTING SOCIAL AND POLITICAL CONDITIONS

Legal challenges were hardly the only motivation for Southern Whites to address educational inequality, but they were the most immediate and persuasive. A rather different concern was declining population, and particularly the loss of Black families and workers. Black migration out of the region had stepped up during the war years, as African Americans moved north and west in search of employment.[23] A continuing exodus in the postwar era prompted some Whites to call for school reform to make communities attractive to African Americans and to preserve traditional sources of labor. The movement of children out of rural areas also made it difficult for districts to plan for the future.[24] At the same time, rapidly advancing mechanization in agriculture reduced the demand for unskilled labor, causing some to call for better education to meet changing job requirements. These issues, however, did not get nearly the same attention as the potential for integration with respect to equalization.[25] In the pronouncements of politicians and school officials, editorial columns and letters to editors, the overwhelming sentiment was one of resisting the threat of desegregation at all costs. This fear was hardly the sturdiest foundation upon which to launch a campaign to remedy longstanding deficiencies in schooling, but it was a start. For many of the region's Black educators, it seemed to represent a change that was long overdue, prompting guarded optimism among many.[26]

For their part, White school leaders quickly recognized the vulnerability of longstanding policies and practices to civil rights litigation against segregated and unequal education. Along with other more liberally minded Whites, they urged state legislatures to act immediately in addressing the manifold problems of Black schools. "The program of Negro education must in the future even more than it has in the past, be promulgated and directed by the Mississippi people," declared a state superintendent in 1947, or "it is clear that it will be done by outside influences and agencies."[27] Similarly, Newbold wrote in 1948 that school leaders "have for a long time been fully conscious of the legal pressures which have been upon them" as they observed events throughout the South. These sentiments were echoed by other school officials and educational experts.[28] Alabama officials estimated that more than 8,000 new classrooms were needed to rectify inequities in schooling, and that massive increases in funding would be necessary.[29] Education agencies throughout the South began drawing up plans for spending more on African American schools. It did not take long for these proposals to reach legislative agendas in most states, marking a historic shift in regional thinking about Black schooling.

Such plans met with a decidedly mixed reception from White legislators and other political leaders, but the growing tide of litigation prompted fears that even bigger changes were possible. Money was always at issue, as the South was clearly the nation's poorest region and it also had the highest level of fertility. More children and fewer funds meant that Southern states were required to spend a larger portion of their general budgets on schooling than other states. On top of that, they also had to operate separate school systems to maintain segregation, which became an ever larger concern.[30] Behind the question of equity, however, lay the threat of integrated education, an alternative that many Southern Whites opposed vehemently. This confluence of events and interests set the stage for important changes in Black education, and high schools in particular. By the end of the 1940s legislation to provide additional funding for African American schools had been introduced in legislatures across the region. It started in Mississippi, where a tentative wave of funding for facilities was launched in 1946, followed by additional resources in 1948 and beyond. Although these measures did relatively little to close the racial gap in resources, as many districts diverted these funds to White schools, they did allow for expansion of some schools and higher pay for teachers.[31]

Equalization was more ambitious in other states in the Deep South, where legislative measures came into view a few years later. The biggest funding shift occurred in Georgia, which had the largest Black population. Following proposals introduced in 1946, inveterate segregationist Governor Herman Talmadge led the fight to pass a $170 million equalization program based on the state's first comprehensive sales tax in 1951. Historians have argued that he used the issue of segregation to mobilize White support for increased spending on all schools, and that improving Black education was a by-product of the effort. A 1950 NAACP federal lawsuit to desegregate Atlanta's schools, *Aaron v. Cook*, also was a source of motivation.[32] But the impact was substantial, partly because Georgia's "Minimum Foundation" program did not leave control of school construction entirely up to local authorities.[33] Similar plans were launched in other states at about the same time, as White leaders proclaimed education essential to the future of the region. It was seen as vital to economic development and gaining political support among the growing middle class, in addition to forestalling the threat of integration.

Of course, the NAACP and other Black organizations aggressively took up equal education as a cause and helped to secure enhancements to Black schools.[34] While White support for these efforts was linked to fears of integration, many African Americans took heart from the promise of new school resources. This occurred despite debates about the wisdom of pushing for equalization rather than integration. For many, gaining tangible improvements to familiar institutions was an attractive proposition, one they were not prepared to dismiss out of hand. After all, it was a dramatic change from the past and represented a material benefit.[35] Assurances from White officials helped. N. C. Newbold told a group of Black educators that North Carolina planned to eliminate "all the remaining differentials at the earliest possible date," and that they could look forward to the future with "a new song in the air and a new star in the sky."[36] Many in the audience no doubt agreed, and it turned out that these sentiments were not entirely misplaced; a significant shift in policy was under way.

A NEW DAY FOR HIGH SCHOOLS

Equalization may have started slowly, but it picked up steam as the NAACP and other civil rights groups pushed for change, and eventually it began to draw national attention. In 1952, the *New York Times* announced that Southern states were going "all out" to improve Black schools across the region.[37] White political leaders were anxious about legal challenges to segregated schooling, and made commitments to sharp increases in spending for African American education. At the same time that governors declared the right to abolish public education if segregation was threatened, they also laid out ambitious plans to devote more resources for Black schools in hopes of making "separate but equal" policies defensible.[38] Georgia education commissioner M. D. Collins declared "Negro schools in this state are being improved much more rapidly and to a greater degree than are white schools." North Carolina had budgeted a million dollars more for Black schools than White ones, and Alabama superintendent W. J. Terry proclaimed the appropriations for African American education "phenomenal." The valuation of Black schools in Arkansas apparently had increased more than 300% since 1940. Similar developments were evident in Florida, Virginia, and even Kentucky. In some states, the *Times* reported, "More progress has been made in the past five years than during the previous fifty."[39] This was embellishment, of course, but for the first time since Reconstruction, states were spending more on certain aspects of Black education—school construction in particular—than on White institutions. To many observers, including the *Times* reporter, it seemed a new day had indeed arrived.

In 1952, Georgia's Division of Negro Education announced measures to eliminate racial differences in funding for teachers, transportation, and textbooks. The cost of instructional services and transportation for White students far exceeded that of Blacks. Although Blacks constituted only 32% of the school population, more than half the state's 3,290 schools were designated as "colored."[40] This meant that most Black students attended small isolated schoolhouses, and much of the improvement effort focused on replacing old, dilapidated facilities with larger, newer ones. This became the principal thrust of equalization. Georgia closed more than 1,200 Black one- or two-room schools in the first half of the 1950s, and other states shuttered thousands more.[41] Most were replaced with modern grade-school facilities, but there were enhancements to high schools as well. In many areas, such developments proceeded under the banner of consolidation, much as they had for White schools in earlier decades. In these cases, a county typically became the unit of administration, with elementary schools organized around a central secondary institution with buses for transportation. This allowed for larger, separate high schools, often housed in new buildings, offering a wider range of curricular options than the older, smaller union schools.[42]

In 1953, the South Carolina Department of Education could report that greater progress was made in consolidating secondary institutions for Black students than for Whites. In particular, it boasted that "nineteen modern, handsomely appointed and fully equipped high schools were or are nearly completed" for African American youth. Altogether, the number of accredited Black secondary institutions had increased in 7 years from 75 to 95 (about 25%), while the number of approved White high schools declined from 299 to 287 due to consolidation. "It is very probable," the report added, "that within the next year as many as ten or fifteen Negro high schools will be added to the list," and more than 30 White institutions would be closed. As the number of newly approved Black secondary schools increased, White ones were disappearing.[43] South Carolina reported eliminating 2,000 small schools by the middle of the decade, and promoted special training for Black administrators assigned to larger facilities.[44]

In other states, improvement to Black schools looked a bit different, but everywhere there was greater emphasis on improved facilities, better transportation, and increased capacity. As more schools achieved accreditation, the overall number of Black institutions declined or remained roughly the same, and 1- or 2-year high school programs disappeared. Georgia aggressively pursued school consolidation, providing new buildings for Black schools and dropping the total number of high schools substantially. By the mid-1950s more than 250 Black secondary institutions, more than a quarter of the state's total, had been closed or merged with others. Altogether, the rate of consolidation for Black schools in Georgia was more than twice that of White ones during this period.[45] Elsewhere, the numbers did not drop as dramatically, and in some places even increased, but new facilities were provided to enlarge capacity. In North Carolina, Black high schools with five or fewer teachers decreased from more than 150 in 1945 to just 54 within a decade. At the same time, the number of Black secondary institutions increased by seven, to 237. The largest number of these schools, roughly half, had between 6 and 11 teachers, the size range of most White institutions. These trends continued in the years to follow, with increased availability of larger institutions for both races.[46] In Alabama and Tennessee, the numbers of Black secondary institutions increased more rapidly than those for Whites, although many smaller schools appear to have remained in both states.[47] At the same time, officials in Mississippi could declare that as a result of reorganization, "the number and size of Negro schools are in a constant state of change," reflecting conditions throughout the region.[48]

Consolidation, of course, called for changes in the way students went to school. Increased busing for Blacks made it possible for them to attend larger institutions, typically located in or near population centers. During the 1950s, the proportion of African Americans bused in North Carolina increased by about 50%. By mid-decade, nearly 45% of the state's Black students were transported at public expense, only slightly less than the proportion of Whites, which was about half.[49] The Mississippi Department of Education reported that more than 4,500 new steel buses had been purchased for transporting rural Black youth, and all transportation needs had been met in 33 counties. Plans were in place to transport even more Black students in other parts of the state. South Carolina officials estimated that the number of African Americans being bused had doubled in 2 years to nearly a quarter of a million.[50] In a short span of time, school consolidation and improved transportation had changed many basic features of Black schooling across the region.

As a consequence, the number of African American high schools receiving state accreditation grew steadily as resources became more widely available. In South Carolina, for instance, the number of state-approved institutions increased by about 50%, to 122, during the first half of the 1950s, with another 32 schools planning to apply for accreditation in 1955. For Mississippi, which had somewhat lower standards, the numbers went from 153 in 1950 to 165 six years later, out of a total of about 260 institutions offering some form of secondary instruction. More than 2,000 new classrooms were added to Black schools, many at the high school level. Similar developments elsewhere helped to widen access and improve the quality of secondary education. Only about half of Alabama's 192 Black high schools were accredited in 1958, but they produced nearly three-quarters of the state's secondary graduates. According to a study at the time, these larger schools featured more curricular offerings and better-trained teachers.[51] In North Carolina, more than 8 out of 10 Black secondary schools were state-accredited at the end of the decade, the region's highest proportion.[52] The number of its Black secondary graduates nearly doubled between 1945 and 1958, while White graduation increased by just 37%. In the latter 1950s, moreover, the proportion of graduates of either race going to college was roughly the same: about 25%. Given developments such as these, there could be little doubt that the capacity of Black high schools throughout the South had been augmented substantially. As South Carolina's superintendent of education noted in 1954, improved funding "has brought us closer to equality of facilities between the races."[53] Even if the level of parity between Black and White schools still varied a good deal, and rarely achieved complete and proper equalization, it was clear that great strides had been taken.

RISING LEVELS OF ATTAINMENT

Signs of change in Black secondary education were plainly evident in regional enrollment figures. Table 2.1 offers a view of conditions in 1960, utilizing the same general categories considered in the previous chapter. Here, too, farming and non-farming, and property ownership and renting, are employed as indicators of social and economic status, pointing to broad distinctions in life circumstances at the time. Black youth are the principal concern; figures for the White population are provided for comparison. Both provide telling benchmarks of progress during the intervening decades.

When compared with figures for 1940, it is clear that critical changes had occurred. First, as suggested above, the region's Black youth had shifted away from farming and greater numbers of them lived in home-owning families. The proportion living on farms of any kind had dropped from half to just 21%, while those living in owner-occupied homes increased from 26% to 40%, approaching two-thirds of the White rate. Perhaps most important, fewer than one in six lived on tenant farms, down from nearly 40%—the largest single category—on the eve of World War II. These figures underscore the big shift away from agricultural employment among Southern Blacks, and improvement in their social and economic status.

Signs of progress also are readily evident in the enrollment figures presented in Table 2.1, which utilizes the same measures of participation and attainment as the previous chapter. The first category of school involvement, enrollment for youth ages 14 to 18, is the proportion of Black and White teenagers enrolled in secondary institutions or graduated. The second, junior-year enrollment or higher (including graduation) for 17-year-olds, indicates the proportion of individuals "on track" to graduate, having maintained an age-appropriate grade level. The numbers in both categories were considerably higher in 1960 than 20 years earlier for both races, but especially for Blacks. This is tangible evidence of the regional impact of equalization, which among other things made high schools more accessible to African Americans.

Altogether, more than half of all high school age Southern Blacks were enrolled in secondary institutions, a milestone of sorts in African American history. This was 80% of the White rate, a dramatic improvement from 2 decades earlier, when it was little better than a third. Less than half of Black 17-year-olds were at the junior year or higher, but this, too, was an improvement over 1940, when it was just half this level. This measure was 72% of the White figure, indicating that African Americans did not succeed at levels comparable to Whites, undoubtedly reflecting the poor social and economic circumstances many still endured.[54]

TABLE 2.1. Southern Black High School Enrollment, Ages 14–17, 1960 (in percentages)

Household Status	Portion of Teen Population		Teen Secondary Enrollment Rate		17-year-old Jr. + Enrollment Rate	
	Black	White	Black	White	Black	White
Non Farm; Home Owner	34	54	64.8	72.1	56.4	71
Non Farm; Non Owner	45	30	47.5	56	39.2	43
Farm; Landowner	6	11	60	72.9	50.4	70
Farm; Non Landowner	15	5	39.7	48.4	26.6	44
Total Region	100	100	53	66	44	61.5

Source: IPUMS data.

The group with the greatest success was youth from home-owning families, whose numbers more than doubled from 1940. Their attendance was 90% of the White rate, and a slight majority of the 17-year-olds appeared to be on track to graduate. Those living on farms had slightly lower numbers, but they made up just 6% of the Black teen population. Among renters, enrollment rates were lower for both Black and White youth, but particularly for African Americans living on tenant farms. Although about 40% of the latter were enrolled in high school, barely a quarter were on track to graduate at age 17, less than 60% of the corresponding White rate. Among non-farm renters, the largest category of Black youth, general enrollment and 17-year-old junior enrollment levels were both within 85% of the rates for White youth. For most African American teens not living on a tenant farm, high school appears to have become a near modal experience by 1960. This, too, was a significant development in Southern Black education, linked to the move away from farm tenancy.

Yet other changes were evident in the enrollment profile of African American youth at this time. The gender imbalance that was so readily evident in 1940 had grown less severe, even among youth on farms. Black enrollments were slightly more than half female (54%), down from nearly two-thirds, with the greatest imbalance still occurring among tenant farm families, with 60% female enrollment. African Americans were a bit more feminized than the White rate of 51%, but considerably less so than in 1940. This points to greater Black male involvement in school than in earlier times. Still, it was among Black tenant farm families, particularly those most reliant on farm income, that male enrollments were lowest, a sign of the continuing need for labor. By comparison, almost

"Equalization" and Secondary Schooling

FIGURE 2.1. Logistic Regression: Factors Contributing to High School Enrollment, Youth, 14–18, Metropolitan South, 1960

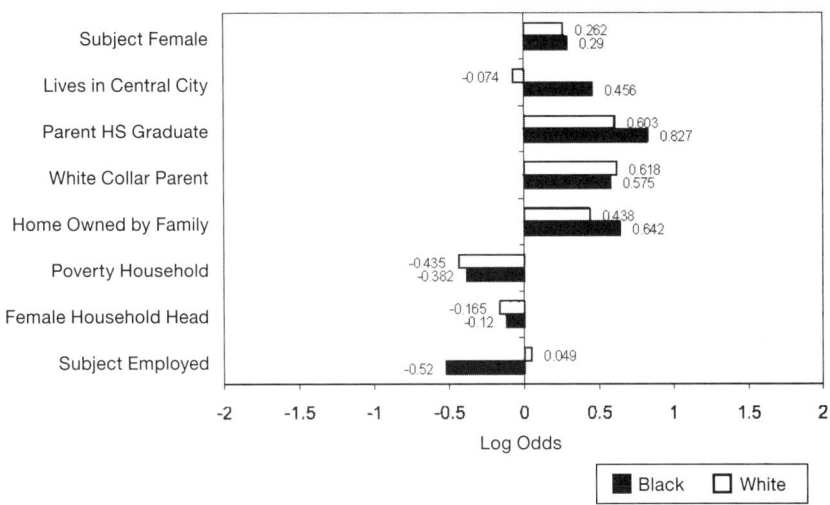

Dependent variable: Enrollment (or not) in high school. All variables significant at .001 level, except Female Headed Household for Blacks and Lives in Central City for Whites, both significant at .05. See Appendix B for additional information.

half (49%) of all secondary enrollments in White tenant farm households were male.[55] The continuing pattern of greater enrollments for girls is evidence of the socioeconomic difficulties faced by many African American families and expectations for young men to help out.[56]

Additional evidence of these problems can be found in Figure 2.1, which presents a logistic regression analysis of high school enrollments for Black and White metropolitan youth in 1960. This figure is similar to Figure 1.1 presented in Chapter 1: Values greater than 0 represent a higher likelihood of attending high school, while values less than 0 represent a lower likelihood. An additional variable has been added for poverty status, a factor that was not available for 1940. In general, the results are comparable to those obtained earlier, although the racial differences are considerably smaller in magnitude. Both Blacks and Whites, it seems, were subject to similar conditions in their school-going behavior, although differences were evident as well. Girls of both races were about 30% more likely to be in high school than boys. Parental education continued to be the most important positive predictor of enrollment for all teens, along with home ownership and parental occupational status. Black offspring of high school graduates were more than twice as likely to attend schools as those whose parents did not graduate; for Whites, the advantage was not as great. For both races, there was a similar advantage for those with parents in white-collar jobs of one kind or another, controlling for parental education. Those in home-owning families were 50% to 80% more likely to attend school than those who rented; it was a slightly less important factor for Whites. Although racial differences in enrollment had closed, social and economic status still appears to have loomed a bit larger in the lives of Black students in 1960 than for Whites.

Other factors represent circumstances that posed obstacles to attending high school. Living in a household below the federal poverty level was the greatest single problem for both races, reducing the likelihood of attendance by 30% to 40%. Living in a female-headed household was an impediment for all youth, with enrollment some 80% to 90% for those with a father present. But the biggest single deterrent—or perhaps alternative—to Black enrollment was being employed, even if it was less an issue than it had been earlier. African American youth with jobs were only about half as likely to attend high school as those who were not employed. Working did not have this effect for Whites, perhaps because many found jobs that were compatible with school. Whites enjoyed wider employment options than Blacks and this extended to youth as well. But this probably did not fully account for the difference. Black and White youth worked generally similar hours, with about half working 29 hours or less per week and a third working less than 14; yet only about a third of Blacks with jobs (34%) were enrolled compared with more than half (54%) of Whites.[57] This suggests that for some African American teens, having a job may have been a welcome alternative to school, although it is also possible that employers were less willing to reconcile work and school schedules for Blacks than for Whites.

From the standpoint of community type, African Americans in central cities were better than 50% more likely to enroll than those living elsewhere, after controlling for other factors in the analysis. Despite the substantial building campaigns to expand Black schooling, this is evidence that high schools were still more accessible in urban centers. In this respect, it appears that urban youth continued to enjoy educational advantages, despite their growing numbers in the wake of migration.

This speaks to the limitations of equalization regarding secondary education, especially where recalcitrant White school boards continued to hold power. Local circumstances also undoubtedly contributed to the lower odds of attendance among Black farm youth. The fact that living in a large city presented no enrollment advantage to White teens is further evidence of this, along with the *greater* likelihood of secondary attendance for White youth in farm households. African Americans living outside the region's central cities were at a disadvantage when it came to secondary education, and this does not appear to have been true for Whites.

These findings point to the continuing importance of the immediate social and economic context in high school attendance for youth of both races, even as enrollment increased for everyone. But going to high school had clearly become a widely observed norm. The lower coefficients for each race in 1960 than in 1940 reflect the wider availability of schooling and the greater propensity of all youth to attend secondary schools. Staying enrolled was somewhat *less* determined by these factors at the end of the 1950s than it had been 20 years earlier.

Most important, racial differences in attainment had been reduced dramatically, but distinctions remained. This is evident in the comparable coefficients associated with major life circumstances in Figure 2.1. Parental education and home ownership remained more important for African Americans than for Whites, although the magnitude of these coefficients was considerably lower than in 1940, suggesting that such factors were less decisive in shaping secondary attainment. It appears that work presented an alluring alternative for more Black than White youth, and that education for African Americans was constrained outside of the cities, but much of the attainment gap evident in 1940 had been closed. Whether such progress could be sustained was another question, of course, but the improvements were incontrovertible.

A GRASSROOTS MOVEMENT

Despite equalization's limitations, a significant shift in school funding did occur and Black children benefited throughout the region. As Percy H. Easom, Mississippi's director of Negro Education, pointed out in 1956, the state's racial gap had closed substantially. The building program had spent more than $21 million on Black schools, nearly two-thirds of it in the previous 2 years. "Never before in the history of the state," Easom exclaimed, "have all the Negro schools received public tax funds for providing teaching supplies and material." This, of course, highlighted the deplorable conditions that had prevailed for decades, prompting Easom to proclaim "staggering progress" since the 1920s.[58] Other White officials echoed this view, no doubt concerned about forestalling desegregation in the wake of the *Brown* decision. Altogether, it was a promising time in Black education, even if the future of Black schools remained uncertain.[59]

Accounts of increased interest in secondary education from African Americans appeared across the region. Much of the momentum for improving Black schools originated locally, where demand for more and better high schools was rooted. In South Carolina, for example, officials reported Black secondary schools making inquiries about accreditation in 1948; eight new ones had been approved, while "others undoubtedly will be added next year and for several years thereafter." The report also noted that districts would have to make financial commitments to make such aspirations tenable.[60] That same year, Newbold reported even greater interest in North Carolina, with the appearance of some 40 "beginning or non-accredited high schools," most of which he predicted would be accredited within 5 years. With this, he felt that most of the state had "a sufficient number of high schools" to serve Blacks, as long as "adequate" transportation could be guaranteed. Looking ahead, he claimed that "not more than a dozen or two others located at strategic points will be needed to have a complete system of public high schools for all Negro children in North Carolina."[61] School officials in other states made similar observations, looking forward to when secondary education would be available to Blacks throughout the region.[62] School consolidation and building programs would eventually fulfill many such dreams, but the impetus would have to come from the districts if new institutions were to succeed. The fact that most did succeed is testimony to local efforts. As sociologist C. Arnold Anderson commented about the South in the mid-1950s, "The major portion of the Negro advance at the secondary level occurred during the last decade."[63]

Yet another sign of rising interest in secondary education was the number of students crowding into the schools. A consistent theme in discussions about the capacity of Black high schools was rapidly rising enrollment. Practically all reports highlighted teeming classrooms and excessive loads for teachers. In South Carolina, for instance, the 1953 state high school report noted that Black teachers were nearly twice as likely to have classes exceeding published guidelines.[64] In 1959, Frary Elrod, superintendent of Jackson County schools in Georgia, reported to the Division of Negro Education a "dire need of additional class room space" and pleaded for a visit to get "first hand information concerning the seriousness of the situation."[65] Apart from inadequate libraries, this was the biggest difficulty for schools seeking accreditation and those trying to maintain it. Even after the school consolidation and building campaigns, complaints about overcrowded Black high schools were commonplace.[66]

Such problems, of course, were symptomatic of inadequate resources, but they also pointed to great interest in secondary schooling among African Americans. Soon after they were established, if seems, schools routinely grew beyond the building and staff capacity limits utilized for accreditation. In some states, new schools were regularly opened in outlying districts well into the 1950s, usually with a modicum of resources, also reflecting a high level of interest. Even as the availability of secondary education was expanding, popular demand among Blacks was outstripping it in many communities.

Evidence of this is clear in Table 2.2, which displays 17-year-old enrollment levels for Blacks and Whites in 1940 and 1960 for Southern states. As noted earlier, in just 2 decades, African Americans had nearly caught up with Whites in high school attendance. This table documents the proportion of 17-year-olds who had reached at least the junior year of high school and were still enrolled or had graduated. As suggested earlier, it can be considered an indicator of graduation rates.

Of course, there was considerable variation across the region on this count, reflecting conditions that existed from one state to another. It is telling, for instance, that Mississippi registered the lowest level of Black attainment in 1940 and still occupied that position 2 decades later. The highest Black rates, on the other hand, were evident in the "upper South" states of North Carolina and Tennessee.[67] These patterns echoed popular opinion, which often held North Carolina a regional leader in educational reform.[68] Mississippi and other Deep South states, on the other hand, were especially poor and often encountered difficulty in implementing equalization measures during the 1950s.[69] History weighed heavily in shaping educational inequality in these parts of the South.

As noted in Chapter 1, many youth in 1940 could not reach the junior-year threshold simply because local schools did not offer more than 2 years of secondary instruction. Table 2.2 reveals that racial distinctions at this level of education were very large, as were overall enrollments. Relatively few youth attained this degree of success for either group, but Blacks were just 27% as likely to reach it as Whites, reflecting the vastly unequal resources available to them.

By 1960, on the other hand, attainment for both groups, measured in this way, had increased substantially. It more than doubled for Whites, but grew more than fivefold for African Americans. This, too, was undoubtedly linked to the additional resources that were made available to all youth, but particularly to Blacks in the wake of equalization. Replacing hundreds of small, abridged secondary programs with larger, modern high schools made it possible for many more Black students to succeed academically. By 1960, African American youth were 70% as likely as Whites to be on track to graduate by age 17. This, too, represented a major step on the road to closing an attainment gap that had existed since the latter 19th century.

There are a number of revealing patterns evident in Table 2.2. States of the upper South exhibited higher enrollment at the start, reflecting smaller numbers of tenant farmers, but other states closed much of the gap by 1960. The "Black Belt" states of Mississippi and South Carolina remained laggards, and Georgia also trailed the regional average, but White

TABLE 2.2. Patterns of High School Attainment, Age 17, Percent at Junior Year or Higher (Including Graduation), 1940 and 1960

State	1940			1960		
	Black Students	White Students	Ratio of Black to White Students	Black Students	White Students	Ratio of Black to White Students
Virginia	7	32	20	47	57	82
Alabama	5	25	20	38	64	59
Arkansas	9	29	31	44	69	64
Florida	8	30	27	43	70	61
Georgia	5	29	17	39	59	66
Louisiana	4	41	10	44	61	72
Mississippi	3	30	10	30	59	51
North Carolina	12	34	35	46	58	79
South Carolina	6	36	17	39	55	71
Texas	15	34	44	52	61	85
Kentucky	3	20	15	55	56	98
Maryland	19	34	56	57	69	83
Tennessee	11	22	50	50	58	86
West Virginia	11	22	20	60	61	98
Regional Total	8	30	27	43	61	70

Source: IPUMS data.
*Oklahoma is excluded because of the low number of black 17-year-olds available for estimating enrollment levels. This accounts for minor differences in the calculation of region-wide attainment rates here and in Table 2.1.

attainment was relatively low in these states, too. Much of this variation was unquestionably linked to the circumstances of Black communities and the students who lived in them. Indeed, the correlation across all 14 states in Table 2.2. between Black attainment and a factor score representing both poverty levels and teens living on farms was -.78, representing more than half the state-level variance in high school success.[70] Equalization did not have the same impact across the South, at least with respect to state attainment levels.

Given this variation, it is clear that certain states performed better educationally than others. The upper South, including Virginia, Tennessee, and especially North Carolina, with a tradition of support for education, offered greater opportunities for attainment. In Mississippi, on the other hand, where about 40% of Black teens lived on farms, it appears to have been especially difficult to complete high school. Neighboring Louisiana and Alabama had more urbanized Black communities, with fewer than one in six teens living on farms, and exhibited correspondingly higher attainment. In states such as West Virginia and Kentucky, with even greater Black urbanization, African American attainment was virtually the same as that for White youth.[71] Although opportunities for secondary schooling dramatically improved in all states, there remained considerable regional variation in the numbers of Black youth who benefitted.

THE GOOD BLACK HIGH SCHOOL

Given the dynamics of growth described above, there can be little doubt that the 1950s and early 1960s were generally a positive time to be working in or attending a Black Southern high school. This is not to say that conditions were ideal, as considerable variation existed across localities, but they had improved considerably in a relatively short time. For the first time, substantial resources flowed from state governments for the improvement of African American schools, including provision of new facilities for secondary institutions. Their pupils were also being prepared in better elementary schools, with greater resources. The old high schools that had started as additions to lower graded schools or training institutions were consolidated into new buildings that rivaled many White facilities in terms of size and appearance, if not always resources. A well-known example is the Caswell County Training School, the focal point of Vanessa Siddle Walker's study of institutional accomplishment, which received more than $245,000 from the state of North Carolina in 1951 for a new facility. Under the able leadership of Nicholas Longworth Dillard, this school eventually enrolled nearly 1,000 students, achieved regional accreditation, and became known for its capable and caring staff. Dillard was the only principal in its 34 years of existence, and Walker's careful accounting of his experiences and leadership provides a vivid portrait of the many strengths of a superior Black institution during this period.[72]

Walker's study may be the best-known examination of Southern Black secondary education, but it is hardly the only one. A growing body of work has produced a fairly consistent picture of the high school experience for African Americans in the pre-integration era, one that emphasizes the support that they received both from their communities and from teachers in the institutions they attended.[73] These studies have also provided a good deal of information about the curricula of Black institutions, their staffs, and the communities that sustained them. The principle themes that have emerged from this body of work have been the academic (as opposed to vocational) orientation of these schools, the high levels of support that students received both in and out of class, the care and concern that teachers and administrators exhibited, and the self-confidence that many students learned despite the discriminatory realities of Jim Crow.[74]

A particularly important topic is the emphasis placed on preparation for higher study. By and large, African American institutions do not appear to have been preoccupied with the vocational or industrial arts education so characteristic of Black education in the era of Booker T. Washington, extending into the 1930s. Although some Southern states emphasized agricultural education for African Americans, the declining farm sector economy made this an ever less important element of the curriculum. Most Black institutions offered a basic core of academic subjects, mainly because anything else would require both specialized teachers and additional facilities. Vocational education called for dedicated space and equipment, and since many institutions started off as modest additions to lower schools, courses frequently were extensions of subjects in the elementary grades. As noted in a North Carolina state superintendent's report in 1950, the curriculum for "a large part of the high schools" was limited to five subjects: English, mathematics, social studies, science, and foreign language. Similar reports were issued in other states concerning the rural schools.[75]

Like Dillard at the Caswell County Training School, local Black educators and their community supporters often did not ask permission of school boards to begin secondary instruction, so there was no official curriculum to be approved. Instead, offerings tended to grow with the school, becoming more extensive and differentiated over time. Since most Black high schools were relatively small, particularly in rural areas, the curriculum remained largely academic in character. The North Carolina superintendent's report noted that unless a school had six or more teachers, it was very difficult to offer any vocational education courses at all.[76] In a survey of Black high school principals in North Carolina during the early 1960s, Frederick Rodgers found that the only vocational course offered in 90% or more of their schools was home economics. Industrial arts, on the other hand, was reportedly offered in 71% of the schools, fewer than those offering foreign language instruction, business courses, or music, each at more than 80%.[77] As this suggests, academic courses typically took precedence. This may have reflected community preferences, but it also was due to state requirements concerning the essential elements of study for accreditation purposes. All Southern states, to one degree or another, demanded a basic academic curriculum for approval. Such courses also were necessary but hardly sufficient for regional accreditation; higher-level academic courses typically were expected for that. For smaller rural schools, even after equalization, vocational education was a luxury that few could afford.

Despite the schools' relatively narrow curriculum, statements of purpose filed with accreditation reports for such schools often highlighted expansive educational principles. For instance, the 1955 goals of the James E. Shepard High School in rural Zebulon, North Carolina, included an emphasis on communication, thinking, citizenship, morality, the "role of science in daily lives," appreciation of beauty, health and safety, leisure activity, and helping "to motivate the child to make satisfactory personal adjustments." The report stated, "Since all youth have certain common needs, regardless of where they live, we try to meet these needs thru the basic courses in the curriculum." It also featured a quote from John Dewey, further evidence of the staff's progressive ideas and their determination to prepare students for a rapidly changing world. Such statements were common in these reports, especially in North Carolina but elsewhere as well. Black educators stayed abreast of developments in the world of professional education, regardless of the modest circumstances of their institutions and communities.[78] This was encouraged by state and regional organizations of Black educators, especially the principals' groups that functioned in most states, often in a semiformal fashion. Due to state policies that sent Black educators to Northern institutions for graduate study, many were quite conversant with progressive ideas and practices. Their regional organizations helped to sustain professional identities and standards, providing networks for the exchange of information and opinion, and offered wider perspective on local conditions and events.[79] Such bonds encouraged the positive, progressive sentiments often expressed in the schools' stated purposes.

There were exceptions to this, of course. Some Black principals complained about teachers who appeared uninterested in learning new ideas, or communities that did not favor plans for accreditation.[80] But the steadily growing numbers of state and regionally approved schools suggests that such problems were rather limited. The general theme of the era was improvement, both in the quality of schooling and the number of students attending and graduating from high school. Some parts of the South exhibited less of an emphasis on academic instruction. In Mississsippi, Eason High in Corinth was staffed with 11 teachers, offered no foreign language instruction, and featured a number of vocational courses. But the local White senior high school did not offer foreign language instruction, either, and it, too, listed many vocational courses. As a rule, it appears that secondary schools had fewer academic resources in Mississippi, the region's poorest state with the largest Black population in proportional terms.[81] In neighboring Alabama, on the other hand, a study of the course offerings of Black high schools in 1958 found that virtually all featured an academic curriculum. Indeed, the author found that size and accreditation were generally unrelated to this, although they did affect the availability of more specialized offerings, especially in math and science.[82] The accumulated evidence suggests that there was relatively little difference in curricular profile between Black and White secondary schools, at least regarding basic courses. The distinctions that existed generally were in more specialized subjects, particularly math and the sciences, as White schools tended to be larger and could offer higher-level classes in these disciplines.

Another important academic strength of Black institutions was staff qualifications, which at this time appear to have been generally equivalent to—if not better than—their White counterparts. There is considerable evidence that Black teachers had closed the racial gap in credentials that existed 20 years earlier. In South Carolina, for instance, the Division of Negro Education reported in 1958 that the number of Black teachers with college degrees had increased from 32% to 92%, and those with master's degrees had grown from 2% to 13%.[83] Similar improvement occurred elsewhere. Census data indicate that the proportion of college-educated Black teachers had surpassed the share of similarly educated Whites in the Southern states by 1960, although it appears that a slightly higher percentage of Whites had graduate training. It is hard to say how Black secondary teachers compared to those in White high schools, but respondents to Rodgers's survey of Black principals in North Carolina indicated that a large majority of teachers in their schools held master's degrees and the highest level of certification. This corresponds to other studies of Black schools during this time.[84] Generally speaking, it appears that better-educated teachers found their way into the secondary institutions, where pay as well as prestige was higher. Therefore, it is probably safe to say that Black high school teachers compared favorably with their White counterparts, at least regarding formal education. There is evidence that Black teachers scored somewhat lower on educational tests utilized by some Southern states to make salary decisions, but it is impossible to know whether this extended to secondary educators, or if it mattered much in terms of instructional effectiveness.[85] From all of the available evidence, it appears that the Black teachers who staffed these schools were highly qualified, and could serve as compelling role models for students interested in pursuing education beyond the high school.

At the heart of the "Good Black High School" research are student accounts of the many positive experiences they had during their secondary school years. In our own interviews with former students, we encountered similar themes. Most dwell upon the support and encouragement that they received from teachers and administrators, and the strict but loving supervision that came from parents, other family members, and the community. This was certainly the case with alumni of Booker T. Washington High in Atlanta, many of whom credited the teachers, along with their parents and neighbors, with providing critical assistance in their success. Brandon Carter attended Washington in the early 1950s and described it as "enjoyable, educational, and . . . motivational." He recalled teachers at Washington who took time to explain academic tasks and to teach "social skills," such as how to eat at a restaurant and "dress for success." His teachers encouraged him to go to college; he received several scholarships, and attended Morehouse and later Tuskegee.

Our interview subjects also discussed the important roles other adults played in the lives of Black youth. Betty Small, who started high school in 1956, described Washington as a place where teachers had strict rules that were reinforced by the larger community. She said it was a place where "you did whatever was expected of you and you went over and beyond," and that in her neighborhood, "there were certain things you would not do, because if you got in trouble and someone saw it, your mother would hear about it." Teachers made time to visit students' homes and discuss their work with parents. Roger Richards recounted similar experiences growing up in Jones County, North Carolina. His teachers were interested in helping all students and devoted additional effort to "slow" pupils. Gloria Chambers, who attended high school in Corinth, Mississippi, and graduated in 1950, said that if students did not do their lessons, teachers would spank them and contact their parents. She remembers having a school choir in the latter 1940s, and an array of student clubs organized by the principal and teachers, despite the fact that institutional resources were meager.[86]

Stories such as these highlight factors accounting for the success of Black schools in this era, notwithstanding the many forms of prejudice faced by students, educators, and their communities. Of course, memories are sometimes sentimental, and dissatisfied former students were undoubtedly less likely to volunteer for oral history interviews, but there can be little question that many individuals benefitted enormously from these institutions. Even though students dropped out for a variety of reasons and those who were interviewed often highlighted the "good times," such accounts are commonplace and underscore the commitment to education as a shared value in Black communities.[87] Large numbers of youth responded positively to these sentiments, devoting time and effort to success in school, and it is evident in a growing body of interview research describing Black high school experiences. This, too, contributed to the growth of Black secondary enrollment and graduation during the 1940s and 1950s. Black high schools provided welcoming and supportive environments for many of the students who came to them, providing learning experiences that would alter their lives in innumerable ways. This is perhaps the most powerful legacy of African American secondary education in this era.

WHITE RESISTANCE AND BLACK SKEPTICISM: THE LIMITS OF REFORM

Despite excitement about the many enhancements to Black schools, it also became quite evident that most Southern Whites supported equalization because of fears about integration. This limited the extent that Black schools could ever truly be made equivalent to those for Whites, simply because there was little underlying commitment to principles of equity. The *New York Times* published a follow-up article on the equalization campaigns in 1954, immediately after the Supreme Court's historic decision in *Brown v. Board of Education*. Citing advances in Virginia, West Virginia, Florida, the Carolinas, Georgia, Alabama, Louisiana, Arkansas, and Kentucky, the *Times* reported that more than $100 million were expended in just four states on operations for Black schools and hundreds of millions more were earmarked for building campaigns.[88] It also noted, however, that even higher amounts were devoted to White education, and that a substantial gap remained in the quality of schooling available to the races. In 1954—a few months after the *Brown* decision—Georgia governor Marvin Griffin urged voters to support a school segregation amendment that he promised would "build protection from strife, unrest, and riot."[89] This, of course, was the other side of "equalization campaigns" across the region. The political compromise in most states required to win support for improvements to Black schools involved substantial funding increases for White education as well. As Robert Cousins declared candidly in 1956, Georgia's expansive building program was designed to provide modern facilities for all the children of the state, and that if some measure of equalization resulted, it was not necessarily intended.[90] Similar points were made in other states, as African Americans noted continuing inequities, particularly when enthusiasm for equalization began to wane and litigation shifted to desegregation.[91] Such was the politics of school improvement in the South at the time. If a rising tide lifted all boats, it was reasoned, the difficult proposition of increased funding for Black education could be sold to White voters, at least at the state level.[92]

While the *Times* was able to point to certain states where funding for Black institutions exceeded funding for Whites at the time, such as South Carolina, it was not true in most of the South, and even in those instances where Black schools received greater support, the benefits were temporary. Historians who have examined equalization in particular states have demonstrated that beyond the principal improvements of the 1950s, the impact of the equalization campaigns never seriously threatened the superiority of White schools. A major reason for this was resistance from White-controlled districts, which typically were asked to contribute funds for new schools and operating expenses and to oversee the allocation of state support. At the start of the period, local districts in Mississippi spent nearly three times as much on White schools as Black institutions, despite state appropriations more or less evenly divided between the races. Even though Mississippi's spending in the 1950s was supposed to result in substantial equalization, some 32 counties spent nothing on Black school construction and half of all new African American facilities were built in the cities of Jackson, Biloxi, and Gulfport.[93]

In many rural areas, local authorities were quite opposed to devoting resources to Black education. In 1957, Lamar Fortenberry, the newly appointed White director of the state's Division of Negro Education, issued a plea that "in order for good relationships to continue between the races, the people of Mississippi, both white and black, must work together toward getting all communities to meet the responsibility of truly equalizing facilities."[94] To Whites in many communities, however, the threat of integration seemed more remote and abstract than the issue of devoting local tax dollars to support African American institutions. Consequently, improvements to Black schools often were limited to state funds, if they were even undertaken at all. In other states, such as Georgia and the Carolinas, state authorities exerted greater pressure to utilize funds, although they were not always successful.[95] This made for a somewhat uneven process of regional change. It also meant that true equalization of education was rarely, if ever, fully realized, as resources for Black institutions lagged. In 1958 the new White head of Georgia's Division of Negro Education declared himself "amazed and dumbfounded at how little they have," more than seven years after the start of the state's "Minimum Foundation" campaign.[96] Local resistance was among the principal impediments to change, and it was formidable indeed.

African American leaders recognized the limitations of the equalization campaigns, and fully realized the depth of White abhorrence regarding integration. Almost from the beginning, there was a healthy strain of ambivalence in Black responses to the idea that Southern states were going to make Black schools fully equivalent to White institutions. As the *Chicago Defender* editorialized in 1951, the "feverish" equalization of Black schools by Southern states did not seem economically feasible, and thus, integration was the only realistic answer to educational inequality.[97] Among many Southern Blacks, years of double-dealing and false promises had left considerable skepticism about the prospects for meaningful change. In 1952, the *Atlanta Daily World* declared, "We doubt if those in authority to expend the school funds will show the alertness to spend sufficiently on the Negro schools, even to make them 'substantially equal.'" Noting that $10 million had been allocated by the legislature for building schools, the paper's editors did not believe it was enough for Black schools alone. "If we are to get the bulk of this money," they wrote, "we must vigorously contend for it." The commentary closed with an emphatic pronouncement that "we must let school officials know we are entitled to EQUALITY and not just mere improvement."[98] As noted earlier, of course, Georgia officials eventually admitted that the building campaigns were never intended to equalize schools.

Reservations about equalization were widely shared elsewhere. Historian Charles Bolton has documented the wary reaction of Black leaders in Mississippi to pledges by the governor and other White political leaders regarding new facilities and more jobs for African American educators. It was widely known that the NAACP had changed course in the early 1950s, dropping equalization as a principal focus and devoting its legal and financial resources to direct attacks on school segregation. Black educators also realized that without the active threat of desegregation, equalization would never move forward in any meaningful way. Similar responses were evident in other states across the region, as equalization was debated as a general strategy.[99] As R. Scott Baker has noted concerning South Carolina, it was only a "showdown over segregation" that "forced reluctant state officials to begin the process of equalizing school facilities." He quoted a local editor, declaring, "The political bosses of this state have never acted decently until and unless they had the club of a policeman over their head, and the only policeman they fear is the federal courts."[100] In the end, Whites simply could not be trusted to provide an equal education for African American children, and even if the school were made more equal, there remained the question of what or who would guarantee that they remain equivalent. As some Black commentators noted, this made the very idea of equalization a questionable proposition.[101]

For many African Americans, the resources that such legislation brought to their communities were certainly welcome, but it quickly became apparent that equalization was hardly the goal of White authorities. Although half a loaf was better than none, it was still just half a loaf. As time went on, it appears that growing numbers of Blacks became dissatisfied with the condition of their schools, even after the improvements that were made possible by state aid. Part of the problem was that many new schools built during the campaigns were visibly inferior to local White institutions. In 1958, the NAACP described the new Black high school in Canton, Mississippi, as "makeshift," decrying its African American supporters for "keeping other Negroes in deplorable conditions."[102] High schools often lacked gyms or auditoriums, as most Black facilities seemed restricted to just one or the other of such amenities. As the *Chicago Defender* noted regarding Mississippi in 1959, "Most Negro schools consist only of classrooms and perhaps a gymnasium, whereas white schools are outfitted with laboratories, visual aids, rooms for special activities such as music and drama, craft shops and many other frills not found in Negro schools." One local critic described the new buildings as "just pretty shells."[103]

Such complaints were widespread. Respondents to Frederick Rodgers's survey of Black principals in North Carolina reported fighting for additional funds for new facilities only to see the bulk of the money devoted to White schools. They also noted that library funds were divided unequally, and Black institutions had to raise their own funds to build and maintain collections, a vital factor in regional accreditation. This continued the longstanding tradition of "double taxation" in Black schooling.[104] As Vanessa Siddle Walker has observed, Black high school principals were continually raising funds and working around recalcitrant White superintendents and boards, vital skills for success in Georgia and other states.[105] And it wasn't just the educators who noticed. Former students recall receiving used textbooks from the White schools instead of new ones, even as they occupied new facilities built with state funds.[106] Despite the promises of equalization, and the hopes that accompanied the state building campaigns, Black high schools still were not generally equivalent to White institutions, even more than a decade after new resources were devoted to improving them.

Perhaps the clearest evidence of this was the number of Black schools that still lacked accreditation in the latter 1950s and early 1960s, and areas of the South that did not offer secondary facilities for Blacks. In 1958, fully half of the respondents to a survey of Alabama Black secondary institutions lacked state accreditation, and only 23 out of 184 were regionally accredited.[107] In Mississippi, a higher number of Black schools were approved by the state, but only seven had earned regional accreditation by 1963. At the same time, virtually all White high schools throughout the South were state-accredited and roughly one-third held regional accreditation. This was incontrovertible evidence of the continuing inferiority of Black secondary schooling, despite the accomplishments of exemplary institutions. Perhaps most frustrating of all, in 1958, the *Atlanta Daily World* reported that 17 counties in Virginia still did not have high schools for their African American students. After all the hue and cry about finally equalizing educational opportunity, some Black youth lacked even the barest opportunity for secondary schooling.[108]

Local authorities often were loath to provide better buildings and amenities for African American students for fear that it would anger the White constituents who had elected them. Until passage of federal civil rights legislation, and the Voting Rights Act in particular, significantly expanding African American political power, there was little redress for local Black communities. In the latter 1950s fewer than 2 percent of Georgia school boards had any Black members, and conditions were similar elsewhere. Short of wielding electoral power, Blacks often suffered frustration in registering complaints about the continuing inequality in schooling throughout the region.[109]

In the end, growing numbers of African Americans came to the conclusion that separate schools never would be able to offer full educational equality. This view was evident in educational testing, an approach to measuring educational outcomes that was being employed more widely throughout the South for a variety of purposes. One of the most consistent patterns in test results was the relatively low performance of African Americans. It was taken by many as evidence that full equalization of educational opportunities would never be attained in a segregated system of schools. As the *Atlanta Daily World* editorialized in 1957, "Buildings alone—however many have been constructed in the past few years—cannot make up for all the inherent and severely perpetrated inequalities under the dual system." Roundly rejecting the idea that test scores reflected differences in innate ability, the paper's editors called for additional school funding and "an accelerated move toward one single school system and one standard of education for all children without taking into consideration the matter of race."[110] In a letter to Georgia's director of Negro Education in 1956, civil rights leader Septima P. Clark described an educators' workshop that identified "a great need for bi-racial channels of communication in the Deep South and a greater need for Negro leadership." She reported that the educators had agreed to hold 12 workshops on integration in 1957, one each month.[111] Although they were not calling for immediate desegregation, statements such as these reflected frustration with the equalization regime and the inherent limitations of the separate but equal doctrine that still prevailed across the South.

Less than 10 years later, the results of the nation's first large-scale assessment of academic achievement, the Equality of Educational Opportunity survey conducted by James Coleman, revealed that Black teens educated in the rural South performed far below every other group considered.[112] This was a quantitative confirmation of what many African American critics of equalization had long suspected: True equality of educational outcomes was never the goal. As the movement to integrate schools pushed forward in the wake of *Brown*, the 1957 Little Rock confrontation, and other incidents, Black support for equalization would continue to wane. Regardless of the great strides it had brought to the regions' Black schools, it seemed ever less likely to produce complete equality of educational outcomes.

CONCLUSION: BUILDING A FOUNDATION FOR THE FUTURE

Between the start of World War II and 1960, high school practically became a commonplace experience for African American youth. Historians have noted the systematic exclusion of Blacks from secondary education prior to the war. Their enrollment in these institutions grew steadily in the 1920s and 1930s, but during the postwar era change became more dramatic. Black education benefited from White fears about preserving segregation, as resources were poured into better access and improved facilities, along with other changes. As suggested above, this appears to have reduced the racial gap in attainment substantially.

Dramatic improvements in Black high school enrollment and secondary attainment, however, did not occur spontaneously; growth did not just represent individual decisions by Black families and their children. Rather, it was the result of an extended struggle to acquire the resources to provide secondary schooling to Black youth. The first phase of this process entailed stretching local assets, converting existing schools to allow some measure of secondary instruction. The institutions that resulted were inferior in many respects to White schools, but they represented a start. These steps demonstrated the dedication and resourcefulness of African American educators, students, and their communities, providing a starting point for future developments in the region.

The next phase came with the so-called equalization campaigns of the late 1940s and 1950s. At this point, it was possible to finally gain some of the advantages that White schools had long enjoyed. These resources were physical, such as buildings, libraries, and laboratories, and they were human, chiefly skilled teachers and administrators. New and improved elementary schools also were critical to the growth of secondary education. African Americans often found helpful allies in White officials who aided the cause, and other Whites who supported them, but there can be little doubt that change was dictated by Black communities and civil rights organizations. Although it is certainly true that attainment was advancing during the 1930s and 1940s, it was only after the threat of litigation over equalization that Southern states began to redress longstanding deficiencies in African American education. Even then, it was a protracted struggle, as local school authorities dragged their feet or simply refused to appreciably improve Black schools. And when new facilities were provided, they soon proved inadequate, as enrollments quickly soared beyond expectations and money was unavailable for further expansion. This, of course, is what ultimately led many African Americans to conclude that equalization of segregated education would never be realized, and that integration was the only effective means of achieving equality in schooling once and for all.

Finally, it is important to emphasize that this was hardly the concluding chapter in the rise of African American attainment. Rather, it was a foundation upon which further developments would build. The change wrought by equalization and the struggle to upgrade Black high schools was ultimately unfinished. Although many institutions flourished, as many as a third of Black high schools in 1960 were unable to achieve even state accreditation. Still fewer were recognized by the regional accrediting agency, the SACS. This does not mean that they were doing a bad job, but it did suggest that their ability to provide an education comparable to that of most White institutions was severely limited. Having unaccredited schools in such large numbers also had serious implications for Black graduates going to college, especially when it came to institutions outside their home states. Addressing this was another step in the development of African American education.

As ever greater numbers of Black youth enrolled in high schools and graduated, they wanted to attend postsecondary institutions in larger numbers. This is just what happened. In the years between 1940 and 1960, Black college enrollments surged in the South, from less than 20,000 to more than 60,000, and increased even more rapidly thereafter.[113] The generation of parents and students who fought to gain access to secondary education during the 1940s and 1950s created a stepping stone for advances in attainment that would develop afterward and the expansion of the Black middle class. Their struggles also readied Black college students to take leadership roles in the civil rights movement, beginning with the sit-in campaigns of the early 1960s.[114] Looking back at this time, it is perhaps easy to forget the many battles that were waged to make the dream of universal secondary education for African Americans a reality. It was in the South that this finally was undertaken on a large scale, and the stage was set for the next steps in the advance of Black educational attainment.

CHAPTER 3

Inequity, Discrimination, and Growth Outside the South, 1940–1960

IN DECEMBER 1943, Robert Queen, a Trenton, New Jersey, lawyer representing the NAACP, petitioned the state's Supreme Court to compel the city schools to admit two African Americans to a White junior high school that was closer to their homes than the Black Lincoln School. The two students, Janet Hedgepeth and Leon Williams, had graduated from different segregated elementary schools, but were assigned to Lincoln despite having to walk 16 blocks to reach it, while Junior High No. Two for Whites was just 2 blocks away. When Mr. Queen inquired about this, he was told "it was the custom" to send Black students to Lincoln.

It did not take the court long to decide in the plaintiffs' favor. Within 2 months, the district admitted Hedgepeth and Williams to the White school and segregated public education in Trenton ended.[1] The practice remained an issue across New Jersey, however, even after the state changed its constitution in 1947 to forbid such segregation.[2] The *Pittsburgh Courier* praised Trenton as a model of evenhandedness and amity, citing the Lincoln case and its integrated schools, including teachers. "Jim Crow, who once directed affairs in the capital of New Jersey," it declared, "is now persona non grata."[3] If change was coming to the South, a new era was dawning for Black education elsewhere, too.

As historian Davison M. Douglas has suggested, an atmosphere of racial tolerance, if hardly complete acceptance, began to influence Black-White relations in much of the North during the 1940s. This contributed to a surge of conflict and litigation against segregationist policies, which had increased dramatically earlier in the century. Like other Northern states, New Jersey had statutes forbidding segregationist school policies but little effort was made to enforce them. It took a concerted effort by the

NAACP to bring many districts into compliance. Similar battles occurred elsewhere, as school integration became a focal point in the Northern civil rights struggle.[4] It marked a growing restlessness among African Americans regarding their status in American society, and recognition of education's importance in preparing for the future.

Trenton's school controversy was just one of many such disputes that occurred in Northern states during the World War II era. Perhaps the most notorious occurred in Hillburn, New York, just 19 miles north of Manhattan, where in 1943 Blacks boycotted two ramshackle segregated grade schools when their children were denied access to modern White facilities. Thurgood Marshall conducted an NAACP investigation that led to a campaign against the town's obstinate leaders, eventually causing the state to close the two schools. This led, in turn, to Whites boycotting the newly integrated grade schools and enrolling in local Catholic institutions. The result was a largely segregated school system once again, but Black students had at least gained access to better facilities. Historians have pointed to Hillburn as symptomatic of Northern struggles against discrimination in education. There were dozens of incidents with Black protest greeted by determined resistance from Whites. Many such conflicts occurred outside of the major cities, in communities that were small enough for frequent contact between the races, but also with rigid status distinctions along racial lines.[5] In most cases, however, the problem of school segregation that provoked them did not extend to high schools.

The dispute in Trenton was a rare instance of protest focused on secondary education, and it concerned a junior high rather than a high school. Most districts outside the South did not operate officially segregated secondary schools, partly because accreditation standards made dual schools expensive. Exceptions tended to occur in places with historic ties to the South, particularly communities from New Jersey to Illinois in counties bordering Southern states, or in Indiana, Missouri, and Kansas, which permitted formally segregated schools. In smaller communities, students from both Black and White grade schools typically attended a single secondary institution, such as nearby Sufferin High for students from Hillburn.[6] This did not mean that racial conflicts were absent from these schools; they just did not become the subject of legal battles or Black protest.

The treatment of Blacks in predominantly White schools had been discussed for years in Northern African American communities.[7] The issues tended to be more subtle than the overt discrimination displayed in Hillburn and Trenton. But anecdotal evidence abounded that White teachers and students were capable of harassing Blacks, subjecting them to various forms of prejudice and even violence, and high schools certainly saw many such incidents. Thus, although secondary schools were more widely available to African Americans, they did not always offer the most hospitable environments.

Despite these challenges, this was a time of expansion in Black education across the North and West, although it occurred differently than in the South. Apart from certain cities, the Black population was smaller and while some districts maintained dual school systems, most found segregated schools cost-prohibitive. Newsworthy racial tensions flared sporadically, but segregationist laws were effectively challenged in courts by the NAACP.[8] In the wake of World War II and growing distaste toward racist ideas, a new discourse on racial understanding was gaining strength. Altogether, it was a hopeful time, one of considerable optimism about the future, even for those attending segregated institutions. Going to school made sense to growing numbers of African American youth, and they reached levels of attainment that were scarcely imaginable in earlier times. Blacks began going to high school as a matter of course, and graduation became a reasonable expectation for many. In this respect, it was a decisive time indeed, laying a foundation for subsequent developments in the expanding purview of African American education.

BLACKS AND SECONDARY SCHOOL ATTAINMENT IN 1940

In 1940, about one in five African American youth lived outside the South. Of this number, nearly 80% lived in the industrial Northeast, spanning the Great Lakes, Middle Atlantic, and New England states. The remaining 20%, about 4% of the national Black population, lived in the Plains states and the West, with the largest numbers in Missouri and California. Unlike Southern Black teens, most did not live on farms or in smaller cities and towns. Nearly two-thirds were in cities at the center of metropolitan areas. As indicated in Table 3.1, African American youth outside the South were about twice as likely to reside in major cities as White teens. Many urban centers had longstanding Black communities, dating to the 19th century or earlier, which grew rapidly due to migration. They also had lengthy traditions of Black education, much of it marked by inequity and discord, legacies that hardly bode well for youth on the eve of World War II.

Larger cities exhibited relatively high neighborhood segregation, often aggravated by the arrival of Southern Blacks, and it extended directly to the schools. Chicago is perhaps the best-known case, largely because it has been so extensively studied, but Detroit, Philadelphia, Boston, Cleveland, Los Angeles, and Milwaukee were also segregated residentially and, consequently, in the schools as well.[9] Secondary school segregation may have been less pronounced in smaller cities, just because local Black communities were smaller. But most Black students attended a limited

TABLE 3.1. Black and White Youth, Ages 14–18, Attending or Graduated from High School Outside the South, 1940 (in percentages)

Region	Portion of Teen Population 1940		Enrollment Rate, 1940		Portion in Central Cities	
	Black	White	Black	White	Black	White
Northeast & Great Lakes	79	70	41	55	65	35
Plains & West	21	30	40	54	66	21

Region	Big-City Enroll Rate		Non-City Enroll Rate	
	Black	White	Black	White
Northeast & Great Lakes	44	59	37	52
Plains & West	44	63	32	52

Source: IPUMS data (Blacks 3% of total youth population).

number of secondary schools because of their restriction to less desirable neighborhoods.

As indicated in Table 3.1, there was little difference between the highly urban and industrial Northeast and the less developed West regarding Black secondary enrollment in 1940. Both areas exhibited attendance rates of about 40%, roughly 14 points (about 26%) lower than the White rate. This, of course, was much higher than the Southern rate of less than 14%, and was close to matching Southern White levels of about 45%. Clearly, secondary education was a good deal more accessible than in the South. Only about one in five of the nation's Black youth lived in proximity to these opportunities, but across the North and West, going to high school was at least an option for many to consider. Most states had ended formal policies of racial segregation by the 1940s, and secondary schools were widely available, if not always hospitable to Blacks. The principal questions with respect to high school were the capacity of families to forgo the earnings of teenage sons or daughters, their willingness to endure White hostility encountered in school, and their interest in this level of education, including requisite preparation for it.

Slightly more than a third of the Black youth in the North and West in 1940 resided outside big cities; most lived in smaller communities in relatively close proximity to Whites. Only about 12% lived outside metropolitan areas and just 6% were on farms. Others were in suburban settings, growing communities immediately adjacent to larger cities. The vast majority of African American households in such places were headed by adults in blue-collar or menial occupations, or household domestic workers. As one historian has suggested, they were the housecleaners, cooks, groundskeepers, and sanitation workers who helped maintain a high standard of living in White suburban communities. Blacks also worked in hotels and restaurants in resort towns, settling in residential pockets within these generally affluent settings.[10] For those families, living outside the city may have afforded an opportunity to own property and enjoy some benefits of a smaller community, but most worked at unskilled jobs and lived with unmistakable racial divisions and firm local status distinctions.

The same types of Black employment existed in big cities, too, but proportionally more Black proprietors and professionals lived in communities large enough to support them. Opportunities for Black professionals elsewhere were limited, as was certainly true for teachers. Positions were rare for African American educators in the non-metropolitan North or West, but they constituted the majority of opportunities for professional Black women. Districts in smaller communities were unwilling to hire them to teach Whites, and often had no more than a grade school or two for Blacks. In fact, openings for Black teachers were also restricted in certain cities, such as Boston, Pittsburgh, and Milwaukee, where school boards resisted adding them to payrolls.[11] Whites also were generally unwilling to patronize Black doctors, dentists, or accountants, making Black clients critical for them. In proportional terms, the Black rate of white-collar employment outside metropolitan areas was about 60% of that in urban centers. Although the numbers of such African Americans in either setting was modest, ranging from 3% to 7%, they could approach a critical mass only in the cities.[12] This had important consequences for urban Black communities, providing a core constituency for high schools and visible role models for academically ambitious students.

Given this, the type of community where Black youth lived affected their chances of attending a segregated secondary school. Because of variability in the size of Black communities, predominantly African American high schools were rare outside the South in 1940, although they eventually became more commonplace.[13] It is telling, consequently, that Black rates of secondary attendance were 23% higher, at 36% versus 44%, in central cities than elsewhere, although the gap in school success was considerably smaller at 25% versus 28%. In general, it does not appear that the less segregated circumstances outside larger cities were any more encouraging to African American students, and in fact they may have been somewhat less heartening.

Much of this geographic difference in secondary enrollment rates may have been due to the economic circumstances of non-urban Black families. Teenagers in these settings were slightly *more* likely to be employed than their city counterparts, 11% versus 9.6%, even among those not living on farms. In particular, relatively low enrollment in the Plains and Western states was largely due to a higher employment rate in non-metropolitan settings, where many worked on farms. These teens were 55% male, an imbalance that indicated agricultural employment. A similar pattern existed for non-metropolitan youth aged 17 and 18 in the North. Life was not any easier for these teens, and it may have been considerably harder, as suggested by higher urban attendance patterns. As in the South, the greatest educational opportunities appear to have existed in the cities.

GOING TO HIGH SCHOOL IN THE NORTH AND WEST, 1940

In the absence of exclusion from schools, the enrollment decisions of African American youth outside the South were shaped by many of the same social and economic conditions that affected White students. By and large, the circumstances of family life exerted considerable influence over persistence in school. This does not mean that discrimination and segregation had no effects, but they were clearly less significant than in the South.

The importance of social and economic factors is evident in Figure 3.1, which offers an analysis of attainment for African Americans and Whites in 1940. This analysis is similar to those in earlier chapters, except that it reports the likelihood of reaching grade 11 or higher, including graduation, for 17-year-olds with various characteristics, holding other factors constant. Examining figures for both races, it is apparent that the biggest effects were associated with family structure and home ownership, broad indicators of social status in American life. Living in households with one of these characteristics, controlling for other factors, roughly doubled the likelihood of reaching this level of attainment. Home ownership appears to have been more important as a positive influence among African Americans, reflecting a Black rate less than half that of Whites (19% versus 48%). The same was true with occupational status, although much variation in attainment for youth of both races was associated with similar socioeconomic characteristics. This was quite a different situation from in the South, where such factors were considerably stronger correlates of enrollment for Blacks, especially parental education. In other settings, where secondary schooling was at least nominally available to

Inequity, Discrimination, and Growth

FIGURE 3.1. Logistic Regression, Factors Contributing to High School Success, Youth, Age 17, North and West, 1940

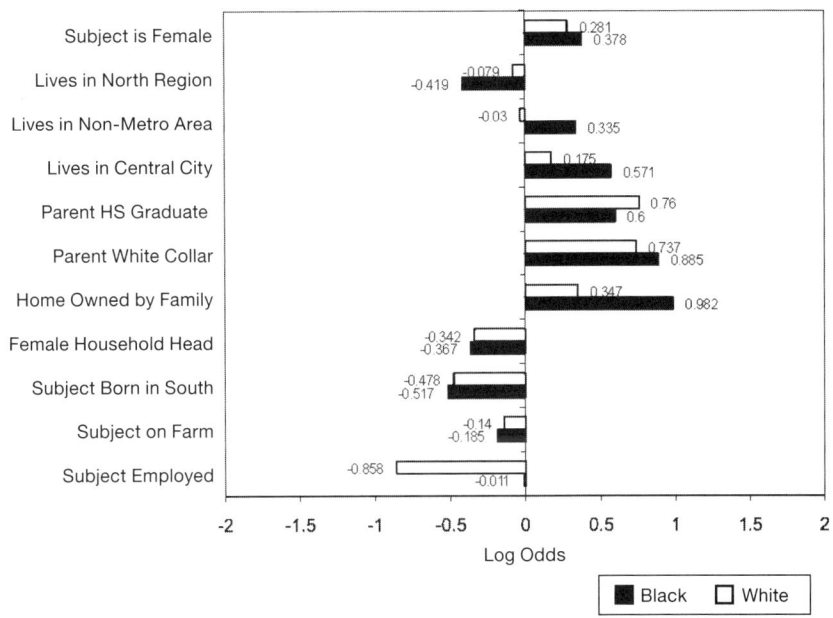

Dependent variable: Enrollment (or not) at the junior level, including graduation. All factors significant at .001 level. See Appendix B for additional information.

all youth, major determinants of success were socioeconomic but not to the same degree. While the offspring of the educated, white-collar, home-owning Black middle class may have represented a core constituency of high schools, particularly in urban areas, Black youth from other households succeeded as well. The fact that more Blacks than Whites occupied the lowest positions in the social structure, of course, meant that the overall Black level of attainment still lagged behind the level of Whites considerably.

Black and White youth also appear to have responded similarly to conditions that inhibited the likelihood of school success, as shown in Figure 3.1. Youth from both races in households without fathers were about equally likely to fall behind or drop out of school, and those born in the South were only about 60% as likely to succeed as those born elsewhere. Since more than twice as many Black youth as Whites did not have a father present (42% versus 18%), the effect of this was considerably greater on African American attainment. Similarly, because Black youth born in the South, at more than 30%, were nearly 14 times the proportion of Southern-born Whites, this factor also had a bigger impact on Black attainment. The negative effect of Southern origins was plain evidence of regional differences in school quality, making it difficult for migrant children of either race to succeed educationally. Their experiences and status became important themes in discussions about racial differences in school performance.[14]

Beyond the shared effects of socioeconomic status, location appears to have had an impact on African American schooling in ways it did not for Whites. Living in the North, as opposed to the West, was a disadvantage for Black youth, controlling for other factors. The advantages of such social class indicators as parental education, occupational status, and home ownership were probably more important there than in the Plains and Western states, where they were less critical to success in school. Residing in a central city was also an advantage, undoubtedly because of the ready availability of high schools. But so, too, was living in a non-metropolitan setting, net of controls for employment, gender, and socioeconomic status, which accounted for much of the lower attainment in these areas.

Apart from these factors, Black youth in smaller cities and towns experienced success in school at rates only slightly lower than those in urban centers. Blacks in both settings did better than their counterparts in suburban communities, the comparison group for these sites. The importance of the location variables is further evidence of the significant role that community setting played in Black educational success. It is revealing, by contrast, that these variables had little association with the likelihood of White attainment at this time. It reflects the generally higher status of Whites and the greater openness of schools to White youth. Even if formal segregation did not exist in most of the North and West, Whites still were the dominant group and clearly felt more comfortable in schools everywhere.[15]

Finally, there is the question of youth employment, which had a much bigger negative impact on White attainment than for Blacks. Unlike the South, where most African American teenagers worked on farms, in the North and West employment was more difficult to secure. The teen job market had been decimated by the Great Depression, and African Americans often faced severe discrimination when competing with Whites for any type of work.[16] Consequently, the employment rate among Black youth was less than three-quarters that of White teens, at about 10%. Moreover, African American youth who held jobs were more likely than Whites to work fewer than 40 hours per week, at 50% versus 40%. Because full-time employment was harder to come by for African Americans, its impact on educational attainment, controlling for other factors, was negligible. Black teenagers seeking work instead of attending school were unlikely to remain enrolled even without a job. For Whites, on the other hand, full-time employment was considered an alternative to schooling for some, even controlling for socioeconomic factors. This, too, is evidence of the many advantages that Whites enjoyed, extending to opportunities in the job market.

Such were the social and economic conditions that shaped African American secondary education outside of the South in 1940. By and large, Black youth in these parts of the country enjoyed access to schools that only a fraction of their Southern cohorts could contemplate. But this did not mean that attending and graduating from high school became commonplace. Little more than a quarter of Black 17-year-olds reached the junior year or higher, as opposed to more than 40% of Whites, testimony to the challenges facing Black families in sending children to school. With fewer resources, less opportunity in the labor market, greater family instability, and weak academic preparation in Southern schools, African American youth were hard-pressed to keep up with Whites. Princeton Elroy migrated north with his family during the late 1940s. He had received only a rudimentary education in Mississippi and was placed in a vocational school in Kansas City, quitting after the 9th grade and joining the military. Other Black students, however, did succeed in school, evidence of their personal resolve, along with that of their parents and communities. Their accomplishments also reflected the efforts of the many dedicated educators who helped them along the way.

RACIAL CONFLICT IN HIGH SCHOOLS

On Tuesday, September 18, 1945, some 800 White students walked out of Froebel High School in Gary, Indiana, to protest the presence of Black students, numbering about 850, a little more than a third of the student body. The incident was precipitated by fighting at a football game the previous Saturday, but the student complaints extended to the principal, whom they later accused of favoring Blacks. Within a matter of days, the strike spread to other buildings, with as many as 2,000 Whites joining by Friday. The response of the school board and other authorities was conciliatory at first, agreeing to meet with protesters and hear their grievances, which included a demand that city high schools be segregated. Previously, African American students had been largely restricted to the all-Black Roosevelt school, which had become severely overcrowded. Although Froebel's Black students had started to participate in a range of activities, including the student council, tensions had been building. The Saturday fight ignited a wave of protest that lasted for months and gained national attention.[17]

Events in Gary were dramatic and received extensive press coverage, revealing the sentiments of many working-class Whites regarding race, education, and social status. Protesters returned to school the following week, after being told that their grievances would be investigated, but they went on strike again in October when Principal Richard Nuzum remained in office. Chief among the complaints was his approval of "mixed white and Negro parties" and that he "ordered the girls' swimming pool opened to Negroes." In making such charges, the students exhibited prejudices shared by many Whites who believed that interracial social contact was either undesirable or morally objectionable. Declaring integration "a degradation of democracy," these students worried that Blacks threatened their "educational advantages" and the standing of their institutions. The high school was an avenue to greater social and economic status, and many feared that African Americans threatened its capacity to convey such benefits. It was a risk that the Gary protesters apparently felt they could not tolerate.

The White students of Froebel included many children of immigrant steel workers, some telling reporters that they resented being labeled with ethnic slurs themselves. This, however, did not make them sympathetic to African Americans. Instead, they worried that prolonged association with Black youth raised the possibility of even further humiliation, threatening their tenuous status as Americans.[18] The pervasiveness of such sentiments became evident when White students at several Chicago secondary schools spontaneously expressed support for the strikers, walking out at Englewood High and demanding a separate building for Blacks at Morgan Park High. Hundreds were involved in each incident. Both schools were integrated and had White student bodies not dissimilar to Gary's protesters.

The *Chicago Defender* reported that White students in New York also expressed sympathy with the strike; doubtless, others did as well.[19] One reason that events in Gary received such wide press coverage was that they touched on questions of interracial contact between young adults. They also brought youthful racial prejudice into the national limelight. The *Defender* labeled the strikers "Gary's Hitler Youth Movement," calling them "teenage racists," and highlighted the readiness of African American students to work for integration despite White attitudes.[20] With this, a metaphorical line was drawn, linking opposition to integration with sympathy for Nazism. Such reasoning gave advocates of integration the moral high ground, especially in light of the war effort, but did little to resolve the status anxiety felt by Whites. Black students were determined to remain in the school.

Eventually, the disputes in Gary and Chicago subsided, integration continued, and the schools moved ahead with Blacks and Whites studying together. Considerable effort was devoted to accomplishing this, however, including visits by popular entertainers Frank Sinatra and Danny Kaye to perform for school audiences, entreating them to cooperate in "the American way."[21] The Congress of Industrial Organizations, representing most of Gary's union members, also made it clear that racial discrimination was a direct violation of its basic principles, and demanded that parents curtail the strike activity of their children. But the events in Gary were hardly isolated incidents, at least with respect to the sentiments they represented. Rather, they were symptomatic of misgivings felt by many Whites about integrated schooling, especially in secondary institutions where dangers of sexual liaison and violent confrontation loomed large, in addition to anxiety about social status and educational quality. Because of this, integrated high schools carried the possibility of volatile social conflict. Educators took note of events in Gary, as African American enrollments across the North and West increased steadily. If rapid integration was likely to produce so much discord, it was practical for many to conclude that it should be avoided as much as possible.

Economist Charles Clotfelter has estimated that about four out of five Black secondary students in North and West non-border states in the 1940s attended schools that were integrated to one extent or another. Based on the National Survey of Black Americans (NSBA) conducted between 1979 and 1992, these data also permitted Clotfelter to calculate the number of Blacks in the typical or "average" school they attended. In the 1940s, he put that figure at a little less than half, some 46%, at the secondary level. This, of course, was a mean around which actual school conditions varied widely. Our own analysis of the NSBA data suggests that African Americans were less likely to encounter Whites in big-city schools. They were only about 60% as likely to attend majority White schools as their non-urban counterparts, and they were liable to be a small minority in schools located in suburbs or non-metropolitan settings.[22] Racial segregation was more commonplace in elementary schools; high schools were larger and drew from multiple elementary buildings, sometimes crossing boundaries between neighborhoods.[23] As a consequence, Black and White students who attended different grade schools often encountered each other in high school, a situation often ripe for misunderstanding and conflict.

Given this, and prevailing racial attitudes in the 1940s, integrated high schools became sites where fears and prejudices often found expression in hostility. Most conflict between Black and White students did not get the press coverage that was devoted to Gary. Much of it occurred in everyday quarrels and scuffles in hallways, playgrounds, athletic fields, or other settings where African Americans and Whites met outside the scope of adult supervision. In these locations, the informal social boundaries of exclusion were enforced between groups, and status distinctions were maintained.

Racial harassment had a long history in Northern high schools. One historian has suggested that it was "impossible for Negro students to remain in primarily white high schools" in Chicago during the 1920s, citing a case where 30 African American students were forced to withdraw due to harassment. As one White student proclaimed, "We didn't give them any peace in the locker room, basement, at noon hours or between classes—told them to keep out of our way—they know where they belong."[24] More than a decade later, circumstances had not changed much, as Black students reported similar treatment from Whites, including teachers. One young woman who attended Chicago's Hyde Park high in the 1930s recalled, "I always knew I wasn't wanted," adding, "There was lots of discrimination" and that "the teachers get it out by giving low marks." As the number of Black students in high schools increased, they met greater resistance from Whites, students and teachers alike.

Clashes also occurred in other cities. In Detroit, Black and White students fought in a "near riot" outside Northwestern High in 1940. Black community leaders and parents complained about mistreatment from White teachers, but additional conflicts between students occurred in subsequent years.[25] Similar incidents broke out in Cleveland.[26] In Los Angeles, some 150 Whites walked out of Fremont High in 1947 to protest the registration of seven African Americans; a Black figure was hanged in effigy. Two years later, another episode occurred in East St. Louis, Illinois.[27] For many African Americans, attending integrated institutions was far from pleasant or positive. One Chicago woman described Englewood High in the 1930s as "a hate center," a description also applicable to many other institutions. Events following the Gary strike suggest that bigoted attitudes toward Black students persisted well into the postwar era.[28]

It would be wrong, however, to conclude that student race relations were always acrimonious. Writing about schools and social stratification in the early 1940s, sociologist W. Loyd Warner and his colleagues suggested that African American students in smaller communities were socially isolated from Whites but suffered little explicit daily prejudice. Some, such as successful athletes, even gained respect and perhaps a degree of acceptance.[29] Although discord and turmoil may have captured the headlines, the Black press also occasionally featured African American success stories at integrated schools. In 1947, for instance, the *Pittsburgh Courier* reported that a Black student named John Hopkins had been elected school president at Jesuit Gonzaga High in Spokane, Washington, while compiling an exemplary academic record. Similarly, in 1949, the *Chicago*

Defender noted that a Black student was elected junior class president in downstate Ottowa, Illinois, where only three African Americans attended high school. The *Defender* reported that African American students had been elected to student offices in Portland and Chicago, and that another had been selected "Boy Governor" of the annual Nutmeg Boys State sponsored by the Connecticut American Legion.[30] In 1950, Alonzo Frazier was the first African American elected "student mayor" of Kansas City, Missouri, on High School Day, during the city's centennial year.[31] The fact that these developments were newsworthy, of course, was evidence of their novelty, but it also reflected the promise of fair play and acceptance that such cases appeared to offer. In the end, however, these instances were exceptions to the general pattern of conflict and discrimination that characterized Black experience in integrated schools.

Reports of African American accomplishment may have been rare, but they pointed to some of the peculiar dynamics of race relations in schools. Most such cases occurred in institutions where Blacks represented a small fraction of the student body and were viewed as less threatening. The Warner study also focused on communities where Black students were few in number.[32] African Americans who succeeded academically or in sports could be safely celebrated in such instances, as racial boundaries were less likely to harden and liberal attitudes could be tolerated. Even in Chicago, where Terry J. Hatter was elected president of Hyde Park High's 1950 senior class, he was just one of two Blacks among more than 200 graduates. These accounts provide additional evidence of how the particular settings of African American experiences were important. They also highlight just how the type of school they attended could be critical in shaping the opportunities Blacks enjoyed. The *Courier* approvingly quoted a Spokane paper, which wondered "how many Negro boys like Hopkins, with the will and ability to succeed, have been crowded back into social oblivion in other parts of the country where prejudice dooms minority races before they have a chance to show their wares."[33] Prejudice certainly existed in Spokane, of course, and the fact that young Hopkins attended a private religious school no doubt contributed substantially to his social and academic success.

IN SEARCH OF TOLERANCE

Most African American secondary students in the North and West, of course, did not attend such accommodating institutions, and there was growing concern about conflict in and around the schools. In the wake of heightened racial and ethnic discord, high schools began developing courses to address racial prejudice and discrimination. As historian Jeffrey Mirel has documented, these efforts were often launched under the banner of a "campaign for intercultural or intergroup education," generally known as intercultural education. Supported by such national organizations as the American Council on Education (ACE) and the National Council for Social Studies, much of this movement was concerned with helping students understand the contributions of immigrants to American society. In the 1940s, however, leaders strove to include materials on African Americans and other victims of discrimination, in response to such violent incidents as the 1943 race riots in Detroit and the anti-Mexican 1942 "Zoot Suit" attacks in Los Angeles, widely publicized incidents of White violence against minority groups.[34] Outside the schools, efforts commenced to prevent further rioting and promote intergroup cooperation and understanding, eventually resulting in more than 1,300 local committees to promote "intergroup relations."[35] Altogether, these developments contributed to a campaign against intolerance and bigotry, aimed at reshaping the national mood with respect to prejudice.

As a consequence, along with the Gary strike and related developments, courses and other activities concerned with intolerance began to appear in schools. Nationally, more than 150 youth projects to promote understanding of human relationships were conducted through the schools, a program developed by ACE. The Chicago Board of Education promoted intercultural groups at high schools across the city, and conferences were held to condemn racial prejudice. The Chicago schools also offered a course on "Intercultural Studies," featuring units on the accomplishments of African Americans. Similar courses were developed in Cleveland, Detroit, Philadelphia, and other cities. New York high schools developed units about the state's anti-discrimination laws, sponsored by the League of Women Shoppers, designed to help Blacks seeking jobs in the retail industry. Youth conferences on intergroup relations were held across the country.[36] Even if these efforts were somewhat sporadic and uneven in impact, the intercultural education movement represented the first national curriculum reform campaign to address racial prejudice and inequity. There can be little doubt that it was a milestone of sorts in African American education, even if it was primarily intended for Whites.[37]

If the goal of the intercultural education movement was to promote greater harmony and understanding, however, it is unclear that it enjoyed much success. Although events as dramatic as Gary's strike did not reoccur, a good deal of violent conflict still marked the interaction of Black and White students in larger cities of the North and West. Typical of most racial clashes at the time, most such incidents were precipitated by Whites attacking African Americans, although Black youth were often ready to respond in kind.

In 1946, for instance, groups of Black and White boys fought at a California high school in summer session, an incident reportedly started by an attack on an African American student. In 1949, football players and others were involved in a "riot" between Black and White students during a game between River Rouge High and Melvindale High in suburban Detroit. Two years later, 30 policemen were required to quell a "free for all fight" involving Black and White students near Philadelphia's Pallestra following a basketball championship game; six were arrested and 15 taken to hospitals, some with stab wounds. Sporting events appear to have been particularly prone to such outbreaks, especially when predominantly Black and White schools competed for athletic honors and passions ran high. Throughout the 1950s, a number of stories about such conflicts appeared in the Black press, which also reported fights between groups of African Americans in similar circumstances. There also were cases of Black students protesting discriminatory treatment of one sort or another. Even with the moderating presence of teachers and administrators, there was the continual possibility of conflict between Blacks and Whites, potent evidence of underlying mistrust and antipathy that plagued race relations in many schools.[38]

Athletic events were hardly the only settings where Black and White students encountered one another with little adult supervision; conflicts erupted in other circumstances, too. In 1951, the *New York Amsterdam News* reported a day-long battle between Black and White students that allegedly started with an attack on an African American on the subway. The fight culminated in a "lunchroom riot," injuring a teacher, and followed by sporadic fighting afterward. Administrators later downplayed the incident but admitted that it started with a racial clash. Similar incidents occurred throughout the decade, typically involving rival groups of Blacks and Whites competing for territory and status in large urban institutions. Cafeterias and athletic fields were repeated points of conflict.[39] Of course, these also were settings for fights between many other groups, and discord often occurred along lines of social class and ethnicity. But the fact that violent conflict continued to arise between Blacks and Whites suggests that racial cooperation and amity were slow to develop in schools.

Eventually, however, greater attention was devoted to improving race relations in schools, especially in the wake of the 1954 *Brown* decision, which marked the end of segregated institutions in many communities outside the South and in states such as Delaware, Maryland, West Virginia, and Kentucky. Because African Americans typically were entering predominantly White institutions, they were usually the victims in violent encounters, not instigators. Although there were notable instances of racial conflict in newly integrated high schools in the latter 1950s, school authorities and law enforcement agencies were particularly attuned to minimizing such clashes and protecting Black students. Intergroup relations courses became popular again in light of *Brown*, especially as more schools became integrated due to African American migration.[40]

As Black neighborhoods slowly expanded into surrounding White areas or started to develop rapidly in new areas of the larger cities, interracial contact in the schools increased accordingly. Tensions continued to exist, but since school integration had become such an important national concern, especially following the highly publicized enrollment of African Americans at Little Rock's Central High in 1957, public opinion outside of the South shifted against Whites who opposed integration. In little more than a decade, White student walkouts such as those conducted by Gary and Chicago students became associated with the past, a less enlightened time, at least until conflicts erupted over court-ordered desegregation and busing in the 1960s and 70s.[41] While everyday clashes between Black and White students continued, and even escalated in the years to come, the ideological circumstances of racial conflict in the schools had changed.[42] In this respect, the decade of the 1950s represented a new era for Black secondary education in these parts of the country as well.

SEGREGATED SECONDARY SCHOOLING, NORTH AND WEST

If most African American secondary students in the North and West attended integrated schools, a substantial minority attended institutions that were principally, if not wholly, Black. In states and municipalities where segregation was not mandated by law, this was generally the consequence of residential segregation, although districts everywhere also actively managed institutions to minimize integration.[43] In Kansas City, Missouri, for example, Lincoln High School was built in an area where, judging from the 1940 census, more than 90% of the city's 42,574 Blacks lived.[44] In places where schools were legally segregated, Black high schools sat at the top of local African American school systems, often carrying a degree of prestige and influence as a result.

Most Northern and Western segregated Black high schools compared favorably with the better African American high schools in Southern states. In border areas stretching from Ohio to Kansas, institutions such as Crispus Attucks High in Indianapolis and Sumner High in St. Louis became renowned in their local communities. Attucks drew national attention in 1955 when Oscar Robertson led its basketball squad to the Indiana championship, one of the country's first Black teams to win a state title.[45]

Dayton, Ohio, established separate Dunbar High in 1933, despite a ruling by the state's Supreme Court against school segregation. A separate secondary school was maintained in East St. Louis, Illinois, and in Cairo to the south.[46] To the west, on either side of the Missouri River, Lincoln High in Kansas City, Missouri, and Sumner High in Kansas City, Kansas, both provided African American students stimulating and supportive environments for academic growth.[47] In Los Angeles, Jefferson High was established as a "minority school," enrolling predominantly African Americans, although Blacks attended other secondary schools as well.[48] Although having just one or two institutions designated for them placed constraints on accessibility for African American youth, it also fostered ties to schools that helped students succeed.

The two metropolitan Kansas City high schools, Sumner and Lincoln, provide instructive examples of how segregated education outside the South provided positive experiences for Blacks. Because employment opportunities for educated African Americans were very limited, each school attracted a faculty with strong academic credentials, most from major Northern colleges and universities. In addition, both schools exhibited a high degree of stability in faculty tenure. As a rule, these were highly valued jobs in the Black community, partly because racially equal district salary schedules, combined with their academic degrees, put them on a par with the best-paid White teachers.[49] Black secondary teachers, as a consequence, tended to remain in place, enhancing their ability to forge ties in local communities, and to accumulate knowledge of the students passing through their classrooms. At Lincoln High, for instance, a cadre of 23 faculty members, some 43% of the teaching staff in 1960, had worked at the school throughout the decade of the 1950s. This was a considerably higher degree of faculty stability than in the city's larger White public high schools at the time.[50] The commitment of educators in these circumstances was an important resource for African American institutions, and for their immediate communities.

Although dropout rates were high by later standards, both Kansas City schools provided exemplars of academic accomplishment. Sumner High, following the lead of two successive principals who were interested in science, performed at a consistently high level in metropolitan science fair competitions, and received national recognition for science education. Lincoln students also won several awards in the science competitions, one arena where Black and White students could contend academically. Indeed, greater Kansas City's two Black high schools each registered more science awards at these events during the 1950s than any area White school.[51] Although both schools maintained sizable vocational programs, and students were given secondhand books and other used materials, growing numbers enrolled in academic or college preparatory courses.

Encouraged by demanding yet supportive teachers, students at both Sumner and Lincoln strove to meet the high standards expected of them, like their counterparts at many other Black high schools.

Alumni from both institutions hold warm recollections of their experiences, particularly regarding their supportive but challenging teachers. Grace Strong graduated from Lincoln in 1947 and fondly recalled teachers who were fair, supportive, and always eager to help students prepare for college. Discipline, order, and school pride were emphasized as well. This was reflected in the daily appearance of the school; Strong said, "Our halls were spotless, nobody dropped trash on the floor . . . there was a minimum amount of noise when classes changed, and nobody was allowed to slam locker doors."[52] Similar themes were reiterated by graduates of Sumner High, who also recalled teachers with high but fair grading standards and who cared deeply about their students. Both schools were highly regarded in their immediate communities, and also drew Black students from nearby districts that paid fees to send them. Strong, for example, said that while she lived 3 to 4 blocks from Lincoln, some of her classmates came from surrounding cities. In many respects, these accounts are comparable to those noted in research on exemplary African American institutions in the South. The good Black high school that has emerged in this literature, it seems, had strong counterparts in the border states and the North.

Elsewhere, a somewhat different pattern of segregation existed: Students from both races attended the same schools but Blacks were excluded from most activities. In 1952, Norma Walsh was among the first Blacks to integrate Washington High School in Kansas City, Kansas.[53] The school was close to home and her mother—aware that courts were starting to rule in favor of racial integration —insisted that her daughter be allowed to enroll there. Walsh recalled, "Sumner was a good school . . . but [my mother] felt like she was paying taxes and the school bus [to Washington] was coming right by [our house] . . . while we were 15 miles from Sumner. Other Blacks were paying to go to Sumner." Although Walsh graduated, she and the few other African Americans who attended Washington rarely participated in activities.

In other instances, schools had a range of extracurricular activities offered on a segregated basis. This was the case at Topeka High, a large institution with a magnificent building serving the capital of Kansas. A separate "colored" basketball team and cheerleading squad existed in 1940, although African Americans did play on the school's varsity basketball and track squads, in larger numbers on the latter. As in the South, this created difficulties for Black athletes and their pep squads, because they were required to travel longer distances to compete against other segregated teams. In the case of Topeka High, this meant going to Kansas

City to play Sumner and Lincoln, and farther into Missouri to compete with other Black schools. Separate Black proms and beauty contests also were held at internally segregated schools. In Topeka, this took the form of different elections for "King and Queen" to preside over proms on the same night but in different rooms.[54]

Yearbooks from this era at Topeka High reveal that African American students were less likely to participate in clubs, student government, and other activities than Whites. Most Black seniors listed just a handful of activities, most notably the Booker T Boy's Club and the Phillis Wheatley Club, segregated groups intended to provide service and leadership opportunities to African American students. A separate "colored" student council was even considered, but did not get administrative approval. The most integrated activity was the track team, which had a nearly proportional representation of Black and White students.[55] Track and field, of course, was a sport that required little contact between participants, and a team could be successful with largely individual or small-group training and practice sessions.

Although a separate African American basketball team may have been unusual, the general pattern of segregation in extracurricular activities during this period was not. Examination of yearbooks for integrated schools during the following decade revealed broadly similar patterns. Sports teams tended to be the most integrated non-academic school activities, although discrimination existed in athletics, too. For example, by the time Harry O'Neal got to Kansas City, Kansas' Washington High in the mid-1950s, only about 50 of the school's estimated 2,000 students were racial minorities, but its swimming pool was closed upon integration. O'Neal was on the football team but was not allowed to play quarterback, although he felt he was best suited for the position. O'Neal recalled other occasions when friends were confident that a Black person had won a particular honor (in his case, "best athlete"), only to find it bestowed upon a White student.[56] While athletic teams were sometimes integrated, other clubs, student government, and theater groups were dominated by White students. This sometimes led to problems, as in Pittsburgh, where African American students protested an "offensive" blackface role in a play performed by White students in 1946.[57] Separate proms and other social events were more characteristic of the border regions, and were occasionally a matter of controversy elsewhere.[58] The racial composition of cheerleading squads was another sensitive issue, with Blacks demanding greater representation.[59] As in Topeka, African Americans often joined their own service organization, and in some schools they participated in band and other musical activities. These patterns, moreover, appear to have persisted well beyond the period in question. Clotfelter found similar tendencies in a survey of nearly 200 schools some 50 years later.[60]

This may have been partly related to social class differences in student background, as more affluent students are more likely to participate in such activities. But formal and informal manifestations of segregation and exclusion within schools, evident in Topeka during the 1940s, apparently continued to characterize integrated secondary schools.[61]

Perhaps the most common form of high school segregation outside of the South and border states, however, resulted from the restriction of most African Americans to certain neighborhoods in bigger cities. This took time to impact secondary education, since high schools served relatively large attendance areas. In 1940, few Northern or Western cities had Black populations large enough to create many wholly African American secondary schools simply on the basis of neighborhood segregation. Chicago was one that did, and its principal Black institutions gained a local reputation that was decidedly more mixed than the institutions in Kansas City. The family of Talmadge Boyd left Birmingham for Chicago in 1919 and in the 1930s he entered Englewood High School, which he described as made up of "predominantly White, working-class children of immigrants."[62] He later attended the racially integrated Phillips High, where teachers were "devoted to the idea that we could learn and they were going to teach us." But as the Black population grew rapidly—and awareness of Black history grew—community leaders suggested naming the school after Jean Baptiste DuSable, the Black explorer who was Chicago's first settler. DuSable became an all-Black high school, built to relieve enrollment pressure at Phillips and provide a second institution to serve the area's rapidly growing African American population.[63]

The 1939 edition of the *Red and Black*, DuSable's yearbook, boasted of graduating the first class to complete all 4 years in the new building. Both Phillips and DuSable acquired reputations for graduating many of the city's prominent Black citizens, and sending a steady stream of students to local colleges and universities. Alumni recollections of the schools are similar in certain respects to those for Lincoln and Sumner High in Kansas City, particularly concerning their thoughtful and well-educated faculty members. Talmadge, for example, remembered the teachers at DuSable and the aspirations they encouraged in students. But unlike formally segregated secondary schools elsewhere in Illinois and in other states, Chicago's Black high schools were staffed by both African American and White teachers. The principal and 50 of the 63 teachers in the 1939 DuSable *Red and Black* were White, but they exhibited few of the prejudices evident elsewhere. While Black students suffered harassment and discrimination in predominantly White schools, at DuSable they could participate in a range of extracurricular and sports activities, including clubs for botany, French, physics, chemistry, and Black history.

Problems arose too. Phillips and DuSable became quite crowded and gained reputations for high dropout rates and discipline problems.[64] Students in these schools also were directed to "remedial" educational programs in the 1950s. As the African American population grew rapidly in the postwar years, other schools shifted from predominantly White to Black, reflecting neighborhood changes on the city's South and West sides. It was a process that occurred in most large urban centers, but became evident sooner in Chicago.[65] In this regard, the city's Black high schools were bellwethers of change that would occur across the North and West.

Even though most states had banned formal segregation of schools, residential segregation eventually resulted in more African American students attending predominantly Black institutions. These tendencies were abetted by district administrators who drew attendance areas to avoid integrating Black and White students. Such practices had a long history, but they gained added resonance in the wake of events like the Gary protests and ongoing incidents of violence. In the minds of many educators, racial conflict and controversy was to be avoided if possible, and integration certainly did not rank very high as a priority before *Brown*. Consequently, Black secondary students soon came to be concentrated in certain schools in Philadelphia, Cleveland, Los Angeles, and Detroit, in addition to Chicago. Boston and Milwaukee had somewhat smaller Black populations, with African American students clustered in schools adjacent to their neighborhoods.[66] These tendencies became a general pattern of institutional development; as Black neighborhoods grew, so did the degree of segregation in many high schools.

School segregation was less pronounced in the West, where the African American population was smaller and less clearly restricted to particular neighborhoods, at least in the 1940s. The city with the largest Black population was Los Angeles, and as noted earlier, the Board of Education there created a separate high school to serve most of its African Americans. Large concentrations of Black students did not start to appear in other schools until after World War II, which saw thousands of African Americans arrive to work in war industries. Oakland to the north also became a destination for migrants, and gained a large Black population in the latter 1940s. McClymonds High in West Oakland served the city's oldest Black neighborhoods, but as the African American population expanded and moved to East Oakland and additional neighborhoods, their numbers in other high schools grew.[67] By the 1950s, certain suburban communities also began to emerge as centers of African American settlement, especially following a federal ban on restrictive covenants. Most of these were "blue-collar" suburbs, featuring relatively low housing costs and easy access to the industrial jobs that Blacks traditionally held. Compton, immediately to the south of predominantly Black Watts in Los Angeles is perhaps the best-known case, but there were others as well. By 1959, African Americans comprised nearly 40% of Compton's population, and were highly segregated in certain neighborhoods. Although suburban Blacks were more affluent and had higher rates of home ownership than inner-city residents, they were not generally welcomed in these settings. There is ample evidence that these suburban Black students were subject to discriminatory and exclusionary behavior by Whites.[68] Just because it took a bit longer to develop, the somewhat lower level of segregation on the West Coast did not always mean that prejudice was less virulent.

PARSING THE ACADEMIC LAYER CAKE

School systems were more highly developed and better funded outside the South, and this proved to be both an advantage and a source of difficulty for African American students. It was a benefit with respect to the availability of schools, the opportunity to attend integrated institutions in many instances, and the quality of amenities such as libraries, laboratories, vocational equipment, and support for extracurricular activities. The difficulty stemmed from the penchant for modern school districts to make extensive use of IQ tests and similar forms of standardized assessment that resulted in many Black students being placed in general, remedial, and vocational "tracks" within schools, often with little encouragement to develop their academic abilities. Moreover, there is considerable evidence that districts devoted fewer resources to schools with large African American populations. As the numbers of Black students increased with migration, Black high schools in cities everywhere became badly overcrowded, with larger class sizes and fewer challenging academic courses. Overall, it appears that the quality of secondary schools serving African American youth declined substantially in many instances, while additional resources were devoted to predominantly White schools. Although the degree of such funding diversions was hardly as egregious as in the South, it was nonetheless substantial, making it even more difficult for Black students to compete with Whites. If high schools were wedding cake institutions sitting atop expanding urban school systems, many African Americans were granted access only to the crumbs.

From the standpoint of curriculum, there is evidence that African American students studied different subjects from those taken by Whites. Black schools in the border states, for instance, sometimes emphasized vocational training more than White high schools. Kansas City's Sumner High featured an extensive array of occupational classes, and Crispus Attucks in Indianapolis provided basic vocational training courses as well.[69] For the most part, however, African American students were no more likely to take such secondary courses than Whites in most districts. As a number of historians have noted, vocational education became popular in a number of districts during the Great Depression, and students of both races took them in hopes of gaining skills to help land a job. The difference came with the type and quality of vocational training that Black and White students received. Kathryn Neckerman has demonstrated that African American students were relegated to less selective vocational schools in Chicago, principally as a matter of segregation. Schools that served the city's Black neighborhoods typically lacked connections with the unions and trade councils that enabled students to get jobs. As it turned out, at least in Chicago, it was the school and not the courses that dictated the likelihood of finding employment in the trades, a distinction linked directly to race.[70]

Vocational education was hardly the only curricular domain where African Americans experienced inequity. They also were disproportionally placed into remedial education courses designed to help students who had failed several classes or performed poorly on tests. This form of curricular differentiation was based on seemingly color-blind criteria of academic performance and cognitive ability, and not arbitrary assignment by race, but had the effect of placing disproportionate numbers of African Americans into these classes. As Neckerman has pointed out, in districts with overcrowded Black schools such as Chicago, this meant that the weakest students often received inadequate resources, contributing to higher rates of failure and dropping out of school. While teachers of remedial students in Chicago were supposed to provide them with individualized attention, large average class sizes often made this very difficult to accomplish. Veteran DuSable teacher Mary Herrick, for instance, reported in 1956 that classes of 30 to 40 students made it especially difficult to work with weaker students, speculating that 18 would be a better number.[71] Less dedicated teachers no doubt devoted limited attention to the needs of such pupils.

Similarly, in their study of curricular differentiation in secondary schools, David Angus and Jeffrey Mirel found that African American students in Detroit during the 1940s were disproportionally assigned to the district's largely custodial "general" track, where they received neither vocational training nor preparation for college. This was the least challenging academic program offered by the schools, and nearly 45% of the city's Black secondary students were assigned to it, as opposed to just 27% of Whites. The effect was to create a clear impression that African Americans were less scholastically capable than Whites, despite the fact that the standardized tests used in making such assignments were intended to assess individuals and not groups.[72] Similar curricular patterns were evident in other cities. The New York City teachers union reported that African American students were "shunted" into vocational and "general" curriculum courses, to prepare for "jobs that they can get."[73] In Cleveland, predominantly Black Central High featured fewer academic courses and extracurricular activities than largely White schools in the district. Like similar schools in other cities, it quickly became overcrowded as its attendance boundaries were drawn to include the most rapidly growing Black neighborhoods. In Milwaukee, academic course offerings narrowed at North Division High as it became more African American during the latter 1950s, as did the number of extracurricular activities.[74]

The emergence of tracking in comprehensive high schools and the rise of specialized urban secondary schools in the postwar era had a significant impact on Black academic experiences. The development of differentiated curricula, with various tracks for students of differing abilities and interests, undoubtedly affected Black students in suburban and non-metropolitan settings, too. Often coming from poverty backgrounds, with lower levels of parental education, and having attended poorly funded, segregated elementary schools, large numbers of African American students were relegated to lower-status courses as tracking systems were adopted by districts.[75] It was a problem that eventually gained attention in light of the relatively poor performance of Black youth on standardized tests. In 1958, the *Chicago Defender* decried the poor showing of African Americans on a statewide exam given by the Illinois State Scholarship Commission to help determine college financial aid awards. Although scores were not reported by race, the *Defender* carefully checked names and addresses of some 750 Chicago students who scored high enough to be considered for scholarships and found only a handful of African Americans. Noting that Blacks performed well in athletic competition, the paper's reporter lamented their apparent academic limitations and did not hesitate in identifying the source of the problem as the schools themselves. "It should be obvious by now to everyone concerned with our school problems," he wrote, "that we have a serious situation on our hands."[76]

This was an apt assessment, as the problems facing Chicago high schools that served African Americans in this era were manifold. As Neckerman and other scholars have shown, predominantly Black schools in big-city districts such as Chicago started to experience higher turnover in their teaching staffs, adding yet another element of instability and uncertainty in academic performance.[77] When combined with large class sizes due to overcrowding and the poor preparation of African American students, the absence of experienced, dedicated, and effective teachers surely made matters even worse. With large numbers of Black students assigned to remedial courses, lacking individualized attention, it is little wonder that the performance of seniors on standardized tests was anemic compared to that of Whites. In the larger school systems outside of the South, many secondary schools serving predominantly Black populations were poorly equipped to promote academic excellence. Consequently, African Americans who managed to succeed in these institutions generally did not reach the same level of scholastic achievement as other students.

The comparatively weak academic performance of African American students in many non-Southern secondary schools pointed to one of the persistent dilemmas in Black education. While most African Americans favored integration as a policy acknowledging their rights as citizens, many were concerned about their children being subjected to unfair competition and harassment from White students and teachers. Some, including W.E.B. DuBois, even argued that integrated education was probably not worth the threat to African American youth that attending school under such circumstances appeared to entail.[78] Segregated schools seemed a safer alternative, as the fond memories associated with predominantly Black institutions seem to suggest. However, high schools with majority African American student bodies generally did not receive the same academic support from school districts as White institutions. They became widely known as inferior schools, offering fewer scholastic options and weaker preparation for postsecondary study. Black secondary students and their families thus faced a difficult choice. They could aspire to the higher standards and advanced offerings of predominantly White schools and brave the risks of aggravation and insult on a daily basis, or they could attend majority Black schools with generally inferior academic reputations.

Of course, for many Black youth, the option of attending White institutions was simply not available because of district policies matching attendance zones to residential segregation patterns. But for those who did have such choices, decisions were rarely easy. As African American families moved to new areas of Northern and Western cities and suburbs, Black youth began attending previously all-White high schools. Particularly after the *Brown* decision, school administrators made more concerted efforts to make such enrollment decisions easier for them. As Clotfelter has demonstrated, survey data indicate that secondary school segregation declined in the North and West during the 1950s. Although attending a predominantly White school was hardly a guarantee of success, especially with widespread tracking policies, it may have offered the possibility of benefitting from somewhat higher expectations, along with an opportunity for first hand experience with the dominant social group. The threat of social ostracism was formidable even to most dedicated students and in the most enlightened circumstances. It is testimony to the fortitude and determination of Black students who were among the first to enroll in these schools, consequently, that segregation decreased across the postwar period. They were the pioneers who helped advance a new vision of racial interaction and cooperation in schooling, one that held the promise of even greater accomplishments for African Americans, most of whom still struggled with the stigma of segregation and presumed academic inferiority.

BLACK SECONDARY SCHOOL ATTAINMENT IN 1960

The social and economic circumstances for African American youth in the North and West changed considerably in the postwar years. Secondary school enrollment increased substantially, more than keeping pace with growing White attendance, even with population growth due to migration from the South. At the same time, African Americans became more concentrated in cities, particularly in the North. These events helped to set the stage for subsequent developments in Black education during the 1960s, the so-called crisis of urban schooling and the expansion of postsecondary education for African Americans.

Perhaps the most basic changes in the circumstances of Black youth in the North and West were linked to population movement. As Table 3.2 suggests, there was a shift in proportional terms to the West by 1960, particularly the West Coast. This process began during World War II and the emergence of defense industries there and it continued during the postwar era. Black secondary enrollment improved dramatically in both regions, closing the gap with White attendance in proportional terms by more than a third, and remained ahead of the South, although the interregional attainment gap narrowed even more dramatically. Altogether, the overall rate of attendance was slightly higher in the West at this time, despite more rapid population growth there.

Overall, the numbers of African American youth in these regions increased rapidly during the decades following 1940, largely because of migration. As indicated in Table 3.2, by 1960 the North and West together represented more than a third of the nation's African American teenagers. The vast majority of migrants settled in the larger cities, such that in 1960 nearly three-quarters (74%) of the nation's non-Southern Black youth lived in urban centers. This was a change from 1940, when more than a third lived outside of such cities. During the postwar era, the nation's Black youth became considerably more concentrated in central city settings, where they lived in largely segregated neighborhoods.

The Black population in the West retained the same level of concentration in urban core areas that it exhibited 20 years earlier, more than

Inequity, Discrimination, and Growth

TABLE 3.2. Black and White Youth, Ages 14–18, Percentage Attending or Graduated from High School Outside the South, 1960

Region	Portion of Teen Population 1960		Attendance Rate 1960		Portion in Central Cities	
	Black	White	Black	White	Black	White
Northeast & Great Lakes	76	64	63	78	76	30
Plains & West	24	36	66	79	65	18

Region	Big-City Enroll Rate		Non-City Enroll Rate	
	Black	White	Black	White
Northeast & Great Lakes	64	78	61	78
Plains & West	68	80	63	79

Source: IPUMS data (Blacks 6% of total youth population).

three times that of the region's White population. As indicated in Table 3.2, about two-thirds of Black teens in the Plains and Mountain states lived in central city neighborhoods, with slightly fewer (62%) in the Pacific States. In the more highly urbanized North, on the other hand, the proportion living in core urban areas exceeded three-quarters. It was in these places that vast urban ghettos defined by racially segregated residential tracts appeared most dramatically in the postwar era, although the West had Black ghettos as well. It was also in these settings that the most severe forms of racial segregation in schooling occurred, including the emergence of additional Black high schools. In ecological terms, there were important differences between Northern and Western cities, and this was reflected to a degree in the patterns of schooling for Black youth associated with these distinctive urban environments.

For many high school–age African Americans living outside central cities in 1960, circumstances had improved considerably. Whereas about half of these teens lived in suburban communities before the war, by the end of the 1950s their numbers grew to two-thirds in the North, while remaining at about half in the West. Home ownership increased in both suburban and non-metropolitan settings for families of Black teens, but especially in the suburbs. Residential ownership for such households exceeded half in the North but approached two-thirds in the West; both were higher than comparable rates in cities and non-metropolitan settings. Perhaps an even better indicator was secondary enrollment rates. As indicated in Table 3.2, the proportion of African American youth attending high school outside the central cities had nearly reached parity with urban enrollment levels by 1960, but suburban rates were even higher. In the West, nearly three out of four (72%) Black youth living in the suburbs were enrolled in 1960, and more than 60% in the North. The former was the highest level of attendance for any group of African American students, approaching 90% of the comparable White rate. On the other hand, enrollment for Black youth outside the metropolitan areas was considerably lower, ranging between 50% and 60%. For these teens, employment rates were higher, particularly in the West, where they were nearly 40% more likely to be working than their suburban peers. Among Black youth living outside the cities, those in the suburbs clearly enjoyed substantial educational advantages.[79]

Secondary education had become more widespread since 1940, and this was evident in factors associated with Black success in school. Figure 3.2 presents the results of a logistic regression analysis of attainment in 1960, similar to the one performed in Table 3.1 Some factors exhibited similar effects 20 years later, such as the advantage held by girls of both races and living on a farm. But the effects of such location variables as region, Southern birth, and urban residence were considerably less important by the end of the 1950s, controlling for other factors, including poverty status.[80] The improved performance of youth born in the South may have reflected improvements in the schools there. The biggest effects were associated with social and economic status, with the most important factor for both Blacks and Whites being parental education. African American youth with at least one high school–educated parent were better than three times more likely to succeed in school than those without one. Those with educated parents holding white-collar jobs, owning their homes and living together were even more likely to be on track to graduate. Black families with these characteristics were nearly twice as likely to live in suburbs as in cities, and such status differences contributed to new patterns of school participation. Broad social class distinctions remained important among African Americans and contributed to a new urban-suburban divide in educational experiences.[81]

By the end of the 1950s, there could be little doubt that the social and economic circumstances of many African Americans living outside of the South had improved. Addressing the graduating class of 1955, the principal of Kansas City's Lincoln High declared that they would have "greater opportunities than those experienced by our former graduates."[82] It was

FIGURE 3.2. Logistic Regression, Factors Contributing to High School Success, Youth, Age 17, North and West, 1960

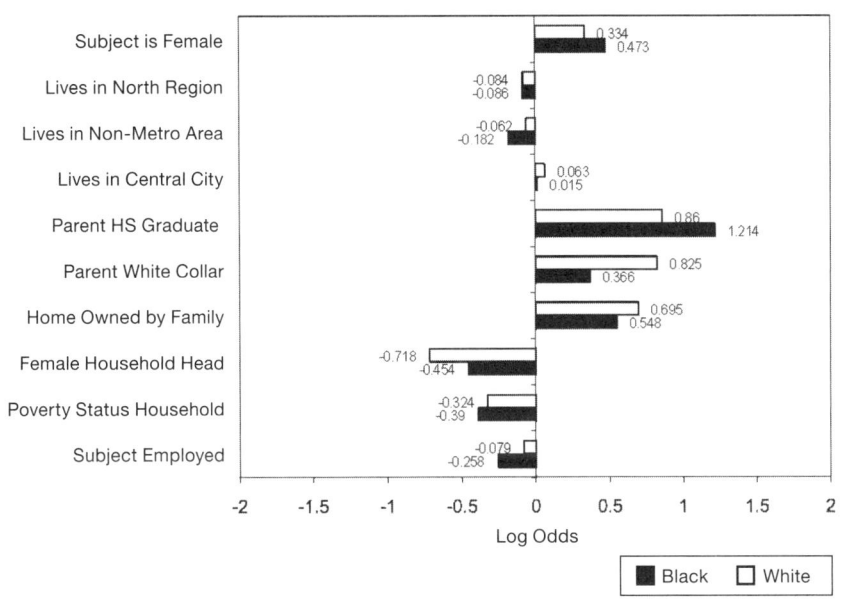

Dependent variable: Enrollment (or not) at the junior level or higher, including graduation. All factors significant at .001 level, except central city residence for Black youth, which is statistically insignificant. See Appendix B for additional information.

an era of rising expectations, and this was reflected in secondary enrollment and graduation rates, which had increased steadily throughout the decade. Problems continued to exist, particularly in the cities, but the future appeared to be brightening. A majority of African American youth attended high school for the first time in history, and in some communities the level of secondary enrollment approached that of affluent Whites. This was no small accomplishment and, like improvements in Southern education, it was a portent of changes yet to come.

CONCLUSION: GROWING ATTAINMENT AND PERSISTENT INEQUALITY

African American teenagers in the North and West benefited from much greater educational opportunities than their counterparts in the South throughout the postwar era. Survey data suggest that the level of segregation in secondary schools was relatively low through much of both regions, and declined through the decade of the 1950s. At the same time, there is considerable evidence that the quality of education in predominantly Black schools in the larger cities declined in this period, particularly in the North.[83] Just how many Black students were affected by these developments is unclear, but the basic storyline appears to be broadly similar in many of the larger cities across the region. With rapid population growth and the movement of African Americans into new neighborhoods, opportunities to attend integrated schools were afforded to growing numbers of students. This also meant that greater numbers were exposed to the greater curricular offerings and higher academic expectations generally associated with White schools.

As the numbers of Black students enrolling in high school and graduating increased, there is evidence of both significant advancement in African American scholarly accomplishment and growing problems associated with segregation and delimited academic expectations. In suburban communities in the West, where integrated schools predominated during this time, African American attainment levels reached historic highs, surpassing White graduation rates in much of the country. This was a picture of what was possible with respect to racial equity in education. In other parts of the North and West, particularly in the rapidly growing ghetto communities of the larger cities, African American students were relegated to the least demanding academic curricula and restricted to overcrowded schools staffed by teachers who often preferred to work elsewhere. The latter experience provided a glimpse of a pattern of institutional change that would become widely associated with urban school systems in the years to come. But in the years before 1960 such places did not yet define secondary education for African Americans outside the South. In the wake of the *Brown* decision and a massive movement of Blacks away from the segregated South, many things seemed possible, and African American youth across the country looked to the future with optimism. With a solid majority attending and graduating from high school for the first time in American history, the world seemed to be their oyster. The years ahead would both confirm that sentiment and pose a major challenge to it at the same time.

Part II

FIGHTING FOR EQUALITY

CHAPTER 4

Black Youth and the Urban Crisis

In 1961, James Conant published a slim book titled *Slums and Suburbs*, which brought to the nation's attention the deplorable condition of Black education in major cities. A past president of Harvard and author of a recent survey of American high schools, Conant wrote with considerable authority. By contrasting schools in wealthy suburbs with those in impoverished urban neighborhoods, he highlighted the inequities that were then becoming characteristic of metropolitan areas. In particular, Conant warned about the "social dynamite" represented by urban youth, especially African Americans in crowded ghettos. As these problems seemed to mount in the years to follow, his words would seem prophetic. It became commonplace to describe urban education as representing a "crisis," especially as growing numbers of Black students appeared in city schools and Whites moved to the suburbs, making schools more visibly segregated and highlighting stark racial inequalities. Indeed, the very term *urban* became increasingly linked to race. These developments marked a shift in the history of Black schooling, from the countryside to the city and to new dilemmas of inequality.[1]

Conant's book fit the temper of the time, as Americans began the 1960s with new awareness of poverty and inequality. Michael Harrington's *The Other America* appeared in 1962, revealing that nearly one-quarter of Americans lived below the recently established federal poverty level and challenging national myths of social equality and shared prosperity. With respect to children, it became commonplace to refer to those in poor households as "disadvantaged" or "deprived," terms that suggested problems stemming from an impoverished environment rather than innate traits. Given this perspective, it was deemed possible to remedy the effects of poverty and inequality through schooling, to overcome disadvantages through compensatory education. Cultural deprivation, disadvantage, inequality, and poverty would become important themes guiding national domestic policy under the Kennedy and Johnson administrations, finding fullest expression in "War on Poverty" programs during the latter 1960s. These developments held important implications for African Americans, who were significantly overrepresented among the poor, but also were engaged in a broad movement demanding equity in many spheres of life, including in education.[2]

The growing focus on poverty, racial inequalities, and "urban crisis," however, obscured an important development: African American rates of high school graduation increased at this time. High school became an everyday experience for Black youth, as their attainment levels steadily converged with those of Whites. This did not mean, however, that Black high school experiences were equivalent to what most other American youth experienced. Inequity continued to be a source of great controversy, first around questions of school quality and desegregation, and later concerning a range of issues, including curriculum and student life.[3] Rising graduation rates were noted by contemporaries, but they also recognized that Black students faced big problems.[4] Addressing these issues would become a focal point of social and political mobilization. If there was indeed a crisis in urban education, Black communities across the country were determined to see that their youth were not among the casualties.

In this chapter, we address persistent racial disparities in education, especially in urban areas, as a backdrop for the growing demands for school desegregation and such related issues as busing students. The *Brown* decision had led to a modicum of integration, most of it the result of simply ending de jure segregation. It brought Black and White students into closer contact, but also helped expose continuing inequities between schools. These pivotal decades also witnessed the advent of campaigns that urged students to complete school. Access to high schools increased for Black youth with continuing migration from the countryside to cities, and from the South to the North and West. Most Black migrants moved into segregated neighborhoods and attended schools that were rapidly becoming overcrowded, underresourced, staffed with inexperienced teachers, and rife with problems. Many predominantly Black urban schools came to mirror conditions in the impoverished neighborhoods where they were located.

Growing frustration over racial inequality and segregation in urban areas set the stage for civil unrest. Beginning in the middle of the 1960s, violent "riots" or rebellions shook urban Black communities, particularly in the North and West, as residents protested police brutality and discrimination in housing and employment. The mainstream civil rights movement, with a longstanding predisposition to nonviolence, was waning, and inner-city neighborhoods became fertile ground for an emerging ideology of Black Power, which proved appealing to many African American youth.[5] Responding to these influences, Black students protested inequality in school resources and curricular priorities, and equity became a major issue facing urban school districts. The question of race came to be a source of dissension, and the high school, long excluded from political life, was confronted by contentious issues of social justice and equality.

A CHANGING URBAN SCENE

Developments in urban education occurred in a rapidly changing social context. Population shifts and their demographic and economic consequences dramatically affected the public schools. The war had barely ended when migration to suburbia began in the nation's largest metropolitan areas. Pressured by housing shortages in central cities and encouraged by policies that stimulated road building and cheap transportation, Americans began flocking to new communities on the fringes of metropolitan areas. Between 1940 and 1960, the suburban population grew by about 30 million, more than twice the increase in central cities. The share of metropolitan population living in big cities dropped from 62% to 51%. This decline accelerated and was labeled "White flight" during the 1960s, and by 1980 only 40% of the country's metropolitan population lived in central cities; everyone else was in the suburbs.[6]

The new suburbanites were disproportionately young, middle-class, and upwardly mobile. They could afford to move into the burgeoning communities on the edge of expanding metropolitan areas and bear the costs of commuting. As suggested above, they also were overwhelmingly White, and consequently, they could buy housing in neighborhoods that effectually barred others. African Americans, on the other hand, were systematically excluded from most suburbs, at first by restrictive covenants and other legal devices, and later by outright harassment and more subtle forms of discrimination.[7] They also were less likely to qualify for the mortgages typically required to purchase suburban homes. As more Whites moved to suburbia, the population of most central cities became older, poorer, and collectively darker in complexion.[8]

As noted in Chapter 3, the urban Black population grew because of migration, with nearly 5 million moving from the South to the North and West by 1970. At the end of the 1950s, almost two-thirds of African American youth lived in the South; 10 years later, it was 57%.[9] At the same time, their proportion in rural settings dropped from about 35% to 22%, with the overwhelming majority in the South. Those living on farms fell from about 20% to less than 5%. By and large, Black youth had come to live in cities.[10] As indicated in Table 4.1, the Black share of the teenage population of central cities grew substantially in this era, nearly doubling in the North and West and increasing by more than 50% in the

TABLE 4.1. Black Population Share, Ages 14 to 19, Central Cities (in percentages)

Year	South	Non-South
1960	24	15
1970	29	22
1980	38	29

Source: IPUMS data.

South. At the same time, movement of affluent families out of the cities reduced the tax base supporting urban schools, contributing to their physical and functional deterioration. This "flight" also contributed to a widespread perception that poverty levels had increased among all groups of city residents but particularly Blacks.[11]

Some middle-class Blacks greeted the arrival of poorer, less-educated migrants with apprehension, believing they jeopardized community progress. Talmadge Boyd, one of our interview respondents, whose parents moved from Birmingham to Chicago in 1918, described the Black population as exploding by the 1950s, leading Chicago city officials to build high rises and racially segregated schools "to contain this new population and control them." Boyd also noted an intensification of visible social-class differences among African Americans, with new migrants falling into the lower class. Donna L. Franklin, in her study of the history of African American families, echoes this observation, pointing to a "moral panic" among Northern middle-class Blacks as their Southern counterparts arrived in cities. The Black press often described migrants in terms such as a "floating, shiftless, and depraved element,"[12] and occasionally published lists of "do's and don'ts" instructing newcomers on proper city behavior. Much of their "inappropriate" behavior was linked to their inability to find work and resulting changes in families. Black women often found work more easily than men, and the number of female-headed households increased. A survey of secondary students in Kansas City noted that Black students frequently reported knowing little about their fathers.[13] Most mothers worked as domestics, and White preferences for live-in maids reduced Black women's time with their own families.[14] Black children were often left without supervision, contributing to impressions of parental neglect both within and outside the immediate community.

In 1940, some 80% of employed African Americans were concentrated in the lowest occupational categories.[15] Some managed to achieve social mobility during the postwar era, but most still occupied the lowest levels of the metropolitan status hierarchy in 1960. Segregation and job discrimination led most migrants to the least desirable neighborhoods, often occupying homes abandoned by Whites bound for the suburbs. The result was growing Black ghetto tracts in most large American cities, linked in the public mind with poverty, crime, and substandard educational institutions. This concentration of Blacks in overcrowded and derelict "slums" contributed to the impression of an "urban crisis" by the latter 1960s, especially in large Northern cities.[16] Terms such as *lawlessness* and *chaos* were applied to urban schools, often alarming middle-class parents.[17] This process of change posed an immense challenge to educators. It meant adapting their institutions to new groups of students and contending with racial conflict, especially in the high schools, and being confronted with ever more vehement demands for integration.

In the North and West, efforts to integrate were largely ineffective due to the changing composition of the urban population and "White flight." Despite protests, school district policies often abetted segregation, with school attendance areas mirroring patterns of residential transition from White to Black.[18] Examining the racial profile of Chicago public high schools in 1963, for instance, Robert Havighurst found that in all but four schools the student body was 90% or more Black or White, even though the district's population was almost evenly divided between these groups. The vast majority of predominantly Black schools, moreover, reported low achievement scores and relatively high dropout rates, a pattern evident in other large cities.[19] Others reports called attention to continuing disparities in resources between White and Black schools. In Newark, an evaluation of predominantly African American Central High in 1973 found old or broken equipment and non-functioning science labs, along with overcrowded classes and a "watered-down" curriculum. Similar reports came from other cities. A host of commentators remarked on negative attitudes of teachers, the dilapidated quality of facilities, and the routine disruptions and occasional violence that marked school days in urban districts. Some focused on the dropout rate, which was higher for African Americans than Whites. In general, high levels of segregation, or "racial isolation," accompanied the movement of Blacks into urban districts, along with clear differences in educational resources and outcomes.[20] These circumstances contributed to public perceptions of the inferiority of predominantly African American institutions. This and a persistent racial gap in high school graduation also brought urban schools into the spotlight through a growing campaign to persuade youth to stay in school.

DISCOVERY OF THE "DROPOUT"

Added to worries about the quality of urban education and racial inequalities was a new concern about teens leaving high school before graduating, or "dropping out."[21] Beginning in the 1950s, government officials issued periodic reminders for children and youth to "stay in school," citing the higher wages and employment rates of graduates. President Eisenhower issued proclamations about the advantages of staying in school, both for the individual student and society, timed to correspond with the start of school in August or September. Other public officials occasionally made similar statements. This continued in the following decade, with John F. Kennedy warning that leaving school early increased the likelihood of "hardship" in life. His brothers, Edward and Robert, were joined by other politicians and officials in admonishing Black junior high students at a Washington "slum" school not to drop out.[22] Lyndon Johnson maintained the tradition, along with prominent members of his administration.[23] Such occasions became more commonplace as greater emphasis was placed on the role of education in national life, and they were increasingly associated with the question of race.

Exhortations against leaving school extended beyond politicians, and efforts to convince young people of the advantages of school became seemingly ubiquitous. In 1961, the Ford Foundation announced that it was giving over a million dollars in grants to large urban school districts for dropout prevention, along with establishing a national clearinghouse to monitor trends. The focus was on the "blighted" or "depressed" areas of big cities, particularly those with large numbers of "Negro migrants" and other "lower income families."[24] Two years later, the Kennedy administration launched a similar initiative, albeit on a smaller scale.[25] The Urban League began conducting annual "back to school" campaigns in major cities, aimed explicitly at Black communities. The group's Chicago chapter noted that dropout rates were especially high in "schools with substantial Negro enrollment," and called upon community groups and parents to help address the problem.[26] Los Angeles Mayor Sam Yorty praised the local Urban League and declared "Back to School Week" for the opening of city's schools in 1963. Such appeals to "stay in school" became a recurring feature in cities during the early 1960s, particularly at the start of each academic year. Eventually, a range of community organizations contributed to these campaigns.[27] In 1964, the *Chicago Tribune* reported that several hundred groups supported rallies on the city's South Side to encourage youth to return to school, including local churches, neighborhood associations, and Boys and Girls Clubs, along with area politicians. Similar responses were evident in other cities, with a clear emphasis on poor and minority neighborhoods.[28]

As public interest focused on dropping out, the issue received greater attention in the media. Television and radio shows in larger cities linked the act of leaving school to juvenile delinquency, a growing public concern. In the fall of 1962, for instance, Chicago's CBS affiliate produced an hour-long documentary featuring teenagers discussing the challenges they faced. Similar programs were aired by other stations, echoing Conant's characterization of inner-city dropouts as socially unstable.[29] In

1964, radio programs sponsored by the Lever Brothers Corporation began on stations serving Black and Hispanic audiences, in 10-minute segments about the pitfalls of dropping out. Aired during peak listening times and featuring celebrity guests, these spots emphasized the economic benefits of school.[30] Additional radio programming was utilized by districts, such as speeches by Martin Luther King in Los Angeles regarding the importance of staying in school.[31]

At the same time, film strips, pamphlets, and other materials were widely distributed in schools to highlight the danger of dropping out. More than 20 million students saw a short U.S. Labor Department film titled "When I'm Old Enough, Goodbye." Similar filmstrips were distributed by state departments of education and larger districts, such as California's "Don't Be a Dropout" featuring comedian Soupy Sales. Some focused on Black youth, others were developed by employers, and most emphasized the connection between graduation and jobs.[32]

By the latter years of the decade, "stay in school" drives had become a routine annual event and a host of politicians, celebrities such as actors and athletes, and public officials participated in them.[33] One former student we interviewed recalled the excitement of Nat King Cole visiting DuSable High School in the 1950s to encourage students.[34] Other African American figures came to play a more visible role in anti-dropout campaigns, especially entertainers and basketball players, signaling a focus on inner-city youth in particular.[35] Singer James Brown released a popular song titled "Don't Be a Dropout," lamenting the difficulties faced by a person without an education. For its part, the Black press kept up a steady stream of articles on staying in school, and about programs designed to assist youth in graduating.[36] Perhaps even more important than adult admonitions, a growing array of educational programs pointed Black youth toward graduation.[37] The earliest were volunteer efforts, often sponsored by churches and other local institutions, providing tutoring and other services to help students address academic problems or return to school.[38]

Employers sometimes developed programs as well, especially if they were interested in recruiting African American youth to the workplace.[39] Corporate sponsors contributed to other efforts as well, along with new federal programs.[40] With the passage of new federal and state legislation in the middle of the decade, including Lyndon Johnson's "War on Poverty," the pace and scale of efforts to encourage high school graduation increased. Many such programs were based in schools, but others were conducted by community groups and other organizations.[41] Antipoverty programs often included provisions to assist dropouts in returning to school, or for counseling students to remain enrolled.[42] Alternative schools, sometimes called "street academies," were designed to help dropouts meet requirements for graduation, or increasingly for a GED.[43]

Encouragement also came with increasing interest from colleges and universities. Beginning in the early 1960s, elite colleges in the North began quietly reaching out to students from "disadvantaged" backgrounds, particularly African Americans.[44] By the summer of 1964, the *New York Times* announced that such opportunities were expanding markedly with support from national foundations, remarking that "emphasis this year on the Negro appears to have reached a new high."[45] Hundreds of institutions sent representatives to college fairs and to schools in the large cities, often with an explicit goal of enrolling Blacks.[46] Assisted by programs such as the federally funded Upward Bound and New York's SEEK (Search for Education, Elevation, and Knowledge), colleges were able to offer assistance to first-generation college students. Passage of the federal Higher Education Act in 1965 provided need-based financial aid and low-interest loans, adding to institutions' capacity to arrange financial support for low-income students.[47] Public institutions in other large cities made similar efforts to boost access to minority students, especially Blacks.[48] Urban commuter students became a larger segment of the collegiate population, and community college enrollments soared. Together, these factors contributed to a dramatic increase in Black college attendance, which grew faster than the White rate throughout the 1960s and early 1970s.[49]

CONTINUING PROGRESS IN ATTAINMENT

Stay-in-school campaigns resonated with parents and leaders in the African American community, where levels of education and attainment gains were issues of considerable importance. Reports of declining dropout rates went hand in hand with coverage of anti-dropout programs and back to school campaigns.[50] A 1970 United Press International story on the front page of the *Atlanta Daily World* declared that Blacks were "closing [the] gap on education." Citing recently released census reports, it noted that the median Black education level had become high school graduation and that the racial gap in attainment rates had shrunk half a year among young people. Similar articles appeared throughout the decade, marking the steady advance of Black students finishing high school and entering college.[51] Such stories conveyed a sense of progress in education and optimism about the future. This was linked to a general expansion of educational opportunity, including federal funding for schools through Title I of the 1965 Elementary and Secondary Education Act and popular early childhood programs such as Head Start.[52] In providing more resources to elementary schools, these measures undeniably helped boost graduation rates as well. By the latter 1970s, the Census Bureau reported

TABLE 4.2. Percent of 17-year-olds Enrolled in Junior Year or Higher (or Graduated), by Race and Region, 1960–1980

Region	1960		1970		1980	
	Black	White	Black	White	Black	White
South	44	62	58	72	67	75
Non-South	55	76	66	82	72	82
U.S. Total	48	72	64	79	69	80

Source: IPUMS data.

that advances in Black education had closed the graduation gap even more, and that fewer African American students were falling behind in school.[53] But these gains were results of more than 2 decades of efforts to encourage students to remain enrolled and work toward graduation. If Black students made remarkable progress, it was due in large part to a sustained community effort.

Despite the many problems they faced, African American students continued to enroll in high school, and growing numbers succeeded there. As indicated in Table 4.2, the national gap between Black and White attainment closed by more than 25% between 1960 and 1970, and it continued to narrow into the 1970s. Among the most important trends of the era was a steady increase in the number of Black students being more or less on track to graduate. This was a development that historians have overlooked, although it was a recurrent topic in African American communities, judging from the press.[54]

The experience of rising attainment, of course, ran contrary to the prevailing narrative of decline and misfortune associated with African American communities and schools. But the thousands of Black youth crowding into urban areas were not leaving high school in proportions as great as in the past. Although Black dropout rates continued to be greater than those of Whites, the differences had diminished. To observers at the time, of course, it often appeared that school conditions were worsening as the number of Black students increased, just because of the overcrowding, higher dropout rates, and lower grades and test scores. We address these conditions below, but while the appearance and academic performance of the schools may have deteriorated, for many African Americans, these institutions represented an improvement over the options that had been available to previous generations. This was not appreciated by contemporaries who bemoaned the "decline" and "hopelessness" of urban schools.[55] In addition, rising educational norms and expectations also contributed to better enrollment rates, as did movement from the countryside to the city and regional out-migration. African American youth were going to high school in greater numbers everywhere, even in the South. Rather than posing a "crisis" in education, in this respect the

TABLE 4.3. Household Social Status, Youth Aged 14 to 18, Central Cities (in percentages)

Year	SOUTH				NON-SOUTH			
	Black		White		Black		White	
	Poor	Middle Class	Poor	Middle Class	Poor	Middle Class	Poor	Middle Class
1960	62	4	26	31	42	12	15	41
1970	40	15	21	40	30	25	16	53
1980	39	23	18	55	34	28	19	53

Source: IPUMS data.
Note: As indicated in the text, "Middle Class" is defined as 2.5 times the poverty level. Families between these levels can be described as "Working Class," another growing segment of the Black population.

urban settings of the 1960s represented new educational opportunities for many Black youth, at least regarding secondary school.

Improved secondary education was part of broader changes in African American life that pointed to a better future, even in the big cities. As indicated in Table 4.3, poverty rates among urban Black teenagers dropped dramatically in the 1960s, and the number of Blacks in middle-class circumstances increased rapidly. Home ownership among urban Blacks went up also, by about 16% during the 1960s and 10% in the 1970s.[56] Destitution declined for all Americans in the wake of Lyndon Johnson's "War on Poverty" at mid-decade, and more importantly, with healthy economic growth. The change was especially significant among Blacks, however, partly because their initial degree of hardship was so severe.[57]

African Americans also benefitted from anti-discrimination legislation, particularly the 1964 Civil Rights Act. Employers began to make more concerted efforts to hire Blacks and provide them with access to better positions, as suggested by Herschel Summers's and Mabel Fountain's experiences, described in the Introduction. Between 1958 and 1973, the proportion of African Americans in the highest-paying job categories more than doubled and those employed in the lowest-paying jobs fell by a third, with improvement most notable among Black women.[58] These developments contributed to the rise of an African American middle class, and also reflected the greater numbers of Black adults with secondary and college credentials. Theirs were the families moving out of the ghettos, buying homes, and increasingly moving into integrated neighborhoods. It was youth from these households who led the growth of Black high school graduation and college enrollments.[59] This was the other side of the "urban crisis" of the 1960s.

Such general improvements were noted in the press, and the central city figures presented in Table 4.3 paralleled national shifts in the status of African Americans.[60] Because poverty remained much higher for Blacks

FIGURE 4.1. Logistic Regression: Factors Associated with Success in School, 17-Year-Olds, 1970 (IPUMS Data)

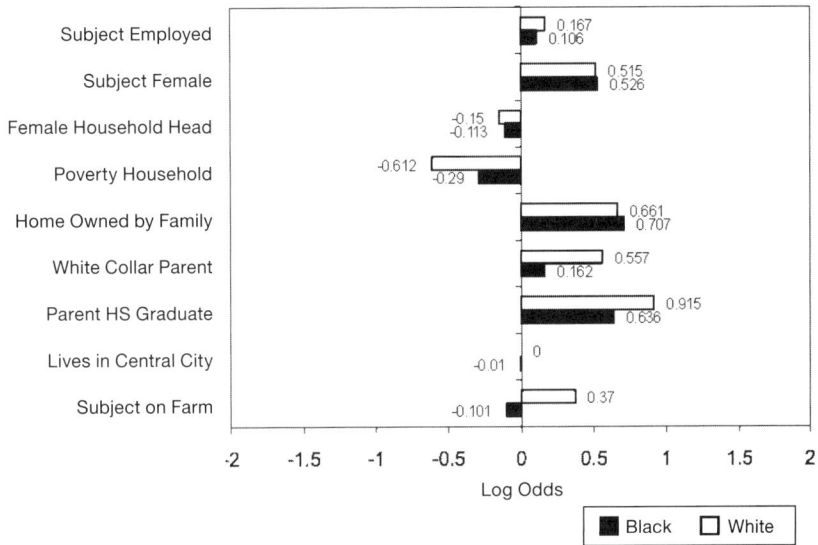

Dependent variable: Enrollment (or not) at the junior level or higher, including graduation. All variables statistically significant at .05 or higher except Lives in Central City for both Blacks and Whites, and Subject Lives on Farm and Subject Employed for Blacks. See Appendix B for additional information.

than Whites, however, the growth of the African American urban population meant that overall destitution often *did* increase in larger cities. Consequently, even if national poverty rates declined for a time, awareness of deprivation was heightened by the growth of sprawling Black ghettos, contributing to impressions of increasing hardship.[61] Like the question of educational attainment, the perception of decline or advance depended upon the perspective of the observer. Despite widespread poverty in many cities, the economic status of African American families was improving. Consequently, what seemed like a "crisis" from one standpoint was, from another view point, progress.

The effects of this were clearly evident in attainment levels. Figure 4.1 presents a logistic regression analysis of educational attainment conducted with national samples of Black and White youth in 1970. This is comparable to analyses conducted in Chapter 3, and focuses on 17-year-olds at the end of the decade, children of the tumultuous 1960s. Once again, the dependent variable is whether or not the subject was enrolled in grade 11 or higher or had graduated. Independent factors are similar to those utilized earlier, including parental educational attainment (high school graduation) and occupational status (white-collar), along with poverty status, home ownership, and family structure (female head). Individual gender (female) and employment status are also included, along with metropolitan residence (central city) and living on a farm.[62]

In general, this analysis shows that social status continued to be a major determinant of success in school for youth of both races. Those with parents who were high school graduates, held white-collar jobs, and owned homes were more likely to have attained this level of schooling than those without such advantages. Conversely, those living in households below the poverty level or with a female head were considerably less likely to succeed in school. Interestingly, poverty appears to have been less of an impediment to educational attainment for African Americans than Whites, despite its much higher incidence in Black communities. This was partly due to the lower rate of school success among all African Americans, but also reflected the rise in Black attainment as well. The important point, however, is that family background factors were decisive in shaping the educational fates of Blacks and Whites alike.[63]

African Americans living on farms—mostly in the South—had a lower likelihood of reaching this level of education, but for the small number of them at this time it was not the major impediment it had been in the past. The opposite was true for Whites on farms, who typically enjoyed higher standards of living.[64] Employment was positively associated with attainment for both groups, but it was not statistically significant for Blacks and appears to have been a bit more compatible with school for White youth, as in earlier years.[65] For both Blacks and Whites, girls performed better academically and graduated at higher rates than boys.[66] With the exception of a non-negative association with Black youth employment, these were familiar patterns in educational attainment, and they continued to hold during this period.

As suggested earlier, living in a central city did not affect the likelihood of youth from either race succeeding, despite the many problems reported in urban schools. This is consistent with overall patterns of enrollment during this time, but it also points to the impact of improved social and economic circumstances, which benefitted Blacks more than Whites. In 1970, poverty and deprivation remained critical impediments to success in school for all youth, but improvements in the status of African Americans were greater than for Whites.[67] And even poor Blacks improved their school success. Consequently, Black youth attended school in greater numbers, staying on track to graduate in spite of the conditions they encountered both in and outside the schools. This is still further evidence of their resolve, and the support they received from parents and other adults in their immediate communities.

LEARNING UNDER DIFFICULT CIRCUMSTANCES

It was one thing to go to school, of course, and another to endure or succeed in the conditions that Black students encountered there. Larger numbers of African Americans appeared in schools each year due to both their rising attendance rates and such other factors as migration and the so-called baby boom, which more than doubled the size of birth cohorts between the 1940s and 1970s. This increase in students represented a challenge to school systems serving Black communities, often leading to badly congested schools, deteriorating facilities, and inadequate staffing. There also were perennial questions about the quality of education in these settings, and the performance of African American students. Eventually, considerable controversy arose over the equality of education and the role of schools in a society marked by continuing racial disparities in status and wealth. Overcrowded and inferior facilities, of course, had long characterized Black schools in both the North and the South. Decades of oversight and neglect contributed to the poor condition of many such institutions, despite Southern equalization campaigns and haphazard efforts of Northern districts to keep abreast of population growth. As Blacks moved into new neighborhoods in the cities, schools began to change, and it was rarely for the better.

Problems linked to overcapacity enrollment varied but were most acute where residential segregation was especially severe. Chicago was among the most segregated cities in the country and the question of overcrowded schools became critical there. As early as 1957, an article in the NAACP magazine *The Crisis* reported that, on average, White elementary schools enrolled fewer than 700 students, while the mean for Black schools was more than 1,200.[68] A 1962 Urban League study found that all but one of the city's largest elementary schools, those with more than 1,600 students, were in Black neighborhoods. By the early 1960s, enrollments in some schools, particularly on the West Side, exceeded 2,000. These schools were placed on double shifts, and more than 80% of the 20,000 students on such shifts reportedly were African American. Overall, class sizes were 25% larger in Black schools. As a consequence, the Urban League found that per pupil expenditures in majority Black schools were only two-thirds those in White institutions.[69] A few years later, a survey by Robert Havighurst of the University of Chicago revealed that "inner-city" elementary schools had the lowest proportion of "regular appointment" teachers, fewer than two-thirds on average, with the others being substitutes. Teachers in these schools also had considerably less experience than in other schools, a median of 4 years compared to a more than 12 elsewhere. The vast majority of Chicago's African American children, more than 80%, attended highly segregated schools (90% or more Black), simply because of longstanding residential isolation.[70] Most children affected by these conditions were in elementary schools, but it was these institutions that fed the city's predominantly Black high schools.

Not surprisingly, overcrowding and related school problems soon became critical issues for Chicago's Black community. In 1963, Edwin Berry, executive director of Chicago's Urban League chapter, declared that African American high school students were getting "no more than a second rate education" because of congested conditions.[71] In the years to follow, similar charges were made about particular institutions, as parents and neighborhood groups protested deteriorating conditions in local high schools. In a 1965 presentation to the board of education, a Marshall High School student claimed that the school was serving twice as many students as its intended capacity. This was a particularly severe case, but levels of crowding in excess of 50% were not uncommon elsewhere.[72] It would not be inaccurate to say that many of Chicago's Black high schools were fairly bursting at the seams.

Congested schools became a focal point of struggles in Chicago and elsewhere. The policy of using temporary structures to accommodate additional students, known as Willis wagons in reference to Chicago's superintendent, became a rallying point in Black protests. The intransigence of district leaders to African American complaints led to massive demonstrations. But the problem of overcrowding did not abate, and in many respects, it grew worse. Chicago had managed to expand facilities in the 1950s and early 1960s, but by the middle of the decade, the district's ability to raise capital for additional building had been exhausted. As in other urban districts, White voters proved reluctant to support substantial improvements as the system became predominantly African American.[73] Consequently, Chicago was unable to add significantly to the stock of secondary institutions available to African American youth. Without integration, overcrowding was virtually a foregone eventuality in light of population growth.

Comparable conditions characterized Black schooling in other cities, even if few were as segregated as Chicago. The Detroit NAACP reported "extreme overcrowding" at Northwestern High School, located in a rapidly growing African American area of the city.[74] Complaints surfaced in Atlanta about overcrowded schools, as hundreds of Black secondary students applied unsuccessfully for transfers to White institutions in early desegregation plans. In cities such as Milwaukee, Cleveland, Newark, and Kansas City, where Black neighborhoods expanded rapidly, crowding occurred principally in elementary schools but occasionally affected secondary institutions as well. Districts also scrambled to find experienced teachers to serve Black students.[75] "Intact busing" schemes were implemented in Milwaukee, Kansas City, Cleveland, and elsewhere to address overcrowding in Black schools, particularly at the elementary level, moving entire classes of Black students to largely White schools to receive instruction in separate classrooms. These measures did not satisfy demands for integration, however, and there was no evidence that instruction improved either.[76] In New York, segregation and overcrowding were most clearly evident in junior high schools, and this, too, became a focal point of community discontent. Secondary schools there experienced fewer such problems after the district instituted a transfer policy allowing students in Brooklyn and Manhattan to choose from a number of institutions, but reports still surfaced about overcrowding at Benjamin Franklin High in East Harlem.[77] Wherever it occurred, crowding students into buildings filled beyond capacity invariably affected the quality of education they received, and added to the challenges facing the educators who served them.

African American objections to congested schools soon became tied to demands for integration. In practical terms, this was a matter of fully utilizing school facilities to serve Black students, as well as a matter of equity and fairness. In Chicago and a number of other cities, activists contended that certain White schools that were adjacent to Black neighborhoods had underutilized facilities. This fueled demands for action and forced districts to relieve crowding and undertake minimal levels of integration.[78] Early desegregation schemes in both the North and South utilized voluntary transfer programs to accommodate shifting demands for secondary education. Such steps typically placed the burden of changing schools on Black students, as their schools exhibited the greatest crowding. It also meant that they were required to contend with hostile receptions in the largely White schools they entered. Conducted in this manner, desegregation was undertaken in piecemeal fashion, with relatively small numbers of African American students "integrating" formerly all-White institutions.[79] Transfers almost never flowed in the opposite direction, as Whites generally avoided going to predominantly African American schools. These and other issues associated with desegregation are addressed in the following chapter.

School boards and district administrators often were reluctant to permit large numbers of African American students to switch schools, fearing White reaction. This prolonged crowding problems and led to frustration in African American communities. At the same time, Whites were typically permitted to transfer when Black students began arriving in a particular high school. Eventually, this dynamic had the effect of changing the racial composition of secondary institutions within a matter of years.[80] It also contributed to the widespread impression that all-Black or mostly Black schools were inferior to predominantly White ones, or that they had declined from earlier years when they served largely White students bodies. This, of course, provided a strong incentive for Whites to abandon schools that were gaining substantial numbers of Blacks. As the populations of secondary institutions underwent this sort of racial transition, there usually was a widespread perception that academic quality had weakened as well.[81]

The theme of declining quality and deteriorating conditions came to be pervasive in urban education, particularly with regard to secondary education. High schools that had been widely viewed as "jewels" of city school systems became associated with discipline and behavior problems and low academic standards.[82] This pattern also characterized certain suburban settings when large numbers of African Americans entered the schools, such as in Compton, California, in the latter 1950s.[83] The reputations of these schools typically were worse than those of Black high schools of previous decades, when a smaller proportion of African American youth attended secondary institutions. Many new students came from deprived rural settings or had been educated in overcrowded elementary schools. This made it difficult to attract and hold the best teachers, and to focus on improving academic performance. Experienced teachers like those who had staffed Black high schools in the past were in high demand, especially when big-city school systems attempted to desegregate faculty ranks. As a result, these schools found it difficult to retain veteran educators, and often were staffed with growing numbers of inexperienced teachers. Although many such newcomers compensated for a lack of know-how with enthusiasm and hard work, the challenges were daunting. Staff turnover became a major problem, leading to complaints from Black communities.[84] Such changes were compounded by problems associated with the densely populated and destitute neighborhoods where many such schools were located.[85]

These developments were evident in the case of Kansas City's Central High School, discussed in greater detail in the next chapter. During this time, the degree of staff turnover at Central increased significantly.[86] Across the decade of the 1950s, slightly more than 20% of the teaching staff remained at the school, a level of stability that indicated a dedicated core group of educators. During the following decade, however, that number dropped to 4%, reflecting a severe erosion of commitment to the school. Judging from faculty pictures in yearbooks, by the latter 1960s, many new teachers were quite young, undoubtedly still early in their careers. Yearbooks from other inner-city high schools reveal similar patterns.[87] This was partly a consequence of district efforts to desegregate school faculties, leading to more teacher transfers, but it also reflected the aversion many teachers felt toward predominantly Black schools.[88] This did not auger well for the scholastic reputation of these institutions.

Academic achievement became a critical concern for Black high schools, at least in terms of public perceptions. Although some institutions had become known for accomplishment in earlier years, few predominantly African American schools were associated with scholastic excellence in the 1960s.[89] This was a consequence both of changes in the student body and conditions in the schools. Rising enrollments meant that a broader segment of the Black community sent its youth to school. Having attended crowded schools, often in shifts, with high levels of staff turnover, it is hardly surprising that these students often scored below district averages on standardized assessments. In the South, where accreditation schemes sometimes placed institutions in categories, African American schools rarely were judged equivalent to White institutions. A 1963 Arkansas study found that Black and White secondary schools were rated the same in only 16% of the state's districts, and no African American school was judged better than neighboring White institutions.[90] Results such as these belied Southern "equalization" campaigns of the 1950s. The example of Caswell County's Training School in North Carolina, which surpassed local White institutions in many respects, was a rarity.[91] While some Black schools may grudgingly have been considered "good" by Whites, most were not.

Such charactertizations held true in the North as well, although accreditation standards there did not formally demark such distinctions. Since few schools failed to receive accreditation, establishing the quality of particular institutions was often tricky. Usually it was a matter of perception and anecdote, occasionally reinforced by test results, along with deterioration of school facilities due to overcrowding and neglect. Occasionally, the issue surfaced in the press. In 1965, the *Chicago Daily News* published a series of articles about conditions at Crane Technical High School, an overcrowded, predominantly Black institution on the city's West Side, operating on three shifts at the time. The school's principal, Thomas J. Farrell, acknowledged that it had "more disorder than others, a larger percentage of inexperienced teachers, fewer textbooks and a dearth of leadership," but maintained that it was "different from many other Chicago high schools only in degree." Students corroborated this while arguing that all students at the school should not be painted with the same brush. One admitted that "standards are low," but also asserted that "we do have students who are learning." She concluded by declaring, "I am not saying Crane gives you a quality education. But how many high schools in Chicago do?"[92] Similar accounts appeared in other cities during these years.[93] As this suggests, a commonplace defense of predominantly African American high schools was to say that they were no worse than other institutions in similar circumstances.

TABLE 4.4, Social and Economic Circumstances of Black and White Central City High School Students, By Year and Region, 1960–1980 (in percentages)

Year and Region	BLACK STUDENTS		WHITE STUDENTS	
	in Poverty	Fatherless Home	in Poverty	Fatherless Home
1960				
South	60	40	16	16
Non South	38	40	10	15
1970				
South	38	30	8	12
Non South	28	34	10	13
1980				
South	33	50	11	22
Non South	32	54	13	24

Source: IPUMS data.

Although this may have served to divert blame from the principal and staff, it also suggested that most such schools were inescapably plagued by these shortcomings.

SERVING THE "DISADVANTAGED"

Behind broad references to the problems of urban schools, of course, was the matter of the children and youth they served. Most educators recognized that student background characteristics profoundly affected both achievement levels and perceptions about particular schools. Poverty was a particularly important consideration, along with the relatively large number of Black fatherless households. Contemporaries used the expression "cultural deprivation" to describe the effect of these conditions, although there was little systematic research on how student background influenced achievement until James Coleman's national survey of achievement in 1966. It was not long, however, before terms such as *culturally deprived* were applied principally to African Americans and other students from racial and ethnic minority groups. Eventually, this practice would lead to controversy, as growing numbers of African Americans objected to the implication that their children were somehow culturally "deficient." In academic circles, the cultural deficiency perspective was criticized as "blaming the victim," and was answered by an interpretive framework focusing on strengths and pride in racial and ethnic identity and culture.[94] Still, there was a growing consensus that poverty and family instability were critical obstacles to academic success for children of all racial and ethnic backgrounds.

A major problem, of course, was the very high incidence of these circumstances among African American students, both in absolute and relative terms. Table 4.4 provides estimates of the proportion of the *students* in central city high schools who lived with household poverty and family instability (distinct from figures for *all* youth in Table 4.3 above). Nearly 40% of urban Black students outside the South in 1960 lived below the federal poverty level, and a similar proportion resided in homes with no father figure, with 20% experiencing both conditions. In a representative Black high school, in that case, some 56% of the students contended with one or both of these circumstances. For schools located in ghettos with greater concentrations of poverty, the figure was undoubtedly higher. The corresponding proportion for Whites was 20%. Although conditions improved in the ensuing years, the incidence of poverty and fatherless households remained two to three times greater among African Americans.[95] The proportion of Black high school students in poverty was even higher in the South, although fatherlessness was slightly lower. As suggested by the analysis in Figure 4.1 earlier, these circumstances were not conducive to academic accomplishment and contributed to White advantages in school success. In this respect, African American students were indeed "disadvantaged," but it was due less to "culture" than to the social and economic conditions associated with widespread residential segregation, continuing discrimination in employment and education, and pervasive prejudice in everyday life. The effects were clearly evident in comparisons of schools.

The impact of this was clear in the few studies that considered Black and White achievement. Systematic assessment of schools was not performed routinely, so evidence is fragmentary. Yet a consistent record of inferior performance among African American secondary students was apparent. Havighurst's 1964 examination of Chicago high schools, for instance, found most Black freshmen enrolled in remedial English, and most Black schools had fewer high scores in reading than the district average.[96] Two years later, in his survey of achievement in a national sample of schools, Coleman found that most Blacks performed well below average in verbal skills, with the lowest scores in the rural South. Overall, White freshmen registered reading levels about two grades higher than African American 9th-graders. Coleman attributed much of this to student background characteristics, particularly parental education and income, along with household structure.[97] But even if schools did not account for much disparity in achievement, it was widely recognized that the academically frail condition of inner-city institutions severely hampered their ability to address the gaps that research revealed.

The publication of Coleman's findings added fervor to desegregation debates, leading many to argue that integration offered the best chances of raising African American achievement. It was a dispute, however, that generally cast predominantly Black schools in a negative light. These were institutions widely seen as a source of problems rather than as a path to improvement for most Black youth. The term *racial isolation* was used to characterize the dilemma of such settings, suggesting that a lack of non-Black peers was inherently problematic.[98] Irrespective of the virtue of these sentiments, their very expression cast doubt on the possibility that predominantly African American schools could succeed academically. Almost by definition, in that case, an all-Black high school was substandard.

James Conant's *Slums and Suburbs* had helped set the tone for such perceptions. Conant documented the poor conditions in predominantly African American schools, focusing on their overcrowded, ill-maintained facilities and poor academic performance. Although he did suggest additional resources were needed for such schools, he also called for more vocational education for Black students. Conant hoped to keep more of them in school, believing that job training would help. He also wanted to relieve unemployment among African American youth, and felt that vocational courses could lead to jobs.[99] But as Princeton sociologist Melvin Tumin pointed out, such prescriptions appeared to offer a decidedly second-class education for Blacks, and were inconsistent with the egalitarian ethos of the post-*Brown* era.[100] Conant's position also was generally incompatible with his earlier recommendations in *The American High School Today*, which endorsed comprehensive institutions that combined academic and vocational courses. To propose that Black secondary schools should be primarily vocational suggested that they were incapable of achieving academic excellence.

In the years to follow, the idea of vocational education became an important theme in national discussions of African American education. In 1962, for instance, a report issued by the Educational Policy Commission called for greater emphasis on vocational courses, among other measures, to serve the needs of the "disadvantaged American."[101] A year later, the Kennedy administration linked vocational education and "civil rights," a turn that influenced state and local policymakers.[102] At the same time, U.S. Commissioner of Education Francis Keppel endorsed national investment in vocational education and job training, aimed specifically at African Americans, to address youth unemployment.[103] This was a theme that was echoed in local programs sponsored by the Urban League and other community organizations.[104] In the minds of many policymakers, it seemed logical to connect vocational education or job training and African American teenagers.

By and large, however, Black community responses to vocational training were ambivalent, if not downright antagonistic. A 1965 *Chicago Defender* editorial wondered about the growing emphasis on job preparation. While finding it appealing in certain respects, the *Defender* expressed concern that vocational courses could foreclose higher education for many Black students. "It is much easier for an adult to learn on the job," the editorial declared, "than it is for him to repair his deficiencies in mathematics, sciences and English after he has left high school." African American leaders also worried that such training was ill suited to an age when job requirements changed quickly due to technology and economic development. There was also concern that Black youth needed preparation for leadership roles, and that vocational education was not a good grounding for such responsibilities. As the *Defender* noted, "'The culturally deprived' child needs an education that will bring him into our culture; and only a basically liberal education that provides the cultural background not available at home will enable him to overcome his handicaps."[105] In other words, job training did not promise to help poor African American students to improve their status.

Part of the problem was evidence that vocational programs did little to help African Americans gain entry to the skilled trades or other high wage occupations. In Chicago, the *Defender* documented widespread discrimination against Black youth attempting to enter the trades through district programs. The schools linked most directly to these jobs did not admit many Blacks, and institutions with large numbers of African Americans, such as Dunbar High, had poor connections to the unions, the traditional conduit for such positions. Similar issues emerged in other cities.[106] Thus, even when they enrolled in vocational programs, African American youth typically faced barriers to employment.[107] This dilemma does not seem to have occurred to Conant, who praised Dunbar as a model institution.[108] But it tempered the response of Black leaders and educators to calls for greater emphasis on vocational education. It was hardly a panacea for Black educational problems, and it appeared unlikely to result in more employment, even in the short term.

There was also the question of academic quality, linked to the perception that vocational education was a "dumping ground" for students who wished to avoid academic courses. In 1967, a New York conference organized by the NAACP issued a statement expressing concern that "we see many of our youth being guided and counseled into vocational training when it is not in their best interests."[109] It did not appear to be preparation for the problems facing African American communities, and many wondered whether Black youth were able to make such critical decisions early in their academic careers. Concerns such as these fueled skepticism about proposals for more Black vocational education. Behind such sentiments was a fear that it could compromise leadership for the future.

Apart from a policy emphasis on vocational education for African Americans, there is relatively little evidence that curricular expectations differed for Black and White students. Historians David Angus and Jeffrey Mirel have argued that academic standards in American high schools were notoriously suspect for students of all races. Their examination of course-taking trends in Detroit found considerable stability across Black and White schools in the 1960s and early 1970s. Despite some differences in mathematics, with White schools offering more high-level courses, there appears to have been little differentiation by race.[110] In New York, Black leaders complained that African American students were underrepresented in the city's selective specialty high schools, particularly highly regarded institutions such as the Bronx High School of Science.[111] But getting into these schools was less a matter of particular courses than performing competitively on citywide examinations. As junior highs in Harlem and other Black areas of the city began to focus on test preparation, more Black students gained admission to specialty high schools. It is telling that curricular offerings in Black and White schools did not become a key issue of contention, at least with respect to questions of equity. The NAACP denounced tracking schemes that assigned Blacks to less demanding courses, calling the practice "a subtle but systematic form of discrimination" that marked students as "intellectually inferior," but Black leaders did not make it a focal point of protest. Despite complaints about large numbers of Black students in the "general" track, along with "compensatory" or "remedial" classes, the courses available in predominantly African American schools appear to have been similar to those in White institutions in much of the country.[112]

To the extent that curriculum was a matter of dispute, it was over the inclusion of such new subjects as Black history and literature.[113] Otherwise, the principal points of conflict were the condition of the schools and the quality of instruction, often delivered by young and inexperienced teachers. This was a consequence of the deplorable conditions that many African Americans endured in high school. The overcrowded buildings, double shifts, and continually changing faculty led many to conclude they were victims of institutionalized racism and discrimination. It was these problems, and not "cultural deprivation" linked to poverty and family structure, that growing numbers of African Americans believed affected their academic performance. In the midst of a national context of protest over similar issues, perceptions such as these contributed a rising level of confrontation and turmoil in the nation's secondary institutions.

AN ERA OF CONFLICT AND PROTEST

The 1960s were years of dissent and conflict around questions of race and civil and human rights. There was unrest over a range of issues, of course, but few engendered as much strife as racial integration and questions of equity and fairness. Schools figured prominently in these controversies, as important points of contact for children and adults from all racial backgrounds and because they represented critical resources for the attainment and maintenance of social status. This was particularly true of high schools, where the students were old enough to grasp the issues and to become directly involved. It is hardly surprising, in that case, that secondary institutions became critical sites of conflict over a range of issues, not the least important being the quality of education that African American students received.

Teenagers have long fought over any number of issues, extending from the petty to the profane, and schools provided a convenient setting to settle grievances as secondary institutions became commonplace. During the 1960s, however, race figured ever more prominently in such conflicts. Physical proximity often permitted such animosities to flare into the open, occasionally resulting in violence. Kevin Dodge attended Kansas City's predominantly Black Manual High, across the street from largely White Westport High, and interracial clashes became so common that the schools scheduled different dismissal times. It was no time for the faint of heart, and although courage and bravado were displayed in abundance, it was not always in the pursuit of high-minded principles.[114]

Predominantly Black urban schools also earned reputations for disruption and violence not related to racial discord. Street gangs became a more visible social problem in ghetto communities, especially with growing sales of illegal drugs, a major concern for educators and police.[115] Reports of guns in schools surfaced more frequently, usually in connection with gangs and sometimes with deadly consequences.[116] This signaled that neighborhoods around Black high schools were becoming more dangerous, leading to demands for security measures and police intervention.[117] Athletic events occasionally became scenes of hostility between groups of students and outsiders, many of them gang members in larger cities.[118] In Chicago, there was even talk of suspending basketball games in the Public School League because of violence, mostly between rival groups of Black students.[119]

Aggression and fighting had long plagued American high schools, particularly in urban settings, but in the latter 1960s and early 1970s, these issues became more clearly linked to race in the public mind. Incidents such as a 1969 "do your thing day" in New York's Bedford Stuyvesant area contributed to this, when windows were smashed and lockers broken by Black and Puerto Rican students.[120] A 1970 survey of 35 cities found that vandalism had increased everywhere, leaving a "trail of broken windows, wrecked furniture [and] flooded corridors," representing a "loss of many millions of dollars." Arrests of students and other youth for destruction of school property increased dramatically.[121] Developments such as these contributed to the discord and tension in urban high schools that was widely considered a sign of the times. They also added to the physical deterioration of facilities and an increase in security measures, yet another source of conflict with students. By 1970, Chicago employed nearly 500 security officers in the schools.[122] Conditions such as these did little to help the reputation of urban high schools, particularly those serving large numbers of African Americans.

The 1960s also were years of protest and spirited demonstrations against discrimination and injustice, especially regarding questions of race and deprivation. The national civil rights movement drew worldwide attention, and demonstrated that significant changes could be achieved by using a variety of tactics. High school students occasionally were participants, typically as "foot soldiers" in demonstrations and other activities organized by adults. Toward the end of the decade, however, students became more active in struggles to change the schools, especially regarding issues they felt affected them directly, such as the conditions of school facilities and the curriculum they studied. Interestingly, it was only after the national civil rights movement started to wind down that student-initiated protests began to increase in frequency and force.

It appears that national civil rights organizations had little role in launching or coordinating student protests, not even providing student leaders with advice. Rather, mobilization of African American secondary students to protest school issues was principally a local affair, although there can be little doubt that activists drew inspiration and ideas from the national movement. The principal youth organization in the larger movement was the NAACP, which operated youth councils in many communities with more than 60,000 members nationally. These local groups were closely monitored by adult chapter leaders, however, who often discouraged militant or confrontational tactics of the sort advocated by more radical students. In a few cases, student protesters were influenced by Black teachers, "nationalist" community organizations such as the Black Panthers, or college groups like the Student Non-violent Coordinating Committee (SNCC). For example, the Panthers were especially influential in Chicago, where they provided advice and support to high school students organizing demonstrations. SNCC was credited with organizing a protest rally in Forest City, Arkansas, where students demanded free meals and books, resulting in nearly 200 arrests.[123] But overall there is no evidence of national coordination of such student activities. Instead, local circumstances and an affinity to militancy appear to have dictated tactics and goals, sometimes over objections from more established civil rights organizations.[124] There is also considerable evidence that parents and teachers influenced them as well.[125] Although it was a movement that was clearly inspired by advocates of "Black Power" on the national stage, it was conditions in the schools that moved this generation of student dissenters to action.

In the opening years of the decade, African American students were often called upon to participate in demonstrations and other protest activities planned by adults or college students. This was the case in Birmingham, Alabama, in 1963, when hundreds of students were called upon to march into the teeth of police dogs and fire hoses, responding with fervor and courage.[126] At about the same time, students were mobilized for school boycotts and mass demonstrations by local groups in Boston, Chicago, and other cities to protest overcrowded and segregated schools. In June 1963, several thousand African American youth in Boston skipped school to protest segregation, many of them attending "freedom centers" in local churches and community centers for lessons on Black history.[127] The following fall, an estimated 300,000 Chicago students boycotted school in a similar protest, organized by a coalition of community organizations.[128] Parallel incidents occurred in New York, Cleveland, and other cities the following year.[129] Altogether, tens of thousands of high school youth participated in these events in Northern cities, demonstrating their potential for mass mobilization around educational issues, a point recognized by civil rights leaders.[130]

Beyond Birmingham, Black students in the South were called upon to assist with community organizing and to participate in demonstrations organized by civil rights groups, particularly the SNCC. In January 1964, for instance, more than 100 Atlanta youth heeded SNCC leader John Lewis's call to "play hooky for freedom," staging a noisy demonstration in the mayor's office to demand improvements at local high schools. Afterward, they conducted impromptu sit-ins at local restaurants, prompting district officials to call upon the police to prevent organizing near schools.[131] A year later, students in Birmingham joined demonstrations to support voter registration, running through the schools and calling on peers to participate.[132] Many Black youth, of course, were also firsthand witnesses to history, as they observed the struggles that defined the decade. In addition to this, they could see the deteriorating condition of their schools and changing public perceptions of the education they were receiving. This would become an important source of motivation in future protests.

As the national civil rights movement floundered in the wake of Martin Luther King's death and a failure to make headway on economic equity, African American students across the country began to demand recognition of their concerns, and to protest the state of the schools.[133] Borrowing tactics and strategies from mainstream civil rights organizations, they employed a range of methods. Walkouts and strikes were popular tactics, as the idea of leaving school, particularly in warm weather, proved appealing to a wide spectrum of students. Sit-ins and other types of direct confrontation with authorities were less widely employed, as they entailed the possibility of hostility or arrest, and perhaps additional repercussions. Given the temper of the times, however, and the widespread familiarity of youth with protest tactics, a relatively small group of instigators could wield considerable influence, particularly if grievances could be clearly articulated.[134] The result was a wave of protest activity that surprised even its organizers at times.

The first rumblings of protest over school conditions started in the middle of the decade. At Chicago's Farragut High, students walked out in February 1966 to protest overcrowded and outdated facilities, along with the food in the lunchroom. The principal declared that they were merely copying a nearby university boycott, dismissing the incident as "just a bunch of kids showing off."[135] A more sobering portent appeared a couple of months later, as students at Detroit's Northern High School declared a strike to protest the school's declining academic standards and the principal's decision to suppress an editorial about the problem in the school newspaper. Jeffrey Mirel has documented how the Northern walkout led to a confrontation with district administrators that polarized the city, helping to undermine public support for the school system. Regardless of their eventual impact, however, such actions by students, encouraged and supported by local civil rights activists, clearly exhibited their power to dramatically challenge adult authority.[136] In years to come, it would prove much harder for those in positions of control to dismiss the demands and behavior of discontented Black students.

The pace and scale of student protest increased with time, and not just among African Americans. The year 1968 was notable, as college students embraced the antiwar movement in ever-larger numbers, and high school youth achieved an important victory in *Tinker v. Des Moines*, allowing greater freedom of expression and independence from adult supervision.[137] In the spring, "a rash" of school boycotts spread across metropolitan New York City. Just north of Manhattan, a district-wide group called "Concerned Black Students of Yonkers" issued an emblematic series of demands, including the elimination of racial prejudice in the schools, requiring teachers to study Black history, and allowing students greater freedom in selecting courses of study. The group also called for Black teachers and administrators, African American representation in student government, and a community governing board. When asked about missing school, a spokesperson described feeling "very strongly that the educational process stopped years ago for black students."[138] The following fall, African American students in Chicago also staged walkouts, ultimately involving more than 20 high schools. An organizing group called "Black Students for Defense" issued demands to Superintendent James Redmond for more Black teachers, courses in Black history, holidays to commemorate Black heroes, and greater influence over school policies. In a statement to the press, an "articulate black militant spokesman" charged the board of education with "educational genocide."[139] Another student declared, "We're getting third and fourth rate educations now," adding, "We might as well stay out of school and educate ourselves in the library."[140]

As the mainstream civil rights movement began to wind down, incidents of disorder shook the cities and more students were affected by the emerging "Black Power" movement, particularly demands that "Black pride" and self-esteem be fostered through education.[141] This newfound militancy and sense of pride sometimes increased interracial conflict, especially as some students declared a willingness to challenge White authority. In Kansas City, Black students staged a march from Central High to city hall, protesting Martin Luther King Jr.'s assassination, a demonstration that turned disorderly. This led officials to close the city schools, marking a new pattern of response to confrontation. Symptomatic of this, our interview subject Kevin Dodge was drawn briefly to the Black Panthers movement. His Kansas City school was located in a White neighborhood and he was routinely harassed by police officers, and even White "minutemen" who tried to restrain Black youth. He joined the Panthers, who "were preaching that nonviolence wasn't working, we need to get violent, arm ourselves to protect ourselves." After a few meetings with other members brandishing "guns and violent talk," he decided against continuing, but his interest in the group bespoke an new attitude among African American students.[142]

Militant sentiments became more commonplace, particularly in Northern institutions. In Philadelphia, Black students and faculty members were arrested in 1968, following an overnight sit-in at Benjamin Franklin High, as "racial unrest spread throughout public secondary schools throughout the city."[143] At the same time, in New York, demonstrations were staged against "alleged racism in public schools in minority group communities."[144] Los Angeles experienced waves of protest between 1967 and 1969, with militant students labeling Black educators who wore shirts and ties and spoke "English instead of slang" as "sellouts."[145] Black and Mexican students repeatedly issued demands for changes in the schools, including more minority faculty members and greater say in school policies.[146] In Mount Vernon, New York, Black students marched to demand courses in African American history, better bus service, and guidance and career counseling.[147] At Chicago's Harrison High School, students protested White teachers offering courses in Black history, arguing, "We don't feel the white teachers can teach the subject properly."[148] Calls for more instruction in Black history and related subjects swept the city, and other districts.[149]

In 1969, a Chicago firm specializing in public opinion and social trends reported a "growing number of racial disruptions" in high schools across the country, referring to protests and clashes between students and authorities. The report noted that demands focused on curricular matters and the composition of the faculty and disciplinary policies, and stated that the boycott was practically a universal tactic. Even though the survey addressed the behavior of both Whites and Blacks, it was an especially apt characterization of protest activities by African American students.[150] In predominantly Black institutions, students were clearly unhappy with the quality of their education and often lashed out in anger. There were other calls for curricular change in Black schools as well, many stemming from community groups pushing for greater emphasis on African heritage.[151] Advocacy of Black pride and racial self-esteem became a hallmark of the time, and a way to explore alternatives to the antipathy many felt toward the deficiencies of conventional schooling.

In the opening years of the 1970s, Black student protests remained regular occurrences in the urban North. Demands for Black administrators and teachers were a consistent feature of these outbursts, along with frustration over poor facilities and the attitudes of White educators.[152] Strikes and boycotts also occurred for other reasons, including dismissal of popular staff members and policies that students found onerous.[153] As one editorial noted, "black students have had sensational success in forcing high school and college administrators to bow to their will," but such accomplishments eventually meant there were fewer complaints to protest.[154] With time, the curricular and staffing issues gave way to longstanding concerns about deteriorating schools and overcrowding. The recruitment of African American educators, along with widespread addition of courses in Black history and literature, meant that these questions eventually ceased to spark much controversy.

As school budgets declined due to eroding property values and middle-class flight to suburbs, the physical state of schools remained a source of turmoil. In 1972, students at Chicago's DuSable High, an especially old facility, staged a boycott to protest its "unsanitary" and "overcrowded" building.[155] A year later, students made similar complaints at Westinghouse High on the West Side, focusing on its "deplorable" condition.[156] Within a month, hundreds protested the cancellation of summer classes because of budget cuts, mainly on the city's largely Black South Side.[157] In short, in the span of a few years, student concern with racial identity and pride, and their infusion into the curriculum, had given way to somewhat more prosaic but perhaps no less pressing issues of tolerable learning environments and the availability of summer courses.

The protest years brought telling changes to the schools. Courses in Black history and culture became far more commonplace, at least for a time, reflecting a surge of interest in those topics on college campuses as well. Numbers of Black teachers and administrators increased, although the problem of faculty turnover in large urban secondary institutions continued to be evident. Black teenage clothing and hairstyle fashions reflected the new "Black pride" sensibility of the times, as "Afro" haircuts and contemporary urban dress found their way into schools. These trends were readily evident in yearbooks, as well as other visual sources from across the country.[158] Indeed, a distinctive Black youth culture, forged in the struggles of the time, was emerging and was quickly embraced by African American high school students.[159] By the latter 1970s, many Black communities had made local institutions into schools they could call their own, focusing improvement efforts on dropouts, drug use, gang activity, and other dangers to urban youth.[160]

Telling regional differences distinguished student conflicts across the country. Protest activity appears to have occurred principally in the North, where most Blacks lived in larger cities and school segregation was highest by 1972. This followed a more general pattern in the larger civil rights movement, as conflict over a range of issues appears to have shifted decisively to the North, beginning in the latter 1960s.[161] In the South and West, there seem to have been considerably fewer such conflicts initiated by students, and a smaller proportion of them attended predominantly Black schools. The emergence of a historically unique Black youth identity, with its own sense of fashion, music, magazines, and media figures, was a national phenomenon. Partly forged in the battles waged in schools across the country, it was a step in the ongoing development of a distinctive Black American identity.

CONCLUSION: COMING OF AGE IN THE 1960S AND 1970S

The 2 decades between 1960 and 1980 represented a time of extensive change in the experiences of Black high school students. At the start of this period, only about half of African American teenagers attended secondary schools, and the vast majority were in highly segregated schools. Enrollment and attainment increased steadily during both decades, narrowing the gap with Whites substantially. In this respect, it was the culmination of a lengthy process of convergence in Black and White education, marking the point when secondary education became a modal experience for African Americans. This was accomplished through the enlistment of community resources, along with assistance from other sources, to see that African American youth recognized the importance of education, and were not distracted by the circumstances they endured both in and out of school.

At the same time that Black enrollments increased, principally in the nation's larger cities, the condition of schools they attended began to deteriorate visibly. This was due to overcrowding, but also to the strained budgets of urban districts, which found it difficult—and often impossible—to build new facilities or improve existing ones. At the same time, turnover among teachers, administrators, and other staff members increased as well. This was partly due to desegregation guidelines that required districts to integrate faculty and staff, particularly those serving large numbers of Black students. It also was a result of teachers choosing to leave these schools in greater numbers, so that urban institutions were served by young and less experienced teachers. This directly affected the quality of Black education, and became a continuing point of contention for both students and adults in affected communities.

Finally, the major pattern of conflict during this time was a function of Black student protest. African American youth made secondary institutions into sites of confrontation over a number of issues, ranging from curricular matters to staffing patterns, and other issues they deemed important to success in school. The course of this mobilization underwent several phases or steps, beginning with students serving as foot soldiers for the mainstream civil rights movement and extending to a groundswell of activism in the latter 1960s. Much of this agitation was focused on getting subjects included in the secondary curriculum and adding more Black teachers and administrators. In later years, these issues appear to have been supplanted by the deteriorating quality of the schools, particularly in larger cities.

By the end of the 1970s, more African Americans were attending high school and succeeding than at any point in history. The steady growth in Black attainment during the 2 decades following 1960 was accompanied by considerable turmoil and conflict, but adversity did not cause large numbers of students to turn their backs on school. Rather, schools represented a battleground and this became a source of motivation. The activism of thousands of students bespoke a commitment to utilizing schools for both personal and collective improvement. Given this, it is little wonder that Black educational attainment increased at this time. The African American secondary school experience had been transformed, and Black youth no longer felt themselves to be outsiders. There were signs of improvement in many schools following the tumultuous 1970s.[162] African American youth had put their stamp on the high school, shaping its organizational and cultural life in many instances, marking something of a culmination to decades of struggle to make Black secondary education better serve community needs.

CHAPTER 5

Battling Segregation

THE HISTORIC *Brown* DECISION marked a turning point in African American education. School integration became the focal point of national debates and, implicitly or explicitly, most local struggles over race and schools. Much has been written about desegregation during the tumultuous years between *Brown* and the latter 1970s. It was a time of massive resistance in the South and conflict elsewhere, and eventual integration in much of the country. As with other aspects of Black education, distinctive regional patterns marked the struggle, although similar issues affected students everywhere. Therefore, we examine high school integration in the North, West, and South, noting distinctions as well as common themes. For example, border states such as Missouri, Kentucky, and Maryland were leaders at the start, but encountered problems with desegregation in time. To illustrate, we consider Kansas City, Missouri, a segregated district prior to 1955. Its uneven progress in school integration was characteristic of many cities. In the North and West, integration of secondary schools remained elusive due to mounting segregation in central city neighborhoods. Progress was most dramatic in the South, however, largely because of successful litigation against intransigent states and districts in the latter 1960s and 1970s.

The concentration of Blacks in urban areas led to school overcrowding, segregation, and inequality in educational resources, and intensified the struggle for desegregation. But regardless of local circumstances, mixing Black and White teenagers for the first time was bound to produce uncertainty and conflict. The extent of these difficulties hinged decisively on the way that adults handled the process, and all too often they failed to ensure that integration became a matter of truly equal opportunity. African American secondary students bore the weight of integration, as they were typically required to change venues, leaving familiar community institutions for schools where they became outsiders. It was a time of awkward and difficult transitions, and considerable conflict, before the social and educational benefits of integrated schools began to be evident. For the first groups of Black students to enter desegregated high schools, integration often was indeed a challenge, but they fought for the principle of equality and paved the way for those who followed.

Although desegregation remained controversial, there is evidence that it contributed to higher-quality school experiences for many African American youth. It may have been difficult to tell at the time, but the first full decade of high school integration yielded lower dropout rates, improved test scores, and higher levels of graduation.[1] In spite of the circumstances, many of the Black students who attended desegregated secondary schools rose to the challenge. This became evident in steadily rising scores on the National Assessment of Educational Progress, attributed in part to their school experiences. It was also reflected in their graduation rates, which continued to converge with those of Whites. If desegregation was hard, it also bore the tangible benefits of educational advancement for African Americans.

INTEGRATION IN THE 1940S AND 1950S

The integration of secondary schools was a point of considerable controversy well before *Brown*. The widely publicized integration of Froebel High in Gary, Indiana following the war highlighted White reactions to attending school with African Americans. Such responses were most palpable in urban areas, where conflict was more likely to occur between working-class White and Black youth as migration brought African Americans to big cities. Elsewhere in the North and West, integrated secondary schools were considerably less controversial, largely because Black youth were relatively few and they posed little threat to existing status distinctions. Less controversy did not mean that integration was universally embraced in principle, however. Rather, it was generally tolerated as a matter of administrative efficiency and compliance with legal requirements. Separate schools for Blacks were forbidden by many states, and deemed impractical in any case due to the small numbers of African Americans in most communities.[2]

Districts that did practice segregation faced increasing pressure from civil rights groups and state authorities. As noted earlier, Davison Douglas has documented a concerted NAACP campaign against segregated schooling outside the South during the 1940s. Combined with a measured improvement of race relations following the war, this resulted in gradual progress in the North and West. There were, of course, certain communities that doggedly resisted integration, such as towns in southern Illinois and others in Indiana and Ohio that practiced segregation in defiance of state laws. But most had been forced to integrate their secondary schools by the early 1950s.[3] Segregated high schools were ended in Arizona and

New Mexico in 1953.[4] By the time of *Brown*, the only remaining all-Black high schools outside the South and certain border states such as Missouri were those serving segregated neighborhoods, mostly in larger cities. Segregation still existed, but its reach had been considerably restricted. Charles Clotfelter has estimated that just 11% of Black youth attended segregated secondary schools outside the South and border states in the 1950s, and probably even fewer at the close of the decade.[5] This was a high point for secondary school integration in these regions, however, as it would decline in the following decade and beyond.

Most African American youth, of course, lived in the South at the time of *Brown*, and because de jure segregation in public schools was practiced across the region, integration was virtually unknown in its high schools. The *Brown* decision was greeted with animosity and vows of resistance in the South, and widespread segregation persisted for more than a decade. When one of our interview respondents, Lorna Tillman, attended Gentry High in Indianola, Mississippi, in the early 1970s, it was still an all-Black school. But in border states such as Maryland, Kentucky, Missouri, and Oklahoma, the reception was considerably more positive. Larger districts in these states moved quickly to formally abolish segregation, opening schools to the *possibility* of integration, if neither the necessity nor the expectation of fully achieving it. In the 1955 *Briggs* decision, federal district judge John Parker ruled in South Carolina that although districts could not bar Blacks from attending school with Whites, they were under no obligation to ensure that integration occurred. The so-called "Parker Doctrine" became a source of desegregation evasion tactics for more than a decade, and it helped to set a very low standard for declaring that integration had been achieved. Due to acceptance of this principle, and because the separation of Black and White students had been so absolute, enrollment of a single Black in a formerly White school was said to represent desegregation at the time.[6]

Using this standard, high schools across the border region were quickly "integrated," as small numbers of African Americans began enrolling as early as the fall of 1954. By and large, their presence was greeted by minor resistance from Whites, students and adults alike, although isolated incidents of violence—or threats of it—did occur.[7] In 1956, an "overall-clad dummy" was hanged in effigy, with a sign cursing the NAACP, from the crossbar of Henderson, Kentucky's Black school's football field, neighboring the town's White high school. Attendance at the newly integrated Weaverton County High had increased to more than 500 students, suggesting that the incident in nearby Henderson was fairly isolated.[8] A modest number of other Southern communities desegregated their high schools immediately after *Brown*, all with relatively small numbers of Black students, such as the college town of Fayetteville, Arkansas.[9]

Baltimore and other cities that voluntarily ended segregation requirements witnessed angry White picketers, and reports surfaced of fights at high schools. These events occurred when Black students entered previously White institutions, which protesters sought to "defend" against incursions.[10] For the most part, however, this process entailed Blacks enrolling in new schools; it rarely led to Whites attending formerly Black schools. This practice was a response to White prejudice, of course, but it also reflected a widespread belief that African American schools were inferior, a view held by most Whites and many Blacks as well. The result was a declining number of formerly White institutions while wholly Black schools remained generally the same, and eventually their student populations increased. In short, from the very beginning, "integration" was largely a one-way transition of Black students moving to a wider range of schools, while Whites remained chiefly in institutions they had historically occupied. In some cases, Whites abandoned schools altogether when Black enrollments grew rapidly.[11] Desegregation, in that case, usually meant more dramatic changes for Blacks than Whites, a theme that would characterize the era.

One upshot was that African American youth had more options for secondary education. For those in Baltimore and other border cities such as Indianapolis, St. Louis, and Kansas City, school desegregation meant that they were no longer restricted to the institutions that were historically designated for them. Many such schools, including Baltimore's Frederick Douglass High and Sumner High in St. Louis, had become overcrowded due to population growth, and the construction of new Black institutions had not kept pace. The availability of additional schools contributed to the growth of African American enrollments, and eventually to higher graduation rates. Although Black attendance in White schools was modest at first, the number of Black students increased rapidly in institutions adjacent to African American neighborhoods.[12] In Kentucky, about a quarter of school systems started desegregation almost immediately, including Lexington and Louisville, which held important implications for secondary education. In rural areas where Blacks did not have separate secondary schools and had to attend elsewhere, some were permitted to enroll in local White institutions. Changes in urban districts were more dramatic. Louisville launched a widely publicized voluntary transfer plan in 1956, and because formerly White schools outnumbered those for Blacks, this new policy presented an opportunity for more Black youth to enroll. Developments such as these increased the availability of high schools for African Americans considerably, even if relatively few benefitted right away.[13]

If high school desegregation started smoothly in most border state communities, it occasioned conflict and violent protest in others. In 1954, Milford, Delaware's school board decided to admit 11 Black students to previously all-White Milford High, but when rumors surfaced about a Black boy asking a White girl to a dance and African Americans wielding knives, White resistance flared. Supporters of integration were threatened, crosses were burned, and Whites were persuaded to boycott the school. Clinton, Tennessee, became another site of confrontation in 1956, when a federal court ordered desegregation to open the school year. Although just 12 Black students were admitted to previously all-White Clinton High, they were confronted by angry mobs and pickets. Intimidation was leveled at their parents and supporters.[14] The National Guard was called into Clay, Kentucky, in response to another protest.[15] These incidents may have been unusual, but their malevolence gained national attention.[16]

Similar clashes occurred elsewhere. In Mansfield, Texas, an irate mob prevented Black students from attending the local White high school, even though there was no other secondary institution in the community. The governor called upon the Texas Rangers to bar Black students from the school, and the Eisenhower administration refused to intervene. The following year, a Black girl was attacked while attending a previously White secondary school in Charlotte, North Carolina, an experience that led her parents to send her north to an integrated Philadelphia institution.[17] These cases also received wide publicity, reminding everyone of the potential for violence with desegregation, as reactionaries declared determination to oppose integration at all costs. In the wake of these events few signs of moderation emanated from the South, and extremists commanded considerable attention.[18]

The best-known instance of conflict over desegregation, of course, occurred with admission of Blacks to all-White Central High in Little Rock in September 1957, leading President Eisenhower to send federal troops to restore order and escort nine African American students to class. The school was patrolled by military personnel for the academic year to ensure student safety, and all city public high schools were closed the following year to forestall integration. This case came to represent a milestone in the campaign to desegregate Southern schools, even if it affected a rather small number of students, largely because of extensive news coverage and federal intervention.[19] Altogether, the struggle lasted several years, punctuated with violent demonstrations and attacks on Blacks and their supporters, occasionally in full view of news media and police. Public displays of White hostility and cruelty and the calm determination of Black students entering the school, exhibited clearly on television, helped to marshal public opinion against Southern extremism. It also demonstrated that many Whites could react to the very idea of integration with ugly malice.[20] After Little Rock, educators across the country were acutely aware of the potential for violence in even modest integration proposals.

Although controversy over desegregation struck all sorts of institutions, high schools seem to have drawn greater adversity than most. Secondary education was an especially contentious battleground, representing a conduit to occupational skills, college, and higher status. High schools also were prime sites for the nation's growing youth culture, which was tied to budding sexuality and rebellious promiscuity.[21] In a letter to the *Washington Post*, a woman expressed deep misgivings about youthful interracial liaisons, declaring that "the modern high school lunchroom is more like a noontime nightclub—with all the hand holding, canned music and going steady."[22] A Virginia segregationist made it plainer still in a 1955 school board campaign, declaring that "unwise attachments can be and often are formed during school years that can result in mixed marriages or worse."[23] Such charges were calculated to incite panic in communities across the region.[24]

White demagogues fanned popular fears about youth from different races engaging in activities that even hinted of intimacy. Bigoted agitators played prominent roles in the incidents at Milford, Clinton, and in other conflicts over high schools. White youth were readily mobilized in defense of the status quo, particularly young men, many clearly disposed to aggressive displays of hateful resistance to integration.[25] Given these circumstances, it is little wonder that high schools became flash points over school integration. Because they brought young people together in a setting believed to be conducive to familiarity, often arousing the combustible passions of youth, early battles over Southern high schools could be particularly volatile. This made the prospects of desegregation appear rather uncertain in the latter 1950s, despite the significance of *Brown* and growing national sentiment against segregated schooling.

Following these early battles, however, the pace of desegregation moved forward gradually with fewer violent outbursts. Extremist conspirators eventually were arrested, tried, and jailed in Tennessee and elsewhere. School bombings in Georgia and other states occasioned widespread condemnation, and helped to persuade moderate Whites to tolerate token integration.[26] Clinton, Tennessee, eventually became a model of success in the national media.[27] But the pace of change was slow and widespread advances in desegregation failed to materialize. The Parker Doctrine held that districts only needed to make the possibility of integration available, permitting students to attend schools regardless of race, and state and local authorities quickly developed an array of measures to make comprehensive desegregation difficult to achieve. These included elaborate procedures for approval to transfer, intimidation tactics to deter Black families from participating, and locating new facilities within White or Black neighborhoods so enrollment trends would follow housing patterns. Extreme pressure was placed on the few Black students who dared to spearhead integration efforts, including almost constant harassment and threats of violence.[28] And when these steps did not succeed in maintaining segregation, Whites simply moved away.

Atlanta was among the first lower South cities to undertake a voluntary transfer plan. Beginning in 1961, after several years of dispute, it was restricted to students in the final 2 years of high school. Just nine Black students were admitted to White schools in the first year, out of more than 250 who applied, but authorities ensured that the transition occurred without incident and the program expanded thereafter.[29] Eventually, larger numbers of African American students transferred to certain White schools, but these became majority-Black institutions within a few years. When this process finally succeeded in enabling students to leave overcrowded Black schools, Whites responded by abandoning the institutions in question. In the words of one historian, it became a matter of proceeding "from segregation to segregation."[30] This was repeated elsewhere as other large districts instituted similar programs in response to federal pressures. In this way, the number of predominantly Black secondary schools began to grow. It was a pattern that would soon become evident in districts across the country where voluntary transfer plans became the focal point of desegregation.[31]

For many African Americans, progress was painfully slow in the years immediately following *Brown*. Utilizing the National Survey of Black Americans (NSBA), economists Michael Boozer, Alan Krueger, and Sari Wolkon concluded that little meaningful integration occurred in the South prior to the mid-1960s, and our own analysis of NSBA data indicates that this was true for elementary and high schools alike.[32] In border states, desegregation was more substantial, but African Americans were highly urbanized and voluntary integration produced just transitory effects in most desegregated schools. In the North and West, integration of secondary schools remained elusive as well, especially as the Black population became concentrated in central city neighborhoods. As historic as the *Brown* decision may have been, its immediate national impact on segregation was modest.

CHANGING HIGH SCHOOLS IN KANSAS CITY

Located near the middle of the continental United States, Kansas City, Missouri, displayed influences of both the North and South in its schools and other institutions. The state mandated segregated schooling prior to 1954, but under pressure from civil rights organizations, the city banned discrimination in other public facilities in 1951 and established a Human Relations Commission. Although much of the White population retained historically prejudicial attitudes, growing numbers supported liberal reform in race relations during the postwar era.[33] Kansas City offers an instructive example of educational change, in that case, demonstrating both the success of high school desegregation and its ultimate demise in a setting representative of the country's larger metropolitan areas.

Kansas City moved quickly after *Brown* to desegregate its schools. On July 29, 1954, its school board eliminated the dual system by establishing new school boundaries, although a plan reassigning students irrespective of race was not unveiled until 1955, starting in the fall. The *Kansas City Star* declared after a year, somewhat prematurely, that "racial integration, a big question mark in September, has proceeded smoothly . . . difficulties have been few considering the fact that there are mixed classes in 40 schools and integrated faculties in three."[34] Still, it was believed to be a momentous step, especially for the schools most immediately affected, such as Central High, the city's oldest public high school. In its 1956 yearbook, the *Centralian*, Principal Paul M. Marshall declared:

> Central has had another great moment this year, and those of us who have been privileged to live it have known the determination of students and faculty that the integration program should succeed at Central. Never once did the leaders of our student body fail to stand fast in their determination that it would succeed. This has been the most interesting year I have experienced in 35 years of educational administration.[35]

Although this may have been Marshall's "most interesting" experience, and it seemed to be an easy transition, it was only the beginning of a process that would transform Central from White to nearly all-Black in less than a decade. Shifting residential patterns changed its clientle, particularly as neighborhoods surrounding it became increasingly African American. This transition also represented greater opportunities for students in the city's historically Black schools, which had become extremely overcrowded, with the advent of access to formerly White institutions.[36] Central's experience, it turned out, would become characteristic of many urban secondary schools, in both the North and South.

Following *Brown* it was widely believed that race relations in Kansas City were generally positive, contributing to what appeared to be a relatively smooth process of school desegregation. Despite the city's legacy of segregation, there seemed to be little overt resistance to the *Brown* decision. But as in other cities, Kansas City neighborhoods had become highly segregated, so even when dual school boundaries were dropped, most schools remained mainly Black or White. By the late 1950s, for example, most Black secondary students still attended Lincoln or Manual high schools, traditionally Black institutions, while only about 10% of new students entering East High were African American, and the school remained principally White through the 1960s. Racial residential patterns dictated this division. Schools serving neighborhoods occupied by the most affluent Whites remained largely immune to integration.[37] This was true at Southwest High, located in a White upper-middle-class neighborhood. Southwest students were known for excelling in athletics and academic achievement and, after graduating, going to the nation's best colleges. The 1964 and 1966 editions of its yearbook showed just one Black faculty member and fewer than 10 Black students, indicating only token integration.[38] Although Black enrollment may have started smoothly at Central and a few other institutions, longer-term prospects were hardly promising.

Schools like Central, previously all-White but located near the city center and in neighborhoods increasingly occupied by Blacks, typically experienced rapid integration. The city's burgeoning African American population, growing from 55,682 to 83,130 during the 1950s, was being displaced by urban renewal into central city areas increasingly perceived as "Black neighborhoods."[39] This trend would continue into the next decade as the Black population pushed to the south and east, raising African American enrollment at Paseo High, just a few miles south of Central, and Southeast High, located farther east. Students were assigned to buildings that served their neighborhoods, and as the population changed, so did the racial profile of schools. Students, however, were allowed to request transfers if they wanted to attend a different institution, and transfers were sought by growing numbers of Whites as the population shifted. In a 1971 report, a local task force concluded that "transfer policies have regularly permitted white parents to remove their children from schools in racially changing neighborhoods and place them in predominantly white schools."[40] Although district policy stipulated that such transfers were not to be utilized for "discriminatory" purposes, such requests were rarely questioned. Administrators and board members feared that challenging them on a large scale could trigger a political backlash and losing more Whites to the suburbs, outcomes they clearly wanted to avoid.[41]

Central's integration started with a few Black students who gradually became included in school activities. The administrative staff and most teachers continued to be White, but there was a measured transition in school activities and the curriculum that reflected the changing population. There were reports of a cross being burned at the start of the school year in 1955, but no other such incidents appear to have occurred afterward. As suggested in Principal Marshall's remarks, however, the school's administration and White student leaders were highly cognizant of the threat of conflict, and worked quietly to preclude it.[42] Although the first group of African American students was small, there were no reports of harassment from hostile Whites. By and large, the first year of "integration" in Kansas City's first public high school appears to have gone quite smoothly.

This situation extended to subsequent years, when the number of African American students began to increase. Student pictures in the 1957 *Centralian* indicate that only 10% of the graduating class was African American, but there was a steady influx in the lower grades and they began to integrate the school's activities. In the 1958 yearbook, there were no Black teachers pictured and no Black students listed in the school's social clubs or literary societies, but Black students had increased their visibility in other activities: 5 of 15 orchestra members, 7 of the 32 Zoology Club members, and 4 of 20 in the French Club. This was a substantial degree of integration in activities that had long defined the extracurricular and social life of the school. As in other desegregating high schools, Central's sports teams also featured a good representation of African American athletes. In many respects, the years between 1954 and 1960 marked an interlude of apparently successful integration at Central, like the initial period of desegregation at other urban high schools.[43]

The transition to a becoming a predominantly Black institution, however, began to unfold rapidly. By 1960, more than half Central's students were Black and in the ensuing years they came to dominate its student profile, constituting more than 98% by 1963. This change reflected the movement of African Americans south and east, as their numbers grew rapidly in the city. It also meant that Whites were moving out of the area. Teachers and administrators changed more gradually, an issue touched upon in Chapter 4. At the start of the decade, only a dozen of the school's 79 teachers were African American, but by 1965 barely half were White. This, too, was more rapid change than in the past, partly a result of district efforts to racially balance its teaching staff. But it also reflected greater teacher turnover; as the student body shifted, so did the faculty. At the same time, the *Centralian* reported a new addition to the building for vocational training and to relieve overcrowding. In subsequent years, practical nursing, electronics, and military science programs became more prominent, signaling a vocational curricular orientation. Eventually, Central would be identified as an academically underperforming school, one serving many students labeled "educationally disadvantaged."[44]

Other schools south and east of the city center underwent similar transitions, from White to integrated to predominantly African American. The transitions occurred because Whites abandoned the schools as they left the vicinity. Such movement was not altogether new, as families always were moving in and out of city neighborhoods. But now White households failed to replace those departing; the new residents were largely African American. South and west of the historic Troost Avenue "wall" separating Black and White areas of the city, affluent White neighborhoods remained racially inviolate and stable.[45] As noted earlier, Paseo High followed Central's path to desegregation and then resegregation as a predominantly Black school in the early to mid-1960s. Large numbers of African Americans eventually enrolled in Southeast High as well.

West of Troost, Southwest High remained the city's most elite public secondary institution, and its last to be integrated. In 1958, Southwest was counted among the top 40 high schools in the nation in terms of National Merit Finalists, and the school play, *Panorama of USA*, included a blackface minstrel act. A few African American students had trickled into the school, but there was little recognition of the broader issue of racial integration. The 1961 edition of its yearbook depicted students safely isolated from broader political and social issues. It noted that despite "the Congo crisis, Castro's Cuba, and Khrushchev's capers" and some debate about Kennedy's narrow presidential victory over Nixon, the students were "comparatively unmoved in their own Southwest environment."[46]

For schools like Southwest, racial integration scarcely seemed to exist in the 1960s, and district leaders did little to change it. Yet the city's expanding African American neighborhoods were among the factors fueling a steady exodus of Whites from Kansas City schools. By the middle of the decade, Blacks were becoming concentrated in largely segregated institutions. Although many Whites were leaving, especially those with children, they remained the largest group of voters and were reluctant to support the district as it became increasingly African American. Tellingly, 1969 marked not only the year when the school population became predominantly Black but also the last time voters approved a school levy.[47] Kansas City's experience demonstrated how racial integration in the cities, particularly in the North where it was expected to proceed relatively smoothly, encountered residential segregation, escalating numbers of poor students, White flight, and declining school revenues. These issues invariably affected the secondary schools serving African American students, and public perceptions of their quality.

In 1965, the district enrolled 18,500 secondary students, one-third Black, yet its high schools remained largely segregated and those schools serving African Americans were often overcrowded.[48] Responding to low test scores and higher dropout rates in predominantly Black schools, the district had announced a "compensatory education" program focused on Lincoln High and its feeder elementary schools.[49] This program marked the start of a series of efforts to address educational problems of Black students, each well intentioned but also contributing to the stigma attached to predominantly African American institutions. The district's leadership offered plans to integrate the schools and the departure of middle-class and affluent Whites continued. The school board tabled systemwide desegregation plans prior to the latter 1970s, and critics argued that enrollment was continually shifted to maintain racial divisions between schools.[50] As noted in a 1971 task force assessment, "Plans that may have given encouragement to integration efforts have been consistently rejected."[51] An influential U.S. Civil Rights Commission report, *Racial Isolation in the Schools*, characterized this response as typical. More often than not, the authors noted, school districts tended "to perpetuate, rather than reduce, separation in the schools."[52]

Protest and controversy over segregation in schools began in the early 1960s, with Black and White activists, including members of the Congress on Racial Equality (CORE), launching pickets and sit-ins at school board offices, demanding greater integration. The district had adopted an "intact busing policy" to relieve overcrowded schools, with Blacks attending White institutions but remaining in separate classrooms. This measure was employed in other cities, and like these districts, Kansas City steadfastly refused to go any further toward a systematic desegregation policy.[53] In 1970, a group of Black students being bused to predominantly White Northeast High marched to the district office to protest violence from Whites and lack of police protection.[54] Their grievances eventually were resolved, but the incident was symptomatic of an uncoordinated and piecemeal approach to desegregation. As in other districts, Kansas City's hand was finally forced when federal mandates required the district to begin busing more students in the 1970s. In the meantime, little change occurred in the racial profile of the city's high schools.[55]

In 1970, the numbers of Kansas City White and Black high school students were nearly even, but 85% of African Americans attended institutions that were 80% or more Black. Southwest High, on the other hand, enrolled just 18 Blacks in a student body of nearly 2,400, a profile similar to other predominantly White institutions in the city. Only two of the city's 10 large high schools, East and Westport, had majority-White student bodies and more than 40 African Americans. Seven years later, to comply with court-ordered desegregation, the district finally attempted to address the issue, but by then much of its White student population had departed. Ultimately, the school board tried to enjoin neighboring suburban districts in a solution to longstanding problems of segregation, finding expression in the federal case *Missouri v. Jenkins*, one of the most ambitious, expensive, and legally contentious desegregation plans of the era.[56]

Despite its relatively calm beginning with school integration, Kansas City eventually joined other communities across the country where desegregation was marked by social protest, violence, and federal intervention. As in Atlanta and other cities, a liberal transfer policy that allowed students to attend high schools by choice made it possible for Whites to flee as the numbers of African Americans grew. Consequently, genuine integration turned out to be a short-lived experience for Kansas City's African American youth, extending for just a few years before formerly White high schools became nearly all-Black. Apart from a few institutions where Blacks and Whites attended together, the city's high schools remained sharply divided by race.

Although Black youth may have gained additional options for secondary school following 1954, when they were limited to just two institutions, public perceptions of the additional schools had been compromised. Paralyzed by worries about angering Whites and contributing to their "flight," school board members and district administrators deflected or ignored demands for greater integration as a remedy to the poor quality of education for African American youth. A 1974 report by the Midwest Research Institute found that "a state of caution that bordered on catatonic" existed among educators in the city because of conflict over school integration.[57] Given this dynamic, with Whites fleeing cities and Black community leaders demanding integration, it was difficult to avoid the conclusion that most city high schools were institutions of last resort, choices that serious students would avoid if possible. Such was the stigma that came to be attached to African American secondary schools in the nation's largest cities, partly a consequence of a failure to realize integration in a stable fashion.

DESEGREGATION AND PROTEST ACROSS THE NORTH

Desegregation efforts during the 1960s and the 1970s began with calls for more equity in resources and relief from overcrowding in African American schools, and shifted to more strident demands for integration to bring about equality in education. Parents and community organizations across the country, but especially in large cities, resorted to public forms of protest such as boycotts and pickets to highlight their concerns.[58] On the 10th anniversary of *Brown*, more than 10,000 Milwaukee Black students boycotted schools to protest de facto segregation, and similar demonstrations occurred in New York.[59] These and related demonstrations were organized by adults, but students were ready participants.[60] It was an era marked by ongoing conflict over civil rights, and school desegregation became a major point of contention.

Responding to the slow process of integration, the Kennedy administration recommended that the 1963 Civil Rights Bill include a title authorizing Justice Department action against schools and other institutions abetting segregation, and support for desegregation initiatives.[61] When approved, Title IV of the Civil Rights Act established a powerful source of pressure for reform, particularly in the South but eventually in districts across the country. Civil rights organizations offered new plans, such as combining Black and White districts in adjoining areas, and a range of other approaches was considered.[62] By 1970, there appeared to be widespread public support for integration, given voice by religious leaders and approval in polls, with many endorsing enforcement of desegregation orders, at least in principle.[63] Most favored racial integration with free-choice transfers between schools in adjoining neighborhoods. But such measures generally proved ineffective, and lawsuits were filed demanding more aggressive approaches, such as changing neighborhood attendance policies.[64] By the end of the 1960s, voluntary transfer plans were giving way to more systematic and compulsory measures, and this would weaken popular resolve. These steps added controversy and much of the resulting public concern revolved around high schools.

New federal initiatives paved the way for more lawsuits against Northern school districts and coincided with growing protest against racial segregation. In Boston, most African American secondary students stayed home to protest segregation and the city's school committee's refusal to address it.[65] A similar demonstration occurred in Chicago, involving even more students.[66] Boycotts, marches, and other protests over desegregation were reported in New Jersey, Ohio, New York, and Wisconsin.[67] Thousands stayed home in Gary, Indiana, demanding, among others things, a citywide integration policy.[68] In New York, a massive boycott kept 464,000 students out of school to reprove the board for sidestepping integration demands.[69] Although New York had few predominantly Black high schools, parents in Harlem demanded integration of junior highs, declaring that segregated schooling was inferior to integrated education. Similar sentiments were expressed elsewhere. Eighty percent of the students in Cincinnati's predominantly Black schools and 40% of those enrolled in Cambridge, Massachusetts, Black schools stayed home for boycotts.[70] In the battle for educational equity in the North, integration clearly inspired a strong endorsement from African Americans, and youth in particular.

In many instances, however, desegregation also met active resistance from Whites. When integration was attempted in historically White secondary schools, parent groups often objected. White parents in Chicago, for instance, denounced "racial violence" that allegedly included physical assault and shooting, leading to a boycott of recently integrated Tilden High for 4 days.[71] At Gage Park High, parents of White students demanded that the district transfer 600 African Americans to the all-Black Englewood High.[72] Bogan High on the city's southwest side was a notorious site of White opposition to desegregation, and parents successfully lobbied school officials to block the transfer of African Americans into the school. This sort of resistance meant that Blacks often encountered hostile environments when they came to new institutions. These were hardly circumstances that encouraged racial harmony. Chicago was infamous for antagonism to nearly any form of integration, but similar conflicts occurred elsewhere. In Detroit, the transfer of 314 Blacks to White schools in 1960 to alleviate overcrowding led angry White parents to keep more than 1,200 children at home.[73] A few years later, Whites in New York boycotted schools to protest integration plans and busing in particular.[74] News reports in the 1970s noted that boycotts by Whites were threatened in Denver and San Francisco.[75] Racial integration often evoked sharp reaction from parents who felt threatened, and not just in the South.

Initial Northern desegregation efforts stalled in the face of permissive school transfer policies, continued residential segregation, White flight, and growing resistance in key cities. A *Chicago Tribune* article reported in 1972 that despite a decade of efforts at school desegregation, a majority of Chicago schools (61%) were either 95% Black or White, and that less than a third of the district's students were White.[76] Overall, Whites were leaving the system faster than African Americans were entering.[77] In other large cities, the press noted that the number of Blacks attending majority-White schools decreased, and civil rights journalist John Herbers described overall desegregation in the North as only "voluntary and token."[78] Other commentators agreed, and tied the process to the movement of middle-class Whites to the suburbs. As desegregation expert Gary Orfield observed, "The effects on public schools are dramatic," as some 13 million people left central cities in the nation's largest metropolitan areas.[79] As the U.S. Commission on Civil Rights later established, "The relative loss of white students was greatest in those districts that had a higher proportion of black enrollment."[80] The pattern of change described in Kansas City high schools earlier was evident across the country.

As voluntary transfer plans proved to be ineffective, the most commonplace strategy for addressing segregation in the latter 1960s became busing students to schools outside their neighborhoods. This occurred everywhere, but affected public opinion most decisively outside the South. Following the 1973 Supreme Court *Keyes* decision, which ruled busing a viable option for overcoming de facto segregation, court-ordered desegregation plans led to more fervor, principally from Whites who objected to "forced busing."[81] Although busing may have had support from the courts, it was not always feasible and was widely denounced by conservative politicians. In some cities, such as Atlanta, plans were scrapped because of residential segregation. Political opponents held that busing should be used as a "last resort" and then only to correct "proven unlawful acts of discrimination." NAACP leader Roy Wilkins described this stance as an "unconscionable assault upon the rule of law,"[82] and it was also condemned by the U.S. Commission on Civil Rights, which argued that desegregation succeeded when supported by community leaders and elected officials.[83] Advocates for integration endorsed the idea that busing was an answer to persistent segregation, and battle lines were drawn.

The public, however, seemed to favor the conservative view. A survey of Chicago residents found that while most Black and White parents supported integration and agreed that Black schools offered lower-quality education, one-third of Black parents and four-fifths of Whites opposed busing children to racially different neighborhoods, responses mirroring national reactions.[84] Although popular opinion continued to favor integration in principle and only a minority of Whites opposed it, the thought of sending children into potentially hostile settings proved alarming to many. Parallel surveys in other cities produced similar results.[85] Busing presented a resolution to the problems of voluntary transfer programs, but made the question of desegregation even more controversial. It quickly became a national issue, a flash point of controversy across the country.[86] Widespread opposition to integration no longer was limited to the South.

Boston became the site of the nation's most volatile anti-busing campaign, although at the high school level most of the controversy concerned just two institutions: South Boston and Charlestown. In 1975, U.S. District Court Judge Wendell Garrity ruled that school authorities had deliberately maintained a segregated system, and anti-busing activists staged a "day of mourning" when the court placed South Boston High in receivership.[87] Garrity imposed an integration plan at the school calling for 1,094 Whites and 358 Blacks to be bused, but attendance the following year fell to 425 and 130, respectively.[88] This began a prolonged and vehement campaign of resistance by Whites, focused on the city's South Side. Mayor Kevin White described busing as the "single most explosive issue in America," and a local journalist observed that it could turn "peaceful, middle-class mothers into street brawlers and normally straight-forward politicians into cowards."[89] But Boston proved to be an anomaly with regard to violent public protest, at least in terms of sustained conflict. While Whites certainly demonstrated vigorously elsewhere, other cities did not experience the same degree of hostility.

Regardless of desegregation's local reception, the merits of racial integration and busing remained hotly contested in the national media, and the discourse that surrounded it often highlighted obstacles to desegregation rather than its advantages.[90] One issue was the increasing numbers of African Americans entering large public school systems and their concentration in certain neighborhoods. As noted earlier, this was largely the result of migration, but the arrival of these largely poor students posed challenges for urban districts. In some areas, their numbers doubled or nearly tripled within a few years,[91] prompting strategies such as the use of mobile units and double shifts in schools. As in earlier years, this contributed to deteriorating buildings, adding to perceptions that Black schools were inferior and that integration would compromise the education of Whites. This added to the rancor over desegregation, sparked private school enrollment, and accelerated White flight. Many Whites claimed that moving away from public schools was not to avoid integration but to find quality schooling for their children, and some noted that even African Americans preferred private institutions.[92] Deteriorating conditions, along with violence, protest, and picketing spotlighted in the media, lent credence to the impression that desegregation posed a threat to children.

Although strife in Boston and a few other places focused national attention on controversy, elsewhere busing plans were greeted with considerably less turmoil. In Cincinnati, more than 600 people were arrested for violent protest against a desegregation plan,[93] but busing started relatively smoothly in nearby Dayton. The same was true of Cleveland, Milwaukee, Detroit, and a number of other larger cities in the mid-1970s. As political scientist Jennifer Hochschild later observed, widespread support from city leaders made desegregation plans more likely to succeed, a point also made by others at the time.[94] A bigger problem lay in the longer-term process of suburbanization, which continued to draw Whites out of central city neighborhoods throughout the 1970s. In the 1974 *Milliken v. Bradley* decision concerning metropolitan Detroit, the Supreme Court ruled that suburban districts were not accountable for segregation in city schools and thus could not be compelled to participate in cross-district busing plans.[95] This decision effectively compromised future efforts to achieve integrated schools, as the number of White students in most big-city school systems dwindled. With relatively few remaining to make integration possible, the pace of desegregation slowed toward the close of the decade.

In the end, Northern desegregation was limited by the unwillingness of Whites to attend school with African Americans in significant numbers, a telling sign of racial prejudice and perceptions of school quality. It became manifest in segregation across the region's larger cities in the 1960s, only temporarily reversed with systematic busing plans in the 1970s. As large public systems became populated by racial minorities, integration without busing across metropolitan areas became even more difficult. Critics claimed that racially integrating schools was pointless when housing remained segregated and Whites left the cities. Describing resegregation, a *Chicago Tribune* columnist argued that schools were simply powerless to integrate in the face of attitudes and population shifts that were larger than the education system itself. Many parents, educators, and community members agreed, suggesting that schools could not be expected to change longstanding problems in society at large.[96]

The U.S. Commission on Civil Rights reported that a majority of districts outside the South underwent significant desegregation between 1965 and 1975, but cities with large Black populations experienced it the least. It was in these settings where conflict over the schools was greatest, and White flight was most likely to occur.[97] The large cities, of course, were where most African Americans outside the South lived, and voluntary transfer programs often made it especially difficult to integrate high schools. As a number of studies have shown, Whites almost never chose to attend predominantly Black schools, and when African Americans in a largely White school approached majority, White flight may have accelerated.[98] Given these dynamics, integration remained an elusive goal. In fact, as indicated in Table 5.1, African American secondary students outside the South appear to have become more segregated with time.

By the latter 1970s, Northern and Western high schools serving communities with large numbers of African Americans were usually Black or White. As suggested in Table 5.1, by the 1970s, African American youth were considerably more concentrated in majority-Black secondary institutions than their predecessors in earlier decades. Segregation was even more pronounced in the cities. According to NSBA data, African Americans who grew up in large non-Southern cities in the 1970s were nearly twice as likely to attend a majority-Black high school as were those who grew up a decade earlier. Whereas about half of respondents who were teens in the 1960s reported attending such schools, two-thirds from the 1970s did so.[99] This indicates that Kansas City was not unusual. Although the movement of Blacks into historically White institutions created brief periods of integration, and opened new opportunities for secondary schooling, integrated education was rarely enduring. This was a bitter lesson for African Americans who had placed so much faith in school integration as a path to educational equity. For many Black high school students in particular, it pointed to the limits of integration as a strategy for social and educational reform.

PYRRHIC VICTORY IN THE SOUTH

In the South, where hundreds of secondary institutions for African Americans had been built and expanded in the postwar era, the majority of high schools remained segregated into the latter 1960s. According to estimates by Clotfelter, more than 90% of Black secondary students in Southern (non-border) states attended segregated institutions in the 1950s, a number that fell to 70% in the 1960s.[100] The latter figure reflects a striking decline in segregated schools in the decade's latter years, and by the early 1970s, most of the region's African American secondary stu-

TABLE 5.1. Distribution of African American Secondary School Students by School Racial Composition, by Decade, NSBA Respondents Growing Up in the North or West, 1950–1980 (in percentages)

School Composition	1950s	1960s	1970s
All Black	15	15	22
Majority Black	23	26	36
Evenly Divided	28	23	19
Majority White	28	29	19
Nearly All White	6	7	4

Sample size=473 (101 in 1950s, 217 in 1960s, 155 in 1970s)
Source: National Survey of Black Americans, 1940–1980. Inter-University Consortium for Political and Social Research, University of Michigan, 1997.

dents attended integrated institutions. Gary Orfield has characterized this as a virtual revolution in Southern education, much of which occurred in a few years.[101]

Passage of Title IV of the 1964 Civil Rights Act gave federal authorities broad powers to promote and enforce school integration, signaling the eventual end of formal segregation in Southern public education. The Elementary and Secondary Education Act, approved a year later, provided considerable government aid to schools, making politicians and educators noticeably more responsive to demands that segregation be ended. Finally, unanimous Supreme Court decisions in 1968 and 1969, *Green v. New Kent County* and *Alexander v. Holmes County*, ruled against a voluntary secondary school transfer plan in Virginia and demanded immediate enforcement of desegregation orders in Mississippi. The threat of denying financial assistance to schools, along with judicial resolve in these rulings, led many Southern Whites to conclude that further resistance to integration was impractical. Diehard opponents chose to send their children to a growing number of "segregation academies" and other private schools, sometimes backed with public funds, and continued to denounce federal mandates. But others eventually acquiesced to the necessity of integration, if not the principle. A new day was dawning in Southern education.

Big changes did not take long to arrive. By 1972, more than a third of all Black students in the South attended predominantly White schools, and the number attending schools less than 90% African American was approaching half (reaching 75% by 1980). NSBA data suggest that figures for high school students were similar. Fewer than 10% of Southern NSBA respondents reported attending all-Black institutions in this period.[102] As indicated in Table 5.2, African Americans in the South during the 1970s were far less likely to attend majority-Black high schools than had been the case in earlier decades. Altogether, fewer than a third of African Americans attended majority-Black schools in the South, as opposed to 70% in the 1960s and 96% in the 1950s. Despite variation from one state to another, the direction of change was unambiguous. In fact, because segregation was increasing in the North and West, the South quickly became the most integrated region of the country. More than a century of segregationist policy had been overturned in a short time, and it readily became evident in the region's high schools.

This remarkable development would eventually help improve educational outcomes for thousands of Black students, but the immediate effect was to pose a number of problems. Because the change occurred so quickly, often under deadlines imposed by federal authorities, adjustments had to be made by teachers, students, and communities rather abruptly. The first order of business was dismantling the dual school systems maintained historically for Blacks and Whites. Schools were consolidated, students reassigned, teachers and other personnel reallocated, and redundant or unnecessary resources (including teachers) purged. Determining just how this was to be accomplished turned out to be a highly sensitive process, as both Blacks and Whites had made considerable financial and emotional investments in local institutions, particularly high schools, which were often focal points of community pride.

In rare instances, historically Black schools were integrated by Whites, which either created a White minority or a racially balanced student body, depending on local residential patterns. The most common pattern, at least at the outset, was to retain existing White facilities for use as senior high schools and assign African Americans to them, where they typically became a highly visible minority. For many Black students, this meant saying farewell to schools they had known in their immediate communities. Black high schools were often converted to junior highs or elementary schools with mixed student bodies. The loss of Black teachers and administrators was yet another point of concern.[103]

Decisions about how to integrate schools were often controversial, especially if it meant closing or changing the status of African American institutions that had existed for decades. Factors cited in favor of utilizing White high schools included their superior facilities, larger size, and more desirable locations, characteristics that African Americans had noted in making demands for integration. As noted earlier, many African American high schools were highly regarded because of the care and concern that educators devoted to students. Fearful of losing the benefits of their institutions' positive qualities, some communities actively resisted the assignment of their youth to local White high schools and the shuttering of Black schools. In Alexandria, Virginia, for instance, Black parents staged a successful boycott to resist a plan to bus "surplus" African Americans to maintain "racial ratios" favoring Whites in city high schools.[104] In other

TABLE 5.2. Distribution of African American Secondary Students by School Racial Composition, by Decade, NSBA Respondents Growing Up in Southern (Non-Border) States (in percentages)

School Composition	1950s	1960s	1970
All Black	90	60.0	9
Majority Black	6	10	21
Evenly Divided	2	13	37
Majority White	1	15	29
Nearly All White	1	2	4

Sample size=562 (163 in 1950s, 240 in 1960s, 159 in 1970s)
Source: National Survey of Black Americans, 1940–1980. Inter-University Consortium for Political and Social Research, University of Michigan, 1997.

instances, resistance to change was more sporadic and focused on particular issues, such as the fate of Black educators.[105] But all such conflicts represented one degree or another of a disquieting anxiety that many African Americans felt with the integration of high schools, especially when closing familiar institutions and sending students into alien and potentially hostile settings.

Katie Hawkins's experience illustrates the difficulties many African Americans faced as schools were being integrated. Katie, who graduated in 1974, recalled starting her sophomore year at Perry County Attendance Center in Mississippi, a segregated school built in 1961. A product of school consolidation and equalization, this facility was a source of community pride. It was relatively new, teachers were caring and supported by parents, discipline problems were few, and it had a good band and other activities. But with integration, Katie was bused to New Augusta High, 15 miles from home and, according to Katie, "old, run-down" and where she was "just a number." Race relations were tense at New Augusta, and when Katie earned the highest average in her senior class, the White principal reluctantly made her valedictorian, publicly apologizing to the White runner-up and naming her "star pupil." Concerns over potential conflict were so great that Katie's father invited friends from the NAACP to attend her graduation.[106]

There were many other such conflicts. Historian David Cecelski has described the remarkable 3-year struggle to preserve a Black secondary school, starting in 1968 in coastal Hyde County, North Carolina. The O. A. Peay School eventually became an integrated elementary school but it was the center of a celebrated community-based struggle. In Tuscumbia, Alabama, historic Trenholm High was closed in 1969 after operating for some 90 years, and its students were assigned to previously White Deshler High. Many teachers were dismissed, and longstanding traditions of the school were discarded. In 1970, students across Georgia protested desegregation plans that threatened Black educators and institutions in 1970.[107] In Austin, Texas, historically Black Anderson High was closed in 1971 after federal authorities ordered busing to achieve integration. Like most other Southern Black institutions, Anderson was unable to attract White students in the district's earlier voluntary transfer integration program.[108] Rather than attempting to force students to attend the school, the district simply closed it, arguing that to bus Whites would only cause them to leave the city or attend private schools. It was a logic that prevailed in many such cases. As Cecelski has noted, the typical result was a bitter outcome of desegregation for Black communities throughout the South. Although a degree of equity had been gained, something quite valuable was also lost.[109] In this respect desegregation was a pyrrhic victory indeed.

Between the latter 1960s and early 1970s, there were dozens of disputes about closing Black institutions across the country. Many found their way into the courts, where clear standards of judgment evolved in such cases. Within this body of case law, arbitrary decisions to close Black schools and reassign their students to predominantly White institutions were generally held impermissible if such actions were found to be discriminatory in intent or held White interests over those of African Americans. *Brice v. Landis* became an important precedent in 1969, when Pittsburg, California, proposed to close Black institutions because Whites objected to sending their children to a Black neighborhood. This was ruled discriminatory, as it clearly upheld a stigma attached to African Americans, contrary to Supreme Court rulings in *Green* and *Brown*.[110] If Black institutions were to be closed during desegregation, the courts held that it must be primarily for educational advantage, operational efficiency, or to enhance the effective use of resources, and not for prejudicial purposes.

In the end, however, the courts did not prevent many districts from closing Black high schools in favor of larger, better equipped, or more centrally located White institutions. The very fact that so many such cases appeared, however, indicated the scope of conflict over this issue, pointing to the widespread propensity of districts to shutter Black institutions when faced with desegregation orders. African American communities were clearly attached to their schools, and fearful of the reception that Black students would find in historically White institutions. At the same time, districts were faced with a dilemma when Whites refused to enroll in Black institutions. This was the case in Austin's Anderson High when most Whites simply failed to show up at the start of school. In Charlotte, the historically Black West Charlotte High did not succeed in enrolling many Whites until it was reopened as a specialized magnet school. Even then, the support of prominent White community leaders was necessary to persuade many to consider it. Such forms of passive resistance were an essential reason why so many Black schools were closed. Although it is not clear just how many such disputes concerned high schools, it appears that threats to shutter secondary institutions inspired strong responses from African American communities, even though the schools were rarely saved.[111]

It seems that the fears and concerns of Black community members about predominantly White schools were well founded. In the South, some White teachers said they would accept at best only a few Black students into their classes, and teacher organizations often suggested that Black educators had received inferior training and were less effective.[112] Teachers also testified that integrated schools led to an increase in disciplinary problems, and that most involved Black children.[113] The overwhelming preponderance of these cases occurred in secondary institutions, where disciplinary action was more likely to entail suspension or expulsion. The incidence of such responses grew rapidly with desegregation, and they involved considerably more Black students than Whites.

Most such cases involved relatively minor infractions as tardiness, talking during class, running in hallways, or breaking other rules. In the words of one observer, they involved "trivial violations of the hidden curriculum; that is, rules with respect to authority or adhering to time schedules, silence and the like."[114] Studies from the 1970s found that African American students were two to four times more likely to be suspended than Whites, and that the numbers went up dramatically with desegregation plans. A report from the Southern Regional Council in 1973 warned about the effect of "an escalating rate of suspensions and expulsions," especially among Black students, both nationally and in the South. Deploring the tendency of some Blacks to drop out in the face of such measures, the authors described the effect as a "push out" of school. The "personal growth and future economic opportunity of young people," they concluded, "is jeopardized by such practices," which they saw as motivated by resistance to desegregation.[115]

In the 1975 case of *Goss v. Lopez*, the Supreme Court ruled that suspended or expelled students were supposed to receive written notification of charges and an opportunity to present their "side of the story," a decision widely interpreted as an effort to control the racial imbalance in disciplinary actions and to curtail their use in opposition to integration.[116] A number of other lawsuits were filed to challenge racially discriminatory patterns in suspensions and expulsions, but courts proved reluctant to intervene further in school disciplinary disputes. In *Hawkins v. Coleman*, the superintendent of the Dallas school system testified that the principal reason for his district's high rates of Black suspension and expulsion was "institutional racism," which led to a judgment against the schools. Even this had little immediate effect on policies and practices, however, as the court did not specify remedies to address the problem. As Judge Sarah Hughes noted, "No court can decree a change in attitudes," and while observers lamented her failure to take more decisive action, this view was symptomatic of judicial approaches to school discipline as a matter of equal rights. Short of completely restructuring the schools, or directly monitoring the conduct of teachers and administrators, the courts lacked a coherent policy response to the problem. Given the controversy that was then raging over busing, it is little wonder that the judiciary was reluctant to begin issuing orders about how to conduct school disciplinary measures on a daily basis.

Regardless of their eventual disposition, however, the appearance of these cases was additional evidence of the challenges faced by Black youth in the wake of desegregation. Large numbers of Black suspensions and expulsions appeared in many instances to be linked to the attitudes of Whites who were predisposed to view African Americans as prone to troublemaking, or simply out of place in historically White schools. For many Blacks, this was yet additional evidence of students being required to bear the principal burden of integration, and having little recourse in a rapidly changing school system.[117] In light of this, some questioned whether integration was the best strategy for improving Black education.

INTEGRATION AND STUDENT CONFLICT

As suggested in earlier chapters, Black and White students had fought periodically in earlier decades, especially at sporting events and other occasions without extensive adult supervision. These conflicts were more likely to occur outside the South, where Black schools competed with White institutions athletically, and groups could encounter one another in school. A different type of clash emerged after *Brown*, as African Americans and Whites started attending school together in greater numbers. Although incidents of violence in the early years of integration were more often precipitated by adults than students, this began to change after 1960.[118] Once the initial blush of controversy had passed, there was an uneasy and occasionally heated accommodation to life in an integrated setting.

In the opening years of the 1960s, the pattern of racial conflict in American high schools continued much as it had during previous decades, if at a somewhat higher level of fervor. Clashes between Black and White students were monitored closely by the African American press, and reports of outbreaks appeared regularly.[119] Some were cases of Whites attacking Blacks, particularly in newly integrated schools or those located in White neighborhoods. In Chicago, for instance, White teens attacked

Black students attending a 1963 graduation ceremony at Calumet High School, where a number of local institutions held commencement exercises in its unusually spacious auditorium. Witnesses reported a large number of Whites "pummeling helpless Negro youth." Similar attacks occurred at John Jay High in Brooklyn, which attracted growing numbers of Blacks in the district's transfer program.[120] On the other hand, Black students occasionally were the aggressors. A columnist for the *Chicago Defender* in 1962 described a "riot" after a Washington, DC, football game between Black and White schools. Apparently upset when their team lost, it was "roving bands of Negro kids who turned the stadium into a bloody battlefield." The shocked correspondent exclaimed, "Ironically, the explosive hate stemmed mostly from my own people." Even in the age of nonviolent civil rights protest, interracial conflict in schools sometimes took a brutal turn, and neither side could claim the moral high ground.[121]

If violence occurred intermittently in the early 1960s, the number and severity of incidents picked up appreciably with time. Gang warfare in "slum" areas of the big cities sometimes spilled into the schools, leading to calls for more security and a police presence.[122] Athletic events also continued to be flash points, especially when Black and White teams competed for championships, as occurred in a 1965 "melee" after a Chicago basketball game.[123] The year 1966 was particularly troublesome, with outbursts reported in Chicago, Los Angeles, Newark, and Manhattan and Brooklyn in New York. Some were "scuffles" involving relatively small numbers and others were "pitched battles" between larger groups, but all reflected mounting racial tensions as Blacks and Whites came into contact.[124] As it turns out, these were portents of even more widespread clashes to come.

The latter half of the 1960s was a time of upheaval and turmoil for African Americans. These years witnessed a fragmentation in the civil rights movement and hundreds of mass outbursts of violence and fury, popularly called "race riots," in urban Black communities across the country. This civil unrest intensified following the assassination of Martin Luther King Jr. in April 1968, when protesters staged angry demonstrations in many cities, looting and burning stores and other businesses.[125] Racial tensions ran high in the wake of these upheavals, which received extensive media coverage.[126] These events inevitably affected the atmosphere in schools, particularly urban secondary institutions. Educators worried about the examples that "rioters" offered to Black youth, but had few answers to the potential for interracial conflict between students.[127] Many schools eventually became battleground sites as Black and White teenagers vented their frustration over desegregation and a range of related issues.

Between 1968 and the early 1970s, racial conflict in high schools appears to have reached a peak in the United States. In the fall of 1970, a survey conducted by United Press International (UPI) found that more than 650 "racially motivated disturbances" had occurred in high schools across the country over the previous 15 months. A front-page story in the *Wall Street Journal* the following spring counted additional cases. Black and White students were the principal combatants in these incidents, although conflicts also were reported between Blacks and Puerto Ricans and Whites and Mexican American students. Officials in some districts reported that such disruptions were declining, while others felt they were on the increase. New York was the scene of almost constant clashes, with "scarcely a week going by without at least a couple of schools being closed to racial disorders." Violence also occurred in suburban areas with the advent of desegregation in those settings. Athletics continued to be critical points of conflict, often the result of "intense emotions aroused" during competition between Black and White schools.[128] Whenever large numbers of Black and White students came together in an atmosphere of rivalry or hostility, the results could be volatile.[129]

These disruptions occurred in a variety of localities and were provoked by a range of circumstances. At Chicago's Calumet High, several students were hurt and others arrested following a "melee" sparked by police attacking a lunchroom celebration of Malcolm X's birthday.[130] In Linden, New Jersey, a fight between two students escalated into a "riot" that spilled into the neighborhood, leading to property destruction and police from nearby towns being called.[131] Blacks entering New York's Canarsie High fought with hostile Whites after being threatened by "a waiting mob outside the school."[132] In Pittsburgh, Pennsylvania, White students loudly booed the first Black homecoming queen at West Miflin's North High, leading to a confrontation with African American athletes.[133] Twenty-one students were arrested at Dorsey High in Los Angeles following an altercation with teachers and administrators over charges of discrimination.[134] In 1969 and 1970, the *Chicago Defender* reported school closings due to racial conflict in Hamden, Connecticut; Ashville, North Carolina; Dayton, Ohio; New Brunswick, New Jersey; Panama City, Florida; Harrisburg, Pennsylvania; and Bogalusa, Louisiana.[135] Closings occurred in other episodes across the country.

As this pattern of conflict unfolded, incidents appear to have become more severe in many respects. A "rock throwing melee" broke out between more than 1,000 Black and White students in Manatee, Florida, following a lunchroom incident.[136] On New York's Long Island, it took three dozen police officers to break up a fight among more than 200 Black and White students, described as a "large scale riot" following an incident involving three individuals.[137] In Greenville, South Carolina, White parents reportedly smashed the windows of a newly integrated school while students fought inside, an incident triggered partly by Black demands that

"Dixie" no longer be played at athletic events, a sore point across the region.[138] More than 150 Black and White students "brawled" in Charlotte, North Carolina, for more than an hour; eventually, seven were arrested for possession of weapons, including rocks, bottles, and hammers.[139] Some 400 students "battled" in Savannah, Georgia, until police intervened with the use of tear gas.[140] In Boca Raton, Florida, Black and White students reportedly "fought with knives and fists, rocks and razors" at two schools over "white power" slogans. Eighteen were injured.[141] In Brooklyn, New York, several Black students were charged with attempted murder when they used knives to protect themselves from a hostile crowd.[142] As the extent of interracial conflict in high schools widened, passions escalated.

Educators in the schools struggled to contain such clashes, and there is evidence that African American students bore the brunt of their efforts. It was in this regard that inequities in suspensions and expulsions were perhaps most glaring. In the 1971 case of *Tillman v. Dade County School Board*, Black and White students were fighting when police pushed the Whites off campus while containing African Americans in the building. As a consequence, all but six of more than 90 students suspended were Black. The following year, another "general melee" between Black and White students in Jackson County, Florida, resulted in a comparable outcome: "Almost all of those disciplined were black." The experiences of Black students in other districts were similar, and the courts and other authorities did little to address the imbalance. Often fighting to defend themselves, African American students were more likely to face punishment—usually by being excluded from school—than White combatants.[143] Whether this had any effect on the incidence of such clashes is an open question, but it did little to make integration a pleasant or appealing process for African Americans.[144] It was a development fraught with conflict for the first groups of students to enter predominantly White schools, in all parts of the country. The determination of these Black students to confront the prejudicial treatment they encountered and to demand respect paved the way for those who followed.

INEQUITY WITHIN THE SCHOOLS

In the latter 1970s, it appears that the level of conflict in desegregated schools diminished appreciably. Reports in the Black press and other sources of clashes between students declined after 1975, a development that some have attributed to the arrival of students who had grown up with desegregation in elementary school.[145] Indeed, the late 1970s and 1980s may have been the high point of desegregated schooling in the United States, at least in terms of the numbers of students involved. Judging from studies conducted at the time and afterward, these years may have also represented something of a starting point for educators who were interested in understanding the challenges of working in integrated schools. As the period of conflict suggested, the problems of negotiating and managing racial interaction in these settings turned out to be far more difficult than most contemporaries had imagined. Rather than representing an end to battles for educational equity, the arrival of desegregation turned out to be the start of yet another struggle to realize the full potential of integrated institutions. It was a process that would extend well beyond the 1970s.

In their 2009 study of the graduates of integrated high schools from this era, sociologist Amy Stuart Wells and her collaborators found that Black and White students retained generally positive recollections about their experiences. Focusing on graduates from the class of 1980, most of whom started high school in 1976, they interviewed more than 500 individuals, including teachers and other community members, asking questions about various dimensions of their experiences and their subsequent reflections about integrated education. By and large, their respondents reported considerably more amicability in high school than their older brothers and sisters had encountered. In most of the schools, the years immediately preceding their arrival were marked by conflict and acrimony between Blacks and Whites, and in some cases Latino students as well. But by the time the class of 1980 arrived, the clashes of the immediate past were receding into institutional memory. In their place stood the new challenges of making integration work in spite of persistent racial inequities, which invariably affected the ways that students interacted.[146]

Researchers in the 1970s did not quite know what to make of desegregation, at least with respect to its effects on students. Although a range of studies were conducted, the research varied a great deal in methodological rigor and purview. Some showed that interracial contact seemed to make racial attitudes and tolerance grow worse, while others documented improvement. Such outcomes inevitably depended upon local circumstances, of course, and as suggested above, conditions in the schools changed with time. Certain findings, however, proved more enduring, particularly with respect to relationships between students from different racial groups. As sociologist Elizabeth Cohen concluded in 1975, there appeared to be a fundamental difficulty at play. Students exhibited a very strong tendency to form friendships with others of the same racial group. As a result, segregation was often re-created within the school, usually in settings where students could congregate informally or without oversight. It was a pattern, moreover, that proved remarkably resistant to adult intervention, as made clear in a range of studies, and did not take long to develop. As Cohen put it, "The school, as presently structured, does not present many opportunities for interracial interaction. Purely social groupings are likely to be racially segregated." This appeared to be true even in institutions where staff members worked conscientiously to encourage social interaction across racial lines.[147] While Black and White students may have ceased fighting in school cafeterias and parking lots, they were not spending much time in one another's company.

The problematic lack of interracial friendships among students in desegregated high schools emerged as one of the most intractable issues in the years that followed. It was aggravated, no doubt, by social class distinctions between students, and by differences in academic interests and backgrounds. Many Black students were tracked into courses with lower academic expectations, including various forms of remedial education, and it did not promote interaction between the groups. The larger problem often became a matter of social standing, with African Americans occupying the lower reaches of the status hierarchy in integrated institutions, even if tracking was not widely utilized. By and large, the social world of most high schools mirrored the class and race distinctions of the larger society, a point confirmed in a number of studies. As Cohen said, the organization of school curricula unintentionally helped to reinforce such distinctions. "Almost every subject," she wrote, "requires the student to exhibit reading, writing, or computational skills," and those "with a lower level of skills . . . will be perceived as having little academic ability in almost every class they attend, even where there is no tracking or ability grouping."[148] In short, the weaker academic preparation of many African American students placed them lower in the student status hierarchy in most institutions, making social interaction even more difficult.

Even when desegregation finally succeeded in bringing students together more or less affably, in that case, there is considerable evidence that interracial contact and exchange was often rather limited. In his study of interracial contact in schools, Clotfelter reported that the extent of within-school segregation in North Carolina after 1970 was greatest at the high school level, a pattern he attributed largely to the effects of tracking students into different classes. In fact, this type of racial separation accounted for the bulk of segregation in secondary schools. Moreover, Clotfelter found considerable evidence of segregation within extracurricular activities in schools, with Whites rarely participating in groups where they constituted a minority. This, of course, was consistent with patterns noted earlier, and the idea that status distinctions continued to shape student experiences in integrated high schools. It also undoubtedly reflected discriminatory attitudes on the part of Whites, and perhaps to a more limited extent, among Black students as well. For many of the latter, school integration was a somewhat mixed blessing. Although it had largely resolved the old problems of inferior facilities and curricular materials such as textbooks, it did not deliver on the promise of bringing students from different racial groups together on terms of general equality. In the words of Wells and her coauthors, many of these high schools were desegregated but not integrated.[149] Given this, it is little wonder that some Blacks began to reassess the benefits of desegregation, and to look back on the all-Black high schools of the past with a degree of nostalgia.

CONCLUSION: TRIAL BY FIRE

School integration was not an easy process in high schools; Black students and their adult supporters were repeatedly required to prove their commitment to educational equality. It was a trial fraught with discrimination and conflict, constrained by White flight and neighborhood segregation, and ultimately, it was compromised by persistent patterns of racial inequity within schools. In the 1940s and 1950s, integration was practiced only in the North and West, even if it was becoming less commonplace in certain cities. In border states, integrated schooling became a matter of choice immediately following *Brown*, leading to generally positive Black student experiences in cities such as Baltimore and Kansas City and to more harrowing encounters in Milford and Clinton. During this phase of desegregation, which began to affect Southern cities such as Atlanta after 1960, African Americans typically found greater acceptance from White students and educators when their numbers were relatively few. When Blacks became a larger part of the student body, Whites were frequently less inclined to accept them, and often abandoned the school. This was a familiar pattern throughout the 1960s and 1970s, as African Americans left the countryside to settle in cities. A small but growing Black suburban population experienced a similar process of school change in these years, as certain blue-collar suburbs became predominantly African American in larger metropolitan areas.[150]

The unrelenting experience of White flight inevitably became a source of considerable consternation for observers who had seen integration as the best hope for equal, high-quality schools. During the 1960s, Black students participated in demonstrations to demand greater access to predominantly White schools and greater equality in education. Eventually, federal and state authorities demanded comprehensive busing programs to address persistent segregation in communities across the country. Within a relatively short time in the early 1970s, a majority of African American secondary students found themselves in desegregated schools. The sudden change was difficult to negotiate both for the students and for their immediate communities. But following a rocky period of conflict and confusion, a more or less stable period of adjustment to newly integrated schools began to set in across the country, but especially in the South. As the *Chicago Tribune* noted, the percentage of African Americans attending majority-White schools in Southern states had doubled from 18% to 39% between 1968 and 1970, but had risen only from 3% to 3.2% in Chicago.[151] By the early 1970s the South, long the bastion of legally enforced segregation, had become the most educationally integrated region of the country, and it was the major cities of the North where "racial isolation" and inequity were most clearly evident.

The watershed moment represented by the *Brown* decision gave way to an ordeal of integration for African American youth concerned with improving the quality of their high school experiences. They endured attacks by racist protesters, harassment by White youth, indifference and hostility from educators, and perhaps most difficult of all, abandonment by their peers of the dominant race. The achievement of integration was a victory won at great cost. Eventually, however, desegregation became a reality for a majority of African American high school students in the 1970s. This did not bring immediate reprieve, but rather it entailed intensified conflict and disappointment, not the least of which concerned the loss of the historic secondary institutions that had served generations before them. But African American students persevered, and many ultimately made desegregation work in their favor.[152] It did not gain widespread or consistent support among Whites, and growing numbers of African Americans came to question its wisdom, but for students who eventually came to realize the fruits of the prior struggles for equal and integrated schools, the results were impressive indeed.

CONCLUSION

The African American High School Experience in Perspective

THE INTEGRATION STRUGGLES of the 1970s, along with the rapid proliferation of Black history and literature courses and widespread demands for more African American educators, provide a telling point of contrast to the condition of Black high schools in 1940. Prior to World War II, secondary education was scarce for African American youth, especially the majority who did not live in cities. Forty years later, it was practically universal in availability, although uneven in quality from one setting to another. The intervening decades were marked by conflict and struggle as African Americans fought, both figuratively and literally, to improve their educational prospects. They strived to realize ever higher standards of accomplishment, given the resources at hand. Their success was plainly evident in rising graduation rates, greater college enrollments, and the development of a substantial Black middle class.

In this concluding chapter, we review our principal findings and place them in a larger historical and conceptual context. In doing this, we try to demonstrate some of the ways in which the major developments in this story were manifest in the lives of individual African Americans at different points in time. We also discuss some of the knottier questions encountered in previous chapters, and speculate about changing perceptions of Black high schools of the past. Finally, we reflect on changes in African American education during the 30 or so years following the end point of this study. Much of the forward momentum that marked the decades prior to 1980, it turns out, was not sustained afterward. This is a point of understandable frustration for many African Americans, particularly those who came of age in an earlier time, as well as other observers. Looking back on the past record of expansion and progress, of course, can help to put more recent developments into a somewhat broader perspective, and perhaps help chart steps for the future.

THE HIGH SCHOOL IN THE HISTORY OF BLACK EDUCATION

Education has long been held as a key to success in American society by Black leaders, families, and civic organizations, but the years between the 1940s and the 1970s were little short of revolutionary in fostering attainment among African Americans. The high school had stood as a critical hurdle in the quest for education for many years. Black schooling, largely at the elementary level, existed before the Civil War, grew in the latter 1800s, and began to blossom in the early decades of the 20th century. But African American secondary schools remained scarce and, where they existed, they were underfunded and offered limited instruction.[1] The "separate but equal doctrine" of *Plessy v. Ferguson* heightened racial inequalities in education. In 1940, more than three-quarters of African Americans lived in the South, most of them in rural communities where secondary schooling was sparse or nonexistent. This was a decisive stumbling block for youth intent upon escaping the oppressive political economy of the region. Still, Blacks eagerly took advantage of the opportunities available to them, while seeking ever-greater equity in educational resources.

As we have shown, during the 1940s, the gap in high school attainment between White and Black students narrowed appreciably and it continued to do so in the ensuing decades. This accomplishment was largely the result of intrepid and persistent efforts by African American parents, communities, and organizations to expand schooling opportunities for Black youth. In earlier decades of the 20th century, they demanded more resources, raised funds to build schools and pay teachers, and insisted that states comply with the "separate but equal" mandate by supporting Black institutions. To preserve segregation, Southern states responded by expanding funds for African American schools. Impressive institutions such as Atlanta's Booker T. Washington, Baltimore's Dunbar, and Indianapolis' Crispus Attucks were established and eventually attracted students from far and wide. But these schools existed mostly in the cities and, especially with substantial Black migration into such areas, could not keep up with the spiraling Black demand for schooling.[2] Consequently, they became overcrowded and the quality of education suffered. Indeed, enrollment beyond capacity in these institutions is testimony to the value that African American families and youth attached to education. The failure of states to meet this growing demand for secondary education among Black students and the widening gap in quality between Black and Whites schools exposed the myth that racially segregated schools could be made equal, and demands for racial integration eventually took center stage in the battle for educational equality.

As indicated in Chapter 2, the Southern equalization campaigns of the latter 1940s and 1950s provided a significant boost to Black secondary attainment. It was a major step in closing the racial attainment gap. This substantial investment in African American education was a consequence of legal battles at the local level, along with persistent agitation by Black communities for better facilities and higher standards. Even if White willingness to provide this level of support was born of fear about integration, the impact was immense. The limits of White largess and readiness to change soon became apparent, but Black high school enrollments climbed to new heights nevertheless. In this respect, "equalization" represented a transformative moment in the history of African American education.

This was a major accomplishment, but it must also be viewed in context. Although the success of these struggles was due largely to African American initiative, it occurred amid a larger process of change. The expansion of high schools, often described as the "second transformation in American education," emerged in the milieu of mounting public interest in educational attainment.[3] Southern states lagged on schooling, struggling to restructure an economy that historically relied heavily on Black agricultural labor. As noted in the Introduction, in 1940 only 46% of White teenagers there graduated from high school, and 14% of Black youth. These rates of attainment, however, were poised for change. Equalization and school consolidation helped, but there were additional factors at play. African American migration to urban areas, searching for employment and social mobility, proved especially advantageous. Millions participated, bringing their children to cities where secondary schooling was readily available.[4] The changing Southern economy and employment uncertainty during the immediate postwar era made attending high school, often in search of marketable skills, more desirable. In subsequent years, widespread campaigns focused on the cities urging youth to stay in school, eventually enrolling thousands in alternative programs. This benefited Blacks and Whites alike, particularly in the South. While attainment climbed for all American youth, these developments were especially important for African Americans.

This process of social change and educational expansion encouraged efforts to improve the schools. Civil rights organizations, community leaders, parents, and students all demanded more resources for Black institutions, employing tactics that ranged from boycotts and walkouts to legal challenges in the courts. It was an era of rising expectations, in employment and civil rights as well as education.[5] As a result, enrollments surged and Black high schools appeared across the country, either as new institutions or as Whites abandoned older schools. As we have noted, these institutions often became points of identification for African American communities and drew families into cities and neighborhoods. Black high schools eventually were able to offer a curriculum comparable to White schools, and they made strides in obtaining accreditation and hiring talented teachers. Former students have spoken glowingly of their experiences in segregated schools, often noting the demanding but caring teachers and the strong sense of community in their neighborhoods. In our own research, Irene Wilson shared a photograph of Eureka High in Hattiesburg, Mississippi, built in 1921 to end the practice of sending Black youth away for secondary school. She boasted of the high standards at Eureka and its many well-known graduates, recounting the learning experiences she enjoyed there.[6] Her recollections were similar to dozens of others we encountered and many more in other studies. This has become an important theme in research on African American education in the 20th century.[7]

Our oral history research did not encounter much avowed desire for racial integration, but as in Wilson's account, it often featured fond memories of what has been called the "good Black high school." The existence of such institutions, of course, has been documented in other studies describing the schools' many virtues, but it is also important to acknowledge their limitations. Although some Black secondary schools may have equaled or even surpassed local White institutions, most did not. Some states, particularly North Carolina, were better than others in supporting African American education. As we have shown, great variation existed across the region, a point difficult to capture in case studies. Given the pride and apparent satisfaction reported with segregated Black high schools, however, it is an open question as to what ultimately prompted the push for racial integration.

It is likely that the "good Black high schools" found in many locales have become somewhat sentimentalized, especially in light of educational changes that unfolded in subsequent decades.[8] Although we in no way undervalue the lived experiences of the many people who recall such institutions, it is also necessary to situate their experiences within a wider context. As noted above, for instance, the vast majority of Black high schools in the South were required to operate with meager resources, severely restricting the quality of education they could provide. There was also the question of accessibility. Census data highlight the often neglected social class distinctions among African Americans, and high schools were more readily available to relatively affluent Blacks. Those who were poor or tenant farmers—which, in 1940, included a substantial majority of the Black population—often had little access to schooling. And even when they were able to attend school, vast racial disparities in the quality of education continued to exist and were clearly documented by contemporaries. Exposing these deficiencies in African American schools underscored demands for racial integration, even after so-called equalization campaigns. All of this must be taken into view when considering the contributions of segregated Black high schools in the past.

HIGH SCHOOLS AND SOCIAL STATUS

By 1960, about half of African Americans teenagers in the South were enrolled in high school but, as we have shown, they hailed disproportionately from non-farm, property-owning families. Our interview subjects Irene Wilson and Gloria Chambers lived in Southern cities but were born into middle-class households with educated parents, which helps explain why they were able to earn high school diplomas. African American youth in less affluent households were less likely to attend or complete high school. Considering social class also helps to situate successful Black high schools in a broader context by highlighting the experiences of those who lacked opportunities for schooling. Indeed, living in poverty was a norm for African Americans prior to the civil rights era, and the majority, especially those who were tenant farmers, spent most of their time eking out a living. For many thousands, especially in rural areas, high schools simply did not exist and productive labor took priority over schooling, even more for sons than daughters. Recall, for example, the Angleton Colored High School in Texas that Jack Jenkins described in the 1940s, a poorly equipped four-room "jumpstart" institution that he attended sporadically. Similarly, Princeton Elroy attended a Skene, Mississippi, school that held class 3 months a year, taught by one teacher with an 8th-grade education.[9] Such institutions were common in the South, even during the 1950s. In 1951, 977 of the 1,152 Georgia schools with only one or two teachers were designated "colored" institutions, and even if many were soon consolidated, others persisted for years.[10] Like Jenkins and Elroy, whose grandparents lived during slavery and later became sharecroppers, many Blacks were lucky to achieve the basic literacy skills that would help them to migrate out of the region. Cities with high schools for African American teens proved attractive to those in search of better opportunities, although these institutions often became overcrowded and less effective as a consequence.

Achieving a superior education in Black communities was often difficult even where schools existed, and this became linked to institutional status. Irene Wilson said that Eureka High School, impressive in size and once the center of the Black community, had gradually become a place for everyone seeking an education, from elementary students to war veterans, typical of the so-called "union schools" discussed earlier. By the late 1950s, it was severely overcrowded and underfunded, years after "equalization."[11] Joseph Williams, an interviewee who attended Atlanta's Washington High, said the school drew students from all over Georgia, many moving in with relatives or friends in order to attend the school. By the time he arrived, Washington High was surrounded with portable edifices to accommodate the steady stream of students.[12] As they struggled to accommodate growing numbers of students, Black high schools soon became highly congested and widely viewed as substandard. The Black youth attending such schools scored lower on standardized tests than Whites; by the 1960s, they were being described as "culturally deprived" and were targets of "compensatory" or "remedial" programs.[13] Regardless of the middle-class standing of many successful students, Black high schools continued to be seen as inferior to their White counterparts.

Despite these problems, secondary education opened the door to opportunity, and completing high school was a major step on the road to social mobility. Most of our interview respondents who graduated sought additional education and some obtained college degrees. Their educational attainment, of course, reflects the tendency of better-educated individuals to participate in such research, but it also corroborated historical trends. Nationally, Black college-going picked up dramatically during the 1960s, as rising numbers of secondary graduates looked to further educational attainment.[14] As mentioned in Chapter 4, employment opportunities were opening in professional, service, and managerial fields in the latter 1950s and 1960s; educational credentials could be helpful and increasingly were required. Females were more likely to finish high school, and teaching was often a career goal. Males dropped out more often, as did our interview respondent Roland Brown, who attended Washington High in the 1940s. Brown recalled enjoying high school but said that his parents, neither of whom had a high school education, emphasized business ownership as the key to success.[15] In general, however, students with such middle-class attributes as home ownership and parents in non-manual occupations exhibited higher levels of success in school.

The relationship of Black educational attainment to social class has been a consistent theme throughout the preceding chapters. By and large, status distinctions within Black communities paralleled those in the larger society, especially after secondary schools became widely available. Parents with higher levels of education and social standing were more likely to see their children graduate from high school. As we have seen, patterns of variation along these lines became more similar to those among Whites and other groups as Black attainment increased. Indeed, by the latter 1970s the major distinctions with respect to secondary attainment appear to have been linked to social class indicators rather than race per se. By this time, of course, integrated education was approaching its highest point and secondary education was more or less universally available to Blacks.[16] It was at this point that it would be reasonable to expect purely racial distinctions in attainment to virtually disappear.

There is considerable evidence that this, in fact, is what occurred. Table C.1 presents the results of an analysis of success in high school (defined in the same way as in earlier chapters) for a sample of all U.S. 17-year-olds living in metropolitan areas in 1980.[17] It employs logistic regression to consider three successive models, each in a separate column in the table. The first simply measures differences between African American students and all others, and subsequent models consider additional variables by simply adding them. The second model examines geographic (or geospatial) factors such as living in the South (compared with non-South) or in a central city (compared to the suburbs), and the third introduces a range of individual social and economic characteristics, ranging from gender to household and parental characteristics to whether or not the individual was employed. These variables have been defined in the same manner as in earlier chapters. By controlling for these factors, it is possible estimate a hypothetically independent effect of being African American on the likelihood of success in school.[18]

This analysis demonstrates how racial differences in educational attainment at the end of this period were affected by factors associated with social and economic status. As indicated in Model 1 in Table C.1, raw racial distinctions in school success were very substantial without controls for geographic or geospatial (GS) and socioeconomic status (SES) factors.[19] Basically, African American students were little more than half as likely as others to be enrolled in their junior year of high school or higher by age 17. But when GS and SES variables were introduced in Models 2 and 3, the negative effect of being African American is diminished. Indeed, in Model 3, the effect of being Black is positive, representing a 31% *greater* likelihood of success in school, after controlling for other factors. This indicates that the negative association between being Black and succeeding in school was principally a function of poverty, differences in family structure, and other factors associated with the relatively low social status endured by many African Americans. The *direct* or isolated effect of race on attainment measured in this way had been generally overcome, at least in the metropolitan settings where most Americans lived at the time. Put somewhat differently, African Americans students who were not poor or living in single parent households or central city settings were at least as likely—if not more—to succeed in school as other students. This is additional evidence of the distance that African American education had come in the years since 1940.

Not all problems were resolved, of course. The geospatial and social and economic status factors in Table C.1 point to the manifold challenges facing many Black youth as they sought to complete their schooling at the end of this period. Living in a central city, in a single-parent household, and in poverty were associated with considerably lower odds of success in school. Rates of poverty and single-parent family structure remained much higher among African Americans in 1980 than among Whites and other Americans. Home ownership levels were better, but many fewer Black youth had parents working in high-status white-collar jobs. Members of the Black middle class had grown in numbers, but there were still significant gaps in wealth and influence when compared with their White counterparts. Perhaps most disturbing, the rapid growth of suburban communities had left many Black households in destitute central city neighborhoods, where the concentration of poverty posed great risk to families and other institutions. In this sample, Black youth in central cities outnumbered those in suburbs by a three to one ratio. Although African Americans were moving to the suburbs in greater numbers, the vast majority remained confined to segregated urban neighborhoods, a situation that sociologists eventually came to describe as "American Apartheid."[20] In the years to follow, many of these problems would grow worse. We revisit these questions below, in turning to the period after 1980.

DILEMMAS OF INTEGRATION

Although African Americans were acutely aware of the strictures of racial segregation, most of our interviews emphasized achieving success within its boundaries rather than pressing for integration. Explaining his perspective on this, Roland Brown said "segregation was terrible, but it didn't bother us at the time. My parents had a business, so I didn't have to be involved. We had our own stores . . . own neighborhood." Indeed, he was surprised that one student in his high school, Martin Luther King Jr., went on to become a civil rights leader.[21] Like Brown, most of our interview subjects seemed to accept segregation as normal; it was the only way of life they had known. But this did not mitigate their desire to obtain a good education and achieve socioeconomic mobility, so the absence of adequate educational resources for African American youth led parents, communities, and state and national organizations to demand more and better schooling.

Access to education itself, moreover, helped fuel an evolving political consciousness that ultimately led to demands for integration. The more education African Americans attained, the more their aspirations grew, ambitions that were often thwarted by racial barriers. Awareness of such

TABLE C.1. Logistic Regression: Factors Associated with Success in School, Metropolitan 17-Year-Olds, 1980 (Log Odds and Odds Ratios)

Independent Variables	Model 1 Race	Model 2 Geo Spatial Factors	Model 3 Social and Economic Status	Odds Ratios Model 3
Subject is Black	-.573	-.379	.270	1.310
Subject Lives in South		-.437	-.426	.653
Subject Lives in Central City		-.315	-.147	.863
Subject is Female			.435	1.545
Parent HS Graduate			.689	1.992
Parent White-Collar Job			.688	1.990
Home Owned by Family			.751	2.120
Household Below Poverty			-.337	.714
Female Household Head			-.474	.622
Subject is Employed			.314	1.369
Variance and Sample Size	Nagelkerke R^2=.012	Nagelkerke R^2=.026	Nagelkerke R^2=.202	

Source: IPUMS data (1980, 1% sample expanded to estimated population figures by use of "personweight" variable). Coefficients are logarithmic expression of odds ratios.
Note: All independent variables are significant at .001 or greater.

obstacles seemed more acute among those who attended high school, and even more if they went on to college. This was frequently illustrated in the narratives of our interview subjects. For example, during her high school years, Grace Strong won a national essay contest and became interested in journalism, but after graduating from college was repeatedly denied a job in the field.[22] Gloria Chambers shared a similar story: After earning her bachelor's degree from Spellman and teaching for a few years, she decided to specialize in speech language pathology. Chambers applied to the University of Southern Mississippi but was turned away because of race. Although she was admitted a little later, she said the state historically had paid tuition for students to attend school elsewhere.[23]

Persistent problems such as these appear to have made Blacks more amenable to integration as a means to advancement. Years later, when Chambers had the opportunity to send her children to a previously all-White school, she did so. Despite her own positive experiences at a racially segregated institution, she equated integration with greater opportunities, and was eager for her children to benefit from it. Her children were among five students to integrate Boyd Elementary School in Jackson, Mississippi, in a "freedom of choice" plan. She explained that her children would "get more exposure" there, and said, "We could see what was coming and we felt that you needed to be able to compete . . . you just need to compete and hold your own."[24] Voluntary integration programs in some Southern cities, especially those involving only a handful of Black students, often proceeded with few incidents. But as we have shown, integrating elementary school children, eventually a norm in many cities, often posed fewer challenges than it did in high schools. Moreover, research reveals significant regional variation in integration experiences, influenced by the history and extent of segregation, the racial composition of schools involved, and the nature of desegregation plans.[25]

Generally speaking, integration initially proceeded more smoothly in non-Southern communities, although there was controversy, and busing sparked protest in the late 1960s and 1970s. As a result of Black protest and legal challenges, by the 1940s, most states outside of the South had ended formal segregation policies, often allowing African American students to attend neighborhood schools. Conflict was more likely to erupt in schools where Blacks constituted a substantial minority, as in Gary's Froebel High, where they numbered a third of the students in 1945. Still, the North became known as a place where Blacks could be educated, and this helped to draw migrants from the South. In the 1940s, Nadine Meyers's parents moved from Arkansas to Missouri, where Nadine and her siblings graduated from high school. Meyers recalled that her mother wanted to ensure that they could get a good education and did so by moving into a reputable school district, which for her family meant living in south Kansas City and attending the predominantly White Southeast High. Only about 15% of the student body was Black in the mid-1960s, but Meyers recalled amiable relationships among students, even while disturbances were occurring in other parts of the city. As suggested earlier, small numbers of Blacks were not very threatening to most Whites; moreover, race-relations courses helped to temper conflict before it got out of hand.[26] Kansas City's East High was at least 30% Black when Kevin Dodge attended in the 1960s, making him feel like a "fish out of water," but he reported fond memories of the school. He found White teachers to be fair and supportive, even more than at the predominantly Black school he had attended. According to Dodge, "East had the better instructors because . . . if they saw you needed help, if they saw you struggling, they would pull you aside and try to explain things to you . . . they didn't mind taking time with you."[27] Amid the confusion and protest over desegregation, there were many quiet success stories of Black achievement and support from White teachers.[28]

Still, efforts to integrate schools generated intense protest and disruptive changes in many communities, and most of the burden was endured by African Americans. As noted in Chapter 5, Blacks were more likely than Whites to leave their schools and neighborhoods for purposes of integration, and thousands of Black teachers lost their jobs instead of being assigned to integrated or White schools. Black students forfeited many traditions that had defined their previous institutions, such as yearbooks, organizations, and culturally oriented activities. They often were seen as invaders in White schools, places where they were neither welcomed nor respected, and subjected to hostility or neglect. Thomas Smith, who was among the Blacks admitted to the Chapel Hill–Carrboro School System, said, "It was a whole new world, going in, being called names, being spit on, hit. . . . I remember one time I was standing in the hall, confused on which way I was supposed to go and this kid walked up and punched me in the stomach, for no reason."[29] The advent of large-scale integration was accompanied by widespread conflict between students, escalating a longstanding practice of interracial violence in secondary schools. Unlike Smith, in the instance recounted above, African American students often defended themselves in such confrontations, giving as much or more than they got. But in many, perhaps most, such cases, they also bore the brunt of institutional responses, and their rates of suspensions and expulsions were more than double those of Whites. For the first generation of Black secondary students to attempt meaningful integration, the experience was fraught with dangers, and threats were posed by White students and educators alike.

Black youth and their parents were willing to risk such hazards, however, if it meant a better education. Freda Jones was 12-years-old when integration came to her community, and her parents enrolled her in a previously all-White school, which they saw as providing a better education. Since no bus service was provided for Blacks, her parents joined with others in their neighborhood and paid for a taxi service. Describing her experience, Jones explained, "It was either benign neglect where they just kind of ignored us or just out and out said silly ridiculous things. I think there was definitely a failure to pay attention to the African-American students."[30] In spite of her treatment, Jones went on to graduate, attended college, and became a university dean. Research has suggested that many Black students who attended integrated schools ultimately did better in subsequent schooling and in the labor market.[31] Succeeding in these circumstances, however, rarely seems to have been easy.

African American students were often assumed to be academically inferior and ill-prepared for success in White schools, and their experiences often served to reinforce such perceptions. They were not always able to meet the demands of the curriculum in White schools. As Ralph Naples said after being one of the Blacks to integrate a school in Raleigh, North Carolina, "We couldn't live up to the expectations of the [White] teachers there. They were piling up a lot of homework on us that we didn't have the resources and time to do. A lot of white kids, they had encyclopedias and dictionaries and stuff in the home. . . . [W]e had to go to the public library, which was quite a distance from the house."[32] By the 1960s, many African Americans in segregated institutions may have been exposed to somewhat less demanding academic standards than in White schools, and there were calls for a greater emphasis on vocational training. This, of course, was controversial, but even when such ideas met resistance, critical questions remained about the quality of predominantly Black schools. Consistently low test scores, especially for Black schools, belied the idea that these institutions had generally high standards.

Much of the difficulty, of course, was due to the high rates of poverty endured by African American students and the growing number of single-parent households in their communities. But important changes had occurred in the schools as well. Desegregation signaled the end of the striving Southern Black high school and in many ways marked the start of new problems. Perhaps the most critical was the loss of dedicated teachers who had committed years to African American institutions. As suggested in Chapter 5, the impact was especially dramatic in urban institutions that had relied upon such staff members. One longtime educator attributed many troubles to White teachers in the late 1960s and 1970s who could not discipline Black students or gain their respect. Jack Jenkins claimed that a handful of Whites came to Kansas City's Sumner High to teach so they could "pay off their school loans and get back to their own schools," but were ineffective with the students: "You need to have a principal who knows how to discipline, and can handle it, or the kids will run over you. They had three White teachers there, and the kids were just running over them." The problem was compounded when teachers left the schools after a short time to teach elsewhere or pursue new careers. As suggested in our interviews, students often could sense when teachers were disengaged or intent upon leaving. It did little to encourage them to do well or to take their studies seriously.[33]

In the end, of course, growing numbers of African American youth did succeed in school, despite the ordeal of integration. The enrollment trend line continued upward a bit through the 1970s, even after attainment levels had largely flattened for Whites. A number of researchers showed that Black graduation rates from integrated schools exceeded those from segregated institutions, a pattern that continued to be evident beyond the period at hand.[34] A part of the explanation for this may be the somewhat higher status of Black families in integrated neighborhoods that sent children to such schools, but even poor Black youth seem to have done better in integrated settings. Ultimately, the success of integration in high schools was a reflection of the resiliency and determination of African American students and their families and communities. Defeating segregation was a stage in the protracted and bitter campaign to achieve educational equity. The fact that this goal is still so distant is evidence of the depth of White intransigence in the face of inequities that continue to exist. Overcoming this remains one of the great challenges to the future of American education, and in recent years progress has been hard to see.

A LEGACY OF PROTEST

Schools are uniquely public institutions, sharing a moral commitment to human perfectibility and civic advancement. They also are open to scrutiny regarding what transpires in and around them. These factors make them particularly apposite sites for the politics of public demonstration. As race became such a volatile issue in the United States, and education was linked to status and security, it is not surprising that schools witnessed such bitter conflicts over these questions. It is hardly original to suggest that many of the grievances and anxieties of the age came to be expressed in these confrontations. And it was students who often were the principal combatants.

Throughout the preceding chapters, we have seen evidence of a political struggle for control of education waged by African Americans and by Whites in a variety of forms. It was manifest in the protest in Lumberton, North Carolina, and the Gary, Indiana, strike against integration, carried out practically at the same time in the fall of 1946. The Lumberton episode was an early step in a long line of such incidents, acts of collective opposition to highlight gross inequity and negligence in schooling. It was linked in spirit to the strike in Farmville 5 years later and to countless other protests against deplorable conditions throughout the period. As suggested in the book's Introduction, these actions were part and parcel of what has become known as the Long Civil Rights Movement, an extended campaign to overcome racial prejudice and exploitation, led by African Americans. For Black students in Lumberton, Farmville, and any number of similar sites, the struggle for better schools was a blow against one of the most palpable signs of oppression in their immediate experience.

For the White strikers in Gary, along with their sympathizers in Chicago and innumerable other settings throughout this period, the stakes may have seemed nearly as high. As suggested in Chapter 3, they perceived the struggle as vital to the preservation of their own status, which seemed threatened by the African American quest for equality. The fear of degradation by association was perhaps greatest among Whites with the least status to lose, immigrant members of the working class. It was their children who led the strike in Gary, even if many of the parents were union members who were ostensibly committed to cross-racial solidarity. In the South, White opposition to school integration was far more sweeping, and it was the social and economic elites who often organized the White Citizens Councils to coordinate resistance. But in all cases, White protest generally was defensive in nature, a matter of opposing change and upholding racial advantages in the face of challenges to segregation. This was the essential dynamic that governed the politics of racial protest in schools across the period in question.[35]

The postwar period, of course, witnessed the beginning of heightened activity in the civil rights movement, a sweeping and sustained mobilization of political resources to bring about change in the degraded status of African Americans. As we have argued, Black students were active participants in this crusade, much of which had little directly to do with schools. They were willing "foot soldiers" for campaigns related to voting rights, housing discrimination, open employment, and a range of other issues that principally concerned adults. For many, the movement was hardly an abstraction, something they read about or saw on television; they were spirited participants and contributors. It was a legacy that foretold greater activism in the schools.[36]

Most of the literature on youth involvement in the civil rights movement has focused on college students. They organized the famous sit-in demonstrations at lunch counters and other segregated restaurants and stores, the "freedom rides" to desegregate bus stations and interstate transport, and strikes on campuses to gain approval of curricula and departments representing the field of Black studies.[37] As noted earlier, rising African American high school graduation during the 1950s and 1960s provided impetus to college enrollment, adding force to the impact of these activities. But during the latter 1960s, African American secondary students also began to agitate for changes in their schools, echoing some of the themes evident in college protests.

Of course, Black students had long engaged in dissent, but at mid-decade, the pace and magnitude of these activities increased dramatically, spreading rapidly across cities and even from one part of the country to another. This upsurge was inspired by the "Black Power" ideology that was then gaining national attention, and eventually by the community control movement, which advocated greater involvement in governance and authority over institutions that directly impacted Black communities.[38] It also was undoubtedly influenced by college protests that occurred at about the same time. High school rebels demanded courses in Black history and literature, more Black teachers and administrators, and a host of other, more mundane changes in schools. They established Black Student Union organizations that continued to agitate for "Black pride" and celebrating milestones in African American history. New fashions and hairstyles appeared in high school yearbooks, reflecting a "Black is beautiful" turn in popular culture.[39] While there was continued interest in desegregation, particularly in the South, it was tempered by a new self-awareness emphasizing the distinctiveness of Black experience.

Between 1940 and 1980, the protest activities of Black high school students shifted from agitation for greater equity and integration to demands for specialized courses and recognition of African American heritage and the significance of Black culture. It does not appear that most Black students renounced integration, but a vocal minority wondered whether it was the best strategy for advancing the cause of Black education. Advocates of integration had realized considerable success as well, especially in the South. As these goals were realized, protest dropped off, and by the end of the period, African American student activism had quieted significantly. Black studies courses had been widely adopted in high schools, even outside of urban areas, and integration appeared to be advancing, or at least was being pursued through the courts. As a number of observers have noted, however, many of the gains made by student protestors proved to be transitory.[40] As was often the case with student movements, their impact dissipated with graduation. Once the major grievances seemed to be resolved, succeeding generations of students turned to different interests and concerns. A long era of Black high school student protest finally ended in the 1970s.

The potent outburst of dissent that marked the latter 1960s and early 1970s marked an apogee to roughly 3 decades of Black student agitation around questions related to the high school. The timing was symptomatic, no doubt, of the decline of the larger civil rights movement. But it also was a portent of the future, a period to follow when secondary schooling would no longer be looked upon as an opportunity or a right denied and, hence, a cause for mobilization and conflict. In its place was a perspective that held the high school as a normative and commonplace experience, one possibly linked to success in the larger society but not necessarily to ideals such as freedom, equality, and justice. This was a turn, we believe, with possibly important implications for the future of African American education.

THE ELUSIVE GOAL OF EQUALITY

Our research has documented a historic narrowing of the Black-White high school attainment gap, due in large part to resolute struggle by African American students and their families and communities. While it is a story of success, the ultimate achievement of racial parity in high school graduation is, unfortunately, not yet a part of it. Although tremendous gains were made in attainment between the 1940s and the 1970s, reflecting the struggle for equality, it appears that the gap in high school graduation rates has remained more or less constant in the decades hence. The civil rights movement offered the promise that extending equal opportunity would eventually result in racial educational and economic parity, but while there have been many gains, these goals have remained elusive.

Several factors account for the persistent racial gap in high school attainment, including White flight, resurgent school segregation, the challenge of providing good education to low-income students, and the fact that some teenagers of all races do not seem to place great stock in a high school diploma. For many African Americans, the years following the 1970s led to more social and economic hardship, including high rates of violence, crime, unemployment, and single-parent families in communities that once exhibited greater stability and solidarity. An early expression of frustration with such problems was revealed in a poem entitled "Unite," written by a student and published in the 1970 *Falcon*, Chicago's Harlan High School yearbook: "Gangs fight gangs; Blacks killing blacks; And laughter rings in my ears—White laughter."[41] Such sentiments would become even more pertinent in the decades to follow.

The study of high school graduation has become a matter of controversy, largely because of the rapid growth of General Equivalency Diploma (GED) programs since the 1970s. Although government statistics on secondary completion rates include GED holders, a growing body of research has cast doubt on the proposition that a GED is actually equivalent to a high school diploma. Considerable caution must be exercised in estimating graduation rates following the 1970s to utilize measures that are accurate reflections of high school graduation and not alternative credentials such as the GED. The most authoritative and comprehensive treatment of this question to date has been performed by economists James J. Heckman and Paul A. LaFontaine, who argue that overall graduation rates have hovered around 76% since the 1970s. Regarding African American graduation, they estimate that "65 percent of blacks and Hispanics leave school with a high school diploma and minority graduation rates are still substantially below the rates for non-Hispanic whites." They also "find no evidence of convergence in minority-majority graduation rates over the past 35 years."[42] In short, progress in raising Black secondary attainment ceased sometime during the 1970s.

Our own analysis of IPUMS data generally corresponds with Heckman and LaFontaine's estimates. Examining the year 1980, we found a secondary graduation rate for Black 19-year-olds of 64%, a bit lower than the proportion of 17-year-old Black youth enrolled in the junior year or greater, at 69%.[43] The graduation rate for non-Hispanic Whites was about 80%, similar to that found by Heckman and LaFontaine for later years. Judging by Heckman and LaFontaine's calculations, progress in raising the level of African American secondary graduation had ended by 1980. Like other American youth, Black high school students did not increase their graduation rate in the closing decades of the 20th century. Large numbers of them completed GED and other alternative credential programs, especially in the prison population. Indeed, Heckman and LaFontaine suggest that the unusually high rate of African American GED completion after 1980 was largely due to individuals accomplishing it while incarcerated. But this was not the same as graduating from high school.[44] The latter 1970s, with successful struggles to transform aspects of the curriculum and to realize the promise of integration, also marked a high point of Black secondary attainment. Regarding the years that followed, the question is why attainment growth stagnated.

Something of a parallel process can be observed in the achievement results recorded by African American 17-year-olds on the National Assessment of Educational Progress (NAEP) during the 1970s and 1980s. As indicated in the book's Introduction, African American reading and mathematics scores rose steadily between NAEP's first administration in 1971 and the mid-1980s, when both indicators reached their highest point of convergence with White scores, which had remained largely unchanged. After that, improvement in Black scores basically ended, and they even declined during the next decade or so.[45] In other words, a similar pattern of rising accomplishment, convergence with White performance, and eventual stagnation came to characterize Black academic *achievement* as well, at least as it was measured by this assessment.

This halt in Black academic progress has received considerable attention in recent years. Explanations vary, extending from worsening social and economic conditions in Black communities, faltering desegregation, a failure of urban schools, and the rise of an African American youth culture glorifying antisocial behavior and denigrating academic accomplishment. Some also suggest that the rise of the GED as a substitute for graduation has led more youth to leave school, especially among Blacks and other minority groups.[46] We believe that each of these factors may well have played a role in the story of African American academic shortcomings, but another contributing factor was the stagnation in educational attainment that began about a decade before the peak NAEP assessments among Black 17-year-olds. The young men and women who scored highest on the assessments, after all, were children of the generation of Blacks who had graduated during the 1960s, when going to high school was still a potentially political act of racial advancement. These were children who grew up in the 1970s, when secondary attainment and desegregation arguably reached their highest points. They entered high school in the 1980s in a stronger academic position than any previous generation of African Americans.[47] Given this, it is little wonder that they did so well. The question of educational progress after the mid-1980s concerns the generations that followed them. These were the offspring of the graduates of the 1970s, for whom going to high school was less a political statement and more a normative or everyday expectation. Although we believe that Black attainment continued to grow during the 1970s, its pace slowed somewhat, and the number of individuals receiving GEDs began to rise significantly. It is possible, in short, that the high school experience came to be viewed a bit differently.[48]

African American high school students of the latter 1980s and 1990s also grew up in a period of mounting social and economic problems in many of their communities. Sociologist William J. Wilson has offered an influential analysis of racial inequality by placing it within the context of economic restructuring, a decline in industrial employment that disproportionately affected the job prospects of African American males. Whereas manufacturing employment offered good opportunities for those with a high school education, and sometimes those with less, the post-industrial economy provided low-wage service jobs that called for a different set of capabilities. Wilson cites findings, for example, that employers often felt African American men lacked the non-cognitive "soft skills," such as meeting and interacting with customers, required for service positions. He also argued that these structural changes were linked to an increase in drugs, crime, and violence in urban areas, contributing to a growing body of research on the "urban underclass."[49]

The most contentious thesis advanced by Wilson was that social class had become more important than race in shaping the life chances of African Americans. While agreeing that historically rooted racism still affected Blacks, Wilson highlighted the growing pace of class polarization among African Americans. Millions were moving into or stabilizing their positions in the middle class, going from the inner-city to suburban communities, leaving behind their economically disadvantaged counterparts. Inner-city areas were stripped of resources, stability, and role models that existed when Blacks of different social classes lived in proximity.[50] The impact of this extended to education. We have shown that the circumstances of family life have historically influenced rates of high school attendance; Black youth living in two-parent, property-owning families had a greater chance of reaching the 11th grade and graduating from high school. As middle-class African Americans left urban neighborhoods, problems in the schools mounted.

Social class polarization is implicated in other trends that help explain educational decline among African Americans. These trends include the loss of racially homogeneous but social class-diverse Black neighborhoods, dramatic changes in the Black family, and increasing urban crime, violence, and incarceration. A central theme in our interviews, and one highlighted in Wilson's analysis, was the demise of the Black community and its ability to exert social control over children. For example, nearly all our interview respondents spoke of a time when cohesive Black communities existed and were unified around the task of keeping children in school. Ruby Arnold graduated from Atlanta's Washington High in 1952 with "high honors" and, like many others, said she simply did not recall many students dropping out of school because parents and the immediate community would not tolerate it. She said, "All your neighborhood encouraged you to go to school, and you couldn't choose to stay out of school . . . your neighbors would not allow it, they would tell your parents . . . everybody was your mother and father."[51] Although such stories were common, our data reveal that dropping out of high school was far from uncommon and was strongly associated with social class. Still, Black neighborhoods were once more class-diverse and cohesive, and they often reinforced the value of education. Since then, class differences among African Americans have grown wider, and many who experienced class mobility have abandoned historic Black neighborhoods. This has resulted in not only a concentration of Black poverty and joblessness in inner-city areas, but the absence of middle-class role models, the demise of extended family networks of support, and a loss of people willing to invest in schools and other community institutions.

Amid the protests of the civil rights era, D. Patrick Moynihan opined that the 40% of African American children then born to single mothers was a major factor in determining racial inequality. This sparked a 30-year controversy about the matriarchal structure of Black families and their functionality. Meanwhile, the percentage of Black children born to single mothers soared from about one-third to nearly 70%, compromising the traditional strength of Black families. The demise of Black marriage has since been a major focus of research.[52] Much of this work has focused on male underemployment and joblessness, although there is also evidence of a cultural ethos of non-marriage, dating to slavery.[53] And as we have noted, children from married, two-parent families exhibit better cognitive development and complete high school more often than those from single-parent households.[54] There appears to be a growing consensus that this has been a key historical factor in the stagnation of Black attainment.[55]

A sense of the magnitude of this question can be gained from statistics presented in Table C.2, which show the changing proportion of 17-year-olds living in single-parent, female-headed households between 1960 and 2000. These figures are a bit different from those for children of younger ages, but clearly demonstrate the historic decline of traditional two-parent families, especially among African Americans.[56] By the end of the 20th century, a majority of Black youth lived in such households, with the number approaching two-thirds in central city settings. The corresponding figures for non-Blacks were considerably lower, although also at historic highs. The concentration of these single-parent households for all families, Black and other, was clearly greater in central city settings, where change occurred at a similar rate for all youth across the period. The extremely high proportion among urban African American youth, however, was an exceptional condition, unprecedented in magnitude. For the first time in recent history, living in a single-parent household of limited means was a preponderant norm for children in many Black communities.

Wilson and other scholars have argued that high concentrations of poverty and single-parent households can have a significant impact on normative expectations in urban communities. These conditions are associated with youth leaving school and becoming involved in violence or gang behavior. Most of our interviewees maintained that fighting in or around the schools was practically unheard of when they grew up, and certainly did not involve guns or other weapons. But the school climate began to change in the 1960s. When Nadine Meyers started school at Southeast in the 1960s, misbehavior among students seldom went beyond occasionally setting a trash can on fire, but by the time she graduated in 1970, it was clear that the school and surrounding area were on the cusp of change. For example, while Black males at Southeast, mostly athletes, "absolutely would not fight," an out-of-school group called the "51st street gang" had started to "terrorize" students. Asked about the cause of these changes, Meyers, like many interview subjects, saw the problem in changing Black families, especially the increase in single mothers.[57] It seemed more difficult for parents to discipline their children, and community cohesion had diminished. Asked why schools had changed so much since he graduated in the 1956, Brandon Carter had a ready list to offer:

> One of the things that I think is that parents don't have enough time to come to PTA meetings; it's not a priority. Second, the laws on the books

have dictated that this generation has rights—by this I mean parents/others can't discipline. Third, kids raising kids, and they don't have any home training. And sometimes parents want to assault teachers. . . . For us, the teacher was always right and we were always wrong. Now that's changed.[58]

Nearly everyone we interviewed offered reasons why the children of subsequent generations seem less respectful, more aggressive, and less interested in school. As with many Americans, most saw single-parent families and weaker communities as the underlying problem, but rarely mentioned broader social forces. For example, structural changes in the economy and the loss of jobs were not mentioned. Neither was suburbanization or White flight, which has isolated Black communities in urban school districts with relatively meager resources. By the early 1990s, about 75% of African American children were attending segregated schools,[59] and research indicates that these institutions have more low-income children, lower scores on standardized tests, less qualified teachers, and fewer advanced courses.[60] In many inner-city settings, all-Black high schools have been labeled "dropout factories," with graduation rates of 50% or lower.[61] These institutions have many problems, but their failings are largely a matter of context. As Richard Rothstein has recently argued, the obstacles facing inner-city children seeking success in school are manifold, and will require a substantial investment in resources to overcome. For those who are *not* interested in school, the obstacles to gaining a productive education are even greater. The conditions faced by today's youth in many central city communities make the "urban crisis" of years past appear mild by comparison.[62]

With so many African Americans contending with circumstances such as these, the road to educational equality is uncertain at best. Yet relatively few Americans, including our Black middle-aged interview respondents, seem to recognize the scope of the problem. There were, of course, other factors that arguably contributed to the demise of Black educational progress. Reagan era cutbacks in college financial aid, for instance, hit African American students particularly hard, reducing incentives for them to focus on school. Budget cuts to urban school districts also send a message that Black education is not a priority, a stark contrast to the civil rights era. City school bureaucracies have historically been slow to respond to failing institutions in African American neighborhoods beset by poverty and crime, and this, too, conveys a message that schooling is not important. In short, the past 30 years or so have not been a time of rising expectations regarding education or just about any other facet of life for many African Americans, particularly those living in inner-city neighborhoods. It may well require another mobilization of public sentiment on the scale of the civil rights movement to raise awareness of these

TABLE C.2. Proportion of 17-Year-Olds in Households with No Father Present, 1960, 1980, and 2000 (in percentages)

Year	BLACK		NON-BLACK	
	Non-City	Central City	Non-City	Central City
1960	37	45	17	20
1980	45	54	18	26
2000	53	65	22	29

Source: IPUMS data.

questions, and to eventually bring about meaningful change. Although the challenges of today are different from those of the past, there may well be some lessons to draw from the era of progressively rising Black educational attainment.

THE IMPERATIVE OF EDUCATIONAL CHANGE

Despite the continuing racial gap in high school graduate rates between Blacks and Whites, the significance of the closing of the attainment gap that started in the 1940s cannot be overstated. In 1940, African Americans graduated from high school at a rate just one-third that of White students, 14% compared to 46%, and an estimated 80% were employed in the three lowest tiers of the occupational hierarchy. Although social class position influenced the likelihood that African Americans in the 1940s and 1950s would have access to and graduate from high school, those who did graduate often went on to attend college and became professionals and community leaders, hastening the emergence of a Black middle class defined largely by educational credentials. Black organizations, parents, and communities fought for all Black children to have equal access to education, whether in segregated or integrated schools, and the high school revolution came to include the majority of African American youth. By 1970, the secondary attainment gap between Blacks and Whites had narrowed substantially, and Blacks were experiencing significant socioeconomic attainment. As Bart Landry has documented, the Black middle class more than doubled between 1960 and 1970, with education being the most important factor in social mobility.[63] By the end of the 20th century, 25% of African Americans had managerial/professional jobs and another 25% had white-collar sales and clerical jobs.[64] Whether these figures can be improved upon without additional improvement in Black education, however, is an open question.

The importance of a high school diploma to socioeconomic success has grown, as today's "post-industrial" economy offers limited opportunities for dropouts. At the same time, the demand for college-educated workers has grown, and the wage gap between dropouts and college graduates has substantially widened. In 2005, the median income of male dropouts was $19,802 and $50,600 for those with a bachelor's degree.[65] But the value of attainment far exceeds monetary advantage; it also is related to other aspects of effective participation in society. Dropping out of school, recently the topic of a White House summit, has been described as the civil rights issue of the 21st century.[66] We find it hard to disagree with this sentiment. In light of the trends described above, the longstanding stagnation in Black educational attainment is a problem in desperate need of attention.

We believe that the experience of the past can inform future efforts to improve attainment levels. Our research has highlighted some of the structural factors that were instrumental in affecting higher rates of graduation among African Americans, such as northward migration, the burgeoning industrial economy, and the growing number of Black high schools. There also was a massive outlay by Southern states for education during the so-called equalization campaigns of the 1940s and 1950s. This was unusual in American history, a concerted, sustained investment in African American schooling. As we have noted, it was often stymied by local school boards determined to maintain White advantages in education, and was accompanied by substantial increases in funding for White schools as well, but it did provide a critical boost to Black attainment at a time when it was becoming ever more important. And improvements in African American education during these years had a measureable payoff in the job market, as we have noted in the book's Introduction. Despite its shortcomings, the impact of "equalization" was historic in magnitude. We believe it can provide a useful reference point for policymakers interested in effecting change in today's largely Black urban schools. For instance, perhaps it is time to consider an equalization campaign for the 21st century, focused on improving inner-city secondary institutions sometimes referred to as "dropout factories."

There were many other factors, of course, that contributed to improvement in Black attainment in the past that can be emulated in the future. As we have indicated, the impact of desegregation was quite positive, despite the often hostile or indifferent response that Black students received in predominantly White institutions. Insofar as integration can be sustained or advanced, it is likely to have beneficial effects in the future as well. The success of desegregation, however, hinges decisively on the willingness of Whites to permit or encourage their children to attend school with African Americans, and history has revealed that large numbers are unwilling to do so. Recent court decisions have indicated that the contemporary judicial and political climate is not encouraging for measures designed to induce or compel Whites to participate in desegregation plans. Because of this, we believe that school integration is likely to have a rather limited impact on improved Black attainment in the immediate future. As critical as it may well be in the long run, the current political context will have to change before large-scale desegregation can be considered a viable path to change. This is an unfortunate fact that must be considered in plans to address current problems in African American education.

Throughout the book, we have emphasized the power of Black organizations, parents, and communities to inspire change and fight for equality, and the determination of students to pursue a high school education, even if it meant attending predominantly White schools where they were unwelcome and at times less prepared to succeed. As suggested above, however, the ability of many Black communities today to engage in such activities to support education has been crippled by structural changes in the economy, particularly the decline of industrial employment in the cities. Black students today may be less likely to see educational change as part of a larger process of social transformation, and consequently, may be less willing to endure the ordeal of integration in the same way as earlier generations did. For this reason, we believe that any effort at "equalization" to redress the educational deficiencies of African Americans in these settings should be linked to comprehensive community-restoration campaigns, to assist families in meeting the many challenges of inner-city life. As Jean Anyon, Richard Rothstein, and others have suggested, it will undoubtedly be necessary to restore the health and vitality of inner-city communities in order to achieve the goal of substantially improving the schools.[67] And to do this will require political determination that probably must be born of a new movement for basic human rights and cross-racial solidarity. In undertaking this, it may be possible to raise expectations for the future once again, just as they were raised to new heights in the past. It may be the only way to harness the remarkable vigor and commitment to success that was so clearly evident during the heyday of African American educational expansion. Given the importance of formal education in today's world, and the well-documented significance of families and communities in supporting the educational process, reclaiming that legacy may well be our best hope for posterity.

APPENDIX A

Oral History Interviews and Other Sources of Information

THIS STUDY DRAWS on multiple sources of data—in-depth oral history interviews that we conducted and/or accessed from archives, newspaper articles, official reports, communication by educators and public officials, high school yearbooks, and quantitative data. Oral history interviews capture the voices and lived experiences of individuals through their own words. These interviews reveal the human agency—the thoughts, emotions, actions, and opinions—of social actors and enable them to become a valued and visible part of the stories written about their times. This component of our study strengthens our findings by adding a dimension of triangulation, gathering data from multiple sources and perspectives as a basis for comparison and analysis, and broadening the scope of the research.

Between 2007 and 2009, we conducted interviews with 42 African Americans, most of whom were high school students in the 1940s through the 1970s. They attended high schools in Georgia, Illinois, Kansas, Mississippi, Missouri, New Jersey, North Carolina, and Texas. Each of them signed an agreement that guaranteed their anonymity and granted us permission to use the interviews in this study, in conformity with our approval from the Human Subjects Committee at the University of Kansas. The names of all the interview subjects used throughout the book, consequently are pseudonyms. Most of those we interviewed were born during the 1930s and 1940s. Our oldest respondent, a retired educator and civil rights activist, was born in 1918, and our youngest, who actively recruited members of her high school alumni association to participate in the study, was born in 1970. Twenty-five (25) were male and 17 were female.

Some of our respondents were recruited via word-of-mouth but the majority by placing ads in African American newspapers and contacting high schools and community organizations. Our interview guide consisted of a few opening questions to gather demographic and background information (such as education and occupation of parents) followed by a set of open-ended questions that focused the high school experiences of our respondents. The interviews were audiotaped and transcribed, and then reviewed and coded for major themes. In addition to the 42 interviews we personally conducted, we also accessed 20 interviews from the Southern Oral History project archived at the Southern Historical Collection in the Wilson Library of the University of North Carolina–Chapel Hill and the Center for Oral History and Cultural Heritage in the McCain Library at the University of Southern Mississippi in Hattiesburg. These interviews were conducted with Black and White respondents who related their opinions about and experiences with racially integrating schools, and who worked in or attended Black high schools during these years.

Our interviews focused on factors related to the growth in high school attendance among African Americans that began in the 1940s, before large-scale desegregation. We found that the interviews offered important insights into the role of secondary schools in the lives of African Americans, and the personal meaning attached to these institutions and the educators who worked in them. Most of our respondents were the first in their families to attend or finish high school, and they were clearly inspired with a sense of pride and upward mobility. They had fond memories of their high school years and emphasized the positive aspects of the racially segregated schools they attended, so in this respect our findings were consistent with a growing body of research on Black high schools in the past. It is also important to acknowledge, however, that focusing on the positive side of the institutions they attended meant overlooking or downplaying less flattering aspects of schooling in the past. It was relatively common, for instance, for interview subjects to recall that practically all of students from their era graduated from high school, but statistical data tell a different story. High levels of academic accomplishment also were recalled, but test scores suggest that this was true of a relatively small number of students. Warm and caring teachers were often featured in the interviews, yet some respondents also acknowledge widespread use of corporal punishment in these institutions, which must have left some students feeling alienated from teachers they perceived as overly harsh. That said, we do not believe our interview respondents intentionally offered biased or misleading reports in describing their experiences, but we do think it is important to reflect on the degree of partiality to pleasant memories evident in their accounts.

Most of our subjects were successful students and went on to lead fulfilling lives after graduation. After all, these are the type of people—

those with positive memories or school—who usually answer the call to participate in studies of this sort. Individuals who dropped out of school, who decided that it held little meaning for them, who objected to the treatment and discipline they encountered, or who could not afford to forego earnings from work, were less likely to come forward to participate. From the standpoint of sampling, in that case, it is important to exercise considerable caution in making generalizations based upon the evidence derived from such sources. For this reason, we believe it is likely that studies relying predominantly on interview data similar to that used in this study may offer a somewhat one-sided vision of Black high schools in the past. We do not believe that this is a problem unique to African American history; nostalgia for the past, collective memory making, and focusing on positive memories of institutions in the past is common. This is even more likely to occur when memories are filtered through the difficulties of desegregation and the perception of declining interest in high school among many students today. As Shircliffe has argued, nostalgia in oral histories provides interview subjects a way to critique present circumstances and reflect on the loss of valued cultural traditions.[1] Thus, we found it critical to balance the use of interview data with information from a range of additional sources.

Examining high school yearbooks, for instance, proved helpful for understanding some of the changes that were unfolding during the process of integration, such as demographic shifts in the student body, levels of participation by African American students in various activities, and emerging cultural and educational trends. Yearbooks, for example, documented higher levels of turnover among administrators and teachers as high schools became more racially diverse, which created less continuity and stability in the 1960s and 1970s than in previous decades. There were often significant gaps in the sizes of the freshman and senior classes, countering the perceptions of our interview respondents that practically no one dropped out. A growing casualness about high school is reflected in shifting patterns of attire, evident in fewer dresses, shirts, khaki pants, and ties, and fewer students bothering to have their yearbook pictures taken. Through yearbooks, we saw striking changes in the types of activities and courses being offered as schools transitioned from all-White to mostly Black, such as more race-relations and vocational classes, fewer language and science clubs, and in some cases, more despair among students about the value of their education and their future prospects for success.

We also utilized hundreds of articles collected from major newspapers, including the *Chicago Tribune*, the *Chicago Defender*, the *Atlanta Daily World*, the *Atlanta Constitution*, the *Pittsburgh Courier*, *New York Amsterdam News*, the *Baltimore African American*, the *Los Angeles Sentinel*, the *New York Times*, and

Oral History Interviews and Other Sources 203

the Washington Post. These publications offered broad coverage of a range of educational issues, both local and national, and enabled us to identify key players and important developments in Black high schools. Using these articles, we documented national efforts urging youth to stay in school, the numerous local programs offering opportunities for dropouts, and growing dissatisfaction with the quality of schools in urban areas, among many other developments. Moreover, we found editorials expressing contemporary views on school integration, and especially the divisive issue of busing, and articles describing the numerous racial clashes at schools, responses by school officials, educators, and politicians, and the various policies aimed at addressing school inequities. While these articles also represented a somewhat partisan viewpoint in many instances, they were an invaluable source of information on a wide range of issues. Interview data alone could hardly capture the full extent of such questions.

Finally, we utilized archival research to consider a wide range of documents from state entities, school board officials, and educators. We visited state archives in several cities and researched records pertaining to educational issues, especially those that revealed racial disparities in the quality of and access to high school and debates over racial integration. At an archival library in Georgia, for example, we reviewed annual reports of the Department of Education to the General Assembly, Directors' Correspondence, and reports from the Division of Negro Education for the 1940s, 1950s and 1960s. From these records, we culled data on school expenditures and enrollment by race, reports that evaluated the quality of various schools and accreditation, and correspondence revealing efforts to equalize educational resources. Although we had to be judicious in picking sites to conduct this research, and there are many archives across the country that we might also have utilized, the documentary sources we did examine provided yet another perspective on the historical development of African American schooling during this time.

In the end, we believe that this combination of sources has provided us with the most trustworthy insights into the development of African American secondary schooling in the past. Oral history interviews have added a great deal to the study, but have proven most helpful in concert with a range of evidentiary materials. As suggested above, of course, we have only utilized a sampling of the readily available historical records concerning African American education in this period, so this study is hardly the final word on the question. Our hope is that it will contribute to the conversation about race and schooling in the United States, and stimulate other researchers to continue investigating the intriguing and maddening history of inequity and Black education.

APPENDIX B

Logistic Regression Analysis of Secondary School Attainment

THESE TABLES PRESENT the results of logistic regression analyses of school enrollment and attainment in Chapters 1–4 of the book. These results are depicted in charts in the text; the following tables provide additional information about the findings of these analyses, including statistical significance, standard errors and estimates of explained variance. The classification cut value in each model was .50. All samples were expanded using the IPUMS "personweight" weighting variable to estimate population parameters. As indicated in Chapter 1, the Log Odds coefficients used to construct the figures in the chapters are simply logarithmic expressions of the Odds Ratios, which are also listed in the tables below.

Table B.1. Logistic Regression of Factors Contributing to High School Enrollment, African American and White Youth, Ages 14–18, Metropolitan South, 1940

Independent Variables	BLACK		WHITE	
	Log Odds	Odds Ratio	Log Odds	Odds Ratio
Subject is Female	.358** (.010)	1.431	.188** (.005)	1.207
Lives in Central City	.640** (.011)	1.897	.151** (.005)	1.163
Parent HS Graduate	1.317** (.031)	3.731	.848** (.009)	2.335
Parent White-Collar Job	.789** (.024)	2.200	.889** (.006)	2.432
Home Owned by Family	.769** (.011)	2.158	.505** (.005)	1.657
Female Household Head	-.468** (.011)	.626	-.132* (.006)	.876
Subject is Employed	-1.270** (.017)	.281	-.589** (.007)	.555

Dependent variable: Enrollment (or not) in high school. Standard Errors are in parentheses.
*Significant at .05 level. **Significant at .001 level. Naglegerke r/2=.166 for Blacks, .142 for Whites.

Logistic Regression Analysis

Table B.2. Logistic Regression, Factors Contributing to High School Enrollment, Black and White Youth, Ages 14–18, Metropolitan South, 1960

Independent Variable	BLACK		WHITE	
	Log Odds	Odds Ratio	Log Odds	Odds Ratio
Subject is Female	.290** (.006)	1.337	.262** (.003)	1.299
Subject in Central City	.456** (.006)	1.578	-.074* (.004)	.929
Parent HS Graduate	.827** (.020)	2.287	.603** (.005)	1.828
Parent White-Collar Job	.575** (.016)	1.777	.618** (.004)	1.855
Home Owned by Family	.642** (.006)	1.899	.438** (.003)	1.549
Household Below Poverty	-.382** (.006)	.682	-.439** (.004)	.645
Female Household Head	-.120* (.008)	.887	-.165** (.004)	.848
Subject is Employed	-.521** (.007)	.594	.049 (.004)	1.050

Dependent variable: Enrollment (or not) in high school. Standard Errors are in parentheses. *significant at .05 level; **significant at .001 level. Naglegerke $r/2$=.147 for Blacks, .138 for Whites.

Table B.3. Logistic Regression, Factors Contributing to High School Success, Black and White Youth, Age 17, North and West, 1940

Independent Variables	BLACK		WHITE	
	Log Odds	Odds Ratio	Log Odds	Odds Ratio
North Region	-.41 (.026)	.658	-.079 (.004)	.924
Non Metro Area	.335 (.040)	1.398	-.030 (.005)	.971
Central City	.571 (.028)	1.770	.175 (.004)	1.191
Subject is Female	.378 (.021)	1.460	.281 (.003)	1.324
Parents High School Graduate	.600 (.051)	1.822	.760 (.007)	2.137
Parent with White-Collar Job	.885 (.040)	2.422	.737 (.005)	2.089
Home Owned by Family	.982 (.026)	2.669	.347 (.004)	1.415
Female Household Head	-.367 (.023)	.693	-.342 (.005)	.710
Subject Employed	-.011 (.031)	.989	-.858 (.005)	.424
Born in South	-.517 (.024)	.596	-.478 (.012)	.620
Subject on a Farm	-.185 (.065)	.831	-.140 (.005)	.870

Dependent variable: Enrollment (or not) at the junior level, including graduation. Standard errors are in parentheses. All factors significant at .001 level. Nagelkerke $r/2$=.125 for Blacks, .126 for Whites.

Table B.4. Logistic Regression, Factors Contributing to High School Success, Black and White Youth, Age 17, North and West, 1960

Independent Variables	BLACK		WHITE	
	Log Odds	Odds Ratio	Log Odds	Odds Ratio
North Region	-.086 (.016)	.918	-.084 (.00)	.920
Non Metro Area	-.182 (.029)	.834	-.062 (.00)	.940
Central City	.015 (.017)	1.015	.063 (.004)	1.065
Subject is Female	.473 (.013)	1.604	.334 (.005)	1.397
Parent High School Graduate	1.214 (.032)	3.366	.860 (.005)	2.363
Parent with White-Collar Job	.366 (.022)	1.442	.825 (.004)	2.282
Home Owned by Family	.548 (.014)	1.729	.695 (.007)	2.004
Female Household Head	-.454 (.014)	.635	-.718 (.005)	.488
Subject Employed	-.258 (.018)	.772	-.079 (.004)	.924
Poverty Status	-.390 (.014)	.677	-.324 (.005)	.723
Born in South	-.141 (.014)	.868	-.491 (.009)	.612
Subject on a Farm	-1.094 (.075)	.335	.417 (.007)	1.518

Dependent variable: Enrollment (or not) at the junior level, including graduation. Standard errors are in parentheses. All factors significant at .001 level, except central city residence for Black youth, which is statistically insignificant. Nagelkerke r/2= .141 for Blacks, .202 for Whites.

Logistic Regression Analysis

Table B.5. Logistic Regression: Factors Associated with Success in School, Black and White 17-Year-Olds, 1970

Independent Variables	BLACK		WHITE	
	Log Odds	Odds Ratio	Log Odds	Odds Ratio
Subject Lives on Farm	-.101 (.022)	.90	.370* (.008)	1.49
Subject in Central City	-.01 (.009)	.99	.020 (.004)	1.02
Parent HS Graduate	.636* (.010)	1.89	.915* (.004)	2.50
Parent White-Collar Job	.162 (.011)	1.17	.557* (.004)	1.75
Home Owned by Family	.707* (.009)	1.92	.661* (.004)	2.03
Household Below Poverty	-.290* (.010)	.78	-.612* (.004)	.54
Female Household Head	-.113 (.015)	.89	-.150* (.006)	.86
Subject is Female	.526* (.008)	1.69	.515* (.007)	1.67
Subject is Employed	.106 (.011)	1.11	.167* (.004)	1.12
Subject Born in South	-.097 (.009)	.91	-.378* (.004)	.68

Dependent variable: Enrollment (or not) at the junior level, including graduation. Standard errors are in parentheses.
*Significant at .05 or higher.
Nagelgerke R^2=.104 for Blacks, .143 for Whites.

Notes

Introduction

1. "School Board's Inaction Hit," *Baltimore Afro-American*, May 5, 1951, p. 1.

2. The story of the struggle in Farmville is told in detail in Richard Kluger, Simple Justice (New York: Vintage Books, 1975), Ch. 19; also see James Patterson, *Brown v. Board of Education: A Civil Rights Milestone and Its Troubled Legacy* (New York: Oxford University Press, 2001), pp. 27–29.

3. Robert A. Margo, "Explaining Black-White Wage Convergence, 1940–1950," *Industrial and Labor Relations Review,* Vol. 48, No. 3 (April 1995), pp. 470–481.

4. Louis Harlan, *Separate and Unequal: Public School Campaigns and Racism in the Southern Seaboard States, 1901–1915* (New York: Atheneum, 1968), Ch. VIII. On Black high schools in the South prior to 1940, see James D. Anderson, *The Education of Blacks in the South, 1960–1935* (Chapel Hill: University of North Carolina Press, 1988), pp. 196–197. On conditions outside the South, see Davison Douglass, *Jim Crow Moves North: The Battle over Northern School Desegregation, 1865–1954* (New York: Cambridge University Press, 2005), Chs. 4 & 5.

5. This estimate is based on calculating graduation rates for 19-year-old youth from the 1940 census, utilizing Integrated Public Use Microdata Series (IPUMS) data from the Minnesota Population Center: Steven Ruggles, J. Trent Alexander, Katie Genadek, Ronald Goeken, Matthew B. Schroeder, and Matthew Sobek, *Integrated Public Use Microdata Series: Version 5.0* [Machine-readable database] (Minneapolis: University of Minnesota, 2010). We are grateful to the IPUMS program for the use of these data.

6. John Modell, *Into One's Own: From Youth to Adulthood in the United States, 1920–1975* (Berkeley: University of California Press, 1991), Ch. 4.

7. John L. Rury, "The Comprehensive High School, Enrollment Expansion and Inequality: The United States in the Postwar Era," in Barry Franklin and Gary McCullough, eds., *The Death of the Comprehensive High School* (New York: Palgrave Macmillan, 2003), pp. 53–72.

8. Alexander W. Astin, *Minorities in American Higher Education* (San Francisco: Jossey-Bass, 1982), Ch. 4.

9. Orley Ashenfelter, William J. Collins, and Albert Yoon, "Evaluating the Role of *Brown vs. Board of Education* in School Equalization, Desegregation, and the Income of African Americans," NBER Working Paper 11394 (2005); David Card and Alan B. Krueger, "School Quality and Black-White Relative Earnings: A Direct Assessment," *The Quarterly Journal of Economics*, Vol. 107, No. 1 (February 1992), pp. 151–200.

10. We discuss this point in greater depth in the book's conclusion.

11. On this point, see Jerome Morris, "Research, Ideology and the Brown Decision: Counter-narratives to the Historical and Contemporary Representation of Black Schooling," *Teachers College Record*, Vol. 110 No. 4 (2008), pp. 713–732.

12. For discussion of this, see Sar Levitan and Robert Taggert, *Still a Dream: The Changing Status of Blacks Since 1960* (Cambridge, MA: Harvard University Press, 1975), Ch. 4. An exception to this is Kurt J. Bauman, "Schools, Markets, and Family in the History of African-American Education," *American Journal of Education,* Vol. 106, No. 4 (August, 1998), pp. 500–531.

13. Michael Klarman, *Brown v. Board of Education and the Civil Rights Movement* (New York: Oxford University Press, 2007), Ch. 7; Raymond Wolters, *The Burden of Brown: Thirty Years of School Desegregation* (Knoxville: University of Tennessee Press, 1992), Chs. 2, 3, & 4.

14. This was recognized at the time and followed by the Black press. "1950 Census to Show Great Race Progress," *Chicago Defender,* March 18, 1950, p. 11.

15. On this point, see John D. Skrentny, *The Minority Rights Revolution* (Cambridge, MA: Harvard University Press, 2004), passim. Jacquelyn Dowd Hall, "The Long Civil Rights Movement and the Political Uses of the Past," *Journal of American History,* Vol. 91: No. 4 (March 2005), pp. 1233–1263.

16. Herschel Summers interview with John Rury, Booker T. Washington High School, Atlanta, GA, June 2007. We use pseudonyms for all oral history interviewees.

17. On the struggle to increase employment prospects for African Americans, and to aggressively fight discrimination both in large corporations and the government, see Sar A. Levitan, William B. Johnston, and Robert Taggert, *Still a Dream: The Changing Status of Blacks Since 1960* (Cambridge, MA: Harvard University Press, 1975). Ch. 13.

18. Mabel Fountain interview with Shirley Hill, Booker T. Washington High School, Atlanta, GA, June 2007.

19. Robert L. Hampel, *The Last Little Citadel: American High Schools Since 1940* (New York: Houghton Mifflin, 1987), passim; William J. Reese, *Origins of the American High School* (New Haven, CT: Yale University Press, 1995), Epilogue.

20. Claudia Goldin and Lawrence Katz, *The Race Between Education and Technology* (Cambridge, MA: Harvard University Press, 2008), Chs. 5 & 6.

21. Anderson, *Education of Blacks in the South,* Ch. 6; Robert A. Margo, *Race and Schooling in the South, 1880–1950: an Economic History* (Chicago: University of Chicago Press, 1990), Ch. 6.

22. William J. Collins and Robert A. Margo,"Historical Perspectives on Racial Differences in Schooling in the United States," in E. Hanusheck and F. Welch, eds., *Handbook of the Economics of Education, Volume 1* (Amsterdam, North-Holland: Elsevier, 2006), Ch. 3; John J. Donohue III, James J. Heckman, and Petra E. Todd, "The Schooling of Southern Blacks: The Roles of Legal Activism and Private Philanthropy, 1910–1960," *Quarterly Journal of Economics,* Vol. 117, No. 1 (February 2002), pp. 225–268; James P. Smith and Finis R. Welch, "Black Economic Progress after Myrdal," *Journal of Economic Literature, 27,* No.2 (June 1989), pp. 519–564.

23. Summers interview with Rury; Fountain interview with Hill.

24. This was recognized by contemporaries; see "Negroes Top Whites Attending College," *Chicago Defender,* August 26, 1950, p. 14.

25. Doug McAdam, *Political Process and the Development of Black Insurgency, 1930–1970* (Chicago: University of Chicago Press, 1999), Chs. 5 & 6; Rebecca de Schweinitz, *If We Could Change the World: Young People and America's Long Struggle for Racial Equality* (Chapel Hill: University of North Carolina Press, 2009), Ch. 5; Claybourne Carson, *In Struggle, SNCC and the Black Awakening of the 1960s* (Cambridge, MA: Harvard University Press, 1981), passim.

26. McAdam, *Political Insurgency,* Ch. 5.

27. Vanessa Siddle Walker, "Valued Segregated Schools for African American Children in the South, 1935–1969: A Review of Common Themes and Characteristics," *Review of Educational Research, 70* (Fall 2000), pp. 253–285; Vivian Morris and Curtis Morris, *Creating*

Caring and Nurturing Educational Environments for African American Children (Westport, CT: Bergin and Garvey, 2000), passim.

28. The work of Vanessa Siddle Walker has been particularly noteworthy in this regard. See her books, *Their Highest Potential: An African American School Community in the Segregated South* (Chapel Hill: University of North Carolina Press, 1996), passim, and, with Ulysses Byas, *Hello Professor: A Black Principal and Professional Leadership in the Segregated South* (Chapel Hill: University of North Carolina Press, 2009), passim. For an overview of this literature, see Vanessa Siddle Walker with Ulysses Byas, "The Architects of Black Schooling in the Segregated South: The Case of One Principal Leader," *Journal of Curriculum and Supervision,* Vol. 19, No. 1 (Fall 2003), pp. 57–58.

29. Kathryn M. Neckerman, *Schools Betrayed: The Roots of Failure in Inner City Education* (Chicago: University of Chicago Press, 2007), Chs 5, 6 & 7; Douglas Davison, *Jim Crow Moves North: The Battle over Northern School Desegregation, 1865–1954* (New York: Cambridge University Press, 2005), Ch. 6; Judy Jolly Mohraz, *The Separate Problem: Case Studies of Black Education in the North, 1900–1930* (Westport, CT: Greenwood Publishers, 1979), Ch. 6; Thomas Sugrue, *Sweet Land of Liberty; The Forgotten Struggle for Civil Rights in the North* (New York: Random House, 2008), Ch. 6.

30. On Chicago, see Neckerman, *Schools Betrayed,* Ch. 4; on Philadelphia, see Vincent P. Franklin, *The Education of Black Philadelphia: The Social and Educational History of a Minority Community, 1900–1950* (Philadelphia: University of Pennsylvania Press, 1979), Part Two; on Detroit, see Jeffrey Mirel, *The Rise and Fall of an Urban School System: Detroit, 1907–81* (Ann Arbor: University of Michigan Press, 1993), Chs. 4 & 5; on Los Angeles, see Judith Rosenberg Raftery, *Land of Fair Promise: Politics and Reform in the Los Angeles Schools, 1885–1941* (Palo Alto, CA: Stanford University Press, 1992), pp. 183–191; on Milwaukee, see Jack Dougherty, *More Than One Struggle: The Evolution of Black School Reform in Milwaukee* (Chapel Hill: University of North Carolina Press, 2004), Chs. 2 & 3; on Boston, see Joseph Cronin, *Reforming Boston Schools, 1930–2006: Overcoming Corruption and Racial Segregation* (New York: Palgrave Macmillan, 2008), Chs. 3 & 4; and on Cleveland, see William D. Henderson, "Demography and Desegregation in the Cleveland Public Schools: Towards a Comprehensive Theory of Educational Failure and Success," *Review of Law and Social Change,* Vol. 26, No. 4 (February 2002), pp. 460–568.

31. There is relatively little research on this point. For relevant case studies, see Jeanne Theoharis, "'I'd Rather Go To School in the South': How Boston's School Desegregation Complicates the Civil Rights Paradigm;" Scott Brown, "The Politics of Culture: The US Organization and the Quest for Black Unity"; and Johanna Fernandez, "Between Social Service Reform and Revolutionary Politics: The Young Lords, Late Sixties Radicalism and Community Organizing in New York City," in Jeanne F. Theoharis and Komozi Woodard, eds., *Freedom North: Black Freedom Struggles Outside the South, 1940–1980* (New York: Palgrave Macmillan, 2003), pp. 125–152, 223–254, and 255–286. Also see John F. Lyons, *Teachers and Reform: Chicago Public Education, 1929–1970* (Urbana: University of Illinois Press, 2008), Ch 6.

32. Princeton Elroy interview with Shirley Hill, Kansas City, MO, June 2008.

33. Ibid.

34. On life for African Americans in the rural South and during the Great Migration, see Stewart Tolnay, *The Bottom Rung: African American Family Life on Southern Farms* (Urbana: University of Illinois Press, 1999), passim, and idem., "Educational Selection in the Migration of Southern Blacks, 1880–1990," *Social Forces,* Vol. 77, No. 2 (December 1998), pp. 487–514. For an overview, see Tolnay's review article, "The African American 'Great Migration' and Beyond," Annual Review of Sociology, Vol. 29 (2003), pp. 209–232, and Calvin L. Beale, "Rural-Urban Migration of Blacks: Past and Future," American Journal of Agricultural Economics, Vol. 53, No. 2. (May 1971), pp. 302–307.

Notes

35. For an overview of the historical origins of this process, see David B. Tyack, *The One Best System: A History of Urban Education in the United States* (Cambridge, MA: Harvard University Press, 1974); for examination of these issues in a prototypical Northern industrial city, see Jeffrey E. Mirel, *The Rise and Fall of an Urban School System: Detroit, 1907–81*(Ann Arbor: University of Michigan Press, 1993).

36. On this point, see John L. Rury, "Attainment Amidst Adversity: Black High School Students in the Metropolitan North, 1940–1980," in Kenneth Wong and Robert Rothman, eds., *Clio at the Table: History and Educational Policy* (New York: Peter Lang, 2009), pp. 37–58.

37. On the quality of secondary education, for both Blacks and Whites, in the postwar era, see David L. Angus and Jeffrey E. Mirel, *The Failed Promise of the American High School, 1890-1995* (New York: Teachers College Press, 1999) Ch. 4.

38. Rury, "Attainment Amidst Adversity," pp. 45–50.

39. Rury interview with Summers; Hill interview with Fountain.

40. David Armor, *Forced Justice: School Desegregation and the Law* (New York: Oxford University Press, 1995), p. 56; Derek Neal, "How Families and Schools Shape the Achievement Gap," in Paul E. Peterson, ed., *Generational Change: Closing the Test Score Gap* (Lanham, MD: Rowman & Littlefield, 2006), pp. 26–46.

41. Paul E. Peterson, "Toward the Elimination of Race Differences in Educational Achievement," in Paul E. Peterson, ed., *Generational Change: Closing the Test Score Gap* (Lanham, MD: Rowman & Littlefield, 2006), pp. 1–25.

42. On the changes in generations, see Signithia Fordham, *Blacked Out: Dilemmas of Race, Identity and Success at Capital High* (Chicago: University of Chicago Press, 1996), pp. 44–45.

43. Mark Berends, Samuel R. Lucas, and Roberto V. Peñaloza, "How Changes in Families and Schools Are Related to Trends in Black-White Test Scores," *Sociology of Education*, Vol. 81, No. 4 (October 2008), pp. 313–344. They argue that improvements in the educational experiences of Black students attending schools with White students accounted for most of the additional reduction in the gap.

44. Michael D. Cook and William N. Evans, "Families or Schools? Explaining the Convergence in White and Black Academic Performance," *Journal of Labor Economics*, Vol. 18, No. 4 (October 2000), pp. 729–754; Armor, *Forced Justice*, pp. 57–58; Peterson, "Toward the Elimination of Race Differences in Educational Achievement," passim.

Chapter 1

1. James D. Anderson, *Education of Blacks in the South, 1860–1935* (Chapel Hill, University of North Carolina Press, 1988), p. 237.

2. Walter G. Daniel, "Availability of Education for Negroes in the Secondary School," *The Journal of Negro Education*, 16:3 (Summer 1947), pp. 450–458; C. Arnold Anderson, "Inequalities in Schooling in the South," *The American Journal of Sociology*, 60: 6 (May 1955), pp. 547–561.

3. Claudia Goldin, "America's Graduation from High School: The Evolution and Spread of Secondary Schooling in the Twentieth Century," *The Journal of Economic History*, Vol. 58, No. 2 (June 1998), pp. 345–374.

4. "Improving Education in the Southern States," Report of the Committee on Negro Education, Ed McCuistian, Chairman, Southern States Work Conference on School Administrative Problems (Tallahassee, FL, 1938), p. 23; Doxey Wilkerson, "Special Problems of Negro Education," Staff Study No. 12, Advisory Commission on Education, (1939), pp. 40–41.

5. See, for instance, "One Third of Counties in Tenn. Fail to Provide High Schools for Negroes," *Atlanta Daily World*, December 23, 1950, p. 5. School officials argued that numbers

were too low to "warrant organization and operation of an upper grade school large enough to be effective," despite legal requirements to provide "equal" education.

6. Edward E. Redcay, *County Training Schools and Public Secondary Education for Negroes in the South* (John F. Slater Fund Studies in Negro Education, Washington, DC: The John F. Slater Fund, 1935), Ch. III.

7. Committee on Education of the Virginia State Chamber of Commerce, "Opportunities for the Improvement of High School Education in Virginia," (November 1943), p. 1.

8. In his analysis of Black schooling in the first half of the 20th century, Robert Margo focuses on property ownership as a proxy for wealth, and also notes the significance of farm status in this era. See Robert A. Margo, *Race and Schooling in the South, 1880–1950* (Chicago: University of Chicago Press, 1990), Ch. 5. Similar points are made by Stewart Tolnay, *The Bottom Rung: African American Family Life on Southern Farms* (Urbana and Chicago: University of Illinois Press, 1999), Ch. 2.

9. E. Franklin Frazier, "The Negro Family and Negro Youth," *The Journal of Negro Education*, Vol. 9, No. 3 (July 1940), p. 290.

10. On conditions early in the 20th century, see Pamela Barnhouse Walters and Carl M. Briggs, "The Family Economy, Child Labor, and Schooling: Evidence from the Early Twentieth-Century South," *American Sociological Review*, Vol. 58, No. 2 (April 1993), pp. 163–181; also see Tolnay, *The Bottom Rung*, Ch. 2.

11. Ira De A. Reid, "General Characteristics of the Negro Youth Population," *The Journal of Negro Education*, Vol. 9, No. 3 (July 1940), p. 284.

12. We focus on 17-year-olds because of the greater propensity of older (18+) youth to move on, leaving school, whether for employment or additional education. The postwar era, of course, was a time of considerable migration between states and regions, as suggested in the book's Introduction. Since most 17-year-olds lived at home, using these individuals also permits us to connect them to characteristics of the parents and parental households in the census data. Generally speaking, the percentage of 17-year-olds enrolled in the junior or senior year or graduated appears to be a fair approximation of the 19-year-old graduation rate in this period. Using IPUMS 1% samples in 1940, 1960, and 1980, we compared the rate of junior and senior enrollment for 17-year-olds and the high school graduation rate (completed senior year) for 19-year-olds. According to the IPUMS data, in 1960, about 60% of 17-year-olds were enrolled in the junior or senior year of high school, and 61% of 19-year-olds reportedly were high school graduates. In 1980, the figures were 77% and 76%. A small portion of 17-year-olds—about 5%—each year had already graduated, accounting for some of the discrepancy in the numbers. Altogether, this pattern conforms to the findings of David Card and Thomas Lemieux, who maintained that "retention rates from the eleventh grade to the twelfth for both men and women are very stable over the period 1968–96, averaging about 95 percent. Rates of high school completion (conditional on having been enrolled in the eleventh grade) are also fairly stable, at around 92–94 percent, although in the last few years the rates seem to have slipped." David Card and Thomas Lemieux, "Dropout and Enrollment Trends in the Postwar Period: What Went Wrong in the 1970s?" In J. Gruber, ed., *Risky Behavior Among Youths: An Economic Analysis* (Chicago: University of Chicago Press), p. 446.

13. This is a point made in Tolnay, *The Bottom Rung*, pp. 45–47, and Margo, *Race and Schooling in the South*, Ch. 6. In the IPUMS data, 29% of the Black males aged 14 to 18 living in property-owning farm families in the South in 1940 were categorized as unpaid family laborers, while 12% were paid. Among those living in tenant households, 18% were paid farm laborers. Among Whites, unpaid family farm laborers represented about 20% of teenage males in both tenant and property-owning farm families.

14. These figures were calculated with IPUMS data. In Cotton Belt states with high farm tenancy (LA, MS, AL, GA, SC) outside of metropolitan areas, Black teachers with no

collegiate training numbered more than a third.

15. On the earlier feminization of secondary enrollments, see John L. Rury, *Education and Women's Work: Female Schooling and the Division of Labor in Urban America, 1870–1930* (Albany: State University of New York Press, 1991), Ch. 1, and David Tyack and Elisabeth Hansot, *Learning Together: A History of Coeducation in American Schools* (New Haven, CT: Yale University Press, 1990), Ch. 5.

16. Frazier, "The Negro Family and Negro Youth," p. 290; Tolnay, *The Bottom Rung*, Ch. 2

17. This statistic was calculated at the state level using the figures in Table 1.3, with state population size as a weight. The unweighted correlation between property ownership and secondary enrollment is .6 and is also statistically significant at the .001 level.

18. These numbers are calculated from IPUMS data. Among Black non-farm youth aged 14 to 18, the employment rate in 1940 was 22.3%. Among Whites, the corresponding figure was 15.3%. The racial difference in youth employment was greatest in the countryside, where 23% of White youth held jobs, as opposed to 37.7% of African Americans. Among non-property-owning African Americans, the youth employment rate was 39.1%, and for males in this group it was 56%, again underscoring the gender imbalance evident in secondary enrollments for households in this category.

19. Anderson, *The Education of Blacks in the South*, p. 160.

20. South Carolina Department of Education, *Report of the Superintendent of Schools, 1945*, "Division of Negro Education" (Columbia, SC, 1945), p. 140.

21. *Sixty Eighth and Sixty Ninth Annual Reports of the Department of Education to the General Assembly of the State of Georgia for the Biennium Ending June 30, 1940* (Atlanta, 1940), p. 6.

22. "Lumberton School Strike," File in N.C. Newbold Papers, Department of Public Instruction, Division of Negro Education, North Carolina State Archives, Raleigh, NC.

23. Adam Fairclough, *Better Day Coming: Blacks and Equality, 1890–2000* (New York: Viking Penguin, 2001), Ch. 10.

24. "Mississippi Schools for Negroes: Facts from a Report to the Executive Committee," Board of Education, *Mississippi Annual Conference of the Methodist Church* (Vicksburg, MS, February 3, 1942), p. 6; *Mississippi State Superintendent Report, 1945–47*, "Division of Negro Education" (Jackson, MS, 1947), p. 41; *Mississippi's Negro Rural Schools: Suggestions for Their Improvement*, P. H. Easom–J. A, Travis, State Agents, Bulletin No. 94 (Mississippi Department of Education, 1938), p. 2.

25. Alabama Department of Education, *Annual Report, 1947* (Montgomery, AL, 1947), p. 70.

26. "A Survey of Public Education of Less Than College Grade in Georgia," *A Report to the General Assembly of Georgia by Its Special Committee on Education* (Atlanta, GA, January 1, 1947), p. 137; M. D. Collins, State Superintendent of Education, *Look at Our Schools as They Are Today*, (Atlanta, GA: Department of Education, 1949), p. 110. On regional trends, see Walter G. Daniel, "Availability of Education for Negroes in the Secondary School," *The Journal of Negro Education*, Vol. 16, No. 3 (Summer 1947), pp. 452–453.

27. Statement on Small Schools, January 13, 1948, Newbold Papers, Division of Negro Education, North Carolina State Archives, Raleigh, NC. A year earlier, Newbold had described some elementary schools as "utterly unfit for human habitation." Speech to Superintendents, August 7, 1947.

28. Mississippi Department of Education, "Public Schools for Negro Children," Prepared by the Division of Administration and Finance, C. J. Crain, Director, Issued by J. M. Tubb, State Superintendent of Education (typescript), J. M. Tubb Papers, Mississippi State Archives, Jackson, MS. On another state, see J. B. Cade, "The Education of Negroes in Louisiana," *The Journal of Negro Education*, Vol. 16, No. 3 (Summer 1947), pp. 361–369. Black one-room schools outnumbered White ones there in 1944 by a 12 to 1 margin.

29. Interview with Professor N. R. Burger, Mississippi Oral History Program of the University of Southern Mississippi, volume 356, 1982, p. 24.

30. *Look at Our Schools*, p. 122; "Report of the Committee on Negro Education," Improving Education in the Southern States, Southern States Work Conference on School Administrative Problems (1941), p. 23.

31. Speech at Florida A&M College, March 7, 1948, Newbold Papers.

32. Alabama Department of Education, *Annual Report*, "School Consolidation," p. 56.

33. "Survey of Public Education of Less than College Grade in Georgia," pp. 135–136.

34. These estimates were arrived at by comparing figures in "Improving Education in the Southern States" and Walter G. Daniel, "Availability of Education for Negroes in the Secondary School," p. 451.

35. On these points see Margo, *Race and Schooling in the South*, Chs. 6 & 7.

36. Jeffrey Mirel and David Angus, *The Failed Promise of the American High School, 1890–1995* (New York: Teachers College Press, 1999), p. 80; Daniel, "Availability of Education for Negroes in the Secondary School," p. 450.

37. Interview with Professor N. R. Burger, Mississippi Oral History Project, p. 25. Burger's interviewer, R. Wayne Pyle, commented that he had heard similar observations from other educators in the state, "that where independence existed there was a lot more freedom in the educational system, a lot more money (and) a lot more drive for the education." Also see interview with Mr. C. J. Duckworth, Mississippi Oral History Program of the University of Southern Mississippi, Vol. 352, (1975), p. 5. Duckworth also maintained that Black property owners took initiative in establishing schools, using Rosenwald funds to provide assistance. This observation, of course, conforms to other studies of the period. See Vanessa Siddle Walker, *Their Highest Potential: An African American School Community in the Segregated South* (Chapel Hill: University of North Carolina Press, 1996), Chs. 2 & 3.

38. On this point, see Vivian Gunn Morris and Curtis L. Morris, *The Price They Paid: Desegregation in an African American Community* (New York: Teachers College Press, 2002), pp. 44–45, which quotes a 1911 speech by the Black Alabama educator G. W. Trenholm advocating this approach over establishing private secondary schools for African Americans.

39. Redcay, *County Training Schools and Public Secondary Education for Negroes in the South*, Chs. I and II. For a discussion of the secondary program offered in country training schools, see Reid E. Jackson, "County Training Schools in Alabama," *The School Review*, Vol. 47, No. 9 (November 1939), pp. 683–694.

40. On this point, see Anderson, *The Education of Blacks in the South*, p. 156, and Morris and Morris, *The Price They Paid*, p. 46.

41. Letter from Robert Cousins to Miss Ruth Morton, December 12, 1941, American Missionary Society Folder, Division of Negro Education Papers, Box 4, Georgia State Archives, Morrow, GA. A new Black high school was finally built in Macon some 9 years later, under very different circumstances, with support from the state. See "$500,000 High School Erected in Macon, GA," *The Pittsburgh Courier*, November 5, 1949, p. 11. Also see the discussion of alternatives in Mississippi, where superintendents recommended "adding high school work to existing elementary schools" while central high schools were planned in some areas." Agitation Deplored as Key to Negro Problem in State," *Jackson Daily News*, June 18, 1946, Percy H. Eason Clipping File, Mississippi State Archives, Jackson, MS.

42. Ellis O. Know emphasized the role of the latter institutions. See "A Historical Sketch of Secondary Education for Negroes," pp. 450–451. For a compelling case study of one such school, see Vanessa Siddle Walker, *Their Highest Potential: An African American School Community in the Segregated South* (Chapel Hill: University of North Carolina Press, 1996), Chs. 1–3.

43. "Public Schools for Negroes," State Department of Education of Louisiana, *Bulletin 614*, October 1946; *Mississippi State School Superintendent's Biennial Report, 1947–49*, "Negro Education," (Jackson, MS, 1949), p. 43.

44. Alethea H. Washington, "Negro Secondary Education in Rural Areas," *The Journal of Negro Education*, Vol. 9, No. 3 (July 1940), pp. 516–517. Programs for training Black

principals were a regular feature of school reports. See, for instance, Georgia Department of Education, *Biennial Report, 1941–2*, Division of Negro Education (Atlanta, GA, 1942), p. 51. On the need for teachers, see Mississippi State School Superintendent, *Biennial Report* (Jackson, MS, 1947), p. 13.

45. Robert L. Cousins, letter to L. M. Sheffer, July 9, 1940, Division of Negro Education Papers, Box 4, Sheffer File, Georgia State Archives, Morrow, GA.

46. Letter from Lexton Lewis to Robert Cousins, August 27, 1945, Division of Negro Education Papers, Box 4, American Missionary Society Folder, Georgia State Archives, Morrow, GA.

47. N. R. Burger noted the same practice in Mississippi, routinely used as a way to maximize the impact of state funds to support the school. Interview with Professor R. N. Burger, p. 23.

48. Grace Graham, "Negro Education Progresses in South Carolina," *Social Forces*, Vol. 30, No. 4 (May 1952), pp. 432, 437; Ernst W. Swanson and John A. Griffin, *Public Education in the South, Today and Tomorrow: A Statistical Survey* (Chapel Hill: University of North Carolina Press, 1955), p. 39. Across the South, the number of Black youth enrolled in high school increased by 54% between 1939 and 1949, with the biggest increases coming in the Deep South, where the African American population was most concentrated and enrollment rates were historically very low.

49. Edward E. Redcay, *County Training Schools and Public Secondary Education for Negroes in the South*, p. 57.

50. See, for instance, discussion of this in the report of the Committee on Education of the Virginia State Chamber of Commerce, "Opportunities for the Improvement of High School Education in Virginia, November 1943, p. 4. This was true for both Black and White schools.

51. See, for instance, the following articles: "600 Ready For BM Graduation Tonight," *Atlanta Daily World*, June 6, 1947, p. 11; "B. T. Washington High School," *Atlanta Daily World*, October 9, 1951, p. 3.

52. The fate of the sports teams of these institutions was a point of concern in 1954; see "High Court Ruling Will Alter High School Sports," *Chicago Defender*, May 29, 1954, p. 24.

53. John Rury interview with Calvin Roberts, Booker T. Washington High School, Atlanta, GA, June 2007; Shirley Hill interview with Grace Simpkins, Booker T. Washington High School, Atlanta, GA, June 2007; Shirley Hill interview with James Hilford, Jackson, MS, June 2008.

54. These figures were derived with IPUMS data from the 1940 census. Graduate work was calculated as 5 or more years of collegiate enrollment. The proportion of central city White teachers with graduate work was under 18%, or about twice the Black level, but the number with college degrees was much closer, at 56% for African Americans and 63% for Whites.

55. For Atlanta, see Georgia Department of Education, *Biennial Report of the Superintendent of Schools, 1940–42* (Atlanta, 1942), p. 152, which shows an enrollment decline from 1,008 to 473 between the 9th and 12th grade among Black students. Similar figures were reported in other urban high schools at the time.

56. See, for instance, "Washington Principal Tells of Needs of School, *Atlanta Daily World*, February 14, 1946, p. 1; "Interest High in Demand for School Probe," *Atlanta Daily World*, June 1, 1948, p. ; and "Officials Deny Charges Made Against High School," *Atlanta Daily World*, June 4, 1948, p. 1.

57. John Rury interview with Brandon Fleming; Shirley Hill interview with Gloria Traynor, Booker T. Washington High School, June 2007.

58. Andrew Weise, *Places of their Own: African American Suburbanization in the Twentieth Century* (Chicago: University of Chicago Press, 2004), Ch. 1; David Goldfield, *Cotton Fields and Skyscrapers: Southern City and Region* (Baltimore: Johns Hopkins University Press, 1989), Ch. 3.

59. See, for instance, Joel Perlmann, *Ethnic Differences: Schooling and Social Structure among the Irish, Italians, Jews, and Blacks in an American City, 1880–1935* (New York: Cambridge University Press, 1988), passim.

60. Georgia Department of Education, *Biennial Report, 1941–42*, "Secondary Education" (Atlanta: Department of Education, 1942), p. 10.

61. North Carolina Department of Education, Division of Negro Education, Mimeographed and Printed Material Files, General Correspondence of the Director, Box 22.

62. Ellis O. Knox, "A Historical Sketch of Secondary Education for Negroes," *The Journal of Negro Education*, Vol. 9, No. 3, (July 1940), pp. 450–451.

63. Georgia Department of Education, *Biennial Report, 1948–50* (Atlanta, 1950), pp. 308–309.

64. Alethea H. Washington, "Negro Secondary Education in Rural Areas," pp. 515–516.

65. State Department of Education of Louisiana, *Bulletin 633*, "Louisiana High School Standards for Organization and Administration," (Baton Rouge, 1947), p. 35.

66. *Mississippi's Negro Rural Schools: Suggestions for their Improvement*, p. 1.

67. See for instance, North Carolina Department of Public Instruction, *Biennial Report, 1948–50* (Raleigh, NC, 1950), p. 37. "A study of the North Carolina Schools has revealed that the central problem in improving educational opportunities for North Carolina youth is the small size of the high schools." In particular, it was noted that the curriculum was generally limited to five subjects: English, math, social studies, science, and foreign language. A South Carolina report from 1946 described the state's high school curricular expectations as "flexible," with only three units in English and one in history required. See South Carolina Department of Education, *78th Annual Report of the Superintendent of Education of the State of South Carolina* (Jackson, SC, 1946), p. 108. On trends across the South in this respect, see Walter G. Daniel, "The Aims of Secondary Education and the Adequacy of the Curriculum of the Negro Secondary School," *The Journal of Negro Education*, Vol. 9, No. 3 (July 1940), p. 470; Alethea H. Washington, "Negro Secondary Education in Rural Areas," p. 516, and Walter G. Daniel, "Availability of Education for Negroes in the Secondary School," pp. 455–456.

68. Louisiana State Department of Education, *Ninety Ninth Annual Report for the Session 1947–8*, Bulletin 658, Negro Education (Baton Rouge, 1949), p. 55.

69. State Department of Education of Louisiana, *Bulletin 633*, "Louisiana High School Standards for Organization and Administration," p. 36.

70. H. Councill Trenholm, "The Accreditation of the Negro High School," *The Journal of Negro Education*, Vol. 1, No. 1 (April 1932), pp. 34–43. On the relationship of the SACS to Black schools, see Vanessa Siddle Walker, *Hello Professor: A Black Principal and Professional Leadership in the Segregated South* (Chapel Hill: University of North Carolina Press, 2009) Ch. 3.

71. Melanie Deane Carter, "From Jim Crow to Inclusion: An Historical Analysis of the Association of Colleges and Secondary School for Negroes, 1934–1965" (unpublished Ph.D. dissertation, The Ohio State University, 1996), Chs. 2 & 3.

72. For discussion of the relatively small number of Black schools that qualified for regional accreditation, see S. L. Smith, "Library Facilities in Negro Secondary Schools," *The Journal of Negro Education*, Vol. 9, No. 3 (July 1940), p. 506.

73. Letter from Hill Ivy, Superintendent of Meridian, Mississippi Public Schools, October 11, 1939, Southern Association of Colleges and Schools Folder, Division of Negro Education, Georgia State Archives, Morrow, GA.

74. From early on, Cousins noted that accredited Black high schools "want to be measured by the same standards by which the White schools are measured." In particular, he reported that "the Negro teachers association in this state prefers the list (of accredited schools) to be small rather than include some schools which do not merit recognition." Let-

ter from R. L. Cousins to T. J. Dempsy, May 30, 1936, Division of Negro Education Papers, Box 4, Dr. D. J. Allman File, Georgia State Archives, Morrow, GA.

75. See the correspondence on this point in November 1939 with R. L. Cousins and various educators, including W. A. Robinson, Southern Association of Colleges and Schools Folder, Division of Negro Education, Georgia State Archives, Morrow, GA.

76. For instance, in a letter to R. L. Cousins, the principal of Booker T. Washington High School in Atlanta explained the measures being undertaken to meet accreditation requirements. Letter from C. N. Cornell, October 30, 1939, Division of Negro Education, Box 2, SACS Folder, Georgia State Archives, Morrow, GA.

77. Alabama Department of Education, *Narrative Report, 1947*, "Negro High Schools" (Montgomery, AL, 1947), p. 78.

78. South Carolina Department of Education, *80th Report of the Superintendent of Public Schools*, "Negro Education" (Columbia, SC, 1948), p. 103.

79. Alabama Department of Education, *Annual Report of the Superintendent*, "Negro High Schools" (Montgomery, AL, 1947), p. 78.

80. North Carolina Department of Public Instruction, Division of Negro Education, Special Subjects, Box 1, Folder: Accrediment of High Schools, 1944–48. North Carolina State Archives, Raleigh, NC. Speech to Superintendents, August 7, 1947, Newbold Papers, Division of Negro Education, North Carolina State Archives, Raleigh, NC.

81. Inequalities on these measures existed in border states as well. In 1944, more than 90% of Kentucky White high schools were accredited, as opposed to 78% of Black institutions. Although this was a considerably higher rate of accreditation for Black schools, the vast majority of them were assigned a "B" rating, while the majority of White schools were given an "A" rating. States in the Deep South did not use a two-tiered accreditation system, but if they had, the results doubtlessly would have been quite similar. Commonwealth of Kentucky, *Educational Bulletin, Kentucky High Schools, 1943–4* (Lexington, KY: State Department of Education, 1944), Appendix 1.

82. Walter G. Daniel, "Availability of Education for Negroes in the Secondary School," p. 455. Daniel may have conflated the two levels of accreditation in compiling his figures, but his basic point about gross disparities is well taken. In South Carolina, for instance, state-approved White high schools outnumbered Black ones in 1947 by nearly a five to one ratio. See South Carolina Department of Education, *80th Report of the Superintendent of Public Schools*, "Negro Education" (Columbia, SC, 1948), p. 81.

83. Georgia Department of Education, *Biennial Report, 1948–50* (Atlanta, 1950), pp. 310–311.

84. S. L. Smith, "Library Facilities in Negro Secondary Schools," p. 509. See also, for instance, North Carolina Department of Public Instruction, *Biennial Report, 1942–3, 1943–4* (Raleigh, NC, 1944), p. 55, which shows secondary library circulation figures favoring White schools by an eight to one ratio, and Alabama Department of Education, *Report of the State Superintendent of Public Schools* (Montgomery, AL, 1947), pp. 5–7.

85. See Walker, *Their Highest Potential*, Ch. 3.

Chapter 2

1. *Daily Minutes of the 1957 Tuskegee Regional Principals Workshop*, July 9, 1957. General Session facilitated by Dr. L. K. Jones of the Tuskegee Institute entitled "Socio-Economic Changes in the Southern Region."

2. Numan Bartley, *The New South, 1945–1980* (Baton Rouge: Louisiana State University Press, 1985), p. 148.

3. Adam Fairclough, *Better Day Coming: Blacks and Equality, 1890–2000* (New York: Penguin, 2001), Ch. 10.

4. *Biennial Report and Recommendations of the State Superintendent of Public Education to the Legislature of Mississippi for the Scholastic Years 1945–6 and 1946–7,* "Negro Education" (Jackson, MS, 1947), p. 39.

5. Alabama Department of Education, *Narrative Report, 1947,* "Education for Negroes" (Montgomery, AL, 1947).

6. See, for instance, Newbold's October 6, 1944, talk to the Raleigh Torch Club, describing equalization as a legal and moral duty, and his December 15, 1946, speech advocating the creation of an equalization fund. Also see his August 7, 1947, speech to superintendents, wherein he calls for state action on the improvement of Black schools, and his speeches of March 7, 1948, at Florida A&M College, and January 31, 1949. All are held in the Newbold Papers, Division of Negro Education, North Carolina State Archives, Raleigh, NC.

7. *Report and Recommendations of the Commission to Study the Question of Negro Higher Education to the Governor, the Legislative Council and General Assembly of Maryland,* (Baltimore, April 1, 1949), p. 3.

8. "Time is Running Out," *Atlanta Constitution*, January 15, 1948, p. 8; Letter from (Mrs.) Madge Carter, Athens, GA. *Atlanta Constitution*, February 7, 1946, p. 10. The fear of intermarriage always was of concern to White Southerners, especially those interested in retaining clear sexual boundaries between the races. On this point, see Peggy Pascoe, "Miscegenation Law, Court Cases and Ideologies of 'Race' in Twentieth Century America" in Martha Hodes, ed., *Sex, Love, Race: Crossing Boundaries in North American History* (New York: New York University Press, 1999), pp. 464–489, and Joane Nagel, *Race, Ethnicity and Sexuality: Intimate Intersections, Forbidden Frontiers* (New York: Oxford University Press, 2003), Ch. 2.

9. James D. Anderson, *The Education of Blacks in the South, 1860–1935* (Chapel Hill: University of North Carolina Press, 1988), Ch. 6.

10. Georgia Department of Education, *Biennial Report of the State Superintendent, 1948–50,* Division of Negro Education (Atlanta, 1950), p. 84.

11. "Equality All the Way," *Atlanta Daily World*, May 1, 1946, p. 6.

12. This body of work has recently been summarized in Adam Fairclough, *A Class of Their Own: Black Teachers in the Segregated South* (Cambridge, MA: Harvard University Press, 2007), Ch. 8.

13. *Sixty Eighth and Sixty Ninth Annual Reports of the Department of Education to the General Assembly of the State of Georgia for the Biennium Ending June 30, 1940* (Atlanta, GA, 1940), p. 6; Alabama Department of Education, *Narrative Report, 1947,* pp. 20–21.

14. Newbold Speech to Superintendents, August 7, 1947.

15. On this point, see Patricia Sullivan, *Lift Every Voice: The NAACP and the Making of the Civil Rights Movement* (New York: The New Press, 2009), pp. 341–343; Fairclough, *Better Day Coming,* pp. 198–199. See also "A $400 Million Baby," *The Chicago Defender*, September 8, 1951, p. 6.

16. For an overview of this process, see Michael J. Klarman, *From Jim Crow to Civil Rights: The Supreme Court and the Struggle for Racial Equality* (New York: Oxford University Press, 2006), particularly Chs. 3, 4, & 5. See also Mark V. Tushnet, *Making Civil Rights Law: Thurgood Marshall and the Supreme Court, 1956–1961* (New York: Oxford University Press, 1996), Chs. 8–11.

17. This issue is discussed extensively in Adam Fairclough, *A Class of Their Own,* pp. 344–353.

18. Patricia Sullivan, *Lift Every Voice: The NAACP and the Making of the Civil Rights Movement* (New York: The New Press, 2009), p. 341, who notes that part of the NAACP strategy in pushing for equalization was to prove segregation financially unviable. Also see Brian J. Daugherty, "'Keep On Keeping On:' African Americans and the Implementation of *Brown v. Board*

of Education in Virginia," in Brian J. Daugherty and Charles C. Bolton, eds., *With All Deliberate Speed: Implementing* Brown v. Board of Education (Fayetteville: University of Arkansas Press, 2008), p. 43; also see Richard Kluger, *Simple Justice* (New York: Vintage Books, 1975), p. 473, and Doxey A. Wilkerson, "The Negro School Movement in Virginia: From 'Equalization' to 'Integration,'" *The Journal of Negro Education*, Vol. 29, No. 1. (Winter 1960), pp. 17–29.

19. "Court Injunctions May Force Mixed Classes in 2 Counties," *Afro-American*, August 7, 1948, p. C4; "Seek Continuation of Va. School Case," *Atlanta Daily World*, November 20, 1948, p. 1; "Equalization Case in Virginia Ends with New Building," *Atlanta Daily World*, September 27, 1949, p. 4.

20. "School Equality Fight Grows; Four States Open Legal Battle," *The Chicago Defender*, May 21, 1949, p. 1.

21. See, for instance, "Crop of School Suits in South," *Atlanta Daily World*, March 14, 1947, p. 1; "The Equal Facilities Suit," *Atlanta Daily World*, August 11, 1949, p. 6; "Request U.S. Judgment in School Case," *The Pittsburgh Courier*, March 19, 1949, p. 23.

22. The availability and quality of Black high schools was a consistent issue in this tide of equalization suits. See, for instance, "Lawyers Score Regional High School in Virginia," *The Pittsburgh Courier*, October 29, 1949, p. 7; or "Interracial Group Pledges to Work for Equalization," *Atlanta Daily World*, October 4, 1949, p. 6.

23. For an overview of migration patterns, see Stewart E. Tolnay, "The African American 'Great Migration' and Beyond," *Annual Review of Sociology*, 2003, 29, pp. 209–232; and idem, "Educational Selection in the Migration of Southern Blacks, 1880–1990," *Social Forces*, Vol. 77, No. 2 (December 1998), pp. 487–514.

24. See, for instance, the discussion recorded among education officials in "Agitation Deplored as Key to Negro Problem in State," *Jackson Daily News*. Migration out of rural districts was also used as an argument against new construction in some rural areas. See Mississippi Department of Education, *Biennial Report*, 1953–55, p. 66.

25. On these points, see Thomas V. O'Brien, *The Politics of Race and Schooling: Public Education in Georgia, 1900–1961* (Lanham, MD: Lexington Books, 1999), Ch. 2.

26. See, for instance, Charles C. Bolton, *The Hardest Deal of All: The Battle Over School Integration in Mississippi, 1870–1980* (Jackson: University Press of Mississippi, 2005), Ch. 2, which also documents the positive response that equalization plans received from many Black educators, including R. N. Burger (p. 61). Also see "Teachers Meet In Kansas City," *The Chicago Defender*, November 23, 1946, p. 19B; "The Equal Facilities Suit," *Atlanta Daily World*, August 11, 1949, p. 6; "Alabamans Ask 7-Point State Civil Rights Program," *The Chicago Defender*, April 16, 1949, p. 5; and "ASTA Head Issues Statement on Aims of the Organization," *Atlanta Daily World*, September 9, 1952, p. 2.

27. *Mississippi State Superintendent Report, 1945–7* (Jackson, 1947), p. 40.

28. N. C. Newbold, Speech at Peabody College, July 28, 1948, Newbold Papers, Division of Negro Education, North Carolina State Archives, Raleigh, NC; also see Newbold's January 31, 1949, speech, in which he points to a series of commissions and reports discussing the need for improvements in Black education. The Southern States Work Conference on School Administration Problems, Improving Education in the Southern States, *Bulletin 1, 1943*, "Negro Education," pp. 36–37.

29. State of Alabama, Department of Education, *Narrative Report of State Superintendent* (Montgomery, AL, 1947), p. 6.

30. O'Brien, *The Politics of Race and Schooling*, Ch. 1; *Improving Education in the Southern States: Report of the Committee on Negro Education*, Ed McCuistian, Chairman, Southern States Work Conference on School Administrative Problems (Talahassee, FL, 1939).

31. Charles C. Bolton, *The Hardest Deal of All*, Ch. 2.

32. Thomas V. O'Brien, "The Dog That Didn't Bark: *Aaron v. Cook* and the NAACP Strategy in Georgia before Brown," *The Journal of Negro History*, Vol. 84, No. 1 (Winter 1999), pp. 79–88.

33. "Georgia to Speed School Expansion," *New York Times*, April 22, 1951, p. 58; "Equal Facilities Never Intended, Cousins Says," *Atlanta Daily World*, July 13, 1956, p. 1; O'Brien, *The Politics of Race and Schooling*, Ch. 2.

34. These were developments widely discussed across the region at the time. See, for instance, "Equal Pay Ordered For La. Tutors," *Atlanta Daily World*, August 1, 1948, p. 1; "Virginia Rushes to 'Equalize' Schools to Avoid NAACP Suits," *Atlanta Daily World*, May 3, 1950, p. 1; "Alabamans Ask 7-Point State Civil Rights Program" *The Chicago Defender (National edition)*, April 16, 1949, p. 5; "Ark. School Plan To Be Presented," *Atlanta Daily World*, February 21, 1952, p. 6.

35. Bolton, *The Hardest Deal of All*, Ch. 3.

36. Newbold Speech, January 31, 1949.

37. "Negro Education in South on Rise: States Going 'All Out' to Raise Standards in Grade and High Schools of Area," *The New York Times*, March 16, 1952, p. 1.

38. "South Acts to Keep Pupil Segregation: "Resistance Movement Formed-Test Case Opens Today in Charleston, S.C.," *The New York Times*, May 28, 1951, p. 16.

39. "Negro Education in South on Rise," *New York Times*.

40. *Annual Reports to the Department of Education to the General Assembly of the State of Georgia*, M. D. Collins, State Superintendent of Education, (Atlanta, June 30, 1952); "Division of Negro Education," p. 68.

41. These figures have been calculated by comparing school reports. See Georgia Department of Education, *Biennial Report of the Superintendent, 1949–50*, "Schools According to Size" (Atlanta, 1950), p. 326, and Georgia Department of Education, *Biennial Report of the Superintendent, 1955–6*, "Schools According to Size" (Atlanta, 1956), p. 342.

42. *Eighty Third Annual Report of the State Superintendent of Education of the State of South Carolina* (Columbia, 1951), p. 12.

43. South Carolina Department of Education, *Superintendent's Report, 1952–3*, p. 50.

44. South Carolina Department of Education, *Superintendent's Report, 1955–6*, p. 33.

45. These figures have been determined by comparing school reports published in 1950 and 1956, with reported numbers of schools offering "high school grades" for Black and White students. See Georgia Department of Education, *Biennial Report of the Superintendent, 1949–50*, "Schools According to Size," p. 326, and Georgia Department of Education, *Biennial Report of the Superintendent, 1955–6*, "Schools According to Size," p. 342.

46. *Biennial Report of the State Superintendent, 1956–58*, North Carolina Public Schools, "Number of Schools" (Raleigh, NC, 1958), p. 27.

47. Martha Hay Vardeman, "A Study of the Relationship Between Size and Accreditation of School and Certain Aspects of the Instructional Program in Public Negro High Schools, Alabama, 1958," (unpublished Ph.D dissertation, University of Alabama, 1959), p. 17; State of Tennessee, *Annual Statistical Report of the Department of Education for the Scholastic Year Ending June 30, 1961* (Knoxville, 1961), passim.

48. Mississippi Department of Education, *Biennial Report, 1957–59* (Jackson, 1959), p. 22.

49. *Biennial Report of the State Superintendent, 1956–58*, North Carolina Public Schools, "Transportation," p. 31.

50. *88th Annual Report of the State Superintendent of Education of the State of South Carolina, 1955–56* (Columbia, SC, 1956), p. 14; Mississippi Department of Education, *Biennial Report, 1953–55* (Jackson, 1955), p. 18.

51. Vardemann, "A Study of the Relationship Between Size and Accreditation of School and Certain Aspects of the Instructional Program in Public Negro High Schools," passim.

52. G. H. Ferguson, "Some Facts About the Education of Negroes in North Carolina, 1921–1960," Division of Negro Education, General Correspondence, Box 1, North Carolina State Archives, Raleigh, NC.

53. *Eighty Sixth Annual Report of the State Superintendent of Education of the State of South*

Carolina, 1953–54 (Columbia, SC, 1954), p. 13.

54. This is evident when multivariate analyses of enrollment and attainment data are conducted for Southern youth of both races together in 1960 using IPUMS data. When controls for poverty status, family composition, gender, parental education, central city residence, and home ownership are introduced, racial differences are reduced to statistical insignificance.

55. These figures were calculated with IPUMS data for youth aged 14 to 17 in the Southern states in 1960.

56. According to IPUMS data, some 96% of the Black tenant households with high school age children were below the poverty line in 1960, compared with about 70% of White households in similar circumstances. Some 25% of these Black households had no male head, as opposed to just 17% of the White households. These conditions may have accounted for the fact that Black male youth were more likely to work as either unpaid (20%) or paid (28%) farm laborers than White youth in either category (15% and 18%, respectively).

57. Estimates of youth employment were calculated with IPUMS data for 1960, excluding individuals who had graduated from school (to determine how work interacted with school). By and large, Black youth were more likely to be employed as laborers or domestic workers and in other menial occupations, which accounted for more than two-thirds of jobs they held, while White teens were more likely to work in service positions such as clerks, salespersons, office workers, attendants, and apprentices of one sort or another, categories comprising about half their employment profile.

58. P. H. Easom, "A Worthy Story to be Told," Manuscript, Percy H. Easom papers, Mississippi State Archives, Jackson, MS.

59. Backward-looking commentaries such as Easom's were not uncommon. See, for instance, G. H. Ferguson, "Some Facts About the Education of Negroes in North Carolina, 1921–60" Division of Negro Education, General Correspondence, Box 1, North Carolina State Archives, Raleigh, NC.

60. South Carolina Department of Education, *Superintendent's Report, 1948*, p. 103.

61. Newbold speech at Florida A&M College, March 7, 1948.

62. *Biennial Report and Recommendations of the State Superintendent of Public Education to the Legislature of Mississippi* (Jackson, MS, 1947), p. 39.

63. Anderson, "Inequalities in Schooling in the South," p. 533.

64. South Carolina Department of Education, *Report of the State Superintendent*, "High Schools" (Columbia, SC, 1953), p. 54.

65. Collection: Negro Education Division, Director's Subject Files, Georgia Archives.

66. Interestingly, during the 1950s, many such reports came from the urban schools, which were receiving an influx of students who had migrated from the countryside. G. H. Ferguson, "Some Facts About the Education of Negroes in North Carolina, 1921–1960." In Mississippi, state officials reported libraries and auditoriums being used for classes in new Black high schools, as enrollments surged past anticipated classroom capacity. Mississippi State Superintendent of Education, *Report and Recommendations, 1955–57* (Jackson, 1957), p. 40.

67. For state-level statistics on enrollment in this period, see Appendix 2.

68. See, for instance, "North Carolina Does It Again," *Atlanta Daily World,* April 27, 1949, p. 6.

69. Bolton, *The Hardest Deal of All,* Chs. 2 & 3.

70. Poverty levels for Black teens in 1960 and the number living on farms were highly correlated across these states (.78), and the factor extracted from a principal components analysis of these variables represented 89% of their variation. This factor was utilized to calculate the correlation reported in the text. Weighted state means of these population parameters (poverty and farm residence), estimated with IPUMS data, were utilized to make these calculations.

71. In Oklahoma, with a relatively small Black population, African American attainment was also quite high compared to Whites. Oklahoma was not included in this analysis because of the small number of Black 17-year-olds in its population, rendering estimates of attainment rates based on 1% samples unreliable. This accounts for the slight difference in overall black attainment levels across the region as a whole in Table 2.1 and Table 2.2.

72. Vanessa Siddle Walker, *Their Highest Potential: An African American School Community in the Segregated South* (Chapel Hill: University of North Carolina Press, 1996), p. 62. Also see Barry F. Malone, "Before *Brown:* Cultural and Social Capital in a Rural Black School Community, W. E. B. DuBois High School, Wake Forest, North Carolina," *The North Carolina History Review* LXXXV:4 (October 2008), pp. 416–447.

73. For an overview of this literature, see Vanessa Siddle Walker, "The Architects of Black Schooling in the Segregated South: The Case of One Principal Leader," *Journal of Curriculum and Supervision*, 19: 1 (Fall 2003), p. 57. For monographs on other schools, see Vivian Gunn Morris and Curtis L. Morris, *Creating Caring and Nurturing Educational Environments for African American Children* (Westport, CT: Bergin & Garvey, 2000), passim; Barbara Shircliffe, *The Best of That World: Historically Black High Schools and the Crisis of Segregation in a Southern Metropolis* (Cresskill, NJ: Hampton Press, 2006), Chs. 3 & 4; and Hattie Thomas Lucas, *Huntington High School: Symbol of Community Hope and Unity, 1920–1971* (Yorkstown, VA: Publishing Connections, 2000), passim.

74. A classic study of Black secondary education in this era is Frederick A. Rodgers, *The Black High School and Its Community* (Lexington, MA: D.C. Heath, 1973), passim, which features interviews with 58 Black high school principals from the latter 1950s and early 1960s in North Carolina. By and large, Rodgers's study affirms many of the themes evident in the work of Walker and other contributors to this literature.

75. North Carolina Public Schools, *Biennial Report, 1948–50* (Raleigh, 1950), p. 37; Committee on Education of the Virginia Chamber of Commerce, *Opportunities for the Improvement of High School Education in Virginia*, November, 1943. p. 1; South Carolina Department of Education, *Superintendent's Report* (Columbia, 1851), p. 80. Also see the rather detailed statistics on courses taken by Black and White students in the State of Maryland Department of Education, *Eighty Fifth Annual Report of the State Board of Education, Showing Condition of the Public Schools of Maryland for the Year Ending 1951* (Baltimore, 1951), pp. 93–101. These figures show rather low Black enrollments in foreign language and higher branches of mathematics. Both Black and White students were enrolled in vocational and industrial arts courses in large numbers.

76. North Carolina Public Schools, *Biennial Report, 1948–5*, p. 38.

77. Rodgers, *The Black High School and Its Community*, p. 37.

78. Philosophy of the James E. Shepard High School, Zebulon, North Carolina (Box 22, General Correspondence of the Director of Negro Education, Southern Association of Colleges and Secondary Schools Accreditation File), North Carolina Department of Public Instruction Collection, North Carolina State Archives, Raleigh. A similar report was filed by the J. W. Ligon Junior-Senior High School in nearby Raleigh, indicating that larger urban schools also exhibited these values. Located in the same box as the Shepard Report. On an early effort to promote progressive principles in Black schools, see W. A. Robinson, "A Co-operative Effort Among Southern Negro High Schools," *The School Review*, Vol. 52, No. 9 (November 1944), pp. 532–542.

79. For discussion of two such groups, see Rodgers, *The Black High School and Its Community*, p. 66, which describes the H. V. Brown Schoolmasters Club in North Carolina, and Walker, "The Architects of Black Schooling in the Segregated South," p. 61, which mentions the "Masters Club" of principals of regionally accredited high schools in Georgia.

80. Duncan, "Some Problems of Union School Principals in North Carolina," p. 13.

81. *Mississippi Teachers Directory, 1959–60*, J. M. Tubb, Superintendent of Instruction

(Jackson, 1960), pp. 11, 23. The *Mississippi School Bulletin, Educational Directory, 1961–62*, (Department of Education, Jackson, 1962) lists just 25 stand-alone Black secondary institutions in the entire state, most of them in the state's larger cities. On Mississippi's relative standing in the region with respect to Black population and education, see Rodgers, *The Black High School and Its Community*, pp. 13–14.

82. Vardeman, "A Study of the Relationship between Size and Accreditation," p. 402.

83. South Carolina Department of Education, *Report of the Superintendent of Education, 1957–58, Negro Education* (Columbia: State of South Carolina, 1958), p. 34.

84. Rodgers, *The Black High School and Its Community*, p. 36. Ninety percent of the principals reported that between 75% and 100% of the teachers in their schools held master's degrees. Also, see Walker, *Their Highest Potential*, pp. 142–143.

85. On the use of exams to judge Black teachers, see R. Scott Baker, *Paradoxes of Desegregation: African American Struggles for Educational Equity in Charleston, South Carolina, 1926–1972* (Columbia: University of South Carolina Press, 2006), pp. 53–60.

86. Brandon Carter interview with Shirley Hill, July 25, 2007, Atlanta, GA; Gloria Chambers interview with Shirley Hill, May 8, 2009, Jackson, MS; Roger Richards interview with Shirley Hill, October 25, 2007, Raleigh, NC; Betty Small interview with John Rury, July 25, 2007, Atlanta, GA. All names are pseudonyms.

87. On the tendency of respondents from this era to reflect nostalgically, see Barbara Shircliffe, "'We Got the Best of That World': A Case for the Study of Nostalgia in the Oral History of School Segregation," *The Oral History Review*, Vol. 28, No. 2 (Summer–Autumn 2001), pp. 59–84.

88. "South Has Made Big Gains in Improving Educational Facilities for Negroes Since '45," *New York Times*, May 18, 1954, p. 22.

89. Directors Correspondence, letter from Marvin Griffin dated October 22, 1954, Georgia Archives.

90. "Equal Facilities Never Intended, Cousins Says," *Atlanta Daily World*, July 13, 1956.

91. "Alabama Seeks Unified Action on School Segregation Case," *Atlanta Daily World*, July 16, 1953, p. 1; "On integration," *Afro-American*, March 21, 1959, p. 19.

92. Bolton, *The Hardest Deal of All*, Ch. 2.

93. Mississippi Department of Education, *Biennial Report, 1953–55*, p. 66; Fairclough, *A Class of Their Own*, p. 414.

94. Mississippi Department of Education, *Biennial Report, 1956–57*, Division of Negro Education (Jackson: State of Mississippi, 1957), p. 40.

95. Ibid.; O'Brien, *The Politics of Race and Schooling*, Ch. 3.

96. Fairclough, *A Class of Their Own*, p. 414.

97. "Time's On Its Last Leg," *The Chicago Defender*, September 29, 1951, p. 6.

98. "A Judicial Delay," *Atlanta Daily World*, January 31, 1952, p. 6.

99. See, for instance, Shircliffe, *The Best of That World*, Ch. 4. Bolton, *The Hardest Deal of All*, Ch. 2.

100. John McCray, quoted in Baker, *Paradoxes of Desegregation*, p. 94.

101. Dean Gordon B Hancock, "Between the Lines: The Old South in Stampede," *Atlanta Daily World*, September 6, 1955, p. 6.

102. "NAACP Blasts 'Makeshift' School as Inadequate," *Atlanta Daily World*, November 8, 1958, p. 1.

103. "Mississippi Cheats on 'Separate, Equal'," *Daily Defender*, April 7, 1959, p. 8.

104. Rodgers, *The Black High School and Its Community*, pp. 77–78.

105. Walker, "The Architects of Black Schooling in the Segregated South," pp. 62–67.

106. Roger Richards interview with Shirley Hill, Raleigh, NC, October 25, 2009.

107. Vardeman, "A Study of the Relationship Between Size and Accreditation of School," p. 17.

108. "17 Virginia Counties Have No High School for Negroes," *Atlanta Daily World,* September 14, 1958, p. 1.

109. On this point, see James W. Button, *Blacks and Social Change: The Impact of the Civil Rights Movement in Southern Communities* (Princeton, NJ: Princeton University Press, 1989), Ch. 1. Fairclough, *A Class of their Own,* p. 415.

110. "An Alarming Challenge to All," *Atlanta Daily World,* August 15, 1957, p. 4.

111. Directors Correspondence; Letter from Septima P. Clark, Highlander Falk School, Monteagle, TN, to Mr. Robert L. Cousins, Director of Negro Education, Atlanta, GA, Division of Negro Education, Georgia State Archives, Morrow, GA.

112. James S. Coleman, "The Concept of Equality of Educational Opportunity" *Harvard Educational Review,* Special Issue on Coleman Report, 1968. Also see articles by Daniel Patrick Moynihan and David Cohen.

113. Dongbin Kim and John L. Rury, "The Changing Profile of College Access: The Truman Commission and Enrollment Patterns in the Postwar Era," *History of Education Quarterly,* Vol. 47, No. 2 (August 2007), pp. 302–327. Enrollment estimates are drawn from IPUMS data.

114. Clayborne Carson, *In Struggle: SNCC and the Black Awakening of the 1960s* (Cambridge, MA: Harvard University Press, 1995), Chs 1 & 2.

Chapter 3

1. "Bias against Negroes Charged in Trenton," *New York Times,* December 7, 1943, p. 21; "Negroes Win School Suit," *New York Times,* February 1, 1944, p. 21.

2. Thomas J. Sugrue, *Sweet Land of Liberty: The Forgotten Struggle for Civil Rights in the North* (New York: Random House, 2008), pp. 175–179.

3. George S. Schuyler, "Trenton Is Showing Ways to End Bias," *The Pittsburgh Courier,* February 28, 1948, p. 2.

4. Davison M. Douglas, *Jim Crow Moves North: The Battle Over Northern School Segregation, 1865–1954* (New York: Cambridge University Press, 2005), Ch. 6.

5. "Negroes Fight Jim-Crow Schools 19 Miles from New York City," *The Chicago Defender,* September 18, 1943, p. 2; Sugrue, *Sweet Land of Liberty,* pp. 163–170.

6. "Negroes Fight Jim-Crow Schools 19 Miles from New York City," *The Chicago Defender,* p. 2. The *Defender* noted that Black and White high school students were initially transported on separate buses, but the practice was quickly ended when Black parents protested.

7. On this point, see Douglas, *Jim Crow Moves North,* pp. 179–186.

8. Ibid., Ch 5.

9. There is an extensive literature on urban education during this era, which touches to one degree or another on the question of school segregation. On Chicago, see Michael Homel, *Down from Equality: Black Chicago and the Public Schools, 1920–1941* (Urbana: University of Illinois Press, 1984), Chs. 3 & 5, and Kathryn M. Neckerman, *Schools Betrayed: The Roots of Failure in Inner City Education* (Chicago: University of Chicago Press, 2007), Ch. 4; on Philadelphia, see Vincent P. Franklin, *The Education of Black Philadelphia: The Social and Educational History of a Minority Community, 1900–1950* (Philadelphia: University of Pennsylvania Press, 1979), Part Two; on Detroit, see Jeffrey Mirel, *The Rise and Fall of an Urban School System: Detroit, 1907–81* (Ann Arbor: University of Michigan Press, 1993), Chs. 4 & 5; on Los Angeles, see Judith Rosenberg Raftery, *Land of Fair Promise: Politics and Reform in the Los Angeles Schools, 1885–1941* (Palo Alto, CA: Stanford University Press, 1992), pp. 183–191; on Milwaukee, see Jack Dougherty, *More Than One Struggle: The Evolution of Black School Reform in Milwaukee* (Chapel Hill: University of North Carolina Press, 2004), Chs. 2 & 3; on Boston, see Joseph Cronin, *Reforming Boston Schools, 1930–2006: Overcoming Corruption and Racial Segregation* (New York: Palgrave Macmillan, 2008), Chs. 3 & 4; and on Cleveland, see William D. Henderson, "Demography and Desegregation in the Cleveland Public Schools: Towards a Comprehen-

sive Theory of Educational Failure and Success," *Review of Law and Social Change*, Vol. 26, No. 4 (February 2002), pp. 460–568.

10. Sugrue, *Sweet Land of Liberty*, p. 176.

11. See Douglas, *Jim Crow Moves North*, p. 175, and Dougherty, *More than One Struggle*, Ch. 1.

12. For a discussion of this focusing on a slightly later period, see George A. Lee, "Negroes in a Medium-Sized Metropolis: Allentown, Pennsylvania—A Case Study," *The Journal of Negro Education*, Vol. 37, No. 4 (Autumn 1968), pp. 397–405.

13. Charles T. Clotfelter, *After Brown: The Rise and Retreat of School Desegregation* (Princeton, NJ: Princeton University Press, 2004), p. 70.

14. Regarding this issue, see Dougherty, *More than One Struggle*, Ch. 3.

15. On this point generally during this time, see Douglas, *Jim Crow Moves North*, Ch. 5.

16. David Angus and Jeffrey Mirel, *The Failed Promise of the American High School, 1890–1995* (New York: Teachers College Press, 1999), Ch. 3; Harvard Sitkoff, *A New Deal for Blacks: The Emergence of Civil Rights as a National Issue: The Depression Decade* (New York: Oxford University Press, 2008), pp. 36–38.

17. "2,000 Students Skip Classes as Strike Spreads," *Chicago Daily Tribune*, September 21, 1945, p. 13; "Pupils in Gary Vote Protest on Principal," *Chicago Daily Tribune*, October 27, 1945, p. 8. Also see Ronald D. Cohen, *Children of the Mill: Schooling and Society in Gary, Indiana, 1906–1960* (Bloomington: Indiana University Press, 1990), pp. 175–186.

18. "Gary Students Reject Truce; Strike Goes On," *Chicago Daily Tribune*, September 27, 1945, p. 10; Meredith Johns, "Gary School Strike Spreads; Whites Ask Ouster of Negros," *The Chicago Defender*, September 29, 1945, p. 1; Richard Durham, "Gary Strikers Like Their Equality White," *The Chicago Defender*, October 6, 1945, p. 1.

19. "'Pupils' Strike in Englewood up to Parents," *Chicago Daily Tribune*, September 28, 1945, p. 14; Earl Conrad, "N.Y. Schools Join Strike," *The Chicago Defender*, October 6, 1945, p. 1.

20. "Gary Hate Strike on Again," *The Chicago Defender*, November 3, 1945, p. 1; "Strike at Gary School Forgiven But Not Forgotten," *The Chicago Defender*, October 13, 1945, p. 1.

21. "Sinatra Pleads in School Strike," *Los Angeles Times*, November 2, 1945, p. 1; Richard Durham, "Frank Sinatra Fails to Break Gary Hate Strike," *The Chicago Defender*, November 10, 1945, p. 1; "School Strikes Halted," *The Pittsburgh Courier*, October 6, 1945, p. 1.

22. This estimate is based on a simple logistic regression of respondent reports on the composition of their schools (recoded as a categorical factor to indicate majority White) on reports of where they grew up outside of the South (recoded to indicate a large city). It is important to note, however, that because just 86 respondents had complete information for the non-South in the 1940s, this finding failed to achieve statistical significance. A similar analysis of NSBA respondents combining the 1940s and 1950s produced an even lower level of contact with Whites for those living in large cities, with a likelihood of less than 50% of suburban and non-metropolitan Black high school students, and with 196 respondents it was statistically significant at .015. For a description of the dataset, see James S. Jackson and Harold W. Neighbors, *National Survey of Black Americans, Waves 1–4.* (Ann Arbor, MI: Inter-University Consortium for Political and Social Research. ISPCR 6668, 1997).

23. Clotfelter, *After Brown*, Ch. 2.

24. Judy Jolley Mohraz, *The Separate Problem: Case Studies of Black Education in the North, 1900–1930* (Westport, CT: Greenwood Press, 1979), p. 133.

25. Michael W. Homel, *Down from Equality*, p. 110; Jeffrey Mirel, *The Rise and Fall of an Urban School System*, pp. 189–190.

26. Willard C. Richan, "Racial Isolation in the Cleveland Public Schools," A Report of a Study Sponsored by the United States Commission on Civil Rights, Case Western Reserve University, 1967, p. 35.

27. "School Head Blocks Student Hate Walkout in Los Angeles," *Chicago Defender*, March 29, 1947, p. 1; "Police Escort Negro Children Away From High School," *Atlanta Daily World*, February 8, 1949, p. 2.

28. Homel, *Down from Equality*, p. 110.

29. W. Loyd Warner, Robert J. Havighurst, and Martin B. Loeb, *Who Shall Be Educated? The Challenge of Unequal Opportunities* (New York: Harper & Brothers, 1944), pp. 12–14.

30. "Negro Elected Student Body President," *The Pittsburgh Courier,* April 26, 1947, p. 12; "Negro President of Juniors Presides at Ottawa Prom," *Chicago Defender,* June 4, 1949, p. 5; "Caley Cook, Athlete, Heads Student Body at Portland's Jefferson High," *Chicago Defender,* June 24, 1950, p. 3; "Wins Top Honor at Boys' State," *Chicago Defender,* July 15, 1950, p. 1.

31. *1950 Lincolnian,* Lincoln High School, Kansas City, Missouri, p. 3. Frazier was described as a "gifted speaker," who planned to study chemistry at the University of Kansas.

32. Warner, Havighurst, and Loeb, *Who Shall Be Educated,* p. 13.

33. "School Prexy Makes Great Record," *Chicago Defender,* January 28, 1950, p. 2; "Negro Elected Student Body President," *The Pittsburgh Courier,* p. 12.

34. Jeffrey E. Mirel, *Patriotic Pluralism: Americanization Education and European Immigrants* (Cambridge, MA: Harvard University Press, 2010), pp. 208–212. Also see Cherry A. McGee Banks, *Improving Multicultural Education: Lessons from the Intergroup Education Movement* (New York: Teachers College Press, 2005), Ch. 4.

35. Davison, *Jim Crow Moves North,* p. 237.

36. These developments were monitored closely in the Black press, and the *Chicago Defender* in particular. See the following *Defender* articles: "Interracial Group at Beaumont High," December 28, 1946, p. 17; "Youth Group Raps Racial Intolerance," January 18, 1947, p. 18; "Fight Bias Through 160 Youth Projects," March 15, 1947, p. 7; "New York Schools Launch Move Against Bias," July 12, 1947, p. 5; "Negro Progress New Course for Public Schools," October 18, 1947, p. 5; "Students to Join Ranks to War on Race Hate," March 7, 1948, p. 7. Also see "Anti Bias Law to Be Taught in High Schools," *New York Amsterdam News,* July 5, 1947, p. 21. On developments in Cleveland, Detroit, and other cities, see Mirel, *Patriotic Pluralism,* pp. 216–222; on Philadelphia, see Vincent P. Franklin, *The Education of Black Philadelphia: The Social and Educational History of a Minority Community, 1900–1950* (Philadelphia: University of Pennsylvania Press, 1979), p. 165.

37. On the limitations of the movement with respect to race, see Banks, *Improving Multicultural Education,* Ch. 6.

38. Again, the *Chicago Defender* devoted particular attention to these incidents, and not just in local schools. See, for instance, the following *Defender* articles: "Deny Tension Set off Riot," November 12, 1949, p. 1; "Cage Fans Touch Off Philly Riot," March 17, 1951, p. 2; "High School Hoodlums," October 2, 1954, p. 11; "Teenage Punks Threaten High School Sports," December 3, 1959, p. A28. Stories appeared in other papers, too; see, for instance, "High School Students Threaten Calif Riot," *Atlanta Daily World,* August 3, 1946, p. 7, and "More After Game Race Trouble Flares on North Side," *Pittsburgh Courier,* October 20, 1956, p. 6. On demonstrations against prejudicial treatment, see "Students Quit Over Racial Slur," *Chicago Defender,* May 2, 1953, p. 5; "Students' Protest Whip Election Bias," *Pittsburgh Courier,* April 7, 1956, p. 6; and "Dance Ban Leads to School Boycott, *Chicago Daily Defender,* May 19, 1958, p. A4.

39. "Franklin K. Lane Race Riot Quelled," *New York Amsterdam News,* January 20, 1951, p. 9; "Lane High School Incident," *New York Amsterdam News,* March 3, 1951, p. 8; "22 School Rowdies Freed," *Chicago Defender,* November 7, 1956, p. 4; "Adults Join in Fight Between Students of Both Races at Gladstone High School," *Pittsburgh Courier,* September 13, 1958, p. 1.

40. James T. Patterson, *Brown v. Board of Education: A Civil Rights Milestone and Its Troubled Legacy* (New York: Oxford University Press, 2002), pp. 75–77; Michael J. Klarman, *Brown v. Board of Education and the Civil Rights Movement* (New York: Oxford University Press, 2007), pp. 105–110; Diane Ravitch, *The Troubled Crusade, American Education, 1945–1980* (New York: Basic Books, 1983), pp. 131–133.

41. As Ravitch notes, "The national communications media, and particularly television,

changed the way these confrontations were perceived by a national audience.... Raw and undisguised racism was revealed as a direct challenge to the American creed." Ravitch, *The Troubled Crusade*, p. 139. On public opinion and the civil rights movement more generally, see Francine Romero, *Civil Rights Policymaking in the United States: An Institutional Perspective* (Westport, CT: Praeger, 2002), Ch. 1.

42. Incidents still occurred, although not on the scale of Gary's. See "Police Set for Harper Violence," *Chicago Defender*, October 1, 1956, p. 1, and "Students Walk out in Wake of Dispute," *Atlanta Daily World*, p. 2, describing cases in Chicago and St. Louis.

43. Douglas, *Jim Crow Moves North*, Ch. 6; Sugrue, *Sweet Land of Liberty*, Ch. 6; Jolley, *The Separate Problem*, Ch. 6.

44. Supplements to the Report on Neighborhoods, Schools & Recreation, 1948. City Plan Commission of Kansas City, Missouri, p. 10.

45. Bob Womack, "Attucks 5 Wins Indiana Cage Title," *The Chicago Defender*, April 2, 1955, p. 10; Stanley Warren, *Crispus Attucks High School: "Hail to the Green, Hail to the Gold* (Virginia Beach, VA: Donning Company Publishing, 1998), passim. Interestingly, DuSable High in Chicago won the Illinois state title the same year; see Ira Berkow, *The DuSable Panthers* (New York: Atheneum, 1978), passim.

46. Douglas, *Jim Crow Moves North*, pp. 214, 248–249.

47. Aaron Rife, "Sumner High School: A History" (unpublished master's thesis, University of Kansas, 2008), passim.

48. Raftery, *Land of Fair Promise*, p. 183.

49. Grace Strong interview with Shirley Hill, July 10, 2007.

50. These figures were calculated by examining faculty photos in high school yearbooks. At predominantly White Central High, only 26% of the faculty in 1960 had been at the school through the prior decade, and at Paseo High the figure was 35%.

51. For discussion of the record of these schools in science education, and their success in metropolitan science competitions, see Rife, "Sumner High School: A History," pp. 86–89.

52. Grace Strong interview with Shirley Hill, July 10, 2007.

53. Norma Walsh interview with Shirley Hill, October 31, 2008.

54. Ashley Holm, "Racial Differences in Student Engagement and Attainment: A Study of Topeka High School, 1939–1984" (unpublished master's thesis, University of Kansas, 2008), Ch. 2.

55. Ibid., pp. 40–45.

56. Harry O'Neal interview with Shirley Hill, October 31, 2008.

57. Elizabeth C. Marshall, "Protest Objectionable Play; Penn Twp. Pupils Walk Out," *The Pittsburgh Courier*, May 4, 1946, p. 1.

58. Elizabeth C. Marshall, "Principal Denies Jim Crow Charge," *The Pittsburgh Courier*, December 14, 1946, p. 4.

59. "German Township High to Choose Cheerleader; Pastor States His Case," *The Pittsburgh Courier*, October 31, 1953, p. 3. Also see Holm, "Racial Differences in Student Engagement and Attainment."

60. Clotfelter, *After Brown*, pp. 140–145.

61. This is corroborated by examining yearbooks from a number of schools in this period in Kansas City and Chicago.

62. Talmadge Boyd interview with Shirley Hill and John Rury, March 17, 2009.

63. Homel, *Down from Equality*, pp. 81–83. Talmadge Boyd interview.

64. Review of DuSable Yearbooks; "DuSable to Get Cheers," *Chicago Defender*, May 24, 1960, p. 19.

65. Neckerman, *Schools Betrayed*, Ch. 7; John L. Rury, "Race, Space, and the Politics of Chicago's Public Schools: Benjamin Willis and the Tragedy of Urban Education," *History of Education Quarterly*, Vol. 39, No. 2 (Summer 1999), pp. 117–142.

66. Drawing attendance zones to minimize racial integration was a widespread practice. See the discussion of this issue in Jolley, *The Separate Problem*, Ch. 6, which deals with Chicago, Indianapolis, and Philadelphia just prior to this era, and Dougherty, *More than One Struggle*, Ch. 4, which deals with Milwaukee a bit later. On Detroit, see Mirel, *The Rise and Fall of an Urban School System*, Ch. 4; on Cleveland, see Richan, "Racial Isolation in the Cleveland Schools," pp. 5 & 6; on Los Angeles, see Raftery, *Land of Fair Promise*, p. 183; on Boston, see Ronald Formisano, *Boston Against Busing: Race, Class and Ethnicity in the 1960s and 1970s*, 2nd ed. (Chapel Hill: University of North Carolina Press, 2003), Chs. 1 & 2.

67. Shawn A. Ginwright, *Black in School: Afro Centric Reform, Urban Youth and the Promise of Hip Hop Culture* (New York: Teachers College Press, 2004). Ch. 3.

68. Raftery, *Land of Fair Promise*, pp. 183–191; John Caughey, *To Kill a Child's Spirit: The Tragedy of School Segregation in Los Angeles* (Itaska, IL: F.E. Peacock Publishers, 1973), Ch. 1; Emily E. Straus, "The Making of the American School Crisis: Compton, California and the Death of the Suburban Dream" (unpublished Ph.D. dissertation, Brandeis University, 2006), Ch. 2; Edna Bonacich and Robert Goodman, *Deadlock in School Desegregation: A Case Study of Ingelwood, California* (New York: Praeger Publishers, 1972), Chs. 2 & 3; Alan B. Wilson, *The Consequences of Segregation: Academic Achievement in a Northern Community* (Berkeley, CA: Glendessary Press, 1969), Ch. 1.

69. On Sumner, see Rife, "Sumner High School," pp. 75–80; on Attucks, see Douglas, *Jim Crow Moves North*, p. 263.

70. Neckerman, *Schools Betrayed*, Ch. 6.

71. Mary Herrick, Citizens School Committee Papers, Box 28, Folder 2, "A Year Experiment with Core for Slow Learners," Chicago Historical Society, Archival Collections.

72. David L. Angus and Jeffrey E. Mirel, *The Failed Promise of the American High School* (New York: Teachers College Press, 1999), pp. 90–91; Neckerman, *School Betrayed*, Ch. 5.

73. Quoted in Christina Collins, *"Ethnically Qualified:" Race, Merit and the Selection of Urban Teachers, 1920–1980* (New York: Teachers College Press, 2011), p. 26.

74. Richan, "Racial Isolation in the Cleveland Public Schools," p. 34; Dougherty, *More Than One Struggle*, pp. 96–97.

75. This was certainly the case in Chicago and Philadelphia; see Neckerman, *Schools Betrayed*, Ch. 6, and Franklin, *The Education of Black Philadelphia*, Ch. 8.

76. Howard D. Gould, "Students Flunk in Biggest Exam," *Chicago Defender*, December 29, 1958, p. A8. As the article pointed out, Chicago's Black students should have had more than 50 scholarship qualifiers on the exam, but the newspaper counted just six.

77. Neckerman, *Schools Betrayed*, p. 96; also see John F. Lyons, *Teachers and Reform: Chicago Public Education, 1929–1970* (Champaign: University of Illinois Press, 2008), pp. 148–149.

78. Douglas, *Jim Crow Moves North*, pp. 195–203.

79. On Black suburbanization in the North and West at this time, see Andrew Wiese, *Places of Their Own: African American Suburbanization in the Twentieth Century* (Chicago: University of Chicago Press, 2004), Ch. 5. For a contemporary perspective, see "Find Negroes Following Whites to 'Suburbia,'" *Chicago Defender*, March 10, 1962, p. 1. Also see Caroline Eick, *Race-Class Relations and Integration in Secondary Education: The Case of Miller High* (New York: Palgrave Macmillan, 2010), Ch. 1.

80. It is clear, of course, that the robust negative effect of Southern birth in 1940 poses a sharp contrast to its considerably more moderate effect 20 years later. Removing controls for poverty status and other factors did little to change this, suggesting that it may have been reflective of improved schooling in the South.

81. Youth with high school graduate parents holding white-collar jobs, owning homes, and living with a spouse represented 17% of suburban teens and just 9% of those in the cities in the North and West, according to IPUMS data. The suburban Black home ownership rate was 63% while the central city rate was 35%. This would partly account for the

disappearance of the big-city advantage so clearly evident in the 1940 analysis. If suburban residence is substituted for central city in the Black equation, it has a positive and significant effect, representing nearly a 20% advantage (.181) in the likelihood of school success, net of other factors. Without socioeconomic controls such as parental education, white-collar employment, and poverty status, the effect of suburban residence rises to nearly a 30% advantage (.281).

82. Message from Principal Earl D. Thomas, *The 1955 Lincolnian* (Kansas City, Missouri, Lincoln High School, 1955), p. 9.

83. This is the argument in two books on Chicago: Neckerman, *Schools Betrayed*, and Homel, *Down from Equality*.

Chapter 4

1. James Bryan Conant, *Slums and Suburbs: A Commentary on Schools in Metropolitan Areas* (New York: McGraw Hill, 1961), p. 146. For a sense of the response to Conant, see "Conant Says Slum Schools Create Dynamite in Cities," *New York Times*, October 17, 1961, p. 1. Also see "Ribicoff Decries School Drop-Outs," *New York Times*, October 20, 1961, p. 35, apparently the first time in this era that the *Times* used the term *urban crisis*.

2. For discussion of the "War on Poverty," see David Zarefsky, *President Johnson's War on Poverty: Rhetoric and History* (Tuscaloosa, AL: University of Alabama Press, 2005), passim; on education, see Diane Ravitch *The Troubled Crusade: American Education, 1945–1980* (New York: Basic Books, 1983), Ch. 5, and Gareth Davies, *See Government Grow: Education Politics from Johnson to Reagan* (Lawrence: University Press of Kansas, 2007), Part I.

3. James Patterson, *Brown v. Board of Education: A Civil Rights Milestone and Its Troubled Legacy* (New York: Oxford University Press, 2002), Ch. 1; Ravitch, *The Troubled Crusade*, pp. 114–120.

4. Eunice S. Newton and Earle H. West, "The Progress of the Negro in Elementary and Secondary Education," *The Journal of Negro Education*, 32:4 (Autumn 1963), pp. 466–484; Robert Singleton and Paul Bullock, "Some Problems of Minority Group Education in the Los Angeles Public Schools," *The Journal of Negro Education*, 32:2 (Spring 1963), pp. 137–145; Walter G. Daniel, "Problems of Disadvantaged Youth, Urban and Rural," *The Journal of Negro Education*, 32: 3 (Summer 1964), pp. 218–224.

5. For an overview of the urban problems of this era and contemporary perceptions of them, see Gary A. Tobin, ed., *The Changing Structure of the City: What Happened to the Urban Crisis* (Bevery Hills, CA: Sage Publications, 1980), passim. On Black Power, see Penial E. Joseph, *Waiting 'Til the Midnight Hour: A Narrative History of Black Power in America* (New York: Holt, 2006), Chs. 6–11.

6. These figures are calculated from data in Bureau of the Census, *Historical Statistics of the United States: Colonial Times to 1970* (Washington, DC: Government Printing Office, 1975), Ch. A; and idem, *1980 Census of Population, Volume 1, Characteristics of the Population, Chapter, Number of Inhabitants, Part I, United States Summary* (Washington, DC: Government Printing Office, 1983), p. 227; also see Fox, *Metropolitan America*, p. 51. On the urban-suburban migration at this time and its effect, see Jon C. Teaford, *The Twentieth Century American City*, 2nd ed. (Baltimore: Johns Hopkins University Press, 1993), passim; also see Kenneth T. Jackson, *The Crabgrass Frontier: The Suburbanization of the United States* (New York: Oxford University Press, 1985), Ch. 12.

7. Melvin Oliver and Thomas Shapiro, *Black Wealth/White Wealth: A New Perspective on Racial Inequality* (New York: Routledge, 1995), Ch. 1 & 2.

8. Fox, *Metropolitan America*, Ch. 2; Jackson, *Crabgrass Frontier*, Ch. 15; Arnold Hirsch, "With or Without Jim Crow: Black Residential Segregation in the United States," in Arnold R. Hirsch and Raymond Mohl, eds., *Urban Polity on Twentieth Century America* (New Bruns-

wick, NJ: Rutgers University Press, 1993), pp. 65–99; and Andrew Hacker, *Two Nations: Black and White, Separate, Hostile and Unequal* (New York: Charles Scribner's Sons, 1992), Ch. 1.

9. For an overview of this process, see Edmonia W. Davidson, "Education and Black Cities: Demographic Background," *The Journal of Negro Education*, Vol. 42, No. 3 (Summer 1973), pp. 233–260.

10. These figures are drawn from IPUMS data for 1960 and 1970. In 1960, some 65% of Black teens aged 14 to 19 lived in the South, with about half living in rural areas and 21% on farms. By 1970, these figures had dropped to 57% in the South, 36% of whom lived in rural areas. Fewer than 10% of non-Southern Black youth in lived in rural areas, and less than 1% lived on farms in this era.

11. On conditions in the cities, see Karl E. Teuber and Alma F. Teuber, *Negroes in Cities: Residential Segregation and Neighborhood Change* (Chicago: Aldine Publishing, 1966), passim; on "White flight," see William H. Frey, "Central City White Flight: Racial and Nonracial Causes," *American Sociological Review*, Vol. 44, No. 3 (June 1979), pp. 425–448.

12. Donna L. Franklin, *Ensuring Inequality: The Structural Transformation of the African-American Family* (New York: Oxford University Press, 1997), p. 82.

13. Isabel Wilkerson, *The Warmth of Other Suns: The Epic Story of America's Great Migration* (New York: Random House, 2010), p. 291; Thomas Ditmars, "Social Composition of the Kansas City, Missouri Public High Schools" (master's thesis, University of Kansas, 1929) p. 57.

14. C. Marks. *Farewell, We're Good and Gone: The Great Black Migration* (Bloomington: Indiana University Press, 1989), p. 46.

15. Dennis Gilbert, *The American Class Structure in an Age of Growing Inequality* (Thousand Oaks, CA: Pine Forge Press, 2008), p. 55.

16. For influential studies of particular cities, see Thomas J. Sugrue, *The Origins of the Urban Crisis: Race and Inequality in Postwar Detroit* (Princeton, NJ: Princeton University Press, 1996), Ch. 1, and Arnold Hirsch, *The Making of the Second Ghetto: Race and Housing in Chicago, 1940–1960* (Chicago: University of Chicago Press, 1998), passim. On urban education, see Harvey Kantor and Barbara Brenzel, "Urban Education and the 'Truly Disadvantaged': The Historical Roots of the Current Crisis," *Teachers College Record,* Vol. 94 No. 2, 1992, pp. 278–314.

17. See, for instance, Herbert McCann, "Why Does a Fine School Decline?" *Chicago Defender*, June 16, 1973, p. 5, and Mrs. Norine Foster, "The Real Reason," *Chicago Defender*, June 19, 1973, p. 13.

18. Jean Anyon, *Ghetto Schooling: A Political Economy of Urban Educational Reform* (New York: Teachers College Press, 1997), Ch. 6; Mirel, *Rise and Fall of an Urban School System: Detroit, 1907–81* (Ann Arbor: University of Michigan Press, 1993), Ch. 6; Gary Orfield, Susan Eaton, and the Harvard Project on School Desegregation, *Dismantling Desegregation: The Quiet Reversal of Brown v. Board of Education* (New York: The New Press, 1997), Ch 1; John L. Rury, "Race, Space and the Politics of Chicago's Public Schools," *History of Education Quarterly* 39:2 (Summer 1998), pp. 117–142.

19. Robert J. Havighurst, *The Public Schools of Chicago: A Survey for the Board of Education of the City of Chicago* (Chicago: Chicago Board of Education, 1964), Ch. X.; Bennett Harrison, "Education and Underemployment in the Urban Ghetto," *The American Economic Review*, Vol. 62, No. 5 (December 1972), pp. 796–812.

20. Anyon, *Ghetto Schooling*, p. 111; Mirel, *Rise and Fall of an Urban School System*, Ch. 6; Michael Stolee, "The Milwaukee Desegregation Case," in J. L. Rury and F. A. Cassell, *Seeds of Crisis: Public Schooling in Milwaukee Since 1920* (Madison: University of Wisconsin Press, 1993), pp. 229–259; Amy Stuart Wells and Robert Crain, *Stepping Over the Color Line: African American Students in White Suburban Schools* (New Haven, CT: Yale University Press, 1999), Ch. 3.

21. For discussion of the origin of the term *dropout*, see Sherman Dorn, *Creating the Dropout: An Institutional and Social History of School Failure* (Westport, CT: Praeger, 1996), Ch.

4. He notes that use of the term appears to have peaked in the 1960s.

22. "'Stay in School' Advice to Teenagers Who May be Looking for Jobs," *New York Times*, September 8, 1957, p. E11; "President Urges Return to School," *New York Times*, September 4, 1962, p. 20; "Two Kennedys Urge Washington Youth to Remain in School," *New York Times*, June 6, 1963, p. 21.

23. "Asks Youths to Return to School," *New York Amsterdam News*, September 18, 1965, p. 30; "Stay in School Drive is Opened by Johnson," *New York Times*, August 26, 1967, p. 15.

24. "Gives Fund to Cut Drop-Outs from Schools," *Chicago Daily Tribune*, July 11, 1961, p. 24. These grants would total more than $7 million in 2009 dollars.

25. "Kennedy Approves $250,000 to Fight School Dropouts," *Atlanta Daily World*, June 12, 1964, p. 1.

26. "Says School Drop-Outs Hurt Nation's Economy," *Chicago Daily Defender*, May 29, 1961, p. 8.

27. "Mayor Lauds Urban League for Stay-in-School Drive," *Los Angeles Sentinel*, August 10, 1961, p. C1; "Mayor Praises Urban League for Its Stay in School 3rd Annual Campaign," *Los Angeles Sentinel*, September 12, 1963, p. A5; "Ministers Join Crusade for Return to School," *Chicago Defender*, August 25, 1962; "Urban League Launches War on Teen Dropouts," *Chicago Defender*, August 24, 1963, p. 3.

28. "Urban League Urges Return for Dropouts," *Chicago Daily Tribune*, August 30, 1964, p. S2; "Dr. Letson Calls for Broad Attack on School Dropouts," *Atlanta Daily World*, April 14, 1963, p. 1; "Mayor Wagner's Efforts Reduce School Dropouts, *New York Amsterdam News*, April 27, 1963.

29. "WBBM-TV Explores 'Drop-Out,'" *Chicago Defender*, November 17, 1962, p. 7; "WGN to Give Documentary on Dropouts," *Chicago Daily Tribune*, September 6, 1961, p. A10.

30. "A Report on Lever's Anti-Dropout Radio Campaign," *Chicago Defender*, June 26, 1965, p. B20.

31. "Dr. King Album Used in Drive Against Dropouts," *Chicago Daily Defender*, October 11, 1962, p. 20.

32. "Labor Dept. Film Helps in 'Drop-Out' Programs," *Chicago Defender*, November 24, 1962; "Don't Be a Dropout Blackout," *Los Angeles Sentinel*, August 10, 1961, p. C1; "Dropout Film to Be Shown to Tilden PTA," *Chicago Daily Tribune*, March 10, 1963, p. SW A19; "Documentary Drops Hint to Dropouts," *Los Angeles Sentinel*, June 3, 1964, p. A7; "Illinois Bell Film Aims at Dropout," *Chicago Daily Tribune*, October 30, 1964, p. E6.

33. "Groups Join to Stop Dropouts," *Los Angeles Sentinel*, January 30, 1969, p. B2; "Cabrini Green 'Back to School, Stay in School' Parade Set," *Chicago Daily Defender*, August 26, 1969, p. 5.

34. James Brown interview with Shirley Hill, March 17, 2009, Chicago, IL.

35. "Lou Rawls Visits Carver to Help Stop Dropouts," *Los Angeles Sentinel*, January 29, 1970, p. B5; "Pros Dazzle to Make the Point: Stay in School," *New York Times*, August 27, 1973, p. 62.

36. Thadeus Stokes, "Don't Be a Dropout," *Atlanta Daily World*, January 20, 1968, p. 6. Also see editorials in the *Los Angeles Sentinel*, "On Curbing Dropouts," June 22, 1965, p. A6; "Solution to Dropouts," June 29, 1965, p. A6; and "An Examination of Our High School Dropouts," *Chicago Defender*, December 25, 1965, p. 7.

37. Dorn expresses doubt that programs such as these appreciably affected the national dropout rate, but does not consider their effect on Black enrollment levels. He does acknowledge, however, that such campaigns may have prevented a number of youth from leaving school. See *Creating the Dropout*, Ch. 5.

38. "Help Potential Dropouts," *Chicago Daily Tribune*, May 9, 1963, p. 21; "Open Pilot Project to Combat School Dropouts," *Chicago Daily Defender*, March 5, 1963, p. 14; "'Y' Teaches Dropouts," *Chicago Tribune*, May 15, 1964, p. J10.

39. "Here is 'Double E' Plan: Jobs and Studies for Dropouts from Schools," *Chicago Daily Tribune*, June 20, 1963, p. 21; "Learn to Earn Project Approved for Fulton Youth," *Atlanta Daily World*, June 12, 1964, p. 1; ""Program for Dropouts Gains Strength," *Chicago Daily Tribune*, February 16, 1964, p. B2.

40. "Encourages Dropouts to Return," *New York Amsterdam News*, January 13, 1968, p. 25; "Training Plan for Dropouts in Cleveland," *Chicago Daily Defender*, January 13, 1968, p. 3; "Summer Program Aims to Keep Kids in School," *Chicago Daily Defender*, June 19, 1971, p. 15; "60,000 Youth in South to Obtain Summer Jobs," *Atlanta Daily World*, May 7, 1970, p. 1; "Second Chance for Dropouts in Project," *Chicago Daily Defender*, October 15, 1969, p. 27.

41. "Boys Club Receives Funds for Dropouts," *Chicago Daily Tribune*, September 20, 1964, p. N1; "Culturally Deprived Youth Studying in Special Schools," *New York Amsterdam News*, October 9, 1965, p. 34; "Dropout Centers Approved by Board," *Los Angeles Sentinel*, January 4, 1968, p. D2.

42. "Job Corps: New Hope for Dropouts," *Chicago Daily Defender*, April 27, 1965, p. 15; "Groom Dropout Pupils to Enter King Center 'Work Study' High School," *Chicago Tribune*, August 7, 1966, p. T4; "New Programs Offered for High School Dropouts," *Chicago Tribune*, November 7, 1968, p. S4; "Jaycees Program Saves Would-Be Dropouts," *Chicago Daily Defender*, January 9, 1969, p. 10; "Atlanta Urban League's School to Industry Program Involves High School Youth," *Atlanta Daily World*, October 17, 1971, p. 9.

43. "How 'Tender Loving Care' Changes Harlem Dropouts," *New York Amsterdam News*, June 29, 1968, p. 28; "Learning to Learn—That's What Is Happening at 'Drop-Out' School," *Chicago Daily Defender*, March 4, 1969, p. 19; "New Academy Opens for H.S. Dropouts," *Chicago Daily Defender*, May 17, 1969, p. 33; "New Approach to Education Brings Students into Classes from Streets," *Pittsburgh Courier*, December 13, 1969, p. 16; "Concerned Clubs to Stage Street Academy Benefit," *Atlanta Daily World*, July 3, 1970, p. 2; "Cabrini Green Alternative School Gives Dropouts Chance to Avoid Streets," *Chicago Tribune*, December 30, 1971, p. N3.

44. Lisa Stulberg and Anthony Chen, "Beyond Disruption: The Forgotten Origins of Affirmative Action in College and University Admissions, 1961–1969" (Unpublished manuscript, University of Michigan, 2008), passim.

45. "The Disadvantaged: New Programs Prepare Students for Advanced Schooling," *New York Times*, August 16, 1964, p. E7.

46. "2,000 College Hopefuls Being Interviewed, May 14: Scholarships Agency Sponsoring Meeting," *New York Amsterdam News*, May 14, 1966, p. 31; "College Aid Offered HS Students," *New York Amsterdam News*, June 24, 1967, p. 23; "University of Chicago Recruits Harlem Kids," *New York Amsterdam News*, January 11, 1969, p. 31; "12 State Colleges Host 500 Boro Students," *New York Amsterdam News*, May 10, 1969, p. 31; "How Harvard Univ Became more Relevant to Blacks," *New York Amsterdam News*, September 6, 1969, p. 8; "Three Thousand Negro Students Meet with College Advisers," *Atlanta Daily World*, April 8, 1971, p. 1.

47. "Agency Seeks HS Grads for City U," *New York Amsterdam News*, September 10, 1966, p. 32; "U.N. Upward Bound Program Gets Lowest Dropout Rate," *Chicago Daily Defender*, September 21, 1967; "Upward Bound Program Helps Youngsters Find Right Path," *New York Amsterdam News*, September 18, 1971, p. B3.

48. "City U Plans to Triple Minority Enrollment," *New York Amsterdam News*, August 10, 1968, p. 2; "Open Admissions . . . Where Now?" *New York Amsterdam News*, July 8, 1971, p. A5; "Project Opportunity to Help Dropouts," *Chicago Defender*, March 20, 1965, p. A4.

49. Dongbin Kim and John Rury, "The Changing Shape of College Access: The Truman Commission and Enrollment Patterns in the Postwar Era," *History of Education Quarterly*, Vol. 47, No. 2 (August 2007), pp. 302–327; Op. cit., "The Rise of the Commuter Student: Growth in Enrollment Among Students Living at Home, 1960–1980," *Teachers College Record*, Vol. 113, No. 5 (May 2011), pp. 1031–1066.

50. See, for instance, "Board Report Shows Decrease in Dropouts," *Chicago Daily Defender*, May 14, 1964, p. 4; "Dropouts Decline, But Problem is Still Serious," *New York Times*, April 10, 1966, p. 151.

51. "23 Million Negroes Said Closing Gap on Education," *Atlanta Daily World*, August 7, 1970, p. 1; "Black College Enrollment Comparable to the Whites," *Atlanta Daily World*, March 27, 1973, p. 3; "Black Education Rises," *Atlanta Daily World*, March 15, 1975, p. 3.

52. See Davies, *See Government Grow*, Chs. 2 & 3.

53. "Find More Blacks Stay in School," *Chicago Tribune*, March 7, 1979, p. A2.

54. On neglect of this point, see John L. Rury, "Attainment Amidst Adversity: Black High School Students in the Metropolitan North, 1940–1980," in Kenneth K. Wong and Robert Rothman, eds., *CLIO at the Table: Using History to Inform and Improve Education Policy* (New York: Peter Lang, 2009), Ch. 2. On the views of contemporaries, see "High School Grads Up 93% in Last Decade," *Chicago Defender*, January 2, 1965, p. 3; "Need Program to Close Gap in Education," *Chicago Defender*, May 15, 1965, p. 5; "Black College Enrollment Comparable to Whites," *Atlanta Daily World*, March 27, 1973, p. 3.

55. See, for instance, Martin Meyer, "Close to Midnight for the New York Schools," *The New York Times*, May 2, 1965, p. SM34, a feature article in the paper's widely read Sunday magazine.

56. As calculated with IPUMS data, the proportion of central city Black youth living in residence-owning households increased from about 36% in 1960 to 42% in 1970 to 46% in 1980. These figures paralleled national trends, although home ownership was consistently about 5% to 10% lower in the cities due to renters. Home ownership was generally 15% to 20% higher among Whites than Blacks.

57. For a contemporary perspective on this, see Reynolds Farley and Albert Hermalin, "The 1960s: A Decade of Progress for Blacks?" *Demography*, Vol. 9, No. 3 (August 1972), pp. 353–370.

58. Sar A. Levitan, William B. Johnston, and Robert Taggart, *Still a Dream: The Changing Status of Blacks Since 1960* (Cambridge, MA: Harvard University Press, 1975), p. 44.

59. Teuber and Teuber, *Negroes in Cities*, p 7; on Black college enrollment during this time, see Kim and Rury, "The Changing Profile of College Access," passim.

60. For instance, "See Rise in Negro White Collar Jobs," *Chicago Defender*, January 9, 1960, p. 22; "Survey Shows Our Income Keeps Going Up," *Chicago Daily Defender*, September 5, 1962, p. 13. On national trends, see Levitan, Johnson, and Taggart, *Still a Dream*, Ch. 3.

61. Here, the IPUMS data tell a somewhat different story for the South, where central city poverty declined substantially during the 1960s, from more than a third to about a quarter of the youth population. Outside of the South, it remained at about 20% through the 1960s and reached nearly a quarter by 1980.

62. Southern birth was controlled for, but not included in the chart due to space constraints. It was not significantly related to African American attainment, but was negatively associated with White attainment. Most youth in this category lived in the South. In separate regressions run for Black and White 17-year-olds living outside the South, however, the South birth variable had similar values for Blacks (-.151) and Whites (-.404), and was not significant for Blacks, suggesting that the effect of this factor was not simply due to differences in schools or the behavior of residents of different regions. For more information, see Appendix B.

63. This point is corroborated by findings reported in Levitan, Johnson, and Taggart, *Still a Dream*, Ch. 4.

64. Fully 85% of Black farm youth in this sample lived in poverty, as opposed to less than a third of White farm youth.

65. African American youth were much less likely to be in the labor force, a reflection of their restricted opportunities for employment. Among 17-year-olds in 1970, 23%

of Black youth were working or seeking employment compared with 39% of White youth, according to IPUMS data. The vast majority were part-time or seasonal jobs.

66. On the growth of female attainment at this time, see Claudia Goldin, Lawrence F. Katz, and Ilyana Kuziemko, "The Homecoming of American College Women: The Reversal of the College Gender Gap," *Journal of Economic Perspectives*, 20:4 (Fall 2006), pp. 133–156.

67. For overall trends in attainment at this time, see John L. Rury, Argun Saatcioglu, and William P. Skorupski, "Expanding Secondary Attainment in the United States, 1940–1980: A Fixed Effects Panel Regression Model," *Historical Methods*, Vol. 43, No. 3 (July 2010), pp. 139–152.

68. "De Facto Segregation in Chicago Public Schools," *The Crisis,* 65 (February 1958), pp. 87–95, 126–127.

69. Mary Herrick, *The Chicago Schools: A Social and Political History* (Beverly Hills, CA: Sage Publications, 1971), pp. 310–312.

70. Robert J. Havighurst, *The Public Schools of Chicago: A Survey for the Board of Education of the City of Chicago* (Chicago: Chicago Board of Education, 1964), Ch. VII.

71. "Urges School Integrate Now," *Chicago Daily Defender*, May 21, 1963, p. 5.

72. "Student Blasts Marshall High," *Chicago Daily Defender*, December 14, 1965, p. 1; "Set School Action in Drive for Additional Room," *Chicago Daily Defender*, April 5, 1965, p. 9.

73. John L. Rury, "Race, Space, and the Politics of Chicago's Public Schools: Benjamin Willis and the Tragedy of Urban Education," *History of Education Quarterly*, Vol. 39, No. 2 (Summer 1999), pp. 117–142.

74. "Parents Stage Protest Over Crowded School," *Chicago Daily Defender*, October 25, 1962, p. 2.

75. See, for instance, the Human Relations Task Force on Civil Disorder, "Three Year Report: The Quality of Urban Life,"(Kansas City, MO: Kansas City Public Library, Missouri Valley Special Collections, October 1971), p. II-1, which notes the shortage of minority teachers facing the district.

76. "Atlanta Ordered to File 'Facts' on School Desegregation; Warren Says Many Deprived of Education," *Atlanta Daily World*, April 11, 1964, p. 1; "School Protests Grow in Cities in the North," *Atlanta Daily World*, September 11, 1963, p. 1; Jack Dougherty, *More than One Struggle: The Evolution of Black School Reform in Milwaukee* (Chapel Hill: University of North Carolina Press, 2004), pp. 94–96; Peter William Moran, *Race, Law, and the Desegregation of Public Schools* (New York: LFB Scholarly Pub., 2005), pp. 33–34; Jean Anyon, *Ghetto Schooling: A Political Economy of Urban Educational Reform* (New York: Teachers College Press, 1997), pp. 94–95; "Newark's Barringer High: Adults Creating Problems," *New York Amsterdam News*, December 2, 1967, p. 1; Willard C. Richan, "Racial Isolation in the Cleveland Public Schools" (unpublished report, Case Western Reserve University, 1967), passim.

77. Bert E. Swanson, *The Struggle for Equality: The School Integration Controversy in New York City* (New York: Hobbs, Dorman & Co., 1966), p. 18; "Here are Schools in Open Door Policy," *New York Amsterdam News*, September 10, 1960, p. 6; "The Revolution Spreads All Over New York," *New York Amsterdam News*, July 27, 1963, p. 1; "Letter to the Editor," *New York Amsterdam News*, July 9, 1966, p. 28.

78. "Bogan High School NOT Crowded, Defender Finds," *Chicago Daily Defender*, September 30, 1963, p. A2.

79. See, for instance, the account of this process in Moran, *Race, Law and the Desegregation of Public Schools,* Ch. 2.

80. "Permissive Transfer Plan No Good, Dr. Friedman Says," *Chicago Defender*, July 2, 1966, p. 5; "Austin Groups Join Forces: Both Segments Urge Board to Stabilize Racial Balance," *Chicago Tribune*, August 10, 1967, p. F1.

81. "Rally to Probe What's Wrong with Compton Schools," *Los Angeles Sentinel*, August 20, 1964, p. D1.

82. See, for instance, "Education in the Slums: A Study of Hyde Park High: A Former Student Gives Inside Account of How Life Is In School Gone to Pot," *Chicago Daily Defender*, March 4, 1967, p. 1; "Dunbar: Segregation's Stepchild," *Chicago Daily Defender*, September 11, 1963, p. A2; "Hoodlum School," *Chicago Defender*, February 20, 1965, p. 11; "Newark's Barringer High: Adults Creating Problems," *New York Amsterdam News*, December 2, 1967, p. 1; "Jefferson High in Crisis," *Los Angeles Sentinel*, October 23, 1970, p. A7; "Boys High: Decline of a Dynasty," *New York Amsterdam News*, February 7, 1970, p. 1.

83. On Compton in this period, see Emily Straus, "The Making of the American School Crisis: Compton, California and the Death of the American Dream" (unpublished Ph.D. dissertation, Brandeis University, 2006), Ch. 2. For a contemporary take, see "What's Wrong with Compton Schools?" *Los Angeles Sentinel*, August 20, 1964, p. D1.

84. "School Board Facing New S. Side Troubles," *Chicago Defender*, August 27, 1963, p. 2; Sherwood Ross, "Willis on Segregated Schools," *Chicago Defender*, August 31, 1963, p. 5.

85. "Abbott School Parents Demand Police Help," *Chicago Daily Defender*, September 16, 1963, p. A6.

86. Figures obtained from Office of the Superintendent, School District of Kansas City, Missouri, "Report on the Progress of Desegregation in the Kansas City Public Schools, 1955–1970. School District Archives, Kansas City Public Library.

87. Calculated by examining *Centralia*, the Central High yearbook for the years 1950 through 1970, Missouri Valley Collection, Kansas City Public Library.

88. This aversion was reflected in accounts written by teachers during this era. See, for instance, Forrest W. Parkay, *White Teacher, Black School: The Professional Growth of a Ghetto Teacher* (New York: Praeger, 1983), especially Chapter 6, in which he describes other teachers. Also see Harold Saltzman, *Race War in High School: The Ten-Year Destruction of Franklin K. Lane High School in Brooklyn* (New Rochelle, NY: Arlington House, 1972), passim.

89. DuSable High School in Chicago, for instance, was known for its prominent alumni, even if its overall academic record was less than stellar. See "DuSable to Get Cheers," *Chicago Daily Defender*, May 24, 1960, p. 19.

90. "Ark. Schools 'Still Separate and Unequal," *Chicago Daily Defender*, October 9, 1963, p. A5.

91. Vanessa Siddle Walker, *Their Highest Potential: An African American School Community in the Segregated South* (Chapel Hill: University of North Carolina Press, 1996), Ch. 6.

92. "Principal Backs Expose of Conditions at Crane," *Chicago Defender*, December 25, 1965, p. 11.

93. See Jeffry Mirel, *The Rise and Fall of an Urban School System: Detroit, 1907–81* (Ann Arbor: University of Michigan Press, 1993), p. 306. On New York, see Christina Collins, *"Ethnically Qualified:" Race, Merit and the Selection of Urban Teachers, 1920–1980* (New York: Teachers College Press, 2011) Ch. 2; Howie Evans, "Boys High: Decline of a Dynasty," *New York Amsterdam News*, February 7, 1970, p. 1.

94. M. K. Asante, *The Afrocentric Idea* (Philadelphia: Temple University Press, 1987), Part 2. For a contemporary perspective, see William Ryan, *Blaming the Victim* (New York: Vintage, 1976), passim.

95. Levitan, Johnston, and Taggart made a similar point in noting that family background factors were critical in determining achievement among African American students; see *Still a Dream*, pp. 89–91.

96. See Rury, "Race, Space and the Politics of Chicago's Public Schools," pp. 127–129.

97. James Coleman, "The Concept of Equality of Educational Opportunity," in Harvard Educational Review, *Equality of Educational Opportunity* (Cambridge, MA: Harvard University Press, 1969), Ch. 1.

98. Diane Ravitch, *The Troubled Crusade: American Education* (New York: Basic Books, 1983), Ch. 4; United States Commission on Civil Rights, *Racial Isolation in the Public Schools*,

Vol. 1 (Washington, DC: U.S. Government Printing Office, 1967), Ch. 1.

99. James Conant, passim.

100. Melvin Tumin, Book Review, *American Sociological Review*, Vol. 27, No. 3 (June 1962), p. 421

101. "'Disadvantaged American' Causes Concern In Educational Circles, "*Chicago Daily Defender*, April 2, 1962, p. 9.

102. "Civil Rights Program For Ind. Schools Prepared," *Chicago Daily Defender;* June 24, 1963, p. 7.

103. "Equal Education Asked By U. S. Aide," *Chicago Daily Defender*, July 2, 1963, p. 13.

104. "Propose Technical Institute for Unemployed Youth, Dropouts," *New York Amsterdam News*, June 20, 1964, p. 5.

105. "Schools and Jobs," *Chicago Daily Defender*, December 29, 1963, p. 15.

106. Mirel, *The Rise and Fall of an Urban School System*, pp. 263–264. Despite these problems, Dunbar was held up as a model by James Conant; see *Slums and Suburbs*, pp. 47–48.

107. "The Dunbar Story—Prejudice Hamstrings the Negro Craftsman's Future," *Chicago Daily Defender*, July 31, 1961, p. 1; "School Bias Keeps Negroes Out of Trades," *Chicago Defender*, January 5, 1963, p. 11; "Technical Education for Negro Must Make Changes," *Chicago Daily Defender*, August 13, 1963, p. A9; "Dunbar: Segregation's Stepchild," *Chicago Daily Defender*, September 11, 1963; Racial Walls in Chicago Built by Labor in Conspiracy with School Bd. Says NALC," *Chicago Defender*, October 12, 1963.

108. Conant, *Slums and Suburbs*, pp. 47–48.

109. "Conference on Vocational Education, New York, NY, March 20, 1967, NAACP Papers, Part IV, Box E15, 1966–68 Folder. Also see "Vocational Education Called Dumping Ground: Dunbar Said to Take 'Any, All Students,'" *Chicago Daily Defender*, April 12, 1967, p. 11.

110. David Angus and Jeffrey Mirel, *The Failed Promise of the American High School, 1890–1995* (New York: Teachers College Press, 1999), Ch. 5.

111. "State Senator Calls for Probe of Exams," *New York Amsterdam News*, March 30, 1963, p. 29.

112. Mirel, *Rise and Fall of an Urban School System*, pp. 255, 301, although he does note that Black students at Northern High School protested the lack of advanced courses available to them (pp. 300–304); National Association for the Advancemtn of Colored People (NAACP) *58th Annual Convention Resolutions*, July 10–15, 1967, Boston, Massachusetts (NAACP, 1790 Broadway, New York, NY 10019) p. 25. The NAACP clearly believed that compensatory or remedial courses were not a suitable response to educational inequality, calling instead for integration.

113. Mirel, *Rise and Fall of an Urban School System*, p. 332. Jonathan Zimmerman, *Whose America? Culture Wars in the Public Schools* (Cambridge, MA: Harvard University Press, 2005) pp. 107–110.

114. Kevin Dodge interview with Shirley Hill, Kansas City, MO, February 20, 2009.

115. "Act to Keep Dope Pushers Out of School," *Chicago Daily Defender*, April 2, 1966, p. 50; "All Out War on Bronx School Dope Sales," *New York Amsterdam News*, March 23, 1968, p. 59; "Tradition, Drugs and Apathy," *New York Amsterdam News*, February 14, 1970, p. 1; "Schools to Adopt Anti-Drug Program," *New York Amsterdam News*, June 27, 1970, p. 30.

116. "More Teen Violence Hits Hyde Park High," *Chicago Daily Defender*, April 16, 1966, p. 1; "Westside: High School Flare-up," *Chicago Daily Defender*, October 12, 1966, p. 3; "Gang Feud Blamed: Gunman Shoots 3 in Parker High," *Chicago Daily Defender*, September 5, 1968, p. 1; "Youth, 19, Shot at Marshall," *Chicago Daily Defender*, May 28, 1970, p. 1.

117. "KOCO Hits Violence: Seeks Probe at Forrestville High," *Chicago Daily Defender*, September 21, 1970, p. 2.

118. "Tensions Mount at Jeff High, School Closes: Groups Meet in Effort to Remedy Problems," *Los Angeles Sentinel*, October 16, 1969, p. A1; "Students Give Views on Prep Bas-

ketball Crisis," *Chicago Daily Defender,* February 14, 1970, p. 30.

119. Lee Jenkins (editorial), "If Violence Can't Be Checked, Prep Basketball Should Be Abolished," *Chicago Daily Defender,* January 31, 1970, p. 1.

120. "One Day Boycott by HS Students," *New York Amsterdam News,* May 10, 1969, p. 29.

121. "Say Vandalism Soars in Schools, *Chicago Daily Defender,* April 2, 1970, p. 2.

122. "Extra Security Ordered for Schools," *Chicago Defender,* September 5, 1970, p. 1; "Cincinnati Educator Outlines High School Crisis," *Chicago Defender,* April 10, 1975, p. 6.

123. "March on Integrated School," *Chicago Tribune,* September 18, 1965, p. S5.

124. There is little written about the youth division of the NAACP in this period. Examination of archival material in the NAACP records at the Library of Congress, however, reveals a good deal of tension between adults in local chapters and Youth Council members intent on addressing problems in the schools. See, for instance, the Saginaw, Michigan Folder, NAACP Papers, Part IV, Box E5, which describes a chapter reprimanding student leaders for staging a sit-in in 1969 to protest police actions in the schools. In another case, a national youth leader wrote to a Greenwich, Connecticut chapter leader about the "separatist problem" among Black youth nationally, and ways to combat it; Greenwich, Connecticut, Folder, NAACP Papers, Part IV, Box E1. On the influence of Black Panthers on events in Chicago, see Jon Rice, "The World of the Illinois Panthers," in Jeanne F. Theoharris and Komozi Woodard, eds., *Freedom North: Black Freedom Struggles Outside the South, 1940–1980* (New York: Palgrave Macmillan, 2003), Ch. 2. Regarding the influence of teachers and others in the Black community, see Dionne Danns, *Something Better for Our Children: Black Organizing in Chicago Public Schools, 1963–1971* (New York: Routledge, 2003), Chs. 4 & 5.

125. Dionne Danns, "Chicago High School Students' Movement for Quality Public Education, 1966–1971," *The Journal of African American History,* Vol. 88, No. 2 (Spring 2003), pp. 138–150.

126. Aldon Morris, *The Origins of the Civil Rights Movement: Black Communities Organizing for Change* (New York: The Free Press, 1984), Ch. 10.

127. "3,000 Skip Classes in Boston Bias Protest," *Chicago Daily Defender,* June 19, 1963, p. 4.

128. Rury, "Race, Space and the Politics of Chicago's Public Schools," p. 132.

129. "N.Y. Boycott Huge Success," *Chicago Daily Defender,* February 4, 1964, p. A3; "60,000 Boycott Cleveland Schools," *Chicago Daily Defender,* April 22, 1964, p. 5; "Over 2000 Students Take Part in Chester Protests," *Pittsburgh Courier,* February 22, 1964, p. 19.

130. Martin Luther King Jr, "The School Boycott Concept," *New York Amsterdam News,* April 11, 1964, p. 10.

131. "Efforts Being Made to Keep High Schoolers in Classes," *Atlanta Daily World,* January 9, 1964, p. 1; "Youth Leaders Plead: 'Learn Civics in Streets' in Atlanta Protest Move," *Pittsburgh Courier,* January 18, 1964, p. 5.

132. "B'ham High Pupils Stage Rights Trek," *Chicago Defender,* January 15, 1965, p. 2.

133. V. P. Franklin, "Black High School Student Activism in the 1960s: An Urban Phenomenon?"*Journal of Research in Education,* 10 (Fall 2000), pp. 3–8; Dwayne C. Wright, "Black Pride Day, 1968: High School Student Activism in York, Pennsylvania," *The Journal of African American History,* Vol. 88, No. 2 (Spring 2003), pp. 151–162. On the decline of the national movement at this time, see Fairclough, *Better Day Coming,* Ch. 15; and McAdams, *Political Process and the Development of Black Insurgency,* Ch. 8.

134. Bo Wirmark, "Non-Violent Methods and the American Civil Rights Movement," *Journal of Peace Research,* Vol. 11, No. 2 (1974), pp. 115–132.

135. "Farragut Protest Expands," *Chicago Defender,* February 19, 1966, p. 1.

136. Mirel, *Rise and Fall of an Urban School System,* pp. 301–303.

137. Richard Arum, *Judging School Discipline: The Crisis of Moral Authority* (Cambridge, MA: Harvard University Press, 2005), passim.

138. "School Boycott Spreads to Yonkers," *New York Amsterdam News*, May 25, 1968, p. 2.

139. "Black Students Plan Big Walkout Today: Fifth Week of School Turmoil Here," *Chicago Daily Defender*, October 14, 1968, p. 3.

140. "35,000 Stage Peaceful School Walkout: Student Protestors Seek More Black Influence Here," *Chicago Daily Defender*, October 15, 1968, p. 3.

141. On shifts in the larger movement, see Fairclough, *Better Day Coming*, Chs. 14 & 15; and McAdams, *Political Process and the Development of Black Insurgency*, Ch. 8.

142. Dodge interview with Shirley Hill; Joshua Dunn, *Complex Justice: The Case of Missouri v. Jenkins* (Chapel Hill: University of North Carolina Press, 2008), pp. 39–40.

143. United Press International, "Students Sit In at Philadelphia High School," *Chicago Daily Defender*, October 24, 1968, p. 12.

144. "NYC's School Picture: It's 'In' to be Out!," *New York Amsterdam News*, December 7, 1968, p. 1.

145. "Jefferson High in Crisis," *Los Angeles Sentinel*, October 23, 1969, p. A7; Judith Kafka, "From Discipline to Punishment: Race, Bureaucracy, and School Discipline Policy in Los Angeles, 1954–1975" (Unpublished doctoral dissertation, University of California–Berkeley, 2004), Ch. 4.

146. "3 Pasadena Schools Face Student Ban," *Los Angeles Sentinel*, March 20, 1969, p. A1; Ruben Donato, *The Other Struggle for Equal Schools: Mexican Americans During the Civil Rights Era* (Albany, NY: SUNY Press, 1997), Ch. 3.

147. "Marching Students Prompt Conferences," *New York Amsterdam News*, February 24, 1968, p. 30.

148. "Blast Whites Teaching Black History," *Chicago Daily Defender*, September 17, 1968, p. 3.

149. See, for instance, "Student Sit-Ins Hit South Shore High," *Chicago Daily Defender*, November 7, 1968, p. 3; "Black History to Be Required at Dunbar," *Chicago Daily Defender*, October 10, 1968, p. 2.

150. "High School Disorders," *Chicago Daily Defender*, September 2, 1969, p. 13. Also see "Teachers Poll Shows Growing Student Unrest," *Chicago Daily Defender*, August 29, 1970, p. 9.

151. "Nation's Schools Still in the Grip of Disturbances," *Chicago Daily Defender*, March 20, 1969, p. 5. On the latter point, see Thomas J. Sugrue, *Sweet Land of Liberty: The Forgotten Struggle for Civil Rights in the North* (New York: Random House, 2008) pp. 473–474.

152. "100 Students Mob School Bd.," *Chicago Daily Defender*, May 7, 1970, p. 3.

153. "School Strife Growing? Arrest 9 Waller Students; Hyde Park Remains Closed," *Chicago Defender*, April 8, 1971, p. 1; "Students Call Off Strike at Lindbloom," *Chicago Defender*, April 24, 1971, p. 1; "Gage Park Peace on Trial Today," *Chicago Defender*, November 20, 1972, p. 1.

154. "Is Black Power Ebbing?" *Pittsburgh Courier*, May 3, 1969, p. 14.

155. "At DuSable High: Hint Boycott 'til Christmas," *Chicago Defender*, December 14, 1972, p. 4;

156. "Step Up Westinghouse Protest," *Chicago Defender*, May 19, 1973, p. 1.

157. "600 Students Protest," *Chicago Defender*, June 26, 1973, p. 3.

158. Evident in examination of yearbooks for 1960 to 1975 Central, Lincoln, and Paseo high schools in Kansas City, MO, and DuSable, Crane, and Austin high schools in Chicago. For discussion of this in a celebrated predominantly Black school, see Aaron Tyler Rife, "Sumner High School: A History" (unpublished master's thesis, University of Kansas, 2008), Ch. 5.

159. Margaret Beale Spencer and Carol Markstrom-Adams, "Identity Processes Among Racial and Ethnic Minority Children in America," *Child Development*, Vol. 61, No. 2, Special Issue on Minority Children (April 1990), pp. 290–310.

160. See, for instance, the struggle on North Division High School in Dougherty, *More than One Struggle*, Ch. 7.

161. McAdams, *Political Process and the Development of the Black Insurgency,* Ch. 8.

162. See, for instance, "New Life for Pittsburgh's Schenley High," *Christian Science Monitor,* January 13, 1986, p. 23; "Learning Returns to Ghetto High School," *News World,* February 19, 1979 (Schomberg Library Clippings File, Fiche 1137).

Chapter 5

1. Research on whether these developments can be entirely attributed to desegregation is mixed. For a global assessment, see Jonathan Guryan, "Desegregation and Black Dropout Rates," *The American Economic Review* Vol. 94, No. 4 (September 2004) pp. 919-943. For contemporary findings, see Robert L. Crain and Rita E. Mahard, "Desegregation and Black Achievement: A Review of the Research," *Law and Contemporary Problems,* Vol. 42, No. 3 (Summer 1978), pp. 17–56, and Gail E. Thomas and Frank Brown, "What Does Educational Research Tell Us About School Desegregation Effects?" *Journal of Black Studies,* Vol. 13, No. 2 (December 1982), pp. 155–174. For a more general commentary, see Charles Clotfelter, *After Brown: The Rise and Retreat of School Desegregation* (Princeton: Princeton University Press, 2004), p. 186.

2. On this point, see Harry Ashmore, *The Negro and the Schools* (Chapel Hill: University of North Carolina Press, 1954), Ch. 8.

3. Davison M. Douglas, *Jim Crow Moves North: The Battle Over Northern School Segregation, 1865–1954* (New York: Cambridge University Press, 2005), Ch. 6; "Crack School Bias in Second Illinois City," *Chicago Defender,* September 27, 1952, p. 9; "Jim Crow Takes Exit at Tamms High School," *Chicago Defender,* October 4, 1952, p. 2; "Another Illinois School Ends Discrimination," *Chicago Defender,* October 18, 1952, p. 4.

4. "Arizona Wipes of School Segregation: Judge Rules Jim Crow High Schools are Unconstitutional," *Atlanta Daily World,* February 17, 1953, p. 1. Also see Ashmore, *The Negro and the Schools,* Ch. 8.

5. Charles T. Clotfelter, *After Brown: The Rise and Retreat of School Desegregation* (Princeton, NJ: Princeton University Press, 2004), Ch. 2.

6. Richard Kluger, *Simple Justice: The History of Brown v Board of Education and Black America's Struggle for Equality* (New York: Random House, 1975), pp. 751–752; James T. Patterson, *Brown v. Board of Education: A Civil Rights Milestone and Its Troubled Legacy* (New York: Oxford University Press, 2002), p. 85. Lorna Tillman interview with Shirley Hill, Kansas City, Missouri , May 8, 2008.

7. Ibid., pp. 73–78; "47 Baltimore schools mixed; D.C. to follow," *Baltimore Afro-American,* September 18, 1954, p. 1.

8. "Hang Effigy in Kentucky School Fuss," *Chicago Defender,* October 13, 1965, p. 1.

9. Andrew Brill, "'Brown' in Fayetteville: Peaceful Southern School Desegregation in 1954," *The Arkansas Historical Quarterly,* Vol. 65, No. 4 (Winter 2006), pp. 337–359.

10. "Violence Flares over School Integration," *Chicago Defender,* October 16, 1954, p. 3; "Police Quell Demonstrators in Wash., D.C. and Baltimore," *Atlanta Daily World,* October 5, 1954, p. 1; "Riots Rage over School Integration," *New York Amsterdam News,* October 9, 1954, p. 1; "No Retreat on Democracy in Baltimore Schools," *Baltimore Afro-American,* October 9, 1954, p. 8. Also see Patterson, *Brown v. Board of Education,* pp. 76–77.

11. Clotfelter, *After Brown,* pp. 24–25; Diane Ravitch, *The Troubled Crusade: American Education, 1945–1980* (New York: Basic Books, 1983), Ch. 4.

12. James G. Fleming, "Racial Integration in Education in Maryland," *The Journal of Negro Education,* 25:3 (Summer, 1956), pp. 273–284; George D. Brantley, "Present Status of Integration in the Public Schools of Missouri," *The Journal of Negro Education,* 24:3 (Summer 1955), pp. 293–309; Lori Bogle, "Desegregation in a Border State: The Example of Joplin, Missouri," *Missouri Historical Review,* 85:4, (1991), pp. 422–440; Paul Lutz, "De-

segregation: A Crisis Without Drama" *Journal of the West Virginia Historical Association*, 10:1 (1986), pp. 16–33.

13. A. Lee Coleman, "Desegregation of the Public Schools in Kentucky—The Second Year After the Supreme Court's Decision," *The Journal of Negro Education*, 25:3 (Summer 1956), pp. 254–261; Peter Khiss, "Fulton, Ky., Quiet as It Integrates," *New York Times*, September 3, 1958, p. 1. Also see Ravitch, *The Troubled Crusade*, p. 131.

14. "Dixie Boils Over Integration," *Chicago Defender*, September 5, 1956, p. 6; Moses Newson, "Lack of Negro High School Led to Clinton, Tenn., Suit," *Chicago Defender*, September 10, 1956, p. 7.

15. "National Guard Moves into Clay, Ky. As Crowd Gathers," *Atlanta Daily World*, September 15, 1956, p. 1.

16. Wilma Dykeman and James Stokely, "Clinton, Tennessee: A Town on Trial," *New York Times*, October 26, 1958, p. SM9.

17. J. Russell Boner, "Mobs Act In Tenn., Texas..." *Chicago Defender*, September 8, 1956, p. 1; "Negroes Daring Mobs in Fight for Mixed Schools," *Pittsburgh Courier*, September 8, 1956, p. 8. Also see Patterson, *Brown v. Board*, pp. 101–104.

18. On the extent of Southern "backlash" following *Brown*, see Michael J. Klarman, *Brown v. Board of Education and the Civil Rights Movement* (New York: Oxford University Press, 2007), Ch. 7.

19. On the crisis at Central High, see Elizabeth Jacoway, *Turn Away Thy Son: Little Rock, the Crisis That Shocked the Nation* (Fayetteville: University of Arkansas Press, 2008), passim.

20. Patterson, *Brown v. Board of Education*, pp. 109–112.

21. On this point, see James Gilbert, *A Cycle of Outrage: America's Reaction to the Juvenile Delinquent in the 1950s* (New York: Oxford University Press, 1988), Ch. 1.

22. Irene Burns, "Separate Schools," *The Washington Post and Times Herald*, September 4, 1958, p. A12.

23. "Election Plea Called Bigotry," *The Washington Post and Times Herald*, November 6, 1955, p. B3. For similar sentiments, see Paterson, *Brown v. Board of Education*, p. 87.

24. Race and sex was a particularly volatile topic in the South. See Peggy Pascoe, *What Comes Naturally: Miscegenation Law and the Making of Race in America* (New York: Oxford University Press, 2010), Chs. 7 & 8.

25. Paterson, *Brown v. Board of Education*, pp. 101–105.

26. Op. cit., pp. 104–105; Thomas V. O'Brien, *The Politics of Race and Schooling: Public Education in Georgia, 1900–1961* (New York: Lexington Books, 1999), Chs. 6 & 7.

27. Margaret Anderson, "The South Learns Its Hardest Lessons," *New York Times*, September 11, 1960, p. SM27.

28. See, for instance, "6 Plan to Quit Mixed School," *Chicago Defender*, September 4, 1958, p. 4A; "Van Buren 13 Drops to 12 as Senior, 16, Leaves Town," *Chicago Defender*, September 10, 1958, p. A4.

29. "School Transfer Forms Sought by 257 Students," *Atlanta Daily World*, May 5, 1961, p. 1; "10 Student Transfers Authorized by School Board," *Atlanta Daily World*, June 4, 1961, p. 1; "Sanders Lashes Geer on Integration Violence," *Atlanta Daily World*, July 7, 1961, p. 6; "4 Arrested at Schools, Freed," *Atlanta Daily World*, September 2, 1961, p. 1; "Peaceful Desegregation Hailed By NAACP Leader," *Atlanta Daily World*, September 14, 1961, p. 5.

30. Alton Hornsby Jr., "Black Public Education in Atlanta, Georgia, 1954–1973: From Segregation to Segregation," *Journal of Negro History*, 76:1–4 (1991), pp. 21–47. Ronald H. Bayor, *Race and the Shaping of Twentieth-Century Atlanta* (Chapel Hill: University of North Carolina Press, 1996), Ch. 7; also see Henry Mark Huie, "Factors Influencing the Desegregation Process in the Atlanta School System, 1954–1967" (unpublished Ed.D dissertation, University of Georgia, 1967), Ch. IV.

31. Reed Sarat, *The Ordeal of Desegregation: The First Decade* (New York: Harper & Row, 1966), Ch. 7.

32. Michael Boozer, Alan Krueger, and Sari Wolkon, "Race and School Quality Since *Brown v Board of Education*," *Brookings Papers on Economic Activity: Microeconomics* (Washington, DC: The Brookings Institution, 1992), pp. 269–338. We conducted an analysis similar to that described in Figure 3 of Boozer, Krueger, and Wolkon, but limited to secondary students in the 1960s.

33. Sherry Lamb Schirmer, *A City Divided: The Racial Landscape of Kansas City, 1900–1960* (Columbia: University of Missouri Press, 2002), Ch. 8.

34. "Policies for transition from system of separate schools to a desegregated school system, 1955."

35. The *Centralian*, 1956 edition, p. 10.

36. "Color of the Class: Desegregating Kansas City Schools," *Kansas City Star*, May 8, 1990, p. 1.

37. Joshua M. Dunn, *Complex Justice: The Case of Missouri v Jenkins*. (Chapel Hill, University of North Carolina Press, 2008), Ch. 2

38. *The Sachem*, Southwest High School (Kansas City, MO, 1964), passim; *The Sachem*, Southwest High School (Kansas City, MO, 1966), passim.

39. Kevin Fox Gotham, *Race, Real Estate, and Uneven Development: The Kansas City Experience, 1900–2000*. (Albany, NY: State University of New York Press, 2002), pp. 114–116.

40. Human Relations Task Force on Civil Disorder, "Three Year Report: The Quality of Urban Life," (Kansas City, MO, 1971), pp. 2–3.

41. Peter William Moran, *Race, Law and the Desegregation of Public Schools* (El Paso, TX: LFB Scholarly Publishing, 2004), Ch. 1; on the process of neighborhood transition in Kansas City at this time, see Schirmer, *A City Divided*, Ch. 8.

42. "Central's Human Relation's Ledger," *Luminary*, Volume XXXIX; No. 12, March 23, 1956, p. 3 (student newspaper)

43. This discussion is based on analysis of yearbooks, the *Centralian*, 1958–1968.

44. Moran, *Race, Law and the Desegregation of Public Schools*, pp. 128–129; *The Centralian*, Central High School (Kansas City, MO, 1965), passim.

45. Gotham, *Race, Real Estate, and Uneven Development*, Ch. 5.

46. *Sachem*, Southwest High School (Kansas City, MO, 1961), p. 4.

47. M. Simon and B. Rodgers, "A high school that just lost its value," *Pitch Weekly*, November 13–19, 1997, pp. 12–16; Rick Montgomery, "Erasing a Tragic History," *Kansas City Star*, June 6, 2010, pp. A1, A10.

48. R. J. Havighurst, "Problems of Integration in the KC public schools: A report to the Board of Education," November 18, 1965. Among elementary school children, African Americans had become the majority.

49. Moran, *Race, Law and the Desegregation of Public Schools*, pp. 116–117.

50. Ibid., Ch. 2; Gotham, *Race, Real Estate, and Uneven Development*, pp. 117–118.

51. Human Relations Task Force, "The Quality of Urban Life," II-3.

52. U.S. Commission on Civil Rights, *Racial Isolation in the Public Schools* (Washington, DC: U.S. Government Printing Office, 1967), p. 59.

53. On intact busing, see Ibid., pp. 56–58; also see Dougherty, *More Than One Struggle*, pp. 94–97, and Dunn, *Complex Justice*, pp. 38-39

54. Susan White, "Can the Kansas City Schools Be Saved? (Or Is It Too Late?), *Kansas City Town Squire*, June 1970, pp. 1–20, 69–73.

55. Dunn, *Complex Justice*, Ch. 2

56. Rick Montgomery, "Erasing a Tragic History," *Kansas City Star*, June 6, 2010, pp. A1, A10.

57. Midwest Research Institute, "Decision Criteria and Policy for School Consolidation." Final Report, March 15, 1974, p. 10.

58. "Boycott Hits Jammed Poe Grade School," *Chicago Tribune*, September 19, 1967, p. A6; "Kinzie Students Protest Addition," *Chicago Tribune*, December 1, 1968, p. SC-A5; "Gary School Center Seized; Officials Meet Boycotters," *Chicago Tribune*, May 18, 1968, p. N5; Peter Negronida, "Pickets Block Pupils, Principal," *Chicago Tribune*, February 6, 1969, p. W10.

59. "10,000 Engage in Milwaukee Pupil Boycott," *Chicago Tribune*, May 19, 1964, p. 24.

60. "End Boycott of Schools in Milwaukee, *Chicago Tribune*, October 22, 1965, p. 3.

61. "Federal Obligation," *Chicago Tribune*, June 20, 1963, p. 8.

62. James Ritch, "Schools Get 9 New Demands," *Chicago Tribune*, April 7, 1964, p. 1.

63. Louis Harris, "The Harris Analyses," *Chicago Tribune*, March 19, 1970, p. A1. Harris reported that 58% of Americans agreed that it was time to enforce laws to integrate schools, and 57% agreed that it would require a "higher authority" to make it happen.

64. James Ritch, "Resume Court Fight on Schools," *Chicago Tribune*, October 24, 1963, p. 1.

65. "3000 Boston Negroes Skip Day of School in Protest," *Chicago Tribune*, June 19, 1963, p. 2.

66. John L. Rury, "Race, Space and the Politics of Chicago's Public Schools: Benjamin Willis and the Tragedy of Urban Education," *History of Education Quarterly* 39: 2 (Summer 1999), p. 132.

67. "Pickets Seek Integration in Three States," *Chicago Tribune*, September 5, 1963, p. 2.

68. "Gary School Boycott Slated for Today," *Chicago Tribune*, May 13, 1968, p. 10.

69. "Negro Pupil Boycotts Planned in 3 Northern Cities," *Chicago Tribune*, February 11, 1964, p. A8.

70. "2 School Boycotts Protest Race Bars," *Chicago Tribune*, February 12, 1964, p. 2. On New York, see Bert E. Swanson, *The Struggle for Equality: School Integration Controversy in New York City* (New York: Hobbs, Dorman & Co., 1966), p. 18.

71. "White Parents End Tilden High Boycott," *Chicago Tribute*, October 2, 1968, p. B4.

72. Dan Egler, "1000 End Boycott at Gage Park," *Chicago Tribune*, November 12, 1972, p. 9.

73. "1200 Kept Out of Schools in Race Boycott," *Chicago Daily Tribune*, October 29, 1960, p. F7.

74. "60% Boycott at Brooklyn School Hit Race Quotas," *Chicago Daily Defender*, April 1, 1963, p. 13; Joseph Zullo, "175,000 Shun New York Schools," *Chicago Tribune*, September 15, 1964, p. 1.

75. "Boston Busing Boycott Is Set," *Chicago Tribune*, September 30, 1974, p. C12.

76. "School Segregation in Chicago," *Chicago Tribune*, December 2, 1972, p. S8.

77. "Permissive Transfer Plan No Good, Dr. Friedman Says," *Chicago Defender*, July 2, 1966, p. 5.

78. John Herbers, "How School Desegregation Stands," *Chicago Tribune*, September 8, 1971, p. 22.

79. Gary Orfield, *Must We Bus? Segregated Schools and National Policy* (Washington, DC: The Brookings Institution, 1977), p. 50.

80. U.S. Commission on Civil Rights, *Reviewing a Decade of School Desegregation: Report of a National Survey of School Superintendents* (Washington, DC: Government Printing Office, 1977), p. 50.

81. "Supreme Court Warns Northern Schools in Bias," *Chicago Tribune*, June 22, 1973, p. B16.

82. "The President's Busing Formula," *Chicago Tribune*, June 26, 1976, p. A8.

83. "US Panel Defends School Busing," *Chicago Tribune*, August 25, 1976, p. 11.

84. Meyer Weinberg, "Can a Committee Do the Job? Integrating Chicago Schools,"

Chicago Tribune, December 5, 1976, p. A1.

85. Franklin W. Neff, "Adult Attitudes Towards Educational Issues: A Summary of Major Findings," *Mid American Observatory* (Kansas City, MO, June 16, 1972, p. 7.

86. For an overview of this, see Orfield, *Must We Bus*, Chs. 5 & 10. Also see Thomas J. Sugrue, *Sweet Land of Liberty: The Forgotten Struggle for Civil Rights* (New York: Random House, 2008) Ch. 13.

87. Meyer Weinberg, "The Quiet Side of the Busing Fervor," *Chicago Tribune*, November 22, 1975, p. S12; "Busing Protest Halts Traffic," *Chicago Tribune*, December 13, 1975, p. S10. For an overview, see Ronald Formisano, *Boston Against Bussing: Race, Class and Ethnicity in the 1960s and 1970s* (Chapel Hill: University of North Carolina Press, 2003), passim.

88. "Unproductive School Busing," *Chicago Tribune*, September 10, 1975, p. A2.

89. Jim Squires, "School Busing—The Issue Politicians Fear Most," *Chicago Tribune*, September 17, 1975, p. 1.

90. On this point, see Argun Saatcioglu and Jim Carl, "The Discursive Turn in School Desegregation: National Patterns and a Case Analysis of Cleveland, 1973–1998," *Social Science History*, 35:1 (Spring 2011), pp. 59–108.

91. Casimir Banas, "Quality Equals Enrollment Rise," *Chicago Daily Tribune*, January 17, 1960, p. NW1; Ronald Koutlak, "Schools Adequate, Officials Say," *Chicago Daily Tribune*, December 30, 1962, p. B7; "Board Asked for School Facilities," *Chicago Daily Tribune*, September 30, 1962, p. SWA1.

92. "More and More Go to Private Schools," *Chicago Tribune*, September 22, 1967, p. 24.

93. "Peaceful Busing in Dallas, Black Boycott in Louisiana, *Chicago Tribune*, August 24, 1976, p. 2.

94. Jennifer Hochschild, *The New American Dilemma: Liberal Democracy and School Desegregation* (New Haven, CT: Yale University Press, 1984), Ch. 5; U.S. Commission on Civil Rights, *Fulfilling the Letter and Spirit of the Law: Desegregation of the Nation's Public Schools* (Washington, DC: U.S. Commission on Civil Rights, 1976), pp. 128–167.

95. "Unproductive School Busing," *Chicago Tribune*, September 10, 1975, p. A2.

96. "School Resegregation," *Chicago Tribune*, March 14, 1966, p. 16.

97. U.S. Commission on Civil Rights, *Reviewing a Decade of School Desegregation*, Chs. IV and V. Also see idem, *Fulfilling the Letter and the Spirit of the Law*, pp. 131–167.

98. This certainly was evident in Detroit and Milwaukee, among other cities. See Jeffrey Mirel, *The Rise and Fall of an Urban School System: Detroit, 1907–81* (Ann Arbor: University of Michigan Press, 1993), Ch. 6; on Milwaukee, see Michael Stolee, "The Milwaukee Desegregation Case," in John L. Rury and Frank Cassell, eds., *Seeds of Crisis: Public Education in Milwaukee Since 1920* (Madison: University of Wisconsin Press, 1993), pp. 229–267. On "tipping points," see Clotfelter, *After Brown*, pp. 110–114, and his earlier article, Charles T. Clotfelter, "School Desegregation, 'Tipping,' and Private School Enrollment," *Journal of Human Resources*, Vol. 11, No. 1 (June, 1976), pp. 281–294.

99. Within the NSBA sample, some 256 respondents reported growing up in large cities outside the South and border states and were of high school age in the 1960s and 1970s. A simple logistic regression of the 1970 decade dummy variable (1970 or not) on the reported racial composition of this group's high schools (recoded to reflect majority-Black or not) yielded a logistical coefficient of .653, reflecting an odds ratio of 1.921. This relationship was significant at the 0.1 level.

100. Clotfelter, *After Brown*, p. 71.

101. Gary Orfield, *Public School Desegregation in the United States, 1968–1980* (Washington, DC: Joint Center for Political Studies, 1983) Ch. 1.

102. One hundred fifty nine NSBA respondents who grew up in the South, excluding border states, were high school age or older in the 1970s and reported the racial composition of their high school. Some 52 (or 33%) reported attending schools with majority-White

student bodies. A nearly equal number, about 30%, attended majority-Black schools, and 37% attended schools that were reportedly about evenly divided between Black and White students.

103. See, for instance, "Integration Hits Negro Teacher Hard, 300 Jobless," *Chicago Defender*, April 10, 1958, p. A9. For a comprehensive discussion of this issue, see Michael Fultz, "The Displacement of Black Educators Post-*Brown:* An Overview and Analysis," *History of Education Quarterly*, Vol. 44, No. 1, (Spring, 2004), pp. 11-45.

104. "Peaceful Busing in Dallas, Black Boycott in Louisiana, *Chicago Tribune*, August 24, 1976, p. 2.

105. See James Bolner and Arnold Vedlitz, "The Affinity of Negro Pupils for Segregated Schools: Obstacle to Desegregation," *Journal of Negro Education* Vol. 40, No. 4 (Autumn 1974), pp. 313–321.

106. Interview with Katie Hawkins, Hattiesburg, MS, May 21, 2008.

107. "Protest Baker County Desegregation Plan," *Atlanta Daily World*, April 5, 1970, p. 1; "'Freedom School' Closed by Covington Police," *Atlanta Daily World*, April 5, 1970; "200 Guardsmen Ordered Into Athens; Augusta Cleans up Riot Debris, *Atlanta Daily World*, May 15, 1970, p. 1.

108. David Cecelski, *Along Freedom Road: Hyde County, North Carolina, and the Fate of Black Schools in the South* (Chapel Hill: University of North Carolina Press, 1994), Chs. 2–6; Vivian Gunn Morris and Curtis L. Morris, *The Price They Paid: Desegregation in an African American Community* (New York: Teachers College Press, 2002), Ch. 6; Anna Victoria Wilson and William E. Segal, *Oh, Do I Remember! Experiences of Teachers During the Desegregation of Austin's Schools* (Albany: State University of New York Press, 2001), Ch. 7.

109. Cecelski, *Along Freedom Road*, pp. 168–171.

110. Thomas S. Martin, "Inequality in Desegregation: Black School Closings," *The University of Chicago Law Review*, Vol. 39, No. 3 (Spring 1972), pp. 658–672.

111. On this point, see Barbara Shircliffe, "'We Got the Best of That World': A Case for the Study of Nostalgia in the Oral History of School Segregation," *The Oral History Review*, Vol. 28, No. 2 (Summer– Autumn, 2001), pp. 59–84.

112. Casey Banas, "Southerners Await School Ruling Effect," *Chicago Tribune*, November 5, 1969, p. B13.

113. "Integration Attacked by 2D Principal," *Chicago Tribune*, January 31, 1969, p. A2; "Dixie Teachers Reveal Their Feelings About Negroes in Integrated Schools," *Chicago Defender*, November 27, 1965, p. 5.

114. Mark G. Yudof, "Suspension and Expulsion of Black Students from the Public Schools: Academic Capital Punishment and the Constitution," *Law and Contemporary Problems*, Vol 39, No. 2, Part 2 (Spring 1975), p. 380.

115. The Southern Regional Council, *The Student Pushout: Victim of Continued Resistance to Desegregation* (Atlanta: Southern Regional Council, 1973), passim.

116. J. Harvey Wilkinson III, "*Goss v. Lopez*: The Supreme Court as School Superintendent," *The Supreme Court Review*, Vol. 1975 (1975), p. 31.

117. For discussion of these issues at the time, see David G. Carter, "Second-Generation School Integration Problems for Blacks," *Journal of Black Studies*, Vol. 13, No. 2, School Desegregation (December 1982), pp. 175–188.

118. On White resistance to change, see Patterson, *Brown v. Board of Education*, Ch. 5.

119. See, for instance, *Chicago Defender* articles on Toledo, Ohio, and Jackson, Michigan: "Ban on Prep Games," *Chicago Daily Defender*, September 21, 1963, p. A 22; and "10 Arrested in Teen Race Riot at Jackson, Mich. High School," *Chicago Defender*, September 21, 1963, p. 18.

120. "Hirsch Teens in Racial Clash After Graduation," *Chicago Daily Defender*, June 20, 1963, p. 6; "Cite Beatings at John Jay High," *New York Amsterdam News*, October 12, 1963, p. 29.

Notes

121. "Segregation Plants Seeds of Riot," *Chicago Defender*, December 12, 1962, p. 8.

122. "Manual Arts High Prepares for a Fall of Study," *Los Angeles Sentinel*, September 26, 1963, p. A2; "Teen War Flashes; One Dead, Seize 20," *New York Amsterdam News*, October 31, 1964, p. 31; "School Issue," *Los Angeles Sentinel*, November 26, 1964, p. A6; "Westside, Englewood Report Gang Fights," *Chicago Daily Defender*, December 1, 1964, p. 3.

123. "600 Rumble at Basketball Game," *Chicago Daily Defender*, April 5, 1965, p. 3; "Hoods Threaten School Sports: High School Games 'Battle Arenas," *Chicago Defender*, January 12, 1966, p. 28.

124. "Avert Riot at High School of Music and Art," *New York Amsterdam News*, January 15, 1966; "Student Violence Grows: Race Riot Flares at Gage Park School," *Chicago Defender*, February 5, 1966, p. 1; Negroes in Park Slope Attacked by Whites," *New York Amsterdam News*, March 12, 1966, p. 19; "Negroes Walk off Duarte High Campus," *Los Angeles Sentinel*, May 5, 1966, p. A1; "A Cool Prevails at Lafayette High," *New York Amsterdam News*, November 5, 1966, p. 27.

125. Doug McAdam, *Political Process and the Development of Black Insurgency, 1930–1970* (Chicago: University of Chicago Press, 1982), Ch. 8.

126. Adam Fairclough, *Better Day Coming: Blacks and Equality, 1890–2000* (New York: Penguin Books, 2001), Chs. 12 & 13.

127. "Opening Schools After Riots Termed Wise Move," *Chicago Daily Defender*, April 9, 1968, p. 5.

128. Louis Cassels, UPI, "High School Tensions Reflect Parents' Viewpoints," *Atlanta Daily World*, November 29, 1970, p. 1; Jeffrey A. Tannenbaum, "Student Mayhem," *Wall Street Journal*, May 11, 1971, p. 1; "Melee Disrupts PL Cage Opener," *Chicago Defender*, January 8, 1969, p. 24.

129. Charles T. Clotfelter, *After Brown: The Rise and Retreat of School Desegregation* (Princeton, NJ: Princeton University Press, 2004), p. 56.

130. "Violence Erupts at Calumet High School: Cops Blamed for Outbreak at School," *Chicago Daily Defender*, February 22, 1968, p. 1.

131. "Linden Rioters Calm; Curfew On," *New York Amsterdam News*, May 3, 1969, p. 2.

132. "Cops Guard Blacks from White Mob: Canarsie Riots Imperil Students," *New York Amsterdam News*, March 1, 1969, p. 1.

133. "Whites Harass Homecoming Queen," *Pittsburgh Courier*, October 11, 1969, p. 1.

134. "Police Called; 21 Arrested at Dorsey High School," *Los Angeles Sentinel*, January 15, 1970, p. A1.

135. "Race Brawl Erupts at High School," *Chicago Daily Defender*, January 28, 1969, p. 20; "Schools Close in PA City," *Chicago Daily Defender*, February 19, 1969, p. 8; "Strife Closes Schools, *Chicago Daily Defender*, March 20, 1969, p. 12; "Close School After Police, Pupil Row," *Chicago Daily Defender*, October 1, 1969, p. 8; "Racial Flare-up Closes Dayton, Ohio High School," *Chicago Daily Defender*, October 2, 1969, p. 16; "Black, White Students Clash; School Closes," *Chicago Daily Defender*, February 14, 1970, p. 2; "Bogalusa Riot Closes School," *Chicago Daily Defender*, September 16, 1970, p. 8.

136. "68 White Teachers Refuse to Transfer to All Black School in Washington," *Atlanta Daily World*, February 6, 1970, p. 1.

137. "Brawls Close L.I. High School," *New York Amsterdam News*, June 12, 1971, p. 30.

138. "Parents Join Violence in School," *Atlanta Daily World*, November 8, 1970, p. 1. Also see "Tensions Erupt at Ala. School," *Chicago Daily Defender*, October 14, 1970, p. 3.

139. "Negro, Whites Brawl at N.C. High School," *Atlanta Daily World*, October 31, 1971, p. 2.

140. "Savannah Students' Third Racial Battle," *Atlanta Daily World*, December 5, 1971, p. 2.

141. "School Racial Brawl Injures 18 Students," *Atlanta Daily World*, February 18, 1973, p. 1.

142. "Black and White Students in Racial Clash at School," *New York Amsterdam News*, December 15, 1973, p. C1.

143. Yudof, "Suspension and Expulsion of Black Students from the Public Schools," pp. 397–398.

144. For a compelling treatment of these issues in a case study of a single secondary school, see Gerald Grant, *The World We Created at Hamilton High* (Cambridge, MA: Harvard University Press, 1990), Chs. 2 & 6.

145. On changing attitudes toward school integration, see A. Wade Smith, "Tolerance of School Desegregation, 1954-77," *Social Forces*, Vol. 59, No. 4 (June 1981) pp. 1256–1274.

146. Amy Stuart Wells, Jennifer Jellison Holme, Anita Tijerina Revilla, and Awo Korantemaa Atanda, *Both Sides Now: The Story of School Desegregation's Graduates* (Berkeley: University of California Press, 2009), passim.

147. Elizabeth G. Cohen, "The Effects of Desegregation on Race Relations," *Law and Contemporary Problems*, Vol. 39, No. 2 (Spring 1975), p. 290.

148. Ibid., p. 296. For a somewhat different perspective, see Caroline Elck, *Race-Class Relations and Integrated Education in Secondary Education: The Case of Miller High* (New York: Palgrave Macmillan, 2010), Part II.

149. Wells et. al. *Both Sides Now*, p. 84.

150. Perhaps the best-known such case is Compton, California, but Paterson, New Jersey, is a somewhat parallel example on the East Coast. On Compton, see Emily Straus, "The Making of the American School Crisis: Compton, California and the Death of the American Dream" (unpublished Ph.D. dissertation, Brandeis University, 2006), Chs. 2 and 3. On Paterson, see Patrick William Martin, "Historical Events Leading to the State Takeover of the Paterson New Jersey School System," (unpublished Ed.D. dissertation, Teachers College, Columbia University, 1996), Ch. 1; and Stan Karp, "Tests and Bullhorns," *The Radical Teacher*, No. 31 (June 1986), pp. 11–15.

151. "South Goes Ahead in School Integration," *Chicago Tribune*, June 18, 1971, p. 12.

152. For early evidence on this point, see Robert L. Crain, "School Integration and the Academic Achievement of Negroes," *Sociology of Education*, Vol. 44, No. 1 (Winter 1971), pp. 1–26. Also see "Education Survey Finds: High Morale Aids Black Students," *Chicago Daily Defender*, February 21, 1974, p. 6, and Guryan, "Desegregation and Black Dropout Rates," passim.

Conclusion

1. James D. Anderson, *The Education of Blacks in the South, 1860–1932* (Chapel Hill: University of North Carolina Press, 1988), Ch. 1; Heather A. Williams, *Self Taught: African American Education in Slavery and Freedom* (Chapel Hill: University of North Carolina Press, 2007), passim.

2. On Dunbar, see Howell S. Baum, *Brown in Baltimore: School Desegregation and the Limits of Liberalism* (Ithaca, NY: Cornell University Press, 2010), p. 45; Stanley Warren, *Crispus Attucks High School: Hail to the Green and Gold* (Indianapolis: Donning Publishers, 1998), passim.

3. On this point, see Claudia Goldin and Lawrence Katz, *The Race Between Education and Technology* (Cambridge: Harvard University Press, 2007), Ch. 6.

4. On Black migration at this time, see Isabel Wilkerson, *The Warmth of Other Suns: The Epic Story of America's Great Migration* (New York: Random House, 2010), Part 6.

5. Harvard Sitkoff, *The Struggle for Black Equality, 1954–1992* (New York: Hill and Wang, 1993), Ch. 5.

6. Irene Wilson interview, May 21, 2008.

7. Vanessa Siddle Walker, "Valued Segregated Schools for African American Children in the South, 1935–1969: A Review of Common Themes and Characteristics," *Review of Educational Research*, 70 (Fall 2000), pp. 253–285.

8. On this point, see Barbara Shircliffe, "'We Got the Best of That World': A Case for the Study of Nostalgia in the Oral History of School Segregation," *The Oral History Review*, Vol. 28, No. 2 (Summer– Autumn, 2001), pp. 59–84.

9. Jack Jenkins interview, February 19, 2009; Princeton Elroy interview, February 29, 2008.

10. Eighty-Second and Eighty-Third Annual Reports of the Department of the General Assembly of the State of Georgia, June 30, 1954.

11. Irene Wilson interview, May 21, 2008.

12. Joseph Williams interview, July 24, 2007.

13. Diane Ravitch, *The Troubled Crusade: American Education, 1945–1980* (New York: Basic Books, 1983), p. 153; Wayne Urban, "What's in a Name? Education and the Disadvantaged American," *Paedagogica Historica*, Vol. 45; 1 & 2 (2009), pp. 251–264; Sylvia L. M. Martinez and John L. Rury, "From 'Culturally Deprived' to 'At Risk': The Politics of Popular Expressions and Educational Inequality in the United States, 1960–1980," forthcoming.

14. Donbin Kim and John L. Rury, "The Changing Profile of College Access: The Truman Commission and Enrollment Patterns in the Postwar Era," *History of Education Quarterly*, Vol. 47, No. 2 (August 2007), pp. 302–327.

15. Roland Brown interview with John Rury, July 25, 2007.

16. On the timing of desegregation, see Charles T. Clotfelter, *After Brown: The Rise and Retreat of School Desegregation* (Princeton, NJ: Princeton University Press, 2004), Ch 7. Also see Gary Orfield, Susan Eaton, and the Harvard Desegregation Project, *Dismantling Desegregation: The Quiet Reversal of Brown v. Board of Education* (New York: The New Press, 1996), Ch. 1.

17. In 1980, three-quarters of American youth lived in metropolitan areas, about 82% of African American youth and 73% of others. Nearly three-quarters of these African American youth lived in central city settings, and a similar proportion of the others lived in the suburbs. These figures were estimated from IPUMS data.

18. Ideally, we would conduct a multilevel analysis to assess the effect of region. In doing this, we found the effects to be largely the same as reported in Table C.1. For an analysis of these patterns, see John L. Rury and Argum Saatcioglu, "Suburban Advantage: Opportunity Hoarding and Secondary Attainment in the Postwar Metropolitan North," *American Journal of Education*, Vol. 117, No. 3 (May 2011), pp. 307–342.

19. Geographic factors concern an individual's *location* in a type of place or region; social and economic status describes the characteristics of his or her household and parents.

20. Lance Freeman, "African American Locational Attainment Before the Civil Rights Era," *City & Community* 9(3) (2010), pp. 235–255; Douglas Massey and Nancy Denton, *American Apartheid: Segregation and the Making of the Underclass* (Cambridge, MA: Harvard University Press, 1998), Ch. 1.

21. Roland Brown interview, July 25, 2007.

22. Grace Strong interview, July 10, 2007.

23. Gloria Chambers interview, May 8, 2008.

24. Ibid.

25. Jennifer Hochschild, *The New American Dilemma: Liberal Democracy and School Desegregation* (New Haven: Yale University Press, 1984), Ch. 5.

26. Nadine Meyers interview, February 26, 2009.

27. Kevin Dodge interview, February 20, 2009.

28. On this point, see the accounts in Kate Willink, *Bringing Desegregation Home: Memories of the Struggle Toward School Integration in Rural North Carolina* (New York: Palgrave, 2009), Ch. 2; for a contemporary urban perspective, see Forrest W. Parkey, *White Teacher, Black School: The Professional Growth of a Ghetto Teacher* (Westport, CT: Praeger, 1983), passim.

29. Thomas Smith, Southern Oral History Project 4007, K-566, p. 7.

30. Freda Jones interview, Southern Oral History Project 4007, K-208, p. 16.

31. See, for instance, Orley Ashenfelter, William J. Collins, and Albert Yoon, "Evaluating the Role of *Brown v. Board of Education* in School Equalization, Desegregation, and the Income of African Americans," *American Law and Economics Review,* 8:2 (Summer 2006), pp. 213–248, and Kenneth L. Wilson, "The Effects of Integration and Class on Black Educational Attainment," *Sociology of Education,* Vol. 52, No. 2 (April 1979), pp. 84–98.

32. Ralph Naples interview, Southern Oral History Project 4007, K-556, p. 2.

33. Jack Jenkins interview, February 19, 2009.

34. Ashenfelter, Collins, and Yoon, "Evaluating the Role of *Brown v. Board of Education* in School Equalization, Desegregation, and the Income of African Americans," passim.

35. On this point, see George Lewis, *Massive Resistance: The White Response to the Civil Rights Movement* (New York: Bloomsbury, 2006), passim. With respect to one of the most prominent desegregation battles of the period, see John A. Kirk, "'Massive Resistance and Minimum Compliance': The Origins of the 1957 Little Rock School Crisis and the Failure of School Desegregation in the South," and Karen S. Anderson, "Massive Resistance, Violence and Southern Social Relations: The Little Rock, Arkansas, School Integration Crisis, 1954–1960," both in Clive Webb, ed., *Massive Resistance: Southern Opposition to the Second Reconstruction* (New York: Oxford University Press, 2005), pp. 76–98 and 203–220, respectively.

36. Rebecca de Schweinitz, *If We Could Change the World: Young People and America's Long Struggle for Racial Equality* (Chapel Hill: University of North Carolina Press, 2009), Ch. 5.

37. Noliwe M. Rooks, *White Money/Black Power: The Surprising History of African American Studies and the Crisis of Race in Higher Education* (Boston: Beacon Press, 2007), Chs. 1 & 2; Joy Ann Williamson, *Black Power on Campus: The University of Illinois, 1965–75* (Champaign: University of Illinois Press, 2003), passim; and Idem, *Radicalizing the Ebony Tower: Black Colleges and the Black Freedom Struggle in Mississippi* (New York: Teachers College Press, 2008), Ch. 7.

38. Peniel E. Joseph, "Introduction: Toward a Historiography of the Black Power Movement," in Peniel E. Joseph, ed., *The Black Power Movement: Rethinking the Civil Rights-Black Power Era* (New York: Routledge, 2006), pp. 1–26; also see David Goldberg and Trevor Griffey, "Introduction: Constructing Black Power," in David Goldberg and Trevor Griffey, eds., *Black Power at Work: Community Control, Affirmative Action, and the Construction Industry* (Ithaca, NY: ILR Press, 2010), pp. 1–22.

39. On this point, see Maxine Leeds Craig, *Ain't I a Beauty Queen? Black Women, Beauty and the Politics of Race* (New York: Oxford University Press, 2002), Ch. 2.

40. Jonathan Zimmerman, *Whose America: Culture Wars in the Public Schools* (Cambridge, MA: Harvard University Press, 2005), Ch. 5.

41. *The Falcon*, Harlan High School (Kansas City, MO, 1970), Introduction (unnumbered pages).

42. James J. Heckman and Paul A. LaFontaine, "The American High School Graduation Rate: Trends and Levels," *The Review of Economics and Statistics,* May 2010, Vol. 92 No. 2, p. 245.

43. This latter figure suggests the possibility of some mild "inflation" in the reporting of attainment in the census, or else a slightly more substantial dropout rate between the junior and senior years of high school. To test the effect of this on the analysis presented in Table C.1, and a possible GED effect, we reran the regression without the 1,729 17-year-olds (5% of the sample) who reportedly had completed the 12th grade but had not finished a year of college, and the results were nearly identical to those reported above. In other words, inclusion of these cases does not appear to have unduly biased the sample. It is possible, of course, that any inflationary effect is due to misreporting of grade attainment rather than graduation, but we are unable to test this possibility with these data.

44. Stephen V. Cameron and James J. Heckman, "The Nonequivalence of High School Equivalents," *Journal of Labor Economics,* 11:1, Part 1 (1993), pp. 1–47.

45. Derek Neal, "How Families and Schools Shape the Achievement Gap," in Paul E. Peterson, ed., *Generational Change: Closing the Test Score Gap* (Lanham, MD: Rowman and

Littlefield, 2006), pp. 26–46. Also see Jaekyung Lee, "Racial and Ethnic Achievement Gap: Reversing the Progress Toward Equity?" *Educational Researcher* Vol. 31, No. 1 (January–February 2002), pp. 3–12.

46. Many of these points are summarized in Chester E. Finn, "Many Causes, No Easy Solutions," in Peterson, *Generational Change*, pp. 198–211. On the GED, see Heckman and LaFontaine, "The American High School Graduation Rate," p. 260.

47. On this point, see Paul E. Peterson, "Toward the Elimination of Race Differences in Educational Achievement," in Peterson, *Generational Change*, pp. 1–25; and Mark Berends, Samuel R. Lucas, and Roberto V. Peñaloza, "How Changes in Families and Schools Are Related to Trends in Black-White Test Scores," *Sociology of Education*, Vol. 81, No. 4 (October 2008), pp. 313–344.

48. Data on GED production for each year following 1970 can be found National Center for Education Statistics, *Digest of Educational Statistics, 2008* (Washington, DC: U.S. Department of Education, 2008), Table 108. On the age distribution of GED recipients, see National Center for Education Statistics, *Dropout Rates in the United States: 2005* (Washington, DC: U.S. Department of Education), Table A-2. The question of changing attitudes about schooling among Black youth is beyond the scope of this work, and hence a topic for additional research.

49. William Julius Wilson, *When Work Disappears: The World of the New Urban Poor* (New York: Vintage, 1997), Part 1.

50. For historical perspectives on this question, see the essays in Michael B. Katz, ed., *The Underclass Debate: Views from History* (Princeton, NJ: Princeton University Press, 1992), passim; also see Wilson's most recent statement, *More Than Just Race: Being Black and Poor in the Inner City* (New York: Norton, 2009), Ch. 1.

51. Ruby Arnold interview, July 25, 2007.

52. James T. Patterson, *Freedom Is Not Enough: The Moynihan Report and America's Struggle over Black Family Life from LBJ to Obama* (New York: Basic Books, 2010), Chs. 2–5.

53. Shirley A. Hill, *Black Intimacies: A Gender Perspective on Families and Relationships* (Walnut Creek, CA: AltaMira Press, 2005), pp. 77–84.

54. Patrick Heuveline, H. Yang, J. M. Timberlake, "It Takes a Village (Perhaps a Nation): Families, States, and Educational Achievement," *Journal of Marriage and Family*, 72: 5(October 2010), p. 1362.

55. See, for instance, the discussion of this in Heckman and LaFontaine, "The American High School Graduation Rate," p. 260.

56. By and large, these numbers are somewhat lower than those for all children, as parents with teenage offspring tend to be somewhat more mature, with somewhat higher marriage rates than is the case with the parents of younger children. Richard A. Bulcroft and Kris A. Bulcroft, "Race Differences in Attitudinal and Motivational Factors in the Decision to Marry," *Journal of Marriage and Family*, Vol. 55, No. 2 (May 1993), p. 347. Note that having children increases the willingness of both Black women and men to marry.

57. Nadine Meyers interview, February 26, 2009. Wilson, *More Than Just Race*, Ch. 2.

58. Brandon Carter interview, July 25, 2007.

59. Carl L. Bankston III and Stephen J. Caldas, "Family Structure, Schoolmates, and Racial Inequalities in School Achievement, *Journal of Marriage and Family* 60(August 1998), pp. 715–723.

60. Charles J. Ogletree, *All Deliberate Speed: Reflections on the First Half Century of Brown v. Board of Education* (New York: W.W. Norton & Company, 2004), passim.

61. Robert Balfanz and Nettie Legters, "Locating the Dropout Crisis: Which High Schools Produce the Nation's Dropouts? Where Are They Located? Who Attends Them?" Center for Research on the Education of Students Placed At Risk, Johns Hopkins University, Report 70, September 2004.

62. Richard Rothstein, *Class and Schools: Using Social, Economic, And Educational Reform to Close the Black-White Achievement Gap* (New York: Teachers College Press, 2004), Ch. 1.

63. Bart Landry, *The New Black Middle Class* (Berkeley, CA: University of California Press, 1987), Ch. 2.

64. Dennis Gilbert, *The American Class Structure in an Age of Growing Inequality* (Thousand Oaks, CA: Sage, 2008), p. 56.

65. U.S. Bureau of the Census, *Statistical Abstract of the United States, 2004–2005* (Washington, DC: U.S. Government Printing Office, 2005), Table 677. For women, the median incomes are $10,613 for those with less than a high school degree and $30,788 for those with a bachelor's degree.

66. A. D. Barnett and K. Chappell, "Education Nation." *Ebony Magazine*, September 2010, pp. 68–84.

67. Jean Anyon, "Race Social Class and Educational Reform in an Inner City School," *Teachers College Record*, Fall 1995, 97:1, pp. 69–94; Rothstein, *Class and Schools*, Ch. 5.

Appendix A

1. Barbara Shircliffe, "'We Got the Best of That World': A Case for the Study of Nostalgia in the Oral History of School Segregation," *The Oral History Review*, 28(2): 2001, pp. 59–84.

Index

NAMES

Alexander, J. Trent, 208 n. 5
Anderson, C. Arnold, 68, 211 n. 2
Anderson, James D., 5, 10, 25, 208 n. 4, 211 n. 1, 218 n. 9, 246 n. 1
Anderson, Karen, 248 n. 35
Anderson, Margaret, 240 n. 27
Angus, David L., 105, 135–136, 211 n. 37, 214 n. 36, 225 n. 16, 228 n. 72, 236 n. 111
Anyon, Jean, 199, 230 n. 19, 234 n. 77, 250 n. 67
Armor, David, 19, 211 n. 40
Arnold, Ruby, 194, 249 n. 51
Arum, Richard, 238 n. 138
Asante, M. K., 235–236 n. 95
Ashenfelter, Orley, 208 n. 9, 248 n. 31, 248 n. 34
Ashmore, Harry, 239 n. 2
Astin, Alexander W., 208 n. 8
Atanda, Awo Korantemaa, 246 n. 146

Baker, R. Scott, 78, 223 n. 100
Balfanz, Robert, 250 n. 61
Banas, Casimir, 243 n. 91, 244 n. 112
Banks, Cherry A. McGee, 226 n. 34
Bankston, Carl L., 250 n. 59
Barnett, A. D., 250 n. 66
Bartley, Numan, 218 n. 2
Baum, Howell S., 246 n. 2
Bauman, Kurt J., 209 n. 12
Bayor, Ronald H., 241 n. 30
Beale, Calvin L., 210–211 n. 34
Berends, Mark, 19–20, 211 n. 43, 249 n. 47
Berkow, Ira, 227 n. 45
Berry, Edwin, 128
Bogle, Lori, 240 n. 12
Bolner, James, 244 n. 105
Bolton, Charles C., 78, 219 n. 18, 219 n. 26
Bonacich, Edna, 228 n. 68
Boner, J. Russell, 240 n. 17
Boozer, Michael, 151, 241 n. 32
Boyd, Talmadge, 102, 118, 228 n. 62
Brantley, George D., 240 n. 12
Brenzel, Barbara, 230 n. 17
Briggs, Carl M., 212 n. 10
Brill, Andrew, 239 n. 9
Brown, Frank, 239 n. 1
Brown, James, 121, 231 n. 35
Brown, Roland, 181, 183, 247 n. 15, 247 n. 21
Brown, Scott, 210 n. 31
Bulcroft, Kris A., 249 n. 56
Bulcroft, Richard A., 249 n. 56
Bullock, Paul, 229 n. 4
Burger, N. R., 35, 38, 214 n. 29, 214 n. 37, 215 n. 47, 219 n. 26
Burns, Irene, 240 n. 22
Button, James W., 224 n. 109
Byas, Ulysses, 210 n. 28

Cade, J. B., 213–214 n. 28
Caldas, Stephen J., 250 n. 59
Cameron, Stephen V., 249 n. 44
Card, David, 208 n. 9, 212 n. 12
Carl, Jim, 243 n. 90
Carson, Claybourne, 209 n. 25, 224 n. 114
Carter, Brandon, 75, 195–196, 223 n. 86, 250 n. 58
Carter, David G., 244 n. 117
Carter, Madge, 218 n. 8
Carter, Melanie Deane, 216 n. 71
Cassell, Frank A., 231 n. 21, 243 n. 98
Cassels, Louis, 245 n. 128
Castro, Fidel, 155
Caughey, John, 228 n. 68
Cecelski, David, 165–166, 244 n. 108
Chambers, Gloria, 75, 180, 184, 223 n. 86, 247 n. 23
Chappell, K., 250 n. 66
Chen, Anthony, 232 n. 45
Clark, Septima P., 80, 224 n. 111
Clotfelter, Charles T., 93, 101–102, 107, 147, 162, 173, 225 n. 13, 239 n. 1, 239 n. 5, 243 n. 98, 245 n. 129, 247 n. 16
Cohen, Elizabeth G., 172–173, 246 n. 147
Cohen, Ronald D., 225 n. 17
Cole, Nat King, 121
Coleman, A. Lee, 240 n. 13
Coleman, James S., 80–81, 132–134, 224 n. 112, 236 n. 98
Collins, Christina, 228 n. 73
Collins, M. D., 60, 213 n. 26, 220 n. 40

251

Collins, William J., 208 n. 9, 209 n. 22, 248 n. 31, 248 n. 34
Conant, James Bryan, 115, 120–121, 134, 135, 229 n. 1, 236 n. 100, 236 n. 107
Conrad, Earl, 225 n. 19
Cook, Caley, 226 n. 30
Cook, Michael D., 211 n. 44
Cornell, C. N., 217 n. 76
Cousins, Robert L., 36–38, 47–48, 76, 214 n. 41, 215 n. 45, 215 n. 46, 217 nn. 74–76, 220 n. 33, 224 n. 111
Craig, Maxine Leeds, 248 n. 39
Crain, C. J., 213–214 n. 28
Crain, Robert L., 231 n. 21, 239 n. 1, 246 n. 152
Cronin, Joseph, 210 n. 30, 224–225 n. 9

Daniel, Walter G., 34–35, 50, 211 n. 2, 214 n. 34, 216 n. 67, 217 n. 82, 229 n. 4
Danns, Dionne, 237 nn. 125–126
Daugherty, Brian J., 219 n. 18
Davidson, Edmonia W., 230 n. 9
Davies, Gareth, 229 n. 2
Davison, Douglas, 210 n. 29
Dempsy, T. J., 217 n. 74
Denton, Nancy, 247 n. 20
Dewey, John, 73
Dillard, Nicholas Longworth, 71–72
Ditmars, Thomas, 230 n. 14
Dodge, Kevin, 137, 141, 185–186, 237 n. 115, 247 n. 27
Donohue, John J. III, 209 n. 22
Dorn, Sherman, 231 n. 22, 232 n. 38
Dougherty, Jack, 210 n. 30, 224–225 n. 9, 234 n. 77
Douglas, Davison M., 83–84, 146, 208 n. 4, 224 n. 4, 239 n. 3
DuBois, W. E. B., 107
Duckworth, C. J., 214 n. 37
Dunn, Joshua M., 241 n. 37
Durham, Richard, 225 n. 18, 225 n. 21

DuSable, Jean Baptiste, 102
Dykeman, Wilma, 240 n. 16

Easom, Percy H., 67, 213 n. 24, 221 n. 58
Eason, Percy H., 214 n. 41
Eaton, Susan, 230 n. 19, 247 n. 16
Egler, Dan, 242 n. 72
Eisenhower, Dwight D., 119–120, 149
Elck, Caroline, 246 n. 148
Elrod, Frary, 68
Elroy, Princeton, 16, 17–18, 91, 180, 210 n. 32
Evans, Howie, 235 n. 94
Evans, William N., 211 n. 44

Fairclough, Adam, 213 n. 23, 218 n. 3, 218 n. 12, 219 n. 17, 245 n. 126
Farley, Reynolds, 233 n. 58
Farrell, Thomas J., 131
Ferguson, G. H., 221 n. 52, 221 n. 59
Fernandez, Johanna, 210 n. 31
Finn, Chester E., 249 n. 46
Fleming, Brandon, 216 n. 57
Fleming, James G., 240 n. 12
Fordham, Signithia, 211 n. 42
Formisano, Ronald, 228 n. 66, 243 n. 87
Fortenberry, Lamar, 77
Foster, Norine, 230 n. 18
Fountain, Mabel, 9–11, 18–19, 124, 209 n. 18
Franklin, Barry, 208 n. 7
Franklin, Donna L., 118, 230 n. 12
Franklin, Vincent P., 210 n. 30, 224–225 n. 9, 226 n. 36, 238 n. 134
Frazier, Alonzo, 95
Frazier, E. Franklin, 27–28, 212 n. 9
Freeman, Lance, 247 n. 20
Frey, William H., 230 n. 11

Garrity, Wendell, 160
Genadek, Katie, 208 n. 5
Gilbert, Dennis, 230 n. 16, 250 n. 64
Gilbert, James, 240 n. 21
Ginwright, Shawn A., 228 n. 67
Goeken, Ronald, 208 n. 5

Goldberg, David, 248 n. 38
Goldfield, David, 216 n. 58
Goldin, Claudia, 9–10, 209 n. 20, 211 n. 3, 234 n. 67, 246 n. 3
Goodman, Robert, 228 n. 68
Gotham, Kevin Fox, 241 n. 39
Gould, Howard D., 228 n. 76
Graham, Grace, 215 n. 48
Grant, Gerald, 246 n. 144
Griffey, Trevor, 248 n. 38
Griffin, John A., 215 n. 48
Griffin, Marvin, 76, 223 n. 89
Gruber, J., 212 n. 12
Guryan, Jonathan, 239 n. 1

Hacker, Andrew, 230 n. 8
Hall, Jacquelyn Dowd, 8, 209 n. 15
Hampel, Robert L., 209 n. 19
Hancock, Gordon B., 224 n. 101
Hansot, Elisabeth, 213 n. 15
Hanuscheck, E., 209 n. 22
Harlan, Louis, 5, 208 n. 4
Harrington, Michael, 115
Harris, Louis, 242 n. 63
Harrison, Bennett, 231 n. 20
Hatter, Terry J., 95
Havighurst, Robert J., 119, 127, 133, 226 n. 29, 231 n. 20, 234 n. 71, 241 n. 48
Hawkins, Katie, 165, 244 n. 106
Heckman, James J., 191–192, 209 n. 22, 248 n. 42, 249 n. 44
Hedgepeth, Janet, 83
Henderson, William D., 210 n. 30, 224–225 n. 9
Herbers, John, 159, 242 n. 78
Hermalen, Albert, 233 n. 58
Herrick, Mary, 105, 228 n. 71, 234 n. 70
Heuveline, Patrick, 249 n. 54
Hilford, James, 215 n. 53
Hill, Shirley A., 209 n. 18, 210 n. 32, 215 n. 53, 216 n. 57, 223 n. 86, 224 n. 106, 227 n. 53, 227 n. 56, 228 n. 62, 231 n. 35, 237 n. 115, 238 n. 143, 239 n. 6, 249 n. 53
Hirsch, Arnold R., 230 n. 8, 230 n. 17

Index

Hochschild, Jennifer, 161, 243 n. 94, 247 n. 25
Hodes, Martha, 218 n. 8
Holm, Ashley, 227 n. 54
Holme, Jennifer Jellison, 246 n. 146
Homel, Michael W., 224–225 n. 9, 226 n. 25
Hopkins, John, 94, 95
Hornsby, Alton, Jr., 241 n. 30
Hughes, Sarah, 167–168
Huie, Henry Mark, 241 n. 30
Hutcheson, Sterling, 56–57

Ivy, Hill, 217 n. 73

Jackson, James S., 225–226 n. 22
Jackson, Kenneth T., 229–230 n. 6
Jackson, Reid E., 214 n. 39
Jacoway, Elizabeth, 240 n. 19
Jenkins, Jack, 180, 187, 247 n. 9, 248 n. 33
Jenkins, Lee, 237 n. 120
Johns, Meredith, 225 n. 18
Johnson, Lyndon B., 115–116, 120, 121, 124
Johnson, Wilbur, 39
Johnston, William B., 209 n. 17, 233 n. 59
Jones, Freda, 186–187, 248 n. 30
Jones, Jasper, 36
Jones, L. K., 218 n. 1
Joseph, Peniel E., 229 n. 5, 248 n. 38

Kantor, Harvey, 230 n. 17
Karp, Stan, 246 n. 150
Katz, Lawrence F., 9–10, 209 n. 20, 234 n. 67, 246 n. 3
Katz, Michael B., 249 n. 50
Kaye, Danny, 93
Kennedy, Edward, 120
Kennedy, John F., 115–116, 120, 134, 155, 157
Kennedy, Robert, 120
Keppel, Francis, 134
Khiss, Peter, 240 n. 13
Khrushchev, Nikita, 155
Kim, Donbin, 224 n. 113, 233 n. 60, 247 n. 14
King, Martin Luther, Jr., 39, 121, 139, 141, 169, 183, 237 n. 131
Kirk, John A., 248 n. 35

Klarman, Michael J., 209 n. 13, 218–219 n. 16, 227 n. 40, 240 n. 18
Kluger, Richard, 208 n. 2, 219 n. 18, 239 n. 6
Knox, Ellis O., 214–215 n. 42, 216 n. 62
Koutlak, Ronald, 243 n. 91
Krueger, Alan B., 151, 208 n. 9, 241 n. 32
Kuziemko, Ilyana, 234 n. 67

LaFontaine, Paul A., 191–192, 248 n. 42
Landry, Bart, 197, 250 n. 63
Lee, George A., 225 n. 12
Lee, Jaekyung, 249 n. 45
Legters, Nettie, 250 n. 61
Lemieux, Thomas, 212 n. 12
Levitan, Sar A., 209 n. 12, 209 n. 17, 233 n. 59
Lewis, George, 248 n. 35
Lewis, John, 139
Lewis, Lexton, 215 n. 46
Loeb, Martin B., 226 n. 29
Lucas, Hattie Thomas, 222 n. 73
Lucas, Samuel R., 19–20, 211 n. 43, 249 n. 47
Lutz, Paul, 240 n. 12
Lyons, John F., 210 n. 31, 228 n. 77

Mahard, Rita E., 239 n. 1
Malcolm X, 170
Malone, Barry F., 222 n. 72
Margo, Robert A., 208 n. 3, 209 nn. 21–22, 212 n. 8
Marks, C., 230 n. 15
Markstrom-Adams, Carol, 239 n. 160
Marshall, Elizabeth C., 227 nn. 57–58
Marshall, Paul M., 152–154
Marshall, Thurgood, 84
Martin, Martin A., 56–57
Martin, Patrick William, 246 n. 150
Martin, Thomas S., 244 n. 110
Martinez, Sylvia L. M., 247 n. 13
Massey, Douglas, 247 n. 20
McAdam, Doug, 12, 209 n. 25, 245 n. 125
McCann, Herbert, 230 n. 18
McCray, John, 223 n. 100

McCuistian, Ed, 211–212 n. 4
McCullough, Gary, 208 n. 7
Meyer, Martin, 233 n. 56
Meyers, Nadine, 184–185, 195, 247 n. 26, 250 n. 57
Mirel, Jeffrey E., 96, 105, 135–136, 140, 210 n. 30, 211 n. 35, 211 n. 37, 214 n. 36, 224–225 n. 9, 225 n. 16, 226 n. 25, 226 n. 34, 228 n. 72, 235 n. 94, 236 n. 111, 236 n. 113
Modell, John, 208 n. 6
Mohl, Raymond, 230 n. 8
Mohraz, Judy Jolly, 210 n. 29, 226 n. 24
Montgomery, Rick, 241 n. 47, 242 n. 56
Moran, Peter William, 234 n. 77
Morris, Aldon, 237 n. 127
Morris, Curtis L., 210 n. 27, 214 n. 38, 222 n. 73, 244 n. 108
Morris, Jerome, 208–209 n. 11
Morris, Vivian Gunn, 210 n. 27, 214 n. 38, 222 n. 73, 244 n. 108
Morton, Ruth, 214 n. 41
Moynihan, D. Patrick, 194

Nagel, Joane, 218 n. 8
Naples, Ralph, 187, 248 n. 32
Neal, Derek, 211 n. 40, 249 n. 45
Neckerman, Kathryn M., 105, 106, 210 nn. 29–30, 224–225 n. 9
Neff, Franklin W., 243 n. 85
Neighbors, Harold W., 225–226 n. 22
Newbold, N. C. (Nathan C.), 33–34, 49, 54–56, 58, 59, 68, 218 n. 6, 219 n. 28
Newson, Moses, 240 n. 14
Newton, Eunice S., 229 n. 4
Nixon, Richard, 155
Nuzum, Richard, 92

O'Brien, Thomas V., 219 n. 25, 220 n. 32, 240 n. 26
Ogletree, Charles J., 250 n. 60
Oliver, Melvin, 230 n. 7
O'Neal, Harry, 101, 227 n. 56

Orfield, Gary, 159, 162–163, 230 n. 19, 242 n. 79, 244 n. 101, 247 n. 16

Parkay, Forrest W., 235 n. 89
Parker, John, 147
Parkey, Forrest W., 248 n. 28
Pascoe, Peggy, 218 n. 8, 240 n. 24
Patterson, James T., 208 n. 2, 227 n. 40, 229 n. 3, 239 n. 6, 249 n. 52
Peñaloza, Roberto V., 19–20, 211 n. 43, 249 n. 47
Perlmann, Joel, 216 n. 59
Peterson, Paul E., 211 n. 44, 211 nn. 40–41, 249 n. 47

Queen, Robert, 83

Raftery, Judith Rosenberg, 210 n. 30, 224–225 n. 9
Ravitch, Diane, 227 nn. 40–41, 229 n. 2, 236 n. 99, 247 n. 13
Reagan, Ronald, 196
Redcay, Edward E., 38–39, 212 n. 6, 215 n. 49
Redmond, James, 140
Reese, William J., 209 n. 19
Reid, Ira De A., 212 n. 11
Revilla, Anita Tijerina, 246 n. 146
Reynolds, Carl V., 32
Rice, Jon, 237 n. 125
Richan, Willard C., 226 n. 26, 234 n. 77
Richards, Roger, 75, 223 n. 86, 224 n. 106
Rife, Aaron Tyler, 227 n. 47, 239 n. 159
Ritch, James, 242 n. 62, 242 n. 64
Roberts, Calvin, 215 n. 53
Robertson, Oscar, 98
Robinson, W. A., 48, 49, 217 n. 75, 222 n. 78
Rodgers, B., 74, 241 n. 47
Rodgers, Frederick A., 72, 74, 79, 222 n. 74, 223 n. 84
Romero, Francine, 227 n. 41
Rooks, Noliwe M., 248 n. 37
Ross, Sherwood, 235 n. 85
Rothman, Robert, 211 n. 36, 233 n. 55
Rothstein, Richard, 196, 199, 250 n. 62

Ruggles, Steven, 208 n. 5
Rury, John L., 208 n. 7, 209 n. 16, 211 n. 36, 213 n. 15, 215 n. 53, 216 n. 57, 223 n. 86, 224 n. 113, 228 n. 62, 228 n. 65, 230 n. 19, 231 n. 21, 233 n. 55, 233 n. 60, 234 n. 68, 234 n. 74, 242 n. 66, 243 n. 98, 247 nn. 13–15

Saatcioglu, Argun, 234 n. 68, 243 n. 90
Sales, Soupy, 121
Saltzman, Harold, 235 n. 89
Sarat, Reed, 241 n. 31
Schirmer, Sherry Lamb, 241 n. 33
Schroeder, Matthew B., 208 n. 5
Schuyler, George S., 224 n. 3
Schweinitz, Rebecca de, 209 n. 25, 248 n. 36
Segal, William E., 244 n. 108
Shapiro, Thomas, 230 n. 7
Sheffer, L. M., 215 n. 45
Shircliffe, Barbara, 222 n. 73, 223 n. 87, 244 n. 111, 247 n. 8, 250 n. 1
Simon, M., 241 n. 47
Simpkins, Grace, 215 n. 53
Sinatra, Frank, 93
Singleton, Robert, 229 n. 4
Sitkoff, Harvard, 225 n. 16, 247 n. 5
Skorupski, William P., 234 n. 68
Skrentny, John D., 209 n. 15
Small, Betty, 75, 223 n. 86
Smith, A. Wade, 246 n. 145
Smith, James P., 209 n. 22
Smith, S. L., 216 n. 72, 217 n. 84
Smith, Thomas, 186, 248 n. 29
Sobek, Matthew, 208 n. 5
Spencer, Margaret Beale, 239 n. 160
Squires, Jim, 243 n. 89
Stokelyclinton, James, 240 n. 16
Stokes, Thadeus, 232 n. 37
Stolee, Michael, 243 n. 98
Straus, Emily E., 228 n. 68
Strong, Grace, 100, 184, 227 n. 49, 247 n. 22
Stulberg, Lisa, 232 n. 45

Sugrue, Thomas J., 210 n. 29, 224 n. 2, 230 n. 17, 238 n. 152, 243 n. 86
Sullivan, Patricia, 218 n. 15, 219 n. 18
Summers, Herschel, 8–11, 18–19, 124, 209 n. 16
Swanson, Bert E., 234–235 n. 78, 242 n. 70
Swanson, Ernst W., 215 n. 48

Taggart, Robert, 209 n. 12, 209 n. 17, 233 n. 59
Talmadge, Herman, 59
Tannenbaum, Jeffrey A., 245 n. 128
Teaford, Jon C., 229–230 n. 6
Terry, W. J., 60
Teuber, Alma F., 230 n. 11
Teuber, Karl E., 230 n. 11
Theoharis, Jeanne, 210 n. 31, 237 n. 125
Thomas, Earl D., 229 n. 82
Thomas, Gail E., 239 n. 1
Tillman, Lorna, 147, 239 n. 6
Timberlake, J. M., 249 n. 54
Tobin, Gary A., 229 n. 5
Todd, Petra E., 209 n. 22
Tolnay, Stewart E., 210–211 n. 34, 212 n. 8, 212–213 n. 13, 219 n. 23
Travis, J. A., 213 n. 24
Traynor, Gloria, 216 n. 57
Trenholm, G. W., 214 n. 38
Trenholm, H. Councill, 216 n. 70
Truman, Harry S, 53
Tubb, J. M., 213–214 n. 28
Tumin, Melvin, 134, 236 n. 101
Tushnet, Mark V., 218–219 n. 16
Tyack, David B., 211 n. 35, 213 n. 15

Urban, Wayne, 247 n. 13

Vardeman, Martha Hay, 220 n. 47, 223 n. 82
Vedlitz, Arnold, 244 n. 105

Walker, Vanessa Siddle, 71–72, 79, 210 nn. 27–28, 214 n. 37, 214–215 n. 42, 216 n. 70, 222 nn. 72–73, 235 n. 92, 247 n. 7
Walsh, Norma, 100, 227 n. 53

Index

Walters, Pamela Barnhouse, 212 n. 10
Warner, W. Loyd, 94–95, 226 n. 29
Warren, Stanley, 227 n. 45
Washington, Alethea H., 215 n. 44, 216 n. 64, 216 n. 67
Washington, Booker T., 72
Webb, Clive, 248 n. 35
Weinberg, Meyer, 243 n. 84, 243 n. 87
Weise, Andrew, 216 n. 58
Welch, Finis R., 209 n. 22
Wells, Amy Stuart, 172, 174, 231 n. 21, 246 n. 146
West, Earle H., 229 n. 4
White, Kevin, 160
White, Susan, 242 n. 54
Wiese, Andrew, 228–229 n. 79
Wilkerson, Doxey A., 26, 30, 211–212 n. 4, 219 n. 18
Wilkerson, Isabel, 230 n. 13, 247 n. 4
Wilkins, Roy, 159
Wilkinson, J. Harvey III, 244 n. 116
Williams, Heather A., 246 n. 1
Williams, Joseph, 181, 247 n. 12
Williams, Leon, 83
Williamson, Joy Ann, 248 n. 37
Willink, Kate, 248 n. 28
Wilson, Alan B., 228 n. 68
Wilson, Anna Victoria, 244 n. 108
Wilson, Irene, 179–181, 193, 247 n. 6, 247 n. 11
Wilson, Kenneth L., 248 n. 31, 248 n. 34
Wilson, William Julius, 194–195, 249 n. 49
Wirmark, Bo, 238 n. 135
Wolkon, Sari, 151, 241 n. 32
Wolters, Raymond, 209 n. 13
Womack, Bob, 227 n. 45
Wong, Kenneth K., 211 n. 36, 233 n. 55
Woodard, Komozi, 210 n. 31, 237 n. 125
Wright, Dwayne C., 238 n. 134
Wright, Johnson, 44

Yang, H., 249 n. 54
Yoon, Albert, 208 n. 9, 248 n. 31, 248 n. 34
Yorty, Sam, 120
Yudoff, Mark G., 244 n. 114

Zarefsky, David, 229 n. 2
Zimmerman, Jonathan, 236 n. 114, 248 n. 40
Zullo, Joseph, 242 n. 74

SUBJECTS

Aaron v. Cook, 59
Accreditation of schools
  Black high school struggles, 45–50
  in equalization campaigns, 61, 62, 67–69, 71, 73, 79–80, 131
Achievement. *See* Black-White achievement gap
Alabama. *See also* Birmingham, Alabama
  desegregation of schools in, 165
  equalization campaigns in, 54, 58, 61, 62, 71, 74, 138–139
  high school accreditation in, 48, 49
  rural high schools in, 30, 34, 38
Alexander v. Holmes County, 163
American Council on Education (ACE), 96
American High School Today, The (Conant), 134
Anderson High School (Austin, Texas), 166
Angleton Colored High School (Texas), 180
Arizona, 146–147
Arkansas, 60, 98, 138, 147, 149
Association of Colleges and Secondary Schools, 47
Athletic programs, 97, 100–101, 137, 154, 169
Atlanta, Georgia, 8–9 139 174, 181
Atlanta Constitution, 54
Atlanta Daily World, 55, 78, 79–80, 122
Attainment. *See* Black-White attainment gap

Baltimore, Maryland, 148, 174, 177
Benjamin Franklin High School (East Harlem), 129
Benjamin Franklin High School (Philadelphia), 141
Birmingham, Alabama, protests in, 138–139
Black cultural awareness, 23, 116–117, 138, 140–142, 176, 186, 189–190
Black high schools
  accreditation struggles, 45–50
  enrollment statistics, 40–41
  equalization campaigns of the 1950s and 1960s, 52–112
  gender imbalance in enrollment, 29–30
  "good Black high schools," 14, 71–76, 100, 179
  jumpstart schools/union schools, 36–38, 180–181
  libraries, 48, 50, 68
  in the North and West, 98–104
  small rural schools in the South, 36–38
  urban schools in the South, 38–45
Black Panthers, 138, 141
Black Power, 116–117, 138, 141, 189–190
Black-White achievement gap, 83–112
  "crisis" in urban education and, 116, 130–131
  Equality of Educational Opportunity survey, 80–81
  family circumstances and, 132–136
  NAEP scores, 19–20, 146, 192–193
  parental education and, 43–44, 67, 88–90, 106, 110, 181–182
  poverty and, 110, 132–136
  property ownership and, 28–31, 35, 41–44, 63–64, 66, 67, 88, 110
  single-parent households and, 44, 89–90, 132–133, 183, 187, 191, 194–196

Black-White attainment gap, 58
Black secondary school attainment in 1960 outside the South, 108–111
  college and, 9, 11–12, 82
  "crisis" in urban education and, 122–132, 143–144
  elementary education in rural South, 31–34
  graduation rates, 4, 5–8, 17–18, 25, 40–42
  improving Black education, 12–16
  outside the South, 5–6, 14–16, 83–112, 122–124, 143–144, 150–151, 178–179
  patterns by state, 70
  process of narrowing, 4, 5–8, 10, 15–20, 63–67, 187–188
  regional differences, 12–16, 63–67, 108
  in the South, 5–6, 10, 12–14, 16–17, 25, 26–31, 34–45, 52–82, 63–69, 81–82
Bogan High School (Chicago), 158–159
Booker T. Washington High School (Atlanta), 8–9, 39, 75, 177
Boston, Massachusetts, 139, 158, 160, 161
Boyd Elementary School (Jackson, Mississippi), 184
Brice v. Landis, 166
Briggs decision, 147
Bronx High School of Science, 136
Brown v. Board of Education, 3, 12, 55, 67, 76, 81, 97–98, 103, 107, 112, 116, 145–147, 151–152, 157, 166, 168, 174, 175
Busing, 26, 33–34, 36, 55, 60–62, 98, 116, 128–129, 156, 159–161, 164–166, 168, 174, 184, 203

California. *See* Los Angeles, California; Oakland, California
Calumet High School (Chicago), 168–169, 170
Caswell County Training School (North Carolina), 71–72, 131
Central High School (Cleveland), 106
Central High School (Kansas City, Missouri), 130, 141, 152–155
Central High School (Little Rock, Arkansas), 98, 149
Central High School (Newark, New Jersey), 119
Chapel Hill—Carrboro School System (North Carolina), 186
Chicago, Illinois
  "crisis" in urban education, 117, 119, 120–121, 127–128, 129, 131, 133, 134–135, 137–143
  desegregation of schools in, 158–160, 175
  equalization campaigns in, 85–86, 92, 94–95, 96, 98, 102–103, 105, 106–107
  student conflict and, 168–169, 170
Chicago Daily News, 131
Chicago Defender, 57, 78, 79, 92, 94–95, 106, 134–135, 169, 170
Chicago Tribune, 120, 159, 161, 175
Cincinnati, Ohio, desegregation of schools in, 158, 161
Civil rights. *See also* Desegregation; Integration; Protests
  equal educational opportunity, 19
  Long Civil Rights Movement (Hall), 8, 188
  NAACP campaign, 3, 8
  national movement, 14–16, 138–141, 157–158, 178–179, 189, 194–197
  in the South, 3, 8, 11–12, 15–16, 54–59, 60, 67, 76–81, 138–141
  vocational education and, 134
Civil Rights Act of 1964, 124, 157–158, 163
Clark University, 9
Cleveland, Ohio, 106, 161
Clinton High School (Clinton, Tennessee), 149, 150, 174
College preparation and enrollment, 9, 11–12, 82, 122, 189
Colored High School (Angleton, Texas), 36
Commission on Civil Rights, 53
Compensatory education programs, 155–156, 181
Congress of Industrial Organizations (CIO), 93
Congress on Racial Equality (CORE), 156
Consolidation campaigns, 33–34, 38, 61–62, 68, 71, 164–165, 178
Cotton Belt, 30
Crane Technical High School (Chicago), 131
"Crisis" in urban education, 17–18, 20, 22, 115–144
  anti-discrimination legislation, 124–125
  anti-dropout programs, 119–122, 123
  busing, 116, 128–129
  curriculum and, 136, 140, 142–143, 144
  educational attainment gains, 122–132, 143–144
  northern migration of Blacks, 16–18, 52–53, 57–59, 116, 117–119
  overcrowding, 128–129, 134, 136, 139, 145, 177
  protests, 116–117, 136–143
  segregated schools, 118–119, 127–132, 138–141
  vocational education tracks, 134–136
  "White flight" to suburbs and, 23, 117–119, 123–124, 161–162, 174–175, 191, 196
Crispus Attucks High School (Indianapolis), 98, 104–105, 177
Cultural deprivation, 115–117, 125–126, 132–136, 138, 181
Curriculum, 71–74, 136, 140, 142–143, 144, 179

Daily Minutes, 53

Index

Davis v. County School Board of Prince Edward County, 3–4
Dayton, Ohio, equalization campaigns in, 98–99
De facto segregation, 157, 159
De jure segregation, 22, 116, 147
Delaware, desegregation of schools in, 148–150, 174
Desegregation, 23, 129–130, 145–175. *See also* Equalization campaigns; Protests *and names of specific cities and states*
   in the 1940s and 1950s, 146–151
   in the 1960s, 136–143, 168–171
   controversy over, 147–151, 156–162, 198–199
   dilemmas of, 183–188
   inequity within the schools, 171–174
   in Kansas City, Missouri, 145, 151–157
   protest across the North, 157–162
   in the South, 162–168
   student conflict, 168–171
   as trial by fire, 174–175
   voluntary transfer programs, 129, 148, 151, 158–160, 162, 163, 166
Detroit, Michigan, 94, 97, 127, 135–136, 140, 161
Dorsey High School (Los Angeles), 170
Dropouts, 99–100, 119–122, 123, 167
Dunbar High School (Baltimore), 177
Dunbar High School (Chicago), 135
Dunbar High School (Dayton, Ohio), 98–99
DuSable High School (Chicago), 102–103, 105, 121, 142

Eason High School (Corinth, Mississippi), 73–75
East High School (Kansas City, Missouri), 152–153, 185–186
Educational Policy Commission, 134
Elementary and Secondary Education Act of 1965, 122, 163
Elementary education, in the South, 31–34, 38–39, 177
Employment
   agricultural, 27–30, 63, 64–67, 69–70, 126
   high school movement and, 4, 9–12, 18–20, 27–31, 66–67, 90–91, 126, 178, 197–198
   northern migration of Blacks, 16–18, 52–53, 57–59, 146
Englewood High School (Chicago), 92, 94, 102, 158–159
Equality of Educational Opportunity survey, 80–81
Equalization campaigns, 21–22, 178. *See also* Integration *and names of specific cities and states*
   academic achievement in, 80–81

accreditation of schools, 61, 62, 67–69, 71, 73, 79–80, 131
African American interest in improving schools, 55–57
assessment and, 80–81, 104–108
busing in, 60–62
consolidation campaigns in, 33–34, 38, 61–62, 68, 71, 164–165, 170
curriculum in, 71–74, 179
dropout rates, 99–100, 119–122, 123, 167
enrollment improvements in, 63–69, 81–82, 87–91
extracurricular activities in, 97, 100–102, 106
facilities upgrades, 55–57, 59–61, 66–69, 76–77, 127
funding in, 54, 59, 60, 62, 67, 76–79, 104
good Black high schools and, 71–76
impact of urban residential segregation, 98–104, 107–108, 127–129
impact on attainment, 63–67, 69–71, 81–82, 198
intercultural education in, 95–98
Jim Crow policies, 11, 20–21, 35, 53, 56, 72
legal actions, 54–59, 60, 67, 76, 81, 97–98, 112, 124–125, 156, 158, 166, 167–168
limitations of, 66–67, 76–81
meanings of "equalization," 55–57
northern migration of Blacks, 57–59
outside the South, 83–112
regional development impact on, 52–55
in the South, 52–82
summary of, 81–82
teacher quality in, 55–56, 74, 143–144
Eureka High School (Hattiesburg, Mississippi), 179, 180–181
Expulsions, 167–168
Extracurricular activities, 97, 100–102, 106, 137, 154, 169

Farragut High School (Chicago), 140
Florida
   equalization campaigns in, 60
   student conflict and, 170–171
Ford Foundation, 120
Frederick Douglass High School (Baltimore), 148
Fremont High School (Los Angeles), 94
Froebel High School (Gary, Indiana), 91–93, 146, 184
Funding of schools
   elementary education in the South, 31–34
   in equalization campaigns, 54, 59, 60, 62, 67, 76–79, 104
   jumpstart schools/union schools, 36–38
   Smith-Hughes funds for vocational education, 37–38, 50

Gage Park High School (Chicago), 158–159
Gaines v. Canada, 56
Gangs, 137, 169, 191
Gary, Indiana
  desegregation of schools in, 146, 158
  equalization campaigns in, 91–93, 96–97, 98, 103, 146
  post-World War II conflicts, 91–93, 96–97, 98, 184, 188–189
Gender
  employment opportunities and, 44, 181
  in equalization movement, 64–66, 87
  high school movement and, 9, 10–11, 26, 29–30, 181
  impact of single-parent households, 44
General Equivalency Diploma (GED), 16, 191–193
General tracks, 17–18, 104, 105–106, 136
Gentry High School (Indianola, Mississippi), 147
Georgia. *See also* Atlanta, Georgia
  desegregation of schools in, 150, 151, 165–166, 174, 181
  Division of Negro Education, 55, 60, 68, 77, 80
  elementary education in, 31–32, 33–34
  equalization campaigns in, 59, 60–61, 68, 70, 75, 76–78, 80
  high school accreditation in, 47–48, 50
  Minimum Foundation program, 59, 77
  rural high schools in, 26, 30, 33–34, 36–37, 38, 180
  smaller high schools in, 45
  student conflict and, 171
GI Bill, 8
Gonzaga High School (Spokane, Washington), 94–95
Good black high schools, 14, 71–76, 100, 179
Goss v. Lopez, 167
Graduation rates, 4, 5–8, 17–18, 25, 40–42
Great Depression, 5, 9, 16, 25, 32, 90, 105
Green v. New Kent County, 163, 166

Harlan High School (Kansas City, Missouri), 191
Harrison High School (Chicago), 141
Harvard Desegregation Project, 247 n. 16
Hawkins v. Coleman, 167
Head Start, 122
Henry McNeil Turner High School (Atlanta), 9
Higher Education Act of 1965, 122
High school movement. *See also* Black high schools
  in the 1920s, 5–6, 16, 25
  in the 1930s, 5–6, 9, 16, 25, 34, 45
  in the 1940s, 7, 9–10, 16–18, 25–51, 85–91, 146–151
  in the 1950s, 7, 8–9, 13–14, 146–151
  in the 1960s, 6, 7, 10, 17–20, 52–82, 108–111
  in the 1970s, 7, 14, 18, 20
  in the 1980s, 6, 7, 19, 20
  achievement gap in. *See* Black-White achievement gap
  attainment gap in. *See* Black-White attainment gap
  college preparation and enrollment, 9, 11–12, 82, 122, 189
  consolidation campaigns in, 33–34, 38, 61–62, 68, 71, 164–165, 178
  in democratic ethos, 9–12
  in economic development process, 4, 9–12, 18–20
  employment opportunities and, 4, 9–12, 18–20, 27–31, 66–67, 90–91, 126, 178, 197–198
  gender and, 9, 10–11, 26, 29–30, 181
  good Black high schools, 14, 71–76, 100, 179
  graduation rates, 4, 5–8, 12–18, 25, 40–42, 191–192, 197–198
  in history of Black education, 177–180
  improving Black education, 12–16
  northern migration of Blacks, 16–18, 52–53, 57–59, 146
  regional differences in education, 12–16, 63–67
  second transformation in, 25
  social status and, 180–183, 193–194
  in the South, 5–6, 10, 12–14, 16–17, 25–82
  trends in, 5–8
  urbanization trend and, 16–18, 52–53, 57–59, 146
  vocational training, 29–30, 37–38, 50, 54–55
Howard University, 34–35, 50
Human Relations Commission (Kansas), 151–152
Hyde Park High School (Chicago), 94, 95

Illinois. *See also* Chicago, Illinois
  desegregation of schools in, 146
  State Scholarship Commission, 106
Indiana, desegregation of schools in, 146, 148, 177
Indianapolis, equalization campaigns in, 98, 104–105
Industrialization, 16–18, 52, 53, 57–59, 146, 193
Integrated Public Use Microdata Samples (IPUMS), 27, 40–41, 192, 208 n. 5
Integration, 145–175. *See also* Equalization campaigns; Protests *and names of specific cities and states*
  in the 1940s and 1950s, 146–151

Index

demands for, 127–132
dilemmas of, 183–188
impact of segregated housing, 22, 98–104
inequity within the schools, 171–174
outside of the South, 145, 151–157, 184–188
protest across the North, 157–162
in the South, 162–168, 183–184
student conflict, 168–171
as trial by fire, 174–175

James E. Shepard High School (Zebulon, North Carolina), 73
Jefferson High School (Los Angeles), 99
Jim Crow policies, 11, 20–21, 35, 53, 56, 72
John Jay High School (Brooklyn), 169
Jumpstart/union schools, 36–38, 180

Kansas City, Missouri
 "crisis" in urban education, 118, 130, 137, 141
 desegregation of schools in, 145, 148, 151–157, 159, 162, 174, 184–186
 equalization campaigns in, 98, 99–102, 104–105, 110–111
Kansas City Star, 152
Kentucky, 60, 71, 145, 147–149
Keyes v. School District No. 1, 159

Lever Brothers Corporation, 120–121
Lincoln High School (Kansas City, Missouri), 98–102, 110–111, 152–153, 155
Long Civil Rights Movement (Hall), 8, 188
Los Angeles, California
 "crisis" in urban education, 141
 equalization campaigns in, 94, 99, 103
 student conflict and, 170
Louisiana, 37, 45–46, 71

Manual High School (Kansas City, Missouri), 137, 152–153
Marshall High School (Chicago), 128
Maryland, 54,56,145, 147–148,174 *See also* Baltimore, Maryland
Massachusetts. *See also* Boston, Massachusetts
 desegregation of schools in, 158
McClymonds High School (West Oakland, California), 103
McLaurin v. Oklahoma, 56
Melvindale High School (Detroit), 97
Michigan. *See* Detroit, Michigan
Midwest Research Institute, 157
Milford High School (Milford, Delaware), 148–150, 174
Milliken v. Bradley, 161
Milwaukee, Wisconsin, 106, 161
Mississippi
 desegregation of schools, 147, 163, 165, 184

Division of Negro Education, 77
elementary education in, 31–32, 33–34
equalization campaigns in, 53–54, 57–59, 62, 69, 70, 71, 73–74, 75, 77–79, 179
high school accreditation in, 48
rural high schools in, 26, 30, 33, 37, 38, 180–181
smaller high schools in, 46
Mississippi Department of Education, 62
Mississippi Methodist Conference, 33
Missouri, 145, 147. *See also* Kansas City, Missouri; St. Louis, Missouri
Missouri v. Jenkins, 156
Morehouse College, 8
Moton High School (Farmville, Virginia), 3–4, 7, 15

National Assessment of Educational Progress (NAEP), 19–20, 146, 192–193
National Association for the Advancement of Colored People (NAACP), 3, 8, 26, 32, 56–57, 59, 60, 78–79, 83–85, 127, 128, 135–136, 138, 146, 147, 159–160, 165
National Council for Social Studies, 96
National Survey of Black Americans (NSBA), 93, 151, 162, 163, 165
Newark, New Jersey, "crisis" in urban education, 119
New Augusta High School (Mississippi), 165
New Jersey, 83–84, 158, 170. See also Newark, New Jersey; Trenton, New Jersey
New Mexico, desegregation of schools in, 146–147
New York Amsterdam News, 97
New York City
 "crisis" in urban education, 129, 136, 137, 140
 desegregation of schools in, 159
 equalization campaigns in, 97
 student conflict and, 169, 170
New York state. *See also* New York City
 desegregation of schools in, 158
 equalization campaigns in, 84, 92, 141
 post-World War II conflicts, 84, 92
 SEEK (Search for Education, Elevation, and Knowledge), 122
 student conflict and, 170
New York Times, 60, 76–77, 122
North Carolina
 desegregation of schools in, 149, 165, 166–167, 186, 187
 elementary education in, 31–34
 equalization campaigns in, 54, 56, 57, 59, 60, 62, 68, 69, 70–71, 71–73, 75, 79, 131, 179
 high school accreditation in, 49–50
 rural high schools in, 34, 38

North Carolina, *continued*
  smaller high schools in, 45
  student conflict and, 171
  within-school segregation, 173
North Division High School (Milwaukee), 106
Northeast High School (Kansas City, Missouri), 156
Northern High School (Detroit), 140
North High School (West Mifflin, Pennsylvania), 170
Northwestern High School (Detroit), 94, 128

Oakland, California, equalization campaigns in, 103
Ohio, 98–99, 146, 158, 161. *See also* Cincinnati, Ohio; Cleveland, Ohio
Oklahoma, 56, 147
Other America, The (Harrington), 115
Overcrowding, 128–129, 134, 136, 139, 145, 177

Parental education, 43–44, 67, 88–90, 106, 110, 181–182
Parker Doctrine, 147, 150
Pasadena High School, 141
Paseo High School (Kansas City, Missouri), 153, 155
Pennsylvania. *See* Philadelphia, Pennsylvania; Pittsburgh, Pennsylvania
Perry County Attendance Center (Mississippi), 165
Philadelphia, Pennsylvania, 97, 141
Phillips High School (Chicago), 102–103
Pittsburgh, Pennsylvania, student conflict and, 170
Pittsburgh Courier, 83, 94
Plantation economy, 16, 27–30, 32, 52–53
Plessy v. Ferguson, 177
Poverty
  Black-White achievement gap and, 110, 132–136
  "crisis" in urban education and, 115–117
  cultural deprivation and, 115–117, 125–126, 132–136, 138, 181
  educational attainment and, 181–183, 187
Prairie View A&M, 36
Protests
  of the 1960s, 136–143
  and "crisis" in urban education, 116–117, 136–143
  desegregation, 147–151, 157–162, 168–171, 184–186, 194–195
  legacy of, 188–190
  post-World War II equalization campaigns, 3–4, 7, 15, 32–33, 56–57, 83–85, 91–97, 101, 103, 189–190
Public School League (Chicago), 137

Racial isolation, 22, 119, 133–134, 156, 175
Racial Isolation in the Schools (U.S. Civil Rights Commission), 156
Redstone Academy (Lumberton, North Carolina), 32–33, 188
Remedial education, 103, 104, 106–107, 136, 173, 181
Residential segregation, 98–104, 107–108
River Rouge High School (Detroit), 97
Rosenwald Fund, 31–32
Rural areas, 26–31, 31–34, 36–38, 177
SEEK (Search for Education, Elevation, and Knowledge), 122
Segregation
  "crisis" in urban education, 118–119, 127–132, 138–141
  dilemmas of integration and, 183–188
  as racial isolation, 22, 119, 133–134, 156, 175
Single-parent households, 44, 89–90, 132–133, 183, 187, 191, 194–196
Slums and Suburbs (Conant), 115, 134
Smith-Hughes funds for vocational education, 37–38, 50
Social status. *See also* Poverty
  high school movement and, 180–183, 193–194
  parental education, 43–44, 67, 88–90, 106, 110, 181–182
  property ownership, 28–31, 35, 41–44, 63–64, 66, 67, 88, 110
  single-parent households, 44, 89–90, 132–133, 183, 187, 191, 194–196
South Carolina
  desegregation of schools in, 147
  Division of Negro Education, 74
  equalization campaigns in, 61, 62, 68, 70, 74, 77, 78
  high school accreditation in, 49
  rural high schools in, 26, 38
  student conflict and, 170–171
Southeast High School (Kansas City, Missouri), 153, 155, 184–185, 195
Southern Association of Colleges and Secondary Schools (SACS), 46–49, 82
Southern Bell, 9, 11
Southern Oral History Project, 201
Southern Regional Council, 167
Southwest High School (Kansas City, Missouri), 153, 155, 156
Spellman College, 184
St. Louis, Missouri, 98, 148
Strikes, 139, 142, 188
Student Non-violent Coordinating Committee (SNCC), 138–139
Suburbanization, 23, 103–104, 109–110, 117–119, 123–124, 196

Index

Sufferin High School (New York), 84
Sumner High School (Kansas City, Missouri), 98, 99–102, 104–105, 187
Sumner High School (St. Louis), 148
Suspensions, 167–168
Sweatt v. Painter, 56

Teachers
  outside the South, 143–144
  Smith-Hughes funds for vocational education, 37–38
  turnover of, 143–144, 154
  in the urban South, 40, 186, 187
Tenant farmers, 27–30, 63, 64–65, 69–70, 180
Tennessee, 61, 69, 70–71, 149, 150
Texas
  desegregation of schools in, 149, 166
  equalization campaigns in, 57
  rural high schools in, 36–37
  secondary education in, 36, 56
Texas Southern University, 36
Tillman v. Dade County School Board, 171
Tiner v. Des Moines, 140
Topeka High School, 100–102
To Secure These Rights (Commission on Civil Rights), 53
Tracking, 17–18, 103–108, 136, 173, 181. *See also* Vocational education
Trenholm High School (Tuscumbia, Alabama), 165
Trenton, New Jersey, post-World War II conflicts, 83–84

Union schools, 36–38, 180–181
United Press International (UPI), 122, 169–170
U.S. Bureau of the Census, 27, 122–123, 250 n. 65
U.S. Commission on Civil Rights, 156, 159–162, 243 n. 94, 243 n. 97
U.S. Department of Justice, 157–158
U.S. Department of Labor, 121
U.S. Supreme Court, 3–4, 56, 159, 163, 166, 167
University of Chicago, 127
University of Southern Mississippi, 184
Upward Bound, 122
Urbanization process. *See also* "Crisis" in urban education
  Black-White achievement gap 1940–1960, 83–112
  equalization campaigns outside the South, 83–112
  northern migration of Blacks, 16–18, 52, 53, 57–59, 146
  residential segregation in, 98–104, 107–108, 127–129

schools in Southern cities, 38–45
urban middle class in, 28, 41
Urban League, 120, 127–128, 134

Virginia
  desegregation of schools in, 150, 163, 164–165, 170, 191
  equalization campaigns in, 56–57, 60, 70–71, 79–80
  Moton High School (Farmville) student strike, 3–4, 7, 15, 188
  rural high schools in, 27
Vocational education
  for Blacks, 17–18, 54–55, 91
  county training schools, 35–36
  "crisis" in urban education and, 134–136
  in equalization campaigns, 54–55, 72–74, 91, 104–106
  in high school movement, 29–30, 37–38, 50, 54–55
  Smith-Hughes funds for, 37–38, 50
Voluntary transfer programs, 129, 148, 151, 158–160, 162, 163, 166
Voting Rights Act, 80

Wall Street Journal, 170
War on Poverty, 115–116, 121–122, 124
Washington, D.C., student conflict and, 169
Washington High School (Atlanta), 181, 194
Washington High School (Kansas City, Kansas), 100, 101
Washington Post, 150
Weaverton County High School (Kentucky), 147
West Charlotte High School (North Carolina), 166–167
Westinghouse High School (Chicago), 142
Westport High School (Kansas City, Missouri), 137
West Virginia, equalization campaigns in, 71
White Citizens Councils, 189
White flight, 23, 117–119, 123–124, 161–162, 174–175, 191, 196
Wisconsin. *See also* Milwaukee, Wisconsin
  desegregation of schools in, 158, 161
World War I, 5, 46
World War II, 5, 7, 16, 25, 63, 81, 84–85, 103
  high school enrollment trends and, 34–38
  postwar economic development, 52–55

Yearbooks, 101, 102, 142–143, 153–155, 186, 190

About the Authors

John L. Rury is professor of education and (by courtesy) history at the University of Kansas, where he teaches courses on the history of American education and related policy questions. He has served as editor of the *American Educational Research Journal* and was elected president of the History of Education Society (1998) and vice president of the American Educational Research Association (for Division F, 1997–1999).

Professor Rury is a social historian whose writing has focused on gender, race, and social inequality in education, with an emphasis on the twentieth century. His books include *Urban Education in the United States* (2005), *Education and Social Change* (2002, 2005, 2009), *Education and Women's Work* (1991), *Seeds of Crisis: Public Schooling in Milwaukee Since 1920* (1993), and *Rethinking the History of American Education* (2008). His work has appeared in *History of Education Quarterly, Historical Methods, Social Science History, American Journal of Education, Review of Research in Education, Teachers College Record, The Journal of Negro Education,* and *Educational Policy,* among other journals.

Shirley A. Hill is professor of sociology at the University of Kansas and holds a courtesy appointment in the Department of Health Management and Policy. She teaches courses on families, medical sociology, social inequality, and qualitative methods. Examining the implications of social inequalities, especially those based on social class, gender, and race, has been the overarching focus of her research in these areas. She has served as president of Sociologists for Women in Society (2008–09).

Professor Hill has published research in medical sociology examining caregiving, gender and health care, access to health care, and health care policies in such journals as the *Journal of Poverty, Gender & Society* and the *International Journal of Health Services*. Her book, *Managing Sickle Cell Disease in Low-Income Families* (1994) also considers issues of inequality in health care. Professor Hill has also published articles and books that examine how racial inequality affects various aspects of African American family life. She is the author of *Black Intimacies: A Gender Perspective on Families and Relationships* (2005) and *African American Children: Socialization and Development in Families* (1999), and her work has appeared in the *Journal of Black Studies, Sex Roles, Journal of Marriage and Family,* and *Journal of Comparative Family Studies,* among other periodicals.